TIN BATHS
HOT SUMMERS
ROCK 'N' ROLL

DAVEY J ASHFIELD

APS BOOKS
YORKSHIRE

APS Books
APS Books is a subsidiary of the APS Publications imprint

www.andrewsparke.com

Cover art by Terry Greenwell

First published worldwide by APS Books in 2021

And now a story of when we were all young: Tin Baths Hot Summers & Rock 'N' Roll...

This is for our lass and the bairns
For without you, I am that clanging cymbal

And in memory of
all those I loved so much and were called home far too early
Mam and Dad
Our Sheila, Christine and Kenneth

and my love to those that remain
Margaret and Stephen

And finally
for all the old gunfighters who shared their lives with me.
In true Shiney Row madness - they refuse to go gently into
the night

This is your story...

FOREWORD

I am honoured that Davey Ashfield has asked me to write a foreword for his book. I am well qualified for the job: Firstly, Davey's grandfather attacked my great great uncle in 1926, and secondly, Davey has confessed that he was, in his youth, an inveterate poacher of pheasants and stealer of bird's eggs on the Lambton Estate!

Davey and I grew up within a mile of each other, and many of the places he references, such as Burnmoor (that's the way I spell it!) church, Stern's the Chemist (where my friend Sandra Willoughby used to work) and indeed Shiney Row itself, are indelibly woven into my childhood memories. We both share the same musical tastes; *American Pie* by *Don McLean* was the first record I bought, and I was heartened to see that some of his favourite musicians were also mine, such as *Mott The Hoople*, *Little Richard*, and *Head Hands and Feet*. When you consider that his favourite Shakespeare quote, about the world being a stage, is also mine, it would appear that we have much in common, despite the fact that he was given the part of *working class lad* and I was given the part of *toff*.

All of which brings me onto my main point, which is that upon the world's stage, all of our paths are liable to cross, physically, spiritually, morally, culturally and even musically, and whether we care to notice it or not, we are all intimately connected by an underlying humanity that bulldozes through all ostensible barriers, such as class, religion, race, economic-you name it. Without getting too serious, it is my belief that the future depends on us humans realising what unites us, as opposed to what separates us.

This book is an important cultural document. Those who grew up in the region will be highly amused by its nostalgic irony, but possibly more importantly, for the rest of the world, despite its light heartedness. it will serve as a record of a culture that is sadly no longer with us, and were it not for this book, would have disappeared from memory altogether within a couple of generations.

Ned Lambton
Earl of Durham

A PARADISE LOST

This story starts at a time when social media and trolling was limited to writing *Davey loves Christine* on the school wall in chalk stolen from your teachers desk. Our word processing tools were a wooden pen dipped in the ink from ink wells in our desks. Our *cloud storage* was a British Empire red arithmetic exercise book in which we wrote our times tables. The height of social climbing was to be appointed a milk monitor and hand out the free school milk to our peers. And, social distancing was limited to avoiding the person who had had a bad hair day with *the nit nurse*. It ends nearly three decades later when the purgatory of real work and my own subprime mortgage took over - when the joy of youth and innocence ended.

These are the stories of the second half of the twentieth century which heralded immense change in the cultural life of millions of people across the developed world. In my experience having lived and worked in much of this wonderful world almost everyone I have met, wherever they live, seems to think these were the best times of their lives. Relative material wealth or nationality seems to have little or no influence on people's nostalgic reflections of joy and happiness of these years. If you were rich or poor, East or West, North or South, the basic memories of good times seem to be the same.

It also fulfils the promise I made to my father and his friends nearly fifty years ago in the Working Men's Social Club of a County Durham pit village. I often sat drinking with them listening to the sometimes tragic but almost always funny tales of their hardship, poverty and working lives and they urged me to write them down before they were lost. Very soon after promising to write their stories their futures, lives and homeland were changed forever. It is time I honoured my promise.

This is an amusing and poignant hybrid memoir of the shared memories of millions of people's youth and also a personal history of a life I have been blessed to share with many wonderful, often crazy, but never boring citizens of the world; a story of times that we will never see the likes of again.

We move on to when we bathed once a week in one tin bath, the summers were swelteringly hot and lasted forever: And the music? Well, unlike Buddy Holly, it hadn't died yet. Back to a Paradise found.

CONTENTS

All the world's a stage,
And all the men and women merely players,
They have their exits and their entrances
And one man in his time plays many parts

William Shakespeare

CHAPTER ONE
HEALTH AND SICKNESS

Well, was it so great in the good old days?

There is a communication that goes around the internet every now and then basically comparing life when we were young and now. It purports that given we ate unclean, out of date food, played in germ-ridden soil and muck and only bathed once a week, lived with every infection known to man, played on live bomb sites, railway lines, rivers, roads and lit fires, set off lethal fireworks, met with rampant paedophiles and were made to go to Sunday school, we survived. Indeed, the article concludes we were healthy and have grown up psychologically normal (well some of us). And the other day the BBC reported that a study shows that we were all much better off in the Fifties, long before balanced diets, Health and Safety and MRI scanners. So, today in the pub I suggested to Charlie a retired docker friend that this proves my theory in this book - that these were great days indeed. However, I had to stand corrected when he pointed out a few home truths.

'Davey, we had rampant Typhoid, Smallpox, TB, Tetanus, every disease known to man. Because of poverty and ignorance we had rickets, lice, scabies, no teeth, scurvy and malnutrition. People still worked seven days in dangerous shit holes like mines, steel works, docks, factories, building sites, fishing trawlers and farms. We lost limbs, eyes and life and were paid bugger all. We couldn't afford clothes and food and forget cars, phones and holidays, they were luxuries. Our kids died at birth stillborn or had congenital diseases and most workers died before or around pension age. And we say this was a golden era!'

He may have a point. But I knew that despite these *minor problems* we were definitely happy. This story starts when we were happy and ends when we still thought that the WHO was a British rock band who told our grumpy parents to *'f'..f'..f'...ade away'*, then smashed up their

1

instruments and drove Rolls Royces into swimming pools. Yes, social distancing and recombinant vaccines were years away then but Charlie's talk of illness and the dangers and misery of work and now, our current pandemic predicament, kicked me into beginning this wonderful story for you with a teaser to jog your memories of hardship and pain. Hopefully, it will remind you that your dear mother and the new UK National Health Service, despite their loving care, competed to kill you off before you ever reached working age and the near certainty of being maimed or of death at work.

DOCTOR THOMAS
'Watch with Mother' and 'Germolene'

I was born in the fifties and lived in a small County Durham coal mining village called Shiney Row. I understood Shiney Row was so named because in the older days the rows of colliery owned homes had black granite front steps. The wives of the coal miners used to wash and polish these steps daily, as did my mother with her Princes Street front step until she passed on. It seems that one day many moons before my arrival kicking and screaming into this *'It's not of this world', Jim'* crazy place, either the Earl of Durham, my grandfather Stripper's nemesis, Lord Lambton, or someone even higher on the aristocratic ladder, perhaps royalty, I don't know for sure, was riding past with their courtiers and saw how *shiney* the steps were and called the place Shiney Row. So now you know.

Some of my early memories of my mother are being nursed by her when sick from Infant school and seeing *Watch with Mother* on our small black and white rented TV set. It is a modern myth that we were never ill those days. I suspect that is purely because we were all treated with home grown potions and cures.

Germolene and *Domestos* killed all known germs. *Germolene* on any cut, graze or bruise would solve today's antibiotic resistance and flesh guzzling germs (MRSA) in a heartbeat. An indication of where things have gone wrong is that my dearest has used *Germolene* since she started teaching forty-five years ago but is now banned from applying it to children's wounds. It needs a nurse and consent from parents with a lawyer's letter in the form of an indemnity from prosecution. For heaven's sake, have they never read, *Just Awful* that lovely children's book by Alma Marshak?

2

Just like the mother in Alma's book, my wife would take a child who was distressed, sit them on her knee and give them a cuddle and it didn't matter if they were cut or bruised. She'd take out a tin of *Germolene* that she kept permanently in her pocket and rub it onto where it hurt and then read to them. Now she can't even put them on her knee without the threat of the sack, physical attack by their guardians or vexatious litigation…no wonder our kids are disturbed.

Fiery Jack was another tin of pure torture and alchemy that my mother would rub onto any aching joint. It burnt like hell for ages. Pitmen in the village used it on their backs for sprains and pains and it was liberally applied to kids for any ache. As I got older and told my mother that I was big enough to apply it myself I'd rub it in before bed to make sure I could play football the next day. Sadly, being male and having the male habit of perpetual genital holding or, as men do, massaging the TV remote these days, often you'd forget your hands were covered with what, for your genitals, was concentrated sulphuric acid. Those of you, male and female, who have inadvertently done this with chilli peppers, will know what I mean.

I always seemed to be watching *Bill and Ben, Andy Pandy* and the other characters from *Watch with Mother* days when I was ill and off school and it always seemed to be winter. We seemed to be unwell those days with things like Mumps, Measles, Scarlet fever, Tonsillitis, toothache and the like. Most of the time many other kids would also be off school at the same time as infectious diseases rampaged through the close knit social groups we lived in. We were kept in the house until the doctor told your mother you could play outside in the street - I guess a forerunner to today's current social isolation and just as terrible to a young child used to roaming back streets and fields in search of fun. We could only play with those who had the same disease as we had.

Doctor Thomas and Doctor Lloyd were our doctors. I always saw Doctor Thomas. He had only one treatment - penicillin. He gave this for everything, along with a horrible tasting yellow coloured medicine which I was forced to drink off a table spoon for every sickness.

If you were ill for anytime it seemed from somewhere came a bottle of *Lucozade*. Certainly, if we ever visited anyone in hospital there was a bottle on the table. *Lucozade* was a treat. It was normally too expensive to drink as refreshment - that would be supplied by *Neds* the local soft drinks business in Penshaw or *Fentimans'* ginger beer pop wagons every Friday when it was Dad's pay day and we could afford it. Curiously, those days *Lucozade* was supplied in orange bottles of about three quarters of a litre specially wrapped in orange clear cellophane, as if it was some mystical valuable potion. Indeed it was. It seemed it was only supplied by licensed Pharmacists, so it must be good for you. In reality it was carbohydrate in coloured water, great for the Krebs cycle, but not so good for *the tooth dominoes* building up in the mouth nor the waist line or now, the diabetic failure of your Islets of Langerhans in the pancreas. We loved it. However, it was rationed to one glass, but sometimes I'd sneak a drink straight out of the bottle. It gave a sugar rush that was like some form of crack cocaine to us innocent kids. Now of course it has been rebranded as a health and sports drink and targeted at healthy people and not the sick and dying. A masterful exercise that *Snickers* brand managers should have listened to because, as we all know, *Marathon* was a much better brand than *Snickers*, which sounds like some perverted male Japanese vending machine-acquired female underwear brand to me. I worry that *Lucozade* will go the way of anything that's actually nice these days; deemed bad for you and to be taxed out of reach of the common gender neutral person by the sugar tax. Let's hope not, if only for old time's sake.

A lot of the time I was treated for aches, pains, sprains and cuts by my mam's or Nana's homemade recipes and potions. The heat burning thing my mother loved to put on any boil, strain or bruise was a *hot poultice*. These came out of tins if I remember and were boiled up to the melting point of human skin and then applied on any injured part of your body to draw out any septic pus that might be hiding in there. They normally drew out all your red blood corpuscles too just before you collapsed from lack of oxygen and anaemia.

Another weird experience I underwent was the result of eating too much food, particularly sugar and bread, and remaining a normal size rather than the shape of an oblate spheroid. The various old ladies sitting in the house with my mother were sure that the unfortunate child 'must have worms' and advised my darling mother to give me a 'worm cake'. I have a vague memory of my mother looking up my bottom for the horrible nematodes and then being forced to eat what if I remember correctly was a chocolate-tasting thing resembling the biscuit part of an *Oreo*. I am convinced she bought these at Yates the bakers in the street but that seems strange if they contained some horrible toxic chemical that nuked tape or round worms. I guess bakers' shops, even in those days before the Thalidomide scandal, shouldn't have been selling such stuff. If anyone knows if Yates did sell them or where they came from let me know.

Our mams had a tough life. When I think of the loving things mothers had to do to keep us little angels safe – picking nematodes out of their loved one's bottoms must rank as the highest example of unconditional love that I can imagine. Worms in your bottom, nits in your hair, scabies on your skin, rickets in your bones - maybe Charlie is correct about the 'good old days'!

Brown paper had major uses those days. If you recall your *Jack and Jill learn to read* books and the nursery rhyme with Jack trekking up the hill to fetch a pail of water, Jack had his broken head wrapped in vinegar and brown paper. If we had a poorly chest and cough, goose fat was smeared on your chest and then it was covered in brown paper. Long before we could afford a fridge the fat was kept in a jar on the stone pantry shelf where all our meat was kept chilled. At school the fat melted as you sat next to the cast iron radiators. We actually had heat at school rather than the freezer which masqueraded as home in the winter and of course the fat dribbled all the way down your shirt and jumper. This caused great embarrassment with the other kids taking the Mickey out of you.

I note now that brown paper costs as much per sheet as gold leaf. Why is that? Anyone know? And a goose at Christmas is more expensive than fillet steak. Times have changed.

At the other temperature extreme another favourite way of relieving sore chapped legs from playing out in freezing ice and snow in winter with short trousers or skirts on was to rub 'cold cream' on them. I now know that cold cream is a moisturising cream but I still wonder if our mothers had some secret recipe that actually was a cream to stop the cold burning. It didn't work too well mind as we sat on top of the fire trying to warm up, and the fire seemed to make it worse.

And where have all the chilblains gone? Everyone seemed to have chilblains those days. My mother suffered terribly from them. Mind you she never tried the cure it seems they used with my docker mate and his chums because they used to urinate on their hands for chilblains. As Charlie said, 'It didn't make the cornflakes taste any better.'

Another illness that seems to have disappeared is tonsillitis. Everyone seemed to have tonsillitis. Now it seems to have mutated to *a strep throat* to be treated by antibiotics. This must have had been a blow for

Ear, Nose and Throat surgeons as they always seemed to be chopping out tonsils and things called adenoids from young children. Adenoids seem to have disappeared like our pet tortoises, the pipes in school dinner liver and *Vesta* beef curry. Did they ever exist? Or were ENT surgeons keeping themselves in work after the beginnings of the NHS? Maybe Lady T sussed them out, and like the school milk she cruelly stole from us kids, they have been deemed economically unsustainable or sold off to private health care. Whatever happened to tonsils and adenoids must have been a blow to the jelly and ice cream industry. The universal post–traumatic care given to these poor kids whose tonsils had been rived out was jelly and ice cream. One wonders if this universal healing therapy could be brought back today. Or maybe the glycerol, sugar and saturated fatty acids would now be deemed unhealthy for really unhappy and suffering children – best give them a slice of tofu and mountain goat yoghurt to cheer them up, eh?

My wife has a beautiful romantic story which surely must make you cry about fate and post-operative stress and pain when her own 'missing' tonsils were chopped out at the age of eight years. She was lying in her hospital bed and her parents had left her alone to spend her first night. These were the days when Matron's ruled hospitals and visiting was just that, visiting - one hour at a specified time and then parents went home. She was alone in her bed during the evening crying in pain and feeling very sad when a young boy of about twelve came over and sat on her bed. He held her hand and sang *Puff the Magic Dragon* to her. She never forgot this kindness and also the boy. And who was the boy? Well, you may well guess...but wouldn't it be a beautiful moving end to this story if it is who the romantics among you hope it was? I won't spoil the end for you.

My dad's favourite medical recipes were his acne, spots and constipation cures. He had an obsession that bowels had to be regular and moved so he boiled up Senna pods and made this into some horrible tasting medicine which we were made to drink every morning. His pièce de résistance however, was a mixture of sulphur and treacle that he boiled and made into a medicine that we drank which cured acne zits. None of these appears to have taken the pharmaceutical industry by storm and we still got spots. We did seem to poo a lot though…

My dear mother-in-law has an old recipe for tonsillitis, sore throats and upper respiratory tract infections which tastes as vile as Dad's brimstone one. My dearest still has nightmares and trembles a lot when she visits her mum if she has any form of cold, cough or sneeze. Even though she is now at a golden age, her mother makes her drink the concoction of sugar, vinegar and whisky every time. As a Corona virus cure I'm not sure, but, in the absence of real beer during lockdowns, the whisky works well to kill the boredom of self-isolation.

Any oil those days was used for medical treatment or for your old bike, not for putting on salads or frying with. Good old fashioned lard and Heinz salad cream were the only oils used in cooking and eating respectively. As for olive oil, well that was warmed up and went in your lug for earache and was never spread on the rabbit food that masquerades as a salad nowadays. And don't get me on about fish oil.

Cod Liver Oil is now the potion to cure all ills par excellence. Eicosapentaenoic acids and Omega 3's are now the essential weapons in health food stores and nutritionists' arsenals against dying early of coronary heart disease caused from all the great tasting but cheap, fatty food we ate before we all became vegans and *Guardian* readers. As young children we kicked and screamed if our mother got the bottle of cod liver oil out with that dreaded silver table spoon. It was bloody horrible. These days as usual everyone has gone soft; they receive their cod liver oil in capsules or a nice piece of pickled mackerel or poached salmon en croute. Then, we had to suffer the horrible stuff off a spoon. I believe it still had bits of liver floating in it. After the spoonful of bile, in true defiance of medical and pharmacological logic, my mother would give me a slice of beef dripping and bread or a sugar and bread sandwich with real butter from the Meadow Dairy to help comfort me and kill the horrible cod liver taste. We had no fear of cholesterol or dental caries then. How we survived the treatments is the real question.

Dentists and Lollipops

Massive amounts of sugar containing foods, brings back the memory of trips to the dentist and like being poorly and off school and 'Watch with Mother' it seemed that we always went to the dentist in winter time. I always had my teeth yanked out by a dentist who looked like Lawrence Olivier in *Marathon Man* and I am sure he may well have been the actual character Lawrence played - Joseph Mengele. I guess I'll never know unless Odessa finally confesses that County Durham was where the Nazi doctor ended up. There were two in succession who arrived and meetings with both were too horrible an experience to care to remember which of them came first..

These trips to the dentist were always in the freezing cold and required a day off school to go to the house of pain. It always seemed wet, cold and windy. My mother took me there and after the horrors of the gas and the extraction she brought me home with a woollen scarf tied across my mouth to stop the 'cold getting in.' Why she worried about that I can never know. The blood gushing out, the threat of flesh eating bugs and the throbbing pain should have worried her more than getting a chill on the gaping wound.

My dentists seemed only ever to pull teeth. There were no other dental procedures like fillings, polishing, scaling etcetera. - only extractions. Maybe he liked pulling teeth and he pulled a lot of mine. Sadly, dental hygiene wasn't big in our family and the diet of sugar and bread, sugar in tea, sugary pop from Ned's pop factory (then changed to Villa pop) and sugar sweets like black bullets, pineapple chunks, pear drops and the like all caused massive caries I guess. Both my parents had no teeth and nor had my older sister. I believe my mother had her teeth all pulled out by the dentist on the kitchen table. Dad? Maybe he had his taken out in the Working Men's Club by the slaughterhouse man who masqueraded as a dentist. I never ever knew.

I was always told it was because of gingivitis or pyorrhoea that all the teeth were yanked out and replaced with National Health dentures. It was a comfort that everyone seemed to think that there was no correlation between bad dental hygiene and bad diet - a mouth full of *dominoes* was just the way of the world. We all thought American movie stars with their massive smiles and bright white teeth were immune to pyorrhoea; it was a British disease.

The smell of the dentist remains with me to this day as does the smell of the gas mask that was rammed over my mouth by the Odessa fugitives. They never used hypodermics and local anaesthetics; they gassed you. The throbbing in the head as I went under also remains as does the taste of blood and salt in my mouth for hours after. However, at the surgery of Hades when you regained consciousness (those of us lucky enough to do so) there was always a bonus. This came in the form of a large sugar lollipop shaped like a tear drop that the smiling nurse gave you while you lay in the chair bleeding profusely with a huge throbbing headache from the nitrous oxide and feeling sick.

If you ever want to know what one of these lollipops looked like, watch the amazingly funny movie *Kung Fu Hustle*. Somehow one of these dentists must have relocated to deepest China in a spirit of dental missionary evangelism and now I know why most Chinese movies show grizzled, lean peasants with teeth like sets of dominoes.

Mind you I grasped this lollipop as if it was my last meal and my mother would then place a hanky over my mouth in a vain attempt to stop the haemorrhaging and wrap the woollen scarf around my face. We then walked the short way from the surgery down the main street to home, me feeling like death but still clutching my lolly hoping that soon the pain and the feeling horrible would go and I could get stuck into my lolly.

It was years later before I realised the error of my ways in sucking pure sugar. Not before losing more teeth from our erstwhile sadists and then visiting a modern dentist in Houghton-le-Spring who started filling and root canal work rather than gassing and riving out. I also still shake my head when I recall to those in bars and to you dear reader the perversity of this story. I marvel at how the dentist with his free sugar comfort lolly generated more business from a brilliant positive feedback mechanism. Basically it was; eat a sugar lolly, get caries, get tooth pulled, eat yet another sugar lolly, get caries, etcetera. This goes on ad infinitum until you end up on the kitchen table like my mother with all your teeth lying in a cake mixing bowl on the sink draining board. Or maybe they were trying to be kind to their patients by giving away sugar lollipops to ease the pain. Let's try to see some good in them should we? My son is studying to be one for God's sake.

The Dentists in the village were not the only source of dental treatment. My father when he first arrived in the village from London experienced many a strange event which on reflection he told me should have sent him hurrying back down to live in the civilized South taking his newly married Shiney Row wife, my mother, with him. Instead he ended up settling in for the long term and witnessed one event in a Shiney Row club which I must admit would have sent me straight to Durham train station to high-jack *The Flying Scotsman*, North or South, it wouldn't matter where. He said it was an amazing sight when he entered the bar that Friday evening with my Grandfather, Stripper. It was full of men, most wearing flat caps and white mufflers, all with pint glasses or smallwhisky shots on the bar or upon small rectangular tables scattered around the sides of the room. The room was a haze of smoke and cauldron of noise as working men began their night of drinking and socializing in the more pleasant environs than a coal mine, shipyard or building site. Many tables had domino boards on them and the clattering of the domino tiles as they were shuffled and knocked on the boards rendered the room across the background cacophony of voices.

The floor was covered in sawdust and many hob nailed boots and shoes had scattered the dust as they scrubbed across the yellow dusty wood of the floor. Seated across from where Dad and my grandfather sat was a seated man with his head being held back by a man behind him and his mouth open wide. Another rather large man seemed to have his hand over the guy's mouth and was tugging at something. When he could see properly through the smoke haze he saw that what he was watching was a tooth extraction - well, an attempt at one.

The large man was twisting and pulling with what looked like elongated pliers which were firmly pushed into the wriggling man's mouth. The man behind was trying valiantly to keep the patients head still as he writhed and threw his head around in abject pain. One more tug and twist and bingo! - out popped the tooth. It was followed by copious amounts of blood which the patient spat out over the sawdust of the floor.

A bar towel was given to the man to stem the bleeding and the small entourage of the patient and erstwhile peripatetic dentist began swilling pints down, plainly happy at their work.

My father asked Stripper: 'Is that man a dentist Bob?'

'Nah. He's a slaughterer. He works at Hodgkiss the butcher's slaughter house in the village.'

'Why doesn't the man go to a proper dentist? Have you not got one in Shiney Row?'

'Aye, we've got Harry, but he's a butcher. Jimmy is better than that bugger and doesn't cost as much. Jimmy practices pulling the teeth all the time on the sheeps and cows heeds he chops off in the slaughter house.'

My great Uncle Tom interjected. 'Jimmy can pull a tooth faster and cleaner than that bloody dentist and he only charges a couple of pints for it. He likes pulling teeth.'

My father looked at the large slaughterer of beasts and saw him holding his pliers in the air, observing the bloodstained tooth clamped within their jaws and his vice like grip. He had a serene and thoughtful look as if he had indeed found his true vocation in life.

Dad reflected on his first observations of life up North and wondered what was next. There was much more horror to come.

GEORDIE CORN
Barbers and Condoms

Trips to the barbers were almost as bad as trips to the dentist. Ours was Geordie Corn. He was situated next door to *The Shoulder of Mutton* pub, across the road from the dentist. *The Shoulder* gained a lot of trade from the dentist because his adult patients mostly went straight into the pub to ease the pain after the ritual gassing and 'howking' out of your canines.

Geordie's place always smelled of *Brylcreem* and cigarette smoke. He smoked incessantly as did his customers and the ceiling and walls were brown with nicotine stains. His seats were brown-stained concave benches with a plywood back all full of small holes, usually fully occupied by men lounging on them smoking, reading the racing pages of the newspapers and listening to Geordie's craic about horses and pit life. Mothers took us when were young and as we grew up we'd go on our own. It was a traumatic experience.

Geordie only knew one haircut; obviously he wasn't trained in haute coiffure, or by *Teazy Weezy*. He'd worked down the pit before taking up his scissors and an entrepreneur's life. A life hewing coal with a pick axe was obviously good conditioning for the finer arts of hair styling. His one cut for boys was the basin cut. Lots of lads had their hair cut at home to save money and the easiest way was to place a basin over the head and hair and cut the hair that dropped from the sides of the upturned basin. Mothers then shaved the sides short, so that in the end your hair looked like an upturned basin on your head; very much Lawrence Olivier in *Henry the Fifth* style. Geordie had mastered this without the need for the basin template. He could also manage a short back and sides too when we got older and this was the only cut he ever did on the men.

As the fashion developed in the sixties for longer hair like *The Beatles* wore, we always hoped that we could persuade Geordie to leave us with some hair on the sides, but to no avail; he carried on with his routine cut. It was in fact pointless talking to Geordie anyway as he never communicated with kids, only with the old men sat around his shop. He cut your hair and never actually looked at what he was doing as he was always turning and talking to the men about horse racing. He normally had the radio on and they'd all be listening to race commentaries. He hacked away at your hair looking at the men in the brown stained holey seats oblivious to your facial expressions or shouts of, 'That's enough off, Mr Corn please.'

He would also have a habitual cigarette in his mouth which when the ash had grown too long he'd knock off with a flick of his fingers, seemingly aiming for the floor, but it always fell onto your head or face. Any shouts or spluttering as the hot ash burnt your face and hair were ignored for a discussion on the three cross doubles and a treble he'd won or lost at Ascot.

Every time I left the barber shop with the same cut, shaved sides and top short. The ritual for the village after a new haircut from Geordie was to have your head slapped by the big lads you bumped into. There was nowhere to hide as a hair cut from Geordie Corn shone like a *Belisha beacon*; the real give away was that always after every cut your head was caked in *Bylcreem*. It didn't matter if you told him you didn't like *Brylcreem*, he always stuck his hands in his huge tub of it and then slapped it on. I have had an intense dislike for *Brylcreem* ever since; memories of the big lads slapping my head and trying to wash the bloody stuff off in the kitchen sink before anyone else wacked you will remain forever.

Sitting in the shop listening to Geordie and the men talking about horses and life we picked up news about the village, the latest fights on weekends, the current football match or what had happened at the pit but every now and then I'd hear things which made no sense to me. After cutting men's hair Geordie always asked them if: 'They wanted anything for the weekend?'

If he got an affirmative I noticed he'd look guilty and then dig into his drawer and hand the man something in a brown bag under the customer's gown. This puzzled me and it took a few more years and a bit of growing up to realise that this was the source of condoms for the men in the village. It still remained a secret rendezvous for family planning right up until Geordie passed on.

Indeed, no one seemed to talk about things like sex or especially contraception. The only chemist in the town was Mr Stern's and condoms were hidden away and could only be purchased by an individual consultation with the great man himself. The men must have got their condoms in secret from Geordie the barber and maybe that's the reason for the large families seen all over then. Not everyone had the courage to face Mr Stern but I heard a story from Jackie Wanless from Penshaw one fine day which made me laugh when he told of one young lad who had to do such a thing.

MR STERN THE CHEMIST
Philadelphia Yard and Honeymoons

Jackie worked in Philadelphia Yard, the engine works where engineering maintenance for the local pits was carried out. A lot of young boys joined as apprentices to the works and it was better paid and more life-prolonging than working down the pit. The young apprentices were always the subject of pranks and jokes by the time-served men. One young lad was getting married and was still innocent in the ways of the flesh as was his young bride. The lads had told him that he needed to make sure he had his condoms for the honeymoon and he'd asked how and where did he get them. They told him Stern's chemist shop, but he'd have to be measured first. He choked on his tea when told this. The lads continued that he must go and be measured otherwise he wouldn't be able to perform with his darling virgin bride. They said that Mr Stern would measure him in the back of the shop and sell him the correct condom size but he'd better hurry up and get to the shop.

So off to the shop went our innocent virgin. He entered and looked around and could only see the ladies working behind the counter. Looking very embarrassed and anxious he asked for Mr Stern. One of the more mature ladies answered him.

'Sorry pet he's not in at the moment. Can I help?'

'Nah Mrs, I really need Mr Stern.'

The ladies knew what was up as this was a common occurrence when the young lads from Yard who had been wound up by their mates came to the shop. They never came to buy perfumes or cold creams or suntan lotion.

'Oh,' the shop assistant said nodding reassuringly at him, 'I know what you need. Come into the back and we'll see if we can help you.'

The young man looked worried but must have thought he would get through this without having to get his todger out so he started to walk to the back end of the shop and store cupboard. The older lady followed him and turned to a pretty young assistant and shouted:

'Emily pet, bring the tape measure will you and will you help this young lad get his pants down and his old man out. You can measure this one.'

The hapless apprentice looked at the lovely young lass picking up a tape measure off the counter and smiling at him and then the other lady who was bidding him to come into the store room and he took off like *The Road Runner* being chased by *Wile E. Coyote*.

Obviously this story spread like wild fire as everyone knew everybody and the shop ladies had done this many times before to unsuspecting apprentices. Jackie never did say how his fellow apprentice got on his honeymoon except to say he now has a family of twelve.

By now you may well be reliving some of your own happy tortures in dentist and doctors' surgeries or looking at the scars left on your withering bodies by your parents' home-made illegal remedies and thinking what was really so good about growing up.

Well many things were and long before we all watched Netflix, or played *FIFA 2020* on our X boxes and watched CGI inspired 3 D amazing special effects, the TV and radio we enjoyed was - shall we say - special.

CHAPTER TWO
CHILDREN'S TELEVISION AND RADIO

Radiograms and Hire Purchase

As a young boy I remember listening to the radio. As I grew older television was there but only as a special event. We played outside most of the time and television was something that your parents let you watch as a treat. Our radio was a radiogram; it also had a record player in it that played 78 revolutions per minute hard vinyl shellac records. The radiogram was rented from the electrical retailer in the main street, as was the television. Someone was on the other day about what happened to *Rumbelows* and *Radio Rentals*; I guess they went the way of other rental shops when credit became more accessible. My parents couldn't raise the money or borrow enough to buy outright and my father had some fear of higher purchase agreements, like many who lived on the breadline. Later he had to try to borrow money as technology moved on and his children's more affluent peer groups, like now I suppose, put pressure on his kids to own better more expensive things. Sometimes he managed it, but most of the time he couldn't so we lagged behind on technology and fashion but as almost all in our streets were in similar dire financial straits it never affected our love of what we had given how hard our parents had worked to get it.

The next step in raising finance was *the Provident loan*, or the *Provvie*. Most people in working class poverty relied on *provvies* for consumer credit as none had bank accounts, and credit cards were non-existent. My parents got a doorstep *provvie* check for my school uniform. It was the only way I could attend Grammar school. I never got a new blazer until fifth form. School uniforms were always bought several sizes too big if you were less well off so you could grow into them. Many had large V-shaped patches in them, sewn in by caring mothers to accommodate the growing teenage body. I still wore my first school athletic vest and the double-sided, green and yellow football strip at nineteen years old for nights out in Newcastle or Sunderland. Always the fashion icon.

I listened to the radio on Sunday mornings. My dad usually took me for a walk every Sunday morning around the paths through the woods (gills) on Lord Lambton's land and he talked to me about life, family, history and nature. Years later, I did the same with my daughter, except I used to push her under the chain link fence to pinch conkers and tell her to run quickly if the gamekeeper came. She reminds me of a lot of these days, along with the fact that for twenty years she never fished with me legally. Old poaching habits die hard.

My father usually took me into the garden before the walk to help him weed, dig, and pick the vegetables for Sunday lunch or to educate me into how things grow. He'd come in and wash and put on his best shoes and his only suit, dress shirt and tie with flat cap ready to go to the Working Men's Club (the Club) for the usual Sunday lunchtime session while my mother prepared the vegetables and Sunday lunch. I listened to the radio while she worked in the kitchen. The shows remain with me now.

BFPO, Family Favourites, Jimmy Clitheroe and The Navy Lark

I am sure BFPO was on mid-morning Sundays and I never knew what BFPO meant except it was some way of people communicating with family who were serving in the forces overseas. The music always seemed relaxing to me as I played with toy soldiers, read comics, painted or did what generally today my dear daughter does now even in her maturity when she comes home. I guess I 'chilled out'. It seemed there were only two channels, the *Light Programme* and The *Home Service*. I enjoyed the following programs more than BFPO stuff and they were, not in any order I can be certain of at this remove, *The Navy Lark* and *The Clitheroe Kid* with Jimmy Clitheroe. I also believe *Around the Horne* was on Sundays but can't be sure. I liked *Around the Horne* but didn't get the sexually explicit innuendos from the cast. It took some growing up to get there but I found them all funny I guess. And now I see the shows have been revised as stage extravaganzas and I am off to see *Around the Horne* very soon. It'll be interesting to see if it's any good but, to confirm my children's despair at me and my membership of the *Old days Grumpy Old Gits' Club*, I bet it isn't - nowt is as good anymore.

Captain Pugwash and Master Bates

I never got into *The Goons* on radio until I was much older I have to say. It took the satirical TV shows *Monty Python's Flying Circus* and *That Was The Week That Was* and *Rowan and Martin's Laugh In* to get me to return to the old radio satire and realise what I had missed. I guess the sexual innuendo and subtlety of homosexual humour in days when it may well have still been an offence to admit to being homosexual was lost on most of us young people who were ignorant of such things. No,

16

in those days, *gay* meant happy, and *a puff* meant being soft. And in my naivety *Captain Pugwash* was only a jolly pirate cartoon character.

Captain Pugwash was on BBC TV. It is still an urban myth that it contained characters like *Roger the Cabin Boy*, *Master Bates* and *Seaman Staines*. There have been libel cases over whether or not it did. Most people of my age I meet will say it did; the law courts found and ruled that it didn't. But I know it did definitely have a *Master Mates* and a *Pirate Willy* in it. It seems it was a student rag/plot to produce the other rude names but it has remained firm in the mythology of my generation. It was the same with *Sooty and Sweep*.

Sooty and Sweep

Sooty was a glove puppet bear and *Sweep* a glove puppet dog. *Harry Corbett* was the puppeteer whose hands were inserted up their orifices and he spoke and interacted with them during the TV episodes. Sweep had an annoying squeaker stuck up his bottom that Harry pushed regularly to intimate Sweep's conversation which Harry translated. My point is not that a grown man would insert his hand up toy animals backsides for a living, although this is a bit strange, it is that he then felt the need to introduce a female to the duo in some form of ménage-a-trois.

Again, when I was young I knew nothing of French kisses or ménages and the strange perversions of our Gallic cousins. Nor did I see anything wrong in having another puppet in the show. In fact the girls loved the new one, a female Panda bear called *Soo*, and they all asked for this toy for birthdays and Christmases. These days it would be called a great brand expansion by the BBC by marketing gurus gaining a new group of viewers and consumers of stuffed Chinese female bears - not necessarily only children either as there are some strange adult people out there in these liberated days as you all know well.

It has taken many years for it to come out that the introduction of a female to the all-male multi species puppet show almost caused the dismissal of the BBC executives responsible and the closing of the show; a heinous crime indeed. It was revealed by the BBC in 2016 that when Corbett suggested introducing a female character in the 1960s, the show's producer Trevor Hill dismissed the idea on the grounds that '…sex would be creeping into the programme'. Miller, the BBC's head of north regional programmes, accused Corbett of orchestrating a campaign in the press for Sooty to be allowed a girlfriend. One of the BBC governors, Dame Anne Goodwin, was also strongly opposed to Sooty having a female friend. In May 1965, Hill wrote to Miller. He said 'I was left in no doubt as to her feelings in this matter.' However, the BBC DG Hugh Carleton-Greene stepped in to allow Soo's introduction and ruled that Sooty having a female friend *was to be allowed - but they must never touch.*

Poor Sooty he must have been very frustrated. His catchphrase of, 'Izzy Wizzy, let's get busy' must have caused him one hell of an amount of sexual angst as he wasn't allowed physical contact whilst Soo spent quite a lot of time with Sweep, who was obviously the dog in the manger in this multi–species, and also cross-cultural, ménage-a-trois.

I am guessing Soo is of Chinese extraction as she's a Panda and her introduction did expand the cross-cultural attraction to a new audience of swinging sixties global village viewers. We may never find out what perverted activities Sweep may still be up to. However, the *Independent* quoted that *Sooty described the start of his perfect day as when 'Soo and Sweep bring me breakfast in bed'.* Sweep has made several statements on the subject, but unfortunately his squeak is intelligible only to the Corbett family and its friends.'

In 1965, even the Director General of the BBC was not ready for a cross-cultural relationship. Soo did eventually appear in the show pregnant years later, but this turned out to be her practical joke on Sooty (oh the cruel, heartless Oriental bitch) involving a cushion up her dress. Sweep squeaked excitedly mocking his friend, giving him a rude gesture with his bent, upturned arm thrusting into the air. I am amazed the producers have not been investigated for the *bear necessity* of this abuse given how poor Sooty was tortured relentlessly for his unrequited love whilst his best friend got stuck into his Pedigree Chum at breakfast time.

Sooty however is made of sterner stuff. Despite his cuckolding, mangy mute mate and his cock-teasing, oriental trollop, he has shown true British spunk through it all and was even one of the first great world leaders to wish Nelson Mandela a happy birthday at the occasion of his 90th birthday. You can see it on YouTube. Let's hope Sooty gets his Panda one day and he manages to *to share her Bamboo shoots and leave* and say his last goodbye in peaceful satisfaction at last - 'Bye bye, everybody…bye bye.'

The Magic Roundabout

A must to watch before the 6 pm News was *The Magic Roundabout*. This was another puppet show which was originally produced in France as *Le Manège enchanté*. It had endearing characters such as Florence, the dopey, curly headed lass. It is famous like *Captain Pugwash* for its adult hidden meanings and innuendos that again may or may not be an urban myth. To us enlightened baby boomers, post the sixties revolution, *Dylan the Rabbit* was actually stoned all the time. He mimicked the stereotype hippy with guitar in hand, doped out of his tiny rodent brain and talking sixties-type hippy stuff as if in a coma, *It's cool man. Far out.* And stuff like that. He may well have been on LSD, but I prefer to think he was a *Mandy* aficionado. *Where's me Mandies, Flo?* gives it away if you search through the episodes.

His mate was *Dougal*, a large fluffy sheepdog-looking hound who liked to eat sugar lumps. His addiction was complete when Dylan in a more lucid moment commented that, 'He started on one sweet, now he's on two bags a day.'

I guess *Zebedee*, a huge coiled spring that used to like *boinging* and every episode asked Florence the dopey lass if she wanted a shag, was still a throwback to the show's French roots. *Boing! Time for bed,* was always the last thing said on the show by the dirty, French, twisted helix. Florence I still believe was a good girl though and never fell for his large Gallic coil.

Children's telly was educational in those days.

Bill and Ben and Andy Pandy

Back to lying sick on the settee watching *Watch with Mother,* I remember *Andy Pandy* being on Tuesday's; *The Flowerpot Men* on Wednesday; *Rag tag and Bobtail* on Thursday and *The Woodentops* on Friday. I am certain *Tales from the Riverbank* was also on, maybe on Mondays.

Andy Pandy was another weird one really who lived in a basket with *Looby Loo* his girlfriend and *Teddy*, a talking bear. He wore his blue and white stripped pyjamas constantly, looking very like a Holocaust victim. He was always prepared though for dirtier duties than sleep, as he was a lot like the debauched and perverted French spring, *Zebedee*, and he couldn't wait to get his girlfriend into bed. Like *Florence*, she was a bit dopey too. He even bragged about it on the day's social media with a song: *Time to go now…Andy Pandy's going to bed,* as the three of them slowly descended into the cosy basket. I mean, like Sooty, what was this all about in those days - cuddly bears, and girl and boy relationships in small enclosed spaces? It is a worry.

Bill and Ben the Flowerpot Men was a precursor to *The Magic Roundabout* and also Dylan's hallucinogenic habit I believe, although I didn't realise it at the time. All they ever said to each other was, *Flob a lob, Weed?* Guess *Flob a lob* was some form of 1950's jive talk or rap term for, *What's up bro, got a lotta…(Weed)?* And of course the whole thing was based around *pot* plants for God's sake…dear me, we were naïve those days.

Blue Peter and Shep

Talking about pot plants reminds me of another great children's show, *Blue Peter*. As my mother taught me that my penis was called my *peter*, I was confused what this show was about. I guess it was educational to learn years later that the *Blue Peter* was also some form of naval flag and the show had little to do with the turning blue effect of swimming in the North Sea on your private parts.

Indeed, it is just as well, as those young males who had the pure torture and pain inflicted upon them by parents who forced them to swim in the sea, their memories would never allow them to watch a TV show which depicted the effects on their developing gonads.

Recently I had a discussion with a blind Scotsman in the pub. He was on holiday on the English Riviera. Interestingly this man was a plumber by trade. I admired his resolution in the light of his disability so recruited him to fit my new bathroom, as my usual handyman, *Burglar Bob*, was banned by the neighbourhood watch, but I couldn't persuade my darling to use him. She struggles with my pub tradesmen for some reason and believes they may all be piss heads like me - blind, or legless, it doesn't matter which — she's a hard woman. Anyway we had drunk several beers of course so the conversation was convoluted but we got onto days gone by and holidays with parents in the frozen sea up North, or in the Lochs of Bonny Scotland. We both shuddered remembering the first moments of entering zero-degree water and freezing your bollocks off whilst your parents told you it was good for you. His father used to make him and his sister climb over moss covered slippery stones and pushed them into the freezing Lochs, bashing their knees, arms and heads on the rocks. He said there was never any sand, purely solid granite. His father never swam with them. Strange that...

The retraction of the testes is *a flight fight reaction* from the autonomous nervous system. It works brilliantly when they are immersed in water at freezing point and indeed that precious *peter* turns a lovely deep blue and retracts to a scale my friend Dicky so eloquently and accurately described as, 'The size of a 0.22 air rifle lead slug.'

Blue Peter TV show hosts Val Singleton and Peter Purves spent most of their time trying to encourage their young viewers to win a *Blue Peter* badge. I knew no one who had won one; just as I knew no one who could ever afford, or find any sticky back plastic. Every item you had to make at home from cardboard boxes, egg boxes, any detritus your mother was about to throw in the bin, had to be stuck together with sticky backed plastic. In Shiney Row, no one could hear you scream, never mind that *Cairns*, the only hardware shop, might supply something that NASA invented. We couldn't afford to buy things like that anyway; we stole most things from *Cairns* if we needed them, like *Airfix* model planes, *Dinky Cars*, fireworks and matches for burning bonfires. But Mr Cairn never had sticky backed plastic, so no one won a *Blue Peter* badge. To this day I know no one who did.

When they weren't showing you how to build space rockets or produce the next Monet, the hosts would be shovelling up dung from the hordes of pets they kept on the show. *Petra* was their first dog and when that hound was wrapped in sticky back plastic, buried in the *Blue Peter* garden and sent off to the dog heaven in the sky, John Noakes brought in *Shep*, looking very like himself, a Yorkshire sheep dog.

Get down Shep! became John's handle over many years as Shep leapt at the other pets trying to eat them or to shag them or leaping on guests who knew little of sticky back plastic.

John decided to upsize on pets and brought in *Dumbo*, the elephant, which promptly covered the whole studio in shit which our lovely John slipped in and fell covering his lean body head to foot in elephantine poo. Yes, *Blue Peter* was educational all right.

To bring back memories, the other night I watched a documentary on the history of *The Flying Scotsman* steam train, at one time the fastest train in the world. And there, in 1966, was John Noakes getting on board in a special *Blue Peter* episode. This was to support keeping the iconic engine in the post-Beecham, *white heat of technology*, diesel train-inhabited tracks of the East Coast Line. *1966 wow!* I didn't think John Noakes had started so early on the show.

In another unbelievable coincidence as I write this bit of my epic I'm listening to BBC Radio 2 and hear it is the Diamond Anniversary of *Blue Peter* soon. It started on 16th October 1958 and tonight they are presenting a Diamond Blue Peter badge in Manchester for the 5000th show. It will be taken there in an armoured truck. It appears there are many badges now of various colours and grades. The show has come a long way from Elephant poo and sticky back plastic: a great British tradition.

Fireball XL5, Thunderbirds, Captain Scarlet and the Mysterons and Stingray

If sticky back plastic was the cutting edge of technology in those days other amazing cardboard technology brought us TV puppet shows loosely mimicking the Marvel super hero type comics and shows like *Superman, Hulk, Spiderman and Batman*. Our puppet heroes were *Steve Zodiac, Troy Tempest, Marina, Lady Penelope, Parker* and many more. We all desired toy *Thunderbirds* to play with and blow up with fireworks. The animation and special effects sadly left a lot to be desired and the CGI technology of today has come a long way from watching these puppets dangling off strings and voice overs out of sync with fish like mouth movements, but to us it was Steven Spielberg, *Star Wars* and *Avatar* all in one. We were easily pleased.

The Clangers: Bagpuss: The Wombles

Once technology moved on in 1968 from a wooden *Pinocchio* and string we began to get even stranger shows using animatronics out of the Stone Age. *The Clangers* were quite bizarre really for the time. They only ate green soup made by *the Soup Dragon*, who interestingly for those male-oriented times was a dominant lady. They also ate blue string pudding resembling long strings of hardened snot which stuck to the underground caves on the planet where they lived. Curiously, they spoke only in high pitched whistles, which we all imitated in playgrounds and the streets. I can still do it now, listen! …*phew, phew, phew, phew…. Phew!* Which means, *Buy this book for your friends please for Christmas.* If I added a subjunctive clause *phew ooh phew* and said the fourth *phew* whistle in a higher intonation in the ablative absolute then it would mean: *I am sick to death of shitting green broth and eating stringy snot: I could murder an Indian.*

These cuddly creatures were made out of wool, obviously knitted or put through one of the used cotton reel bobbins that my mam used to put pins into and string wool through to make long bits of woven material. My lovely wife knits the characters of The Nativity for charity - Shepherds, Wise Men, Angels, Sheep, etcetera. and now I can see clearly they resemble *The Clangers*. Indeed her baby Jesus is a dead ringer for Baby Clanger and her Wise Men's camel the spit of the Soup Dragon. I may well start my own Clangers show with these woolly imitations - Spielberg and George Lucas, *DreamWorks*, *Pixar*, who needs them? Like the BBC, I too can spend absolutely sod all on actors, special effects and animatronics and still create something that millions of people will remember and adore.

Similarly, *Doctor Who* utilised special effects we could replicate easily. We used to make amazing replicas of *Daleks* from large cardboard boxes with egg boxes stuck on the sides. And Dad's drain plunger as *the exterminator* gun. Sadly in the streets of Shiney Row when you heard the lads start the chant *Exterminate! Exterminate!* it always ended up in a mass fight, with *The Doctor* getting kicked to death. Sadly living somewhere that resembled an MMA cage fighter's arena, they meant it! No happy endings with *The Doctor* saved by his helper or a friendly alien. Curiously, there was never any girl *Doctor's helper* with a mildly romantic subplot in our shows - only violent young male mayhem which the girls watched amusingly whilst playing with their *Cindy Dolls* or skipping down the street playing *Bays*, a game more familiar to posh people as *Hopscotch*.

Two more shows that were created from the BBC Director General's wife's curtains and old cushions were *Bagpuss* and *The Wombles* - the licence fee was in safe hands in those days.

William Tell, The Saint, The Avengers and Robin Hood

These more serious *live people* shows were also favourites and it is the music that tends to stay in the memory rather than any episode. *William Tell* started with the huge flugelhorn blowing and then the song; *Come away, come away, come away, with William Tell...* and then the infamous scene of William shooting the apple off the boy's head with his crossbow. I loved the baddy, *Lamburger Gessler*. He was *Willoughby Goddard* in real life, huge and shaped like a gigantic Swiss cheese with a pock-marked holey face to match who made *Jabba the Hut* look like Gandhi. *Con Kellet* of the future *Comrades Club* stories in later chapters was similar and often called Gessler, but not to his face! Unlike the amiable criminal Con, Gessler was a real baddy.

Robin Hood starred the iconic Dicky Greene, never heard of again, but everyone our age remembers who played Robin Hood. Again the music sticks in the brain:

> *Robin Hood, Robin Hood, riding through the glen.*
> *Robin Hood, Robin Hood with his band of men.*
> *Feared by the bad, loved by the good,*
> *Robin Hood, Robin Hood, Robin Hood*

I can't remember a single episode but we all loved it.

Roger Moore in *The Saint* was much more an adult show and we all loved to be able to stay up the watch it. A bit like a *Man from Uncle* with Robert Vaughan and *Mission Impossible* which were exciting and adult, a lot more interesting than men running around in tights, or huge fat bastards making another man in tights shoot *Granny Smiths* apples off poor, tortured young boys' heads.

When we acted the parts outside in the streets, we all wanted to be Illya Kuryakin from *The Man from Uncle* He seemed cool for some reason, despite our indoctrinated hatred of all things Russian or German. To us all foreigners were baddies. I guess David MacCallum wasn't too great at character acting; he always seemed very British in our eyes.

Steed of *The Avengers* fame of course was an archetypal Englishman. In fact those days on TV you hardly ever got anyone on TV who didn't look and speak like an English public schoolboy. Regional accents were only for extremely thick people, cheeky cockney Tory voting and West Ham supporting racists in that show which has absolutely no chance of being repeated on normal TV these days, *Till Death Do Us Part*, or dodgy cockney rag and bone men in *Steptoe and Son* or for lusty adulterous gardeners in D H Lawrence adaptations, with the scenes of rough Northern passion highly censored back then. Real English gentlemen played all the proper drama roles like *Steed*, *The Saint*, and *Raffles* the Jewel thief. Even James Bond was a posh Jock (never trust a posh Scotsman as my Glaswegian mate Denis says). And in any American movies or TV show Englishmen were always posh and cruel, heartless, evil, cowardly, deceitful, racist and effeminate. In fact, you name any character trait that represented the direct opposite of the all

American hero or the oppressed Irish or Scottish, and the English were it. Nothing much has changed today to be fair.

Colour TV and Westerns

The High Chaparral was the first program I ever watched in colour. We couldn't afford a colour TV but my Aunty Winn who had moved out of Paddington, London to the leafy and posh suburbs of Pinner, had one. I watched it at my annual holidays at her semi-detached mansion. This would be around 1969 I guess. I find on the web that colour TV had been in the UK since 1967. I was amazed that she had a TV that didn't have a wire aerial sitting on the telly that one had to move around and twist to get a clear picture. Also the buttons were press type buttons to change the channel and you twisted the button to tune in the picture. Ours had a dial if I remember which you twiddled with at the same time trying to twist and move the wire aerial. Only a circus contortionist or an Asian barmaid could get their bodies in the position necessary to get a clear picture of *Doctor Who* and his *Daleks*.

And who remembers valves? The TV and radiogram repair man seemed to be always in the house replacing burnt out valves. I guess when the Japanese swamped us with modern *Total Quality* manufactured transistors these repair people became redundant. One wonders how we won the war with good old British manufactured valves in our aircraft and ships radios. They lasted as long as the paintwork on a 60's and 70's British made car. Mind you we loved the used valves the repair man gave us or we stole out of dumped old tellies as kids - they exploded in magical loud bangs when thrown at Penshaw lads or at some grumpy old folks front doors. You couldn't do that with the new transistor radios that came from the cruel-heartless Japanese. We were indoctrinated by comics, war movies and our parents' war memories that the Japanese were evil but it never seemed to stop our parents buying their new radios. The magnets in the old cathode ray tubes were also great playthings for young kids and the tube itself blew apart brilliantly with a 0.22 air rifle slug. You can't do that now with your flat screen telly.

The other thing that was lost forever with the transistor and micro chip revolution was Dad twiddling with the back of the telly to try to get it the screen to stop jumping up and down. This I recall now in a rare moment of lucidness was an attempt to alter the vertical hold knob. It never seemed to work and the telly repair man was called out yet again. And twiddling with TV knobs reminds me of Saturday nights some time after this valve repair time in the eighties and nineties when we spent hours trying to get the tracking right on video tape recorders (VHS) that were playing a new video rental. My lovely daughter never fails to remind me of this when I am taking an eternity with the remote to select a Netflix movie.

As an aside my daughter told me last night of a cartoon image going around on the internet of the skeleton of a man sitting on a sofa with a TV remote in his bony hand. He died of starvation trying to choose what movie to watch on Netflix!

In the VHS days my great friend Eddy and I would roll into the house staggering with the drink late evening after yet another Saturday afternoon of relentless misery watching our football team and clutching a brand new rented version of *Indiana Jones* or *Back to the Future* from Blockbusters. We'd both eat our tatie pot and then put the movie in the video for everyone to watch. Inevitably the screen would show some tracking issue and the men would take it in turns to lie on the floor and twiddle the tracking, swearing and cussing and trying to get the bloody thing to stop jumping. Eventually we'd fall asleep and one of Eddy's or my kids would then twiddle for a second or two and fix the tracking and the two families would watch the movie to the sound of the men snoring; only to wake up just as Clint shoots his last baddie, muttering, 'Bugger it. Have we missed Match of the Day?'

Nothing much has changed, except now it is the bloody buffering of Wi-Fi signal on the Netflix or Prime movies. It drives me insane. 'Get a faster broadband' you say - well, we don't have fibre, cable or even valves here yet. I had a faster Wi Fi in Borneo than here in deepest Devon.

Despite the wonder of our audiovisual technology, in 1969, my Aunty Winn's first colour TV was so wonderful and amazing and it was like watching the movies to me. Going to the 'pictures' was a such a special treat when we were small school children and a welcome break from the ritual torture of learning times tables, doing arithmetic problems and being beaten half to death by your teachers. I must move on from audiovisual pleasure to the happy days of school and childhood.

CHAPTER THREE
EARLY SCHOOL DAYS

Bull's Eyes and Stotty Cakes

My mother took me on the first day of school and all I can remember is being taken me down *the black path*, a path that lead from the top of our estate. The walk to school was about ten minutes and it went through Smithies' farmer's field, past the Hodgkiss's slaughter house and butcher's field, where the heads of the animals used in the slaughter man Alfie's Shiney working men's club dental practice were often left. We older kids used to hop over the fence and extract the bulls eyes out of the severed heads to put down the girls' shirts or frighten the lasses on the way to school. We'd also stick them in the teacher's desk drawer to scare the hell out of the more softer teachers who wouldn't resort to the usual teacher assault and battery with a cane, or wooden ruler or board rubber…happy memories of jolly japes like that.

Hodgkiss's butcher's shop where the bulls eyes came from sat on the main and only shopping street in the village. The slaughter house was at the back. Over the years we experienced many beasts running down our street with blood oozing out of them, as they managed to escape the attentions of the village psychopaths trying to slaughter them. They'd run down bellowing, spoiling our football game, or knocking over the dustbins we used as cricket wicket, with men covered in blood and detritus chasing them armed with cleavers and stun guns.

Nothing much changed in the seventies and eighties after the slaughter house was shut, except the men running down armed and covered in blood were normally the local youth (sons of the slaughter house psychopaths) chasing strangers from Washington, Sunderland and surrounding villages. Oh for the joys of a post-Iron Lady pit village life you may say. Nothing much has changed I hear, so maybe you can take a visit and experience the ambience one day after reading this tale. Take your humane killing stun gun with you though.

In winter the black path froze over in parts and we slid down it making slides in the ice which we'd go up and down many times often arriving late for school. Unsuspecting old people of course would slip on these icy death traps and I guess we were the cause of many a fractured hip or wrist. But sliding down the black path was a fond memory.

My mother not only took me that first day at school but brought me home at lunchtime for lunch (dinner to us; dinner was tea, and anything late evening was supper) and took me back and brought me home again for tea. After that first day I went and came back myself. In those days, there was no such thing as Nursery school and we went to school at five years old. Our mothers looked after us until then. Many mothers didn't work, that was a father's role, if he wasn't on welfare or in jail. My mother cooked, washed and cared for me until I went to school. I am never sure when I first stayed at school for dinner, but I remember mostly coming back in winter at tea time.

Normally, we'd be wrapped up in duffle coats, wearing home-made tank top jumpers and balaclavas and sliding most of the way on ice and snow, or getting soaked in freezing rain. We were always kicking footballs with friends or generally causing nuisances of ourselves to the local populace. What I really remember most was the smell of food as you opened the front door which was never locked. I don't think I ever had a key to our house until I left home to go to college. We were not the latch key kids of the modern era for sure.

Anyway, the smell I remember most was of my mam's stotty cakes. She cooked these in her open range oven after making bread and cakes. I am not sure if it was every school day, but it seemed like it to me. The memory of the taste of them, red hot, with melted butter soaked in still delights me today.

For those of you who know little of North East cuisine a little explanation of how to make a stotty. Here is a Michelin star gourmet taster menu for you. Sadly I have lost my mam's recipe but I spotted several recipes on the new cyber world of *Google*. One site has the nearest one to my mother's recipe that my sister and I recall. It is from Karen at www.lavenderandlovage.com.

Stotty is bread. It was made from left over dough for normal bread kneaded into flat cakes then put into a hot oven that has been turned down after making bread. Karen then describes the process: *where it is baked in an initial burst of heat before continuing to cook as the oven cooled. This baking method is what gives the Stotty Cake it's crusty but soft exterior and yet a rather pleasant chewy crumb and that unique 'Stotty' taste too. A cake it is not, but a simple and homely regional loaf of bread.*

I have to say that the Stotties I have eaten over the years from Greggs, other bakers or in pubs etcetera. have never come up to standard of my mam's homemade ones. They are close but different, not chewy enough and some have the flavour of soft bread. Like Karen, my mother also had a *BE–Ro* cookbook and she made cakes from the recipes in it a couple of times a week and the smell-triggered memory of fresh bread, Stotties and cakes when coming home from school remains with me today sixty odd years on. It was Paradise.

MRS RODGERSON
Poetry and Oor Wullie

I was lucky at early school I guess. I had great friends from the close-knit streets we lived in and I was good at football and could look after myself so had little problems with boys of my age. Only the older sociopaths gave you grief. I was also very sporty and quite bright so found school life and work not difficult at all.

I loved my second year junior school teacher Mrs Rodgerson but probably didn't realise it then as it was not politically correct in our limited culture to enjoy poetry, music and literature. But I remember the small snippets of the Arts that she brought to our lessons like yesterday. I would have been about eight when she introduced me to the poetry of John Masefield. We all had to recite his poems. I particularly liked *Cargoes*. It always made me think of distant lands and tropical paradises (I was to live there eventually so I thank Mrs Rodgerson for putting the seed into my head) and exotic animals and materials. Back then, Newcastle might as well have been Swaziland to us, as all we knew was our own and a couple of the other pit villages we fought with, so even *Dirty British coasters with coals from the Tyne* seemed exotic.

Bobby Shaftoe and Bonnie Prince Charlie

Mrs Rodgerson taught all subjects but she always had time in the afternoon to sit us down and read books, recite poetry or sing songs. Her son was called Haydn and she spoke about him a lot in her lessons. I now understand having children of my own how much she must have loved him. Sadly we all took the piss out his name and assumed he must be soft because he played the piano and had a soft name. I do hope they both were blessed in their lives. I owe her a lot. Particularly, as she loved teaching us local folk songs like *Bobby Shaftoe*; One verse stays with me to this day:

Bobby Shaftoe's gone to sea,

With silver buckles on his knee;
He'll come back and marry me,
Bonny Bobby Shaftoe!

Bobby seems to have come from Spennymoor in County Durham and was a Member of Parliament, so I guess he moved up in the world and got his silver buckles. I doubt he left London though for the hedonistic delights of a pitman's daughter in Spennymoor.

Another local song was *The Keel Row*. All about the men who rowed the keel boats containing coal on the Tyne. Something we would never see in our lifetimes because by the time we had found that the Number 39 bus would take us to that far off land of Newcastle, eight miles away, they like the coal they carried, had long gone.

Curiously we always sang Scottish songs as well. Indeed we seemed to have a lot of Scottish culture around us during those days. A lot of people read the *Sunday Post*, a Glasgow newspaper and most of us got a *Broons* annual for Christmas off Santa and the following year, an *Oor Wullie* annual, both of which were compilations of the cartoon strips in the Scottish paper. And joy of joys just this week I have received a copy of *The Broons* annual through that cyber delivery service *Amazon* sent by my best friend Denis from Glasgow in an attempt to cheer me up in social isolation. Indeed, it did and then yesterday a copy of *Ma Broon's Cook Book* arrived for my wife packed with old and ancient recipes from the depths of *The Wee Krankie's* Independent Caledonia of how to cook mince and potatoes.

We used to eat lots of mince and potatoes at school dinner and afterwards feeling very soporific in the afternoons, Mrs Rodgerson would wake us up by singing and reciting poems, especially Scottish songs like *Speed Bonny Boat*.

Speed, bonnie boat, like a bird on the wing,
Onward! the sailors cry;
Carry the lad that's born to be King
Over the sea to Skye.

Times Tables and Canings

School wouldn't have been school then if you couldn't remember reciting your times tables daily. Mrs Rodgerson and all of our junior school teachers had a league table of where their children were on the learning scale of their two to twelve times' tables. We recited a table everyday and were moved up and down the league depending on how accurate you were. It was a bit like *Top Gear* and the celebrities who try to score the fastest lap with a car. Instead of Jeremy Clarkson taking the piss out of you for being useless in those days it was the teacher and your humiliation depended on how sadistic they were. You were either verbally humiliated in front of all or hit with a ruler or blackboard rubber. These days my darling wife teacher tells me that this is now unacceptable and you can be incarcerated in Durham Jail with rapists, murderers and literary agents and book critics for such negative behaviour towards the poor cherubs. You have to encourage children with positive feedback, stroking their inner person and self-esteem and reward them for failure. Very much like the real contractors in my book *A Turkey and One More Easter Egg* when I think about it! The only positive stroking we got at school was from a cane or ruler.

Indeed, looking back, how on earth did the teachers get away with the overt violence and, without doubt, the perverted pleasure some weirdos got from beating the hell out of small kids? I guess it was the norm; remember our law makers in the UK had mainly grown up in Public (private for the non-British reader) Schools where regular thrashings and rogerings by your prefects and teachers made you a man and helped you gain a stiff upper lip and enjoy a great batting average. Such torture and abuse ensured you retained a long lasting pride in your old school as you took up the 'white man's burden' and ruled the natives across the red coloured parts of the world in your school atlas.

Maybe we have gone a bit too soft on our kids on many things particularly health and safety regimes. As my beloved reminds me, her first Headmistress at Grindon Infant school corrected her in her first job when she suggested to the darling old lady that she thought that the modern teaching practice she had recently learned at college prohibited her sending the boys and girls outside in the freezing North East winter with short trousers and skirts on. Her leader's response was, 'Don't be silly girl, my boys have never caught pneumonia through their knees.'

She was correct of course. We didn't.

However, in those 'good old days', it was not unusual for teachers to hurl board rubbers at your head, slap your legs, whack you over the hand or backside with canes which they all seemed to have handy next to their desks. One of the worst implements of torture to be beaten half to death by was the heavy T-shaped blackboard ruler.

Recently in the *Grumpy Old Gits'* corner of the bar I was told about *Killer Phillips*, a psychopathic teacher who used to have several canes in a bucket. As children were hauled up by the neck to face his wrath, he'd take out each cane and whip it in the fluid movement he'd perfected. If he wasn't happy he'd put it back and take another one. He tortured his victims for minutes as they waited bent over the desk for excruciating pain to come. When he was happy with the weight, spring and lethality of the cane, he thrashed the unfortunate pupil as hard as he could – then broke into an ecstatic sweat as he finished.

Charlie said: 'He acted like 'Zorro' in the movies, whipping his canes in the air like a sword before choosing one and then thrashing you half to death'.

It seems *Killer* was a woodwork teacher and this correlates with my own research on woodwork teachers. Our Grammar School woodwork teacher Mr Dagg and our metalwork teacher Mr Dodd, had perfected the art of battering you with implements of wood or metal honed in the form of rapiers or broadswords. I remember having my hair held in a vice for most of the lesson while getting beaten by my half-made coal fire shovel, a particular favourite of torture from Mr Dodd who seemed to have an avid dislike of Led Zeppelin type haircuts and boys with poor iron riveting technique.

As we grew up it became a rite of passage and badge of honour for the more intransigent and unstable boys in the school to try to outdo the other boys and girls with the amount of beatings they got. Again I have a scientific correlation in human behavior here, as with my directly proportional relationship theory between how late someone stayed out when their mother called them in for bed (or if they never went to Sunday school) and how many years in Borstal they did. The number of deliberate canings they got is directly proportional to the years they subsequently spent in Franklin and Durham Jails. I have the mathematical proofs.

Mrs Rodgerson was the teacher who gave me a very basic understanding of the Arts without resorting to ritual violent abuse. Not the more avant-garde style of painting and literature that frankly is lost on me, but basic poetry, singing and literature. She read to us most afternoons. The first two books I still remember were, *The Secret Garden* and *The Bluebird*. I read them both years later and sadly they were lost on me, but then, when in the throes of childhood, I loved my days with Mrs Rodgerson as she read to us every afternoon, they were classics to my uneducated and naïve eight year old school mind.

Those days one teacher taught you everything. Music, Reading, Spelling, Arithmetic, Problems, English, etcetera. I can't remember if we had a special teacher for sport as we seemed to play only football every day. I was on the school team from day one and the captain. The great bonus was I was called out of class early by a male teacher to go to play away matches much to the jealousy of the non-players. I can never remember training or coaching. We just seemed to turn up and play a game.

It may well have been in Mrs Rodgerson's class that we changed from wooden pens with nibs to blue handled ball point pens. The old pens were like quill pens with ink pots in each of our wooden desks. The blue ball point was a revolution in technology to rival smart phones these days. Sadly it made the ink monitors redundant. Their important job was to fill the ink wells each day but as they were not as militant as the Luddites and sadly not having the then political clout of their fathers' *National Union of Miners* they were cast into history with their first experience of redundancy. The lucky ones managed to get a milk monitor job, two of whom carried the crate full of a third of pint bottles of free milk into the classroom at morning break, pushed a wooden straw into each bottle and handed them out to their classmates. I also remember eating free *Digestive* biscuits around this time at school. Not sure when that smashing pleasure was stopped but I believe it was before I left for Grammar School and the first milk was *snatched* by *Darling Harold*. For those of you who know nothing of free school milk or late twentieth century politics, Mrs Thatcher who became Prime Minister of the UK in 1979 was forever termed *the milk snatcher* for stealing the school milk, a horrendous crime against humanity, but it was Harold Wilson, the then Labour Prime Minister who first pinched the milk for teenagers in 1968 when millions of baby booming adolescent youths were guzzling it in gallons. I know I was.

Dear me, I have just realised, it was a Labour Prime Minister making miners' milk monitor kids redundant. God knows what the Tory *Daily Mail* or *Sun* would make of that these days. If I was his special Downing Street advisor, and my eye sight had improved enough, I'd send a brief from my coffee shop in Barnard Castle to *The Guardian* and spin it as the Government's major vegan policy change in managing our children's health...first remove the fatty cholesterol free milk and then the methane-farting, ozone-depleting cows.

Girls seemed to carry things in satchels those days. I can't remember any boy having anything but a towel bag. We must have carried our football boots and strip in something? Maybe haversacks? But I only remember haversacks when I went into senior school and then we painted the names of our favourite rock bands on them. On mine was Free and Jethro Tull. We all seemed to have towel bags at junior school but I really can't remember what we carried in them. I can't remember ever showering in junior school so maybe the towel was for washing hands or a bloody nose. I guess we did use our own towels those days at school for ablutions and things and my memory has just faded for what they were used for.

Recently I met a fellow North East lass from Blyth, Northumberland, who drinks in my local pub now with her Dorsetshire husband. This causes him much stress as we love to talk about what I am documenting in this book – the great times we had when we were young up North. Her accent gets more and more Geordie as the wine goes down and the stories are told and it really chews him up as he can't understand a word we say. One day I will buy him a 'Geordie Passport' so he can come up one day and see how great the place is and 'lorn te tarrk proppa'. I used to carry this at all times and I'm not sure if it exists now but the part where you have to tick what your marital status is always made me chuckle. The choice: Please tick the box: *Married....or Happy.*

...Anyway the point of this is that this lady prompted my memory again of schooldays and reminded me how they all loved to go outside for a class in the summer. This was indeed a great thing, to be let out of the class and sit on the school field and be taught with daisies and dandelions galore around, and for me - raging hay fever.

Sadly, after another hot summer (they were all hot those days of course) and outside classes among the daisies singing Scottish songs and quoting John Masefield we had to leave Mrs Rodgerson and move up to Year Three juniors where little art was talked of but a lot of war.

MR LISTER
'Don't mention the war'

Mr Lister was the next teacher after Mrs Rodgerson. We never seemed to sing or read poetry much with him. He was the football teacher and managed the junior team. He talked about seeing poverty-stricken, hungry kids kicking balls that were made out of rags in Singapore, Thailand, Indonesia and other places that we could only dream of and he would tell us how lucky we were. It all seemed too far away for us. It was History and particularly *The War* parts of it he seemed to be obsessed with.

He was a nice man if I remember right, tall, gaunt and even then I could see he wasn't quite well. He had been in the Far East during the war and it was clear that his life in the South East Asian jungles and Japanese prison camps had left him mentally scarred. His lessons were always interrupted with references to *The War*. He was never very negative about the Japanese or ever put over his obvious pain at their expense but he told so many tales about the East and the war in general.

I loved to hear these stories of strange foreign lands, animals, and people. I guess that living in a small pit village with little that was exotic but a lot of strange people, Mr Lister's reminiscences were a motivation to get out and try to meet normal people. I failed as you can read in all my past novels.

MR TELFORD
Morris Dancing and School Toilets

In the final year at junior school we gained a strange teacher new to the school, Mr Telford. He was unusual in that he had a beard. I knew no one who had a beard then. He was also unusual as he liked dancing. I knew no one who liked dancing either, so he was definitely weird.

Mr Telford was famous in that he stopped football in his lessons and introduced Morris Dancing. He was universally decried as a sadist and a puff. Mind you none of us knew who or what a puff was. A puff meant someone who didn't play football or fight or was a sensitive human being and not a vicious psychopath like most of my young school chums. Effeminate people were, well...soft. Homosexuality and anything linked to sex was a mystery that we all thought we knew about but didn't. There was no sex education or biology in junior school that I can recall, only English, Maths (which was Problems and Mental Arithmetic) and General Knowledge - the prize which I won every year I am proud to say and still have the encyclopaedias that I was awarded as a testimony to my father's talks at night and when we walked around

Lambton's three gills (woods) every Sunday morning talking about life before he went to the Club.

And of course we played only one sport. We played nothing else at school but football. Once a year we had a sports day where we all had to run and do silly games. Games like the egg and spoon race, the sack race, the bean bag race and hula hoops if I recall. I could never work out what a bean bag was. The only beans we ate were Heinz or Dad's broad or runner beans and they felt nothing like what was hidden in the bag. It remained a mystery for a few years until I met a young lass who ate nothing but grass and beans that came from the mystical bean bag. She introduced me to where the beans were magically born and sold, places like delicatessens, pulse and spice shops...of course the relationship didn't last.

At the Sports' day, the lads all slinked off to kick a football until coerced into competing with the girls. It was the same with Mister Telford's dancing. All the boys universally hated dancing. We were forced to pick girls to dance with and this was worse than our regular visits to the dentist. I always picked the girl who I didn't like. This was a ploy to ensure that no one would suss out that I really did like a couple of girls - a nightmare if anyone found out as you'd have things chalked all around the school playground and coal houses about your and your girl; this was a mega embarrassment for a ten or eleven year boy. Note: we didn't have spray paint in those days, only chalk that we stole from the blackboards or teachers desks or ripped out of plaster board that we wrecked in our habitual playing and thieving raids on the new house building sites that were a consequence of the 1950's baby boom.

School in that last year before senior school was still fun though. Mr Telford started to treat us as young adults. He was trying to develop a sense of pride in our local culture, in ourselves and how to live and communicate in a world outside of our close knit, narrow experiences. He was the first person who sat me down and told me of my weaknesses and strengths and treated me like a young adult and encouraged me to use the communication and leadership talents that he saw in me. For his teaching and counsel I am grateful to him. However, his bloody dancing was still horrible; even with Christine as a partner. Mr Telford scarred us for life. These days he would have been arrested for child cruelty.

Those last junior school memories are happy for me, Morris Dancing the exception. There were bad days of course but they were dwarfed by the fun days. Playing out in the playgrounds was ok if you were not a target for bullying I guess. But I can't really remember same age bullying, we all seemed to get on, even the strange boys and girls, the really poor, the really smelly, the really thick, and the posh from the posh houses seemed to get on. Of course some lads were classed as softer than others and maybe got picked on and there were frequent fights between those of us who were thought to the best fighters but that seemed normal between boys moving up the pecking order. But outright bullying didn't seem prevalent in that community then. It changed later at Grammar school but at Shiney Juniors, most of the time we played out in the playground, the school field and particularly the toilets.

Toilets and Peeing Competitions

School toilets were always a place of fun for boys. Our toilets were outside and open-roofed. We used to see how far we could pee up the wall and the best of the lads could always pee over the wall onto the girls in their toilets. It was great fun to hear them scream as one of us hit the target. Peeing long distances vertically is something in which men retain some superiority over our fairer sex. I guess men are still good for that at least.

We had a competition for who could pee the farthest up the wall and hopefully over it. As we all know size didn't matter - well that's what we tell the wife - it was bladder sphincter control and how much you could hold in your foreskin that mattered to create a massive foreskin balloon of pee and develop huge internal pressure by nipping the end of the foreskin. I always thought that the circumcised of the world are at an evolutionary disadvantage for peeing over toilet walls and for God's sake surely it cannot be normal to let old men in beards and long robes chop bits of your dick off!

Toilets are a fascination to the assembled insane in the bars I have habitually lived in since an early age. Men seem to have a fixation on toilets and particularly British men. As the Red Baron told Blackadder in *Blackadder goes Forth*: 'How lucky you English are to find the toilet so amusing. For us, it is a mundane and functional item - for you, the basis of an entire culture.' And so it is. Memories of toilet paper are also a huge discussion point for some of us.

IZAL Medicated Toilet Paper

Those of us who remember outside toilets and having to do our business in potties under the bed or endure the long freezing cold walk over ice-covered backyards to the outside loo, have vivid memories of toilet function. My grandad's outside privy in Barrack Row was particularly traumatic to me. The door didn't lock and was only a half door anyway so you sat there with another old person next door with his or her drawers down their ankles, head popping over, normally with a cigarette in the mouth and newspaper in hands. Listening to the strains and sounds of evacuation and my God, the smells! It still puts me into some Freudian neurotic catatonia. But I guess it was the toilet paper that most of us remember.

Toilet paper those days was either newspaper cut up, or if you were posh, and certainly in all school toilets, it was *Izal* medicated toilet paper. It was very distressing to try to read the news on the small sheets of newspaper because as you got to an interesting part it ran out and the sheets were never ever put in the order the editor placed them in the paper. Also the class of paper was important, *Scots Ken*, a friend from *The Castle* pub, now sadly deceased, told me in the pub his father from Glasgow would never use *The Glasgow Herald* because the print came off on your arse. This prompted another Mensa type discussion about why now we never have newspaper to wrap your fish and chips in. Most blame the Europeans and health and safety legislation of course.

Now those of you who have grown up with soft, absorbent, sweet smelling toilet tissue that cleans your bottom quite well will have no idea what it was like to smear your own faeces all over your arse and lower back with the wonderful non-stick and slippery *Izal* sheets of paper. Nothing stuck to these *Izal* sheets, especially poo, which surely one would have thought should be a prime necessity for toilet paper.

Winter was hell for those of us having to cross snow and ice cobbles or frozen mud to the outside loo. But winter was infinitely more magical then for some reason despite the hardship of permanent cold and we move on to those magical days.

CHAPTER FOUR
WINTER, CHRISTMAS AND NEW YEAR'S EVE

Sledging and Sliding

On cold nights now I sometimes drift to memories of the glow in the frosty night air of the yellow incandescent street lights which were spaced every twenty yards or so on wooden telegraph poles on our two streets. I clearly see children launching themselves down icy slides time and again from the top to bottom of the road, sometimes sliding well over thirty metres down the slope. In those days very few had cars in our council estate as we were probably one of the poorer areas around and therefore we were never bothered by many cars interrupting the fun. If the ice and snow was packed hard we took sledges we or our fathers had made using steel runners from 'borrowed' materials from the Pit or from Philadelphia Yard, the engineering works for the various mines which employed men from the village.

Freezing Bedrooms and Oven Shelves

It seemed to be always freezing in winter. Our house was like most were those days - pretty much unheated except for a fire in the sitting room (lounge) which was part of the Rayburn coal oven system on which my mother cooked and baked. If you moved more than three feet from the fire you froze. Dad sat right on the fire in his own easy chair; no one else ever sat in it. My mother, my sisters and I sat on the small two seater settees and two soft stools (pouffees) in front of the fire. My sisters, being twelve and fourteen years older than me, soon married and it was my mam and me on the settee, freezing to death most nights while Dad roasted next to the fire. There was always a pecking order for the nearest to the fire. All fathers always won; as they did with dinner time and bath time. They always ate and bathed first.

The bedrooms were like meat freezers. Two had open fireplaces in them but Dad never lit them because it would cost too much in coal, so we froze. Mam would heat up the oven shelves from the fire oven before bed and then wrap them in a towel and place them under the two tonne weight of blankets and coats that were placed on the bed in a vain hope of keeping you warm through the freezing night. The coats were ex-Army World War Great Coats which had failed to keep Hitler's Russian Winter War army warm never mind us poor children facing the howling North wind. Unlike Cock Robin we had no wings to tuck our heads under and we lay pressed into the bed by the weight of the coats and blankets unable to move under the pressure which pinned us to the bottom pink, yellow and white stripy flannelette sheet.

Today I am in awe of the Scandinavians who introduced us to that marvellous invention, the Quilt, or Duvet, I never know what the correct version is - but who cares - one can lie in bed and move around freely without the risk of that now unknown medical condition: *Great Coat-induced deep vein thrombosis.*

Mornings were torture. The windows had ice on the inside and when your mother called you to get up for school, you'd peer out from the mound of coats and blankets, unable to feel your legs or move, and see the white icy smoke of your breath in the orange bedroom light, thinking, 'Oh no, not again!' Then with immense effort you'd push the blankets and coats up a few inches and try to squeeze out of bed before the weight became too much and you collapsed back onto the bottom sheet and mattress. You had to make another Herculean effort at bedtime to squeeze back into them and slide into the relative warmth before your young developing gonads were frozen forever.

The inside window panes always had beautiful ice patterns on them which I'd scrape off to look out at the weather and the two streets which were still illuminated by the yellow fluorescent lights. It looked bleak most school mornings. I have never liked winter since growing up - scarred for life by freezing dark school mornings and even worse, the ritual ice walk to the bathroom for the morning's ablutions.

The bathroom was at about Absolute Zero, and as in the movie 'Alien', 'No one could hear you scream' when you splashed the frozen sink water over your face. We had no shower, only a bath, and you only had one bath a week on a Sunday night after *David Kossoff's Bible Stories*, so we washed in the sink. Sadly my own teeth were ignored both night and morning hence the visits to the dentist up the street who was almost certainly the missing Josef Mengele. I got dressed in front of the sitting room fire which Dad lit before going off to work. My dear mother attempted to warm my vest up in the oven in a futile attempt to save me from the hypothermia I'd develop walking to school through the ice-lined and eerie foggy, yellow, lamp-lit streets in short trousers. In an attempt to ward of hypothermia I usually wore a home-made knitted tank top, balaclava and duffel coat.

It was 1975 before we ever had the benefit of central heating in our Princes Street fridge and then that was a disaster. The council decided that as the country and times had moved on from living and dying in abject fear of winter they'd upgrade their properties. We were moved out of the house whilst they modernised each street by street of the whole estate. Everyone was so excited that we would finally be warm in winter; especially my mother who suffered badly with Reynaud's syndrome and was perpetually cold and in pain. And indeed, the houses were modernised and a full electric central heating system installed. Joy of joys everyone thought - until winter hit and the bills came through.

Sadly in their wisdom, and I will be kind here with my opinion, the council had chosen one supplier and installer for the heating system which was an electric storage system with a large storage unit which blew out warm air. The problem was that the unit couldn't store enough heat to maintain the temperature in the throes of a North East winter. Rather a stupid design fault you may think given the fact it had been freezing testicles off in winter for as long as councillors had been sitting in Houghton-le–Spring's council chamber.

The other rather strange decision was to use electricity in the first place, given we were bang centre of the coal belt and 75% of the tenants worked in the National Coal Board and received free coal. One wonders now if they knew of Baroness Thatcher's plans to close the only source of heat, work and self- respect for their constituents and therefore were masters of economic forecasting and strategic contingency planning. Well, who knows now, but all of a sudden houses were warmer, but only for few hours, and tenants received huge electricity bills which very few could pay. Certainly my mother couldn't, as my father died that same year the heating was installed and she had no income but his pension of seven pounds a month. So she switched off the heating and ran a Calor gas heater and when the ice started to form on the windows again, yet once more again suffered horribly with her Reynaud's syndrome.

Even as I write this I can't help wondering about the motive for that complete cock up on the heating front. Later when most of the miners and associates had been thrown out of work and therefore received no free coal, the council in their convoluted wisdom took out the doomed electric heaters and put in coke fired central heating but only in a few streets. My poor mother never had her heating changed and she died without ever experiencing a warm house. I'm sure she's enjoying a warm centrally-heated bathroom and lying under a warm duvet in

Heaven and possibly those who put in the electric heating system are roasting too, but somewhere else, and without the duvet.

Penshaw Hill and Broken Hips

As winter's shadowy fingers took their grip our thoughts turned to sledging in the two streets we lived in. Our slides went from top to bottom and I now realise why there were so many old people with broken hips those days – the street was purely one skating rink. The poor old buggers had to walk up every day to go to the other 'street', that was the main street where the shops were, so they had to shuffle their old bones up pure sheets of ice, while kids hurled down at them not caring who or what they hit.

Some of the grumpier, or perhaps on reflection, wiser ones threw boiling water or salt on our slides in an attempt to stop the orthopaedic mayhem that resulted from our tilt at a *Torville and Dean* gold medal. We threw icy snowballs at them or put cold water on their front steps at night, waiting for it to freeze in the hope that when they came out to get the milk off their doorstep they'd go head over heels. As you know, kids are horrible creatures.

The other favourite place for sledging was down Penshaw Hill about three quarters of a mile from my house. On the top of this hill sat Penshaw Monument, a folly built in the form of the Parthenon, the original being the one placed on The Acropolis in ancient Greece. The Penshaw Parthenon wasn't built in honour of the Gods but in honour of the Earl of Durham. It was designed to have a statue of him on top, but I was always told he ran out of his tenants' rent money to build it. No doubt historians will correct me but it sounded right to me as young lad.

This hill you can see from the two roads which head up from the South to the North East of England, the A19 and the A1. Years later that monument announced to me and my family after long drives from the South that we were nearly home. It still does for many. Although the *Angel of the North* has gained more fame, 'Pensha' Monument will always mean more to me.

CHRISTMAS
Snow and Toys

All over the world people remember Christmas as some romantic past idyllic time, whether you lived in the tropics or the frozen North.

To us, it always seemed to be cold and there was snow around. Certainly at New Year it always seemed to be snowing. Records show that age and probably beer induced nostalgia has dimmed the actual facts and it didn't snow as much as we like to remember, but that's what we *do* remember, so sod the Meteorological Office. I can remember the deep freeze of 1963 as we made igloos out of snow blocks, built multiple snowmen and had many snow ball fights. Of course a hidden stone in some snowballs was saved for those we particularly disliked. I am sure Christmas Eve was always cold and snowing. Maybe it's only nostalgia but I have distinct memories of carol singing for money and looking out of my bedroom window at the snowflakes falling through the air, twinkling and brilliant white against the yellow fluorescent sky from the street lights glowing incandescently on their wooden poles.

Somehow my father always managed to save or borrow enough money to make sure we had a proper Christmas with gifts and food. Everyone has their own way of celebrating Christmas; ours now has lots of my dearest's traditions in it, mixed with a few of mine and many the kids have thrown in.

Santa and Nylon Stockings

With my family we always spent it together and we always opened presents early Christmas morning. As a young boy I used to sleep with my mam and dad and couldn't wait for the morning. I woke up middle of the night and saw in the dim moonlight the books that Santa had left on their dressing table or the boxes of toys lying on the floor and tried to identify the ones I'd always I hoped I'd get. We never had a sack, only a nylon stocking of my mother's that Santa would fill up, always with an orange or tangerine at the bottom. Sometimes I'd hear Santa stumbling around opening wardrobe doors as if looking for presents hidden in there: the daft bugger - surely he had them already in his sack? He also seemed a bit tipsy to me, maybe it was the glasses of sherry and whisky he'd been given with his Christmas cake in all the houses he'd been before ours? If I was lucky when I woke up I'd be told to go downstairs where Santa might have left a bigger present and sure enough there might be a bike or a *Scalextric* And many presents stayed in the memory long after the years have dimmed many more important memories.

Johnny Seven Gun, Scalextric and Subbuteo

I loved my *Johnny Seven* gun. This had 7 different weapons on it which to maim and kill the plastic toy soldiers or cowboys and red Indians or indeed my young friends.

I also loved my *Scalextric GP* motor racing track and cars. I played this all day and every day in the small back sitting room we had. My brothers-in-law told me years later that they refused to play with me because of my temper if they won. Plus the swear words were worse than they'd heard down the pit. Something that was a great surprise because when I was older I never ever swore in front of my parents, and neither did my father ever swear in the house. I only ever heard him swear a couple of times when he was pissed and fell off a stool in the club when I was old enough to drink with him.

Santa brought my son a *Scalextric* some years later in the 1990's (well, I had added it to his letter that went up the chimney hoping Santa would bring me back my old memories). Sure enough Santa brought it but my darling boy was never that interested in it; computer games and videos were taking over, and I have to say I'd lost a lot of the enthusiasm I'd had when the racing game was the white heat of technology in my youth. I think it got added to the list of disappointing nostalgic items that weren't as good as they seemed when they, and we, were new to this earth. They were given to jumble sales, or the really new retail ventures that were sweeping the country in the eighties and nineties, car boot sales. Playing with Santa's version that year definitely wasn't as good as the evening I had spent in a Pharmaceutical company team building event in Whites Hotel, London ten years earlier where the six lane race track was almost as big as the Nurburgring with bridges, chicanes, tunnels and cars that actually stayed on the track at high speed. And we had the actual hero of F1 motor racing commentators, Murray Walker, including his famous microphone, commentating on our attempts to beat each other to pole position and the final podium. I have to say the copious amounts of drink may have affected my driving skills and if I remember I crashed into Buster Knuckle's car much to the psychopathic medical rep's angst, and my team's terror, as he squashed my car like a scrap yard mechanical crusher in his gnarled hand before chasing us around the track.

I played with my own soccer *Subbuteo* day and night with Dad and with the lads in the streets. We played each other's mini gangs in teams. I guess those days it was the equivalent now of on-line *FIFA 19*. We had no *X-Box, Play Station,* or *Nintendos* then, and the only Wi Fi I had was the string I used to tie between two empty tin cans. Gussy would take one end into his bedroom over the street and I'd have the other tin can in mine. We talked to each other down this Neolithic Wi Fi system at night when we were supposed to be asleep. I guess teenage on-line gaming and smart phones are more efficient nowadays but we loved it. I think we got the idea from a comic or *Blue Peter.* Comics often provided ideas to improve our poor low tech lives. *The Topper* once gave out a free brown paper wiz bang thing which cracked loudly when you flicked it fast with your hand. Millennium kids, eat your heart out, we knew what real technology was.

I only had the red and blue *Subbuteo* players but some luckier lads had real coloured strips of proper teams, mostly Sunderland and a few Newcastle. This table game was a played on a green baize cloth using little plastic footballers with solid plastic semi circles for feet which you flicked to move them and to kick the football. We all became skilled at flicking the players and could cunningly curl them around other players and hit the ball on various edges and cause it in turn to curl or spin. Sadly my original has been missing these last 56 years but a couple of years ago Santa added one to my younger son's Christmas list - he's been kind to me that man, must be a mind reader. I played my three kids most of the day before Christmas dinner, and relatively sober too, but sadly I've lost the mojo and was thoroughly beaten. Even my daughter beat me - beaten by lass for God's sake! What next - girl's football? Dear me a girl might end up playing the part of Dr Who or commentating on Rugby.

I also loved my *Meccano* set. I spent hours trying to make the tractors, cranes, airplanes and other things from the technical drawings in the box, usually with mates from the street. My ambition was to get a set with an engine for Christmas as only one lad richer than us had the posh set with engine and millions more nuts, bolts and things. I never did - must have been on the naughty list too many times But, like the *Scalextric* and the *Subbuteo* somehow a *Meccano* set got added to my older son's Santa list one year by his fairies - obviously I had been a good boy that year. I was delighted, but sadly, like the *Scalextric,* he only played with me a few times. We finally built what I'd always wanted, a crane with a motor engine. I wanted to build an airplane with an engine but he became disinterested and went back to singing and reciting his Times Tables in bed and trying to develop an algorithm on his Casio mathematical calculator for the monthly pocket money compound interest that I owed him. Not surprisingly, he's a corporate lawyer now; I guess building cranes that could lift a box of *Swan Vesta* matches were lost on him.

I have recently found out that the Meccano Company also made *Dinky* cars and *Airfix* models which reminded how I attempted to relive my youth yet again when I bought my daughter an *Airfix* model of *The Victory*, Lord Nelson's flagship for us both to make. I loved making *Airfix* models when young. I built most of the world war airplanes and ships. The tiny pots of *Humbrol* paints were expensive, but you got a lot out of one pot for the smaller models. My lovely daughter and I finally managed to build our Victory, and after searching a model shop in Newcastle, I found a small tin of copper coloured paint and she painted the ship's bottom to finish it perfectly. I think our large retriever hound savaged it, sails, rigging and rollocks some few days later. I never tried again.

My daughter also loved the *Etch A Sketch* that Santa's fairies added to her list before winging its way up our chimney to the North Pole. There was always something quite comforting about shaking the device and magically, the caveman-like drawings you have made disappear and you are left with a blank screen ready to draw yet another terrible likeness of a horse or a cat. That feeling is almost as good as popping bubble wrap - but not quite.

Josephs Sports and Toy shop in Sunderland was a source of special treats, bought for with months of pocket money saving or Christmas presents. Model *Dinky* cars were special. I watch the Antique Road show now and people wheel in boxes of *Dinky* cars untouched and unopened worth thousands. We bought *Corgi* cars I think, as they were cheaper and all of mine were used in some games in the street where they would be smashed into other kids cars, shot down the road into drains and coalhouses, and stamped on by psychopathic big boys. Sadly, I don't even remember what happened to my Corgi, James Bond *Goldfinger* Aston Martin DB5, 'The best boy's toy of the year in 1965' – without doubt the classic of all kids cars. We all loved to press the button and see how high our car would shoot the evil, inscrutable Asian henchman through the roof from the passenger ejector seat. The car is lost forever, like my Dinky cars and my pet tortoise. And also my *Hornby* train set which was never very big like the ones you see on Antiques Road show now worth £100K but might well have bought me more beers than the royalties of my books do if I'd been wise enough to have kept it.

Snooker and Home Brew

One year in the mid sixties Santa brought me a billiard table which we put in the back room on an old kitchen table. It was approximately 5 foot long by 3 foot wide but to me it was like a real table and I played my dad night after night billiards and snooker. I have never been a good loser, as my brothers-in-law can testify and also the lads who took a thump around the head with a cricket bat if they bowled me out. Dad ended up banning himself from playing with me as he beat me most nights and he couldn't take the resulting temper tantrums. As a result the table was stored for many years.

The game was then immortalised by a new TV station, BBC 2. Those days we only had two stations (yes, folks, it's true, we only had two). And you pressed one of two buttons to get each channel. What did men do those days with no remote to cuddle? Oh it was so different back when BBC 2 launched in 1969 and two years later put on the iconic *Pot Black* with Ted Lowe the whispering commentator. As Ray Reardon and Fred Davis battled it out in the first snooker games ever televised. Whispering Ted is immortalised for his comment to the enthralled TV audience: 'For those of you watching in black and white; the brown ball is behind the yellow.'

My table was resurrected in my teens, as by then I used the back room to study and also as a boy's den with a vinyl playing record player in it. I brought back out the snooker table so that my mates and I could play on it listening to the latest underground progressive rock music and drinking beer.

By the age of thirteen I had learnt to make home brewed beer and wine. My dad had shown me and I fell in love with the art of brewing - and sadly drinking the fruits of my labours. The wine was made from fruits and vegetables from the garden or from what I pinched from other peoples gardens. My most ambitious wine project was to make Birch sap wine. I had a wine making book handed down from my dad's mother's family in rural Bedfordshire which was over 60 years old and it had all the old recipes in it. Birch sap was one. I sneaked onto Lord Lambton's land in the first of his three woods, which we called a gill, and cut V-shaped channels in the Birch tree bark with my pocket knife and a long vertical channel which the V's ran into. At the bottom of the vertical I nailed a small tin can. I did this to several trees and went back to collect the sap which I then used as an ingredient for the wine along with wheat or rice and a few raisins I think. It tasted bloody awful.

Many years later when I lived in Singapore, I visited a rubber plantation in Malaysia and watched them do the same as I'd done nearly 40 years before on the belted Earl's land. I was told to be careful as there were Tigers still roaming the area. I laughed - Tigers couldn't have been as fierce as Lord Lambton's head keeper, George Wilson, and his junior gamekeepers who would routinely beat you if they caught you with a poached pheasant or push the birds' eggs down your throat that we'd snaffled from the aristocrat's gill. They got their comebacks mind. Shiney lads have long memories.

Hamlet cigars, Ronson lighters and Old Spice

Gifts for parents at Christmas were always problematical, 1) because of money and 2) what the hell to get them. I'd try to save up my pop and beer bottle collecting money or paper round money and my dad would help out if I asked. Mam would let me use her catalogue and buy something for about six pence a week over 52 weeks. I know that many people did the same from the Brian Mills catalogue as it was the only credit they could gain. Many of us remember the classic presents that all parents got from Santa.

Hamlet cigars were ubiquitous and greatly valued by fathers the world over. It was only when I started going to the Club with my dad that I realised how many parents got *Hamlets*, or the smaller *Tom Thumbs*, as Christmas presents because the bar smelt of cigar smoke which was unusual as it was normally cigarette fumes of *Silk Cut, Players Capstan Full Strength, Woodbines or Embassy.* Nobody smoked cigars except on Christmas day. The TV advertisement was a Christmas special for many and come on now let's all whistle it, to the tune of, *Air on a G String* and finally the classic line, *Happiness is a Cigar called Hamlet.*

The Club also smelt of *Old Spice* shaving cream or after shave. *Old Spice* was also advertised heavily in the Christmas build up with hunks of American men, surfing and splashing their chiselled chins with the smelly liquid from the red bottle. Very few of our dads used after shave lotion at all and few used cream and none had ever surfed in the freezing North East coast to my knowledge. They all used soap from a lather pot and a badger hair brush to apply it. But at Christmas they all smelled of *Old Spice*. However, a revolution happened in the seventies when they launched *Brut* aftershave and deodorant.

Brut was the younger man's *Old Spice* and took the market from *Old Spice* for the young fathers and young teenagers like me. It was supposed to be sexy and smell good to women; whereas *Old Spice* smelt like a mix of Geordie Corn's barber shop floor and *Brylcreem*. It was advertised by Henry Cooper, the only man to have knocked down Mohammed Ali (well he was Cassius Clay then) and supposedly his broad cockney accent and naked torso made it seem macho. The slogan that *Our 'Enri* slurred out in his boxer's cockney hard man drawl was the iconic *Splash it orl over*. It was an acquired taste is all I will say, and I believe it has since been resurrected by that other 'ball grabbing' macho cockney hard man, Wor Vinny. *Blue Stratos* smelly came later to the next generation and I remember the smell of this at many Boxing Day football matches along with nylon shell suits and trainers as Christmas pressies for the supporter glitterati of the football grounds across the country.

Cigarette lighters were particularly valued by parents, *Ronson* seemed to make the best and you could buy table sitting ones or pocket ones, for either sex. I think my mother bought Dad one once but he never really used it as the flints kept falling out or he ran out of petrol or butane gas or whatever fuelled the thing. He liked matches or wooden spills lit from the coal fire.

Mothers tended to get food or bath things and chocolates or biscuits and one year when we had finally got a fridge on hire purchase from the electric shop in the village I bought her a pack of frozen peas as I thought these were new and exciting! She smiled and thanked me joyfully as only mothers can as she put the packet into her new fridges tiny freezer compartment. Chocolates were normally *Milk Tray* or *Black Magic*, *Quality Street* or *Cadbury's Roses*. Again the adverts sold them to the masses. *Milk Tray* were always showing a man dressed in a black tight body stocking and mask who stole into the ladies bedrooms and left them by their bed...*All Because the Lady Loves Milk Tray*.

One wonders if you can have men stalking women like that these days and stealing into their personal space in the middle of the night. Indeed, on discussing this very subject the other day in the pub we came to the conclusion that a lot of what was taken to be normal male behaviour in the *good old days* would not be allowed now, especially the pervert stalker in *My Fair Lady* who often walked up and down poor

Eliza's street, stopping and 'staring through her window. For God's sake, he'd be hung up by the gonads now. And Roy, the Teignmouth Yank, then broke into a new, quite haunting lyric for the song, *I often stalk down the street you live*. Dear me, Bernard Shaw never expected his character to end up as a pervert, 'porvort in Durham pitmatic vernacular', and sexual predator.

Black Magic always was associated with love and courting lasses, a bit soft really for us lads to give our mothers, so we gave them *Quality Street*. If Ena Sharples on *Coronation Street* could eat them, then so could our mothers. And yes, everyone still loves the purple one, and everyone fights to get them. My mother loved us so much that she would only take one. A parody of the *Rollo* advert; *Would you give someone your last purple one?'*

As kids we loved selection boxes with all the favourites in *Mars Bars, Aero, Galaxy, Cadburys Flakes, Smarties, Milky Way, Caramac, and Milky Bars* - you name it they were gobbled with glee and on top of dripping, turkey and Christmas pud, they made many a young child sick. But it was worth it.

Kitchen Gadgets for Christmas

If my mother was lucky she would also get some great gadgets that lasted about one month after Christmas. They were mainly advertised in the build-up to the festive season. The more bizarre seemed to come from the USA. The most frequently advertised would be automatic choppers that would chop, slice, dice any known vegetable or fruit and also fingers. My mother would use it once or twice for making broth then revert back to 50 years of tradition and chop the vegetables with a knife into the size and shape she and her mother had done for years. The device would disappear into some black hole where all American kitchen devices ended up.

The *Goblin Teasmade*, renamed the *Swan Teasmade* was another addition to the black hole. My dad bought one for Christmas but for some reason he still kept getting up at the same time every morning, coming down stairs, lighting the fire and making a cup of tea from the kettle on the fire.

Then there was *Breville* toasted sandwich maker. This was a wonderful thing as it followed the trend in pubs in the 1970's to provide toasted sandwiches to enlightened customers who prior to the seventies could only eat crisps or pickled eggs in a pub. No one has scampi and chips in a basket now either. They seem to have disappeared with toasties and our lost tortoises. No one I knew had a clue what scampi was; we were used to tiny things called shrimps which we bought at the seaside soaked in vinegar. You could also buy them in the Club in tiny packets if you were daft enough to give up the money you could have spent on a pint. Like crisps, only peanuts and bags of these shrimps were eaten until toasties and scampi in a basket arrived, but only by the lasses; men didn't eat while they were drinking. This would be seen as a working mans faux paux as bad as passing the port to the right or holding your lass's hand while you take a stroll. It wasn't until I fished for a living with my crazy brother-in-law, whom I introduce to you later, that I realised what a scampi was.

It was the first Chinese who arrived in the seventies who actually educated me into their use as food. We often caught an Angler fish, an ugly looking bugger which we almost always threw over the side or cut up for bait for the crab pots as no normal person would eat anything where I lived but cod and chips. One day we left one in the boat and when we arrived back at Seaham harbour dock as I sold my crabs and fish on the roadside to the general passing public these newly arrived Chinese went crazy to offer me money for it. It seems that in another world this fish was called Monkfish and its tail was the ideal ringer for scampi and that's what the Chinese put in their scampi dishes. Try doing that now with the price of monkfish!

Back to devices, as Santa had brought my mother a *Breville* we could have toasties anytime we wanted at home and not the Club – even the men. For some reason yet again ours disappeared into the device black hole. I have no idea why. But nothing much changes with kitchen devices. I am sure we bought a toasty device three years ago and I have searched for it now as I write having remembered that we had one. Curiously it too seems to have slipped down some event horizon and joined the now passed Stephen Hawking in his own black hole in the sky. My mother's Electric carving knife Christmas present went the same way when the blades became blunt one week into January.

I wonder if these devices are all taken by the aliens who stole our pet tortoises, as these poor reptiles seemed to disappear without trace too.

Christmas Dinner and TV

Now everyone seems to have real feasts at Christmas with much food and drink and exotic food. We were more simple really. My mother did the cooking with my sisters. Dad went to the Club. Later I went with him with the brothers-in-law and my mates. We ate about 2.45 pm after having been thrown out of the Club at 2 pm. We listened to the Queen - my father and mother liked to listen but frankly those days the Royal family weren't too popular with the younger generation or many of local populace. We were basically hard left of Marx and Engels and Royalty were far too posh and linked to the Southern Establishment which had oppressed the North East forever to worry about that propaganda. Willy Hamilton, soon to be a famous MP and rabid anti-monarchist, lived two doors down from Stripper and my Nana. He used the same outside toilets and tin baths as us all and cut up newspaper to wipe his bum. He went to my alma mater, Washington Grammar School, so had to be a canny lad. He ended up a Member of Parliament after his family headed to up to Fife, Scotland and work the mines there. He seems to have lost the faith and became a closet Tory and royalist apologist years later according to cyber stuff I read now. But, I think, like the last election result, it probably happens to a lot of people in the end of days - his mind went.

As we grew up most of us kids knew nothing about politics in general but as young adults we started to understand the communities around us and the Socialist roots of our grandparents and parents. Most only read *The Daily Mirror*, or the *Football Echo,* and only for the football and racing pages. *The Sunderland Echo* was only for births and deaths and to learn who had been banged away for fighting; that was all it ever wrote about anyway. My mother and sisters loved to read it every night when they gathered around the table after work. Comments from my mother like, 'Poor bairn, 5 years in Durham Jail. He must have been full of the drink. His mam will be to take away,' about the perpetrator of a serious attack on a young lad, with no care or mention of the poor victim, just the effect on the perpetrator's mother. This drove my new fianceé (who you may gather had not grown up in Shiney and had not been an avid reader of the *Sunderland Echo*) to leave the house for good for her own bleak flat in the Bohemian metropolis of Otto Terrace, Sunderland.

Recently, my dear sister has carried on this trait of peculiar greetings hailing from my old homestead. Most times when I call her first words are not, 'How are yeah deeing David?' or 'How's the kids?' But, 'you'll nivva kna weeze deed David.'. The last call was the usual, ' Hello David, guess wee's deed...' Then she will told me the name of someone who I had known from the village who had been murdered recently and continued, 'They didn't just kill him you kna. They murdered him...' Seems the alleged assailants didn't just batter him to death but had used weapons. And that isn't quite cricket, is it?

I rest my case about my exile from my home asylum.

There was no internet or social and political diversity so our political views were based on family history and community peer group bias. No one I grew up with that I recall now had any other view than that of Nye Bevan - Tories were vermin and the establishment were out to keep us as slaves. All changing now mind behind the 'Red Wall'. However, one man's truth is another one's Downing Street's chief advisor, so as its Christmas let's move on to more fun things and I paraphrase Mark Antony who once lied to a load of fratricidal politicians – 'Let's bury Caesar, let loose the joys of Christmas and enjoy the good things that all genders do'.

Christmas vegetables came from the garden and the turkey from Hodgkiss the butcher. Or when frozen meat became de rigueur in the shops, frozen turkey which came from the Walter Wilson supermarket. As these turkeys were half the price of a real one, we switched from Hodgkiss butchers. We always had a piece of pork which sometimes came from men my dad knew from the Club who fattened up pigs on the allotments and then Snack would bash them, like the greyhounds, on the head with a lump hammer and Alfie the slaughterhouse man/dentist would butcher them. Sadly, few health and environment inspectors those days you may say; or indeed RSPCA.

Christmas pudding was also bought, can't remember my mother making them. We never had exotic sauces for puddings, only *Birds Custard*. It took me years, and only when meeting my dearest, to eat anything but custard. Amazingly, her family had rum sauce, which was gorgeous and alcoholic too. These days we alternate between brandy cream, brandy sauce, ice cream or rum sauce. Posh folk now you may say and I guess you're correct.

Days of the working men's club have long gone, so now I only have a few beers with my kids in the various lunatic asylums masquerading as pubs down here and then go back home.

We also watch the Queen. I am now an avid watcher of *The Crown* and *Downton Abbey*. Wee Willie Hamilton would turn in his tin bath. How times have changed. I see much good in Queen Bess; she is without doubt worth every penny and a good person. I admire her even though I could never ever have seen me supporting the royal establishment in those halcyon days before 1980 when Thatcher pinched my school *Gold Top* milk and turned my homeland into a Japanese car factory

My mother did make Christmas cake which was gorgeous after being fed with sherry every few weeks - we couldn't afford brandy - through holes placed in it with a knitting needle. It was eaten after dinner for tea when the men had all gone to bed to sleep off the hard work of drinking and eating, leaving the women to wash up and watch TV in peace. When my nephews and niece came into the family my sisters were pretty tired after getting up early during the night or even at midnight to open presents so they would dose off while the little horrors watched a kids programme. The men, exactly like male lions, slept until time to get up and go out to the Club again. It was a hard life for them.

My favourite food at Christmas was always dripping and bread. My mother collected the turkey fat and pork fat from the cooked meats she'd cooked the night before and mixed them as liquid until it solidified. Christmas breakfast was for me, my sisters, brothers in law and then nephew and nieces always dripping and bread. Marvellous stuff and it put a real lining on the stomach for the drinking ahead. You may guess we were not sylphlike offspring of our two slim parents: living proof that it's not genes but calories that make you fat! I still eat it to this day for Christmas day breakfast, much to the disgust of her indoors and the youngest of my offspring.

I guess most of us silver surfing oldies remember TV at Christmas. As a kid I watched any Disney that might come on, but those days access to these movies was not as easy as now. As a young kid I played a lot with my toys and gifts while Dad was at the Club or he was in bed after dinner and mother and sisters finally managed to sit down and watch telly. I really only went out to play in the street when I got a new football or boots and one year I actually got a football strip bought from Josephs in Sunderland; a full Sunderland AFC kit. This had to be put on and played with outside with other lads who had a new ball or boots as presents. Football strips those days were very rare. We never wore them to a match like everyone does now, only to play football with. They all had long shirt tails and long sleeves too and never fitted you. And they all were made of heavy cotton which absorbed all water and handicapped you by adding another stone of weight along with the leather boots and wooden studs.

Christmas afternoon there was always a blockbuster on of some movie that had been on general release to movie theatres but from years ago, never as recent as now on Netflix. And there was also Morecambe and Wise. Evenings were always spent watching these iconic comedians and some of their Christmas shows remain classics to this day. Now our younger global village citizens also enjoy the past Christmas *Fools and Horses,* which remain iconic and global in their appeal. Eric, Ernie, Rodney, Del Boy, Trigger and all will remain etched in the Christmas memory of millions around the world. We still put on *The Vicar of Dibley's Christmas Dinner Incident* every year but have given up on the Brussels sprout eating competition. Turned soft you may say...and you are correct.

Carol singing for money

The build-up to Christmas included carol singing at neighbours houses, not for any Yuletide ambience or Dickens style wassailing, but purely for money. We never had much luck prising money out of our local council house or colliery house neighbours as none of them had any. Also few gave much thought to carols anyway; most were heathens bordering on satanic. Therefore my best church friend Paul Stoker and me would head down to the newly built Leech, the builder's private houses where he lived and try our luck there. Here we had success as the owners actually liked carols and had money to give us.

That was until we sang at one door and rang the bell (this was a luxury, no one had bells where we lived, you banged on the door which was always open anyway). We looked through the glass door and saw a man running down the stairs and he hurled himself at his lock and flung open the door. He slapped Paul across the head, ignoring Paul's open hand in anticipation of a few pennies placed in it and hurled abuse as we quickly turned and ran as fast we could down his drive followed by his bellowing voice: 'You young bastards! I've spent hours getting the bugger to sleep and you wake him up with your bloody caterwauling. Bugger off before I get the polis!' Yes, the Christmas spirit wasn't entirely great all those years ago, *The Krankies* were alive and well in many houses.

I never saw a real tree in anyone's house; everyone had plastic ones, if they had any at all. Our decorations were paper streamers and paper bells. We had some tinsel that Mam would put on the tree but not much. The tree lights were glass coloured, some in the shape of snow-covered houses, Dickens style lamps or red or blue petal shaped bulbs and decorations were plain round baubles with some tinsel. The tree normally got knocked over every New Year's Eve by some drunken dancing or fighting idiot and sadly the lights and ornaments have never survived those days, which is a pity because we have 80 year old decorations from my wife's extended family still to this day. I guess, as they didn't drink or invite sociopaths from the streets into their lovely home, they were rather more careful with their real Christmas tree and lights than us.

Sunday School and Collection Money
These days, for reasons, if you continue to the end of this epic, I may tell you about, I go to Church regularly. I love advent and Christmas and attend most services and events. My lovely wife has taught young children all her life so she is used to nativity plays as she arranged and supervised so many at school and watched all three of our children in their own nativities. I can never remember a nativity at school at all. Whether this is a mental block, or at Shiney Row we didn't do them I can't say. The first nativity I attended was my own daughters and subsequently my sons'. Sadly due to work commitments I missed many. In my later years running my own consultancy and getting back a family life I made more effort to attend as it is an emotional and valued time that I wished I'd spent more time doing.

None of my family was into Church so I guess Christmas was purely a commercial holiday for them and me. However, as a young boy I was made to attend Sunday school, despite neither parent ever going to Church. Like many parents they still thought it was correct to send their kids to Sunday school.

I hated going. The main reason was not a spiritual one but that I had to leave playing with the other boys in the street and come in to be washed by my mother and put on short trousers and shirt and tie. It was awful when she called me in from football or burning down things around 'the front' to get washed and dressed. The boys would take the mickey and as I left the house all dressed, hair combed and carrying my collection money, the older boys would try to slap me and try to take it from me. No one ever succeeded as I was still a handful even in my short trousers, sleeveless knitted jumper white shirt and red tie but it was a walk of torture every Sunday.

I met Paul Stoker at the top of the street, my best friend, and we walked the few hundred yards to St John's Chapel. But on the way we'd try to put our collection money into the two outside chocolate vending machines and bubble gum machines at Richardson's newsagents. I became really good at pulling the chocolate machines drawer where the chocolate bar came out and not putting money in. The drawer would open slightly and there was enough chocolate showing to be sliced off with my pocket knife. I now ask a few prayers of forgiveness for the church collection money that never found its way to the collection plate. I also ask for a little forgiveness for my actions to the poor old folks and kids who put their hard earned pocket money into Richardson's chocolate machine and expected a full chocolate bar for their sixpence but only ever got three quarters of one.

It is strange that I attended a strict no alcohol Methodist chapel and my sisters were both married in the Station Road chapel down from Stripper's house, yet Dad drank like a fish and never attended church. I never understood why he insisted we all go to Chapel. The coal fields and mining culture of the North East and Wales have much in common and one thing which I came to realise was that despite the reputation for massive drinking in the population of both areas, Methodism, a teetotal creed, seemed to have prevalence over other religions in both areas, Maybe it was the fact that Charles Wellesley wrote so many iconic hymns and the Welsh and the North East miners like to sing – especially when pissed!

My first public speaking was to say 'my piece' at Sunday school. This was a piece of the bible that you had to learn and recite. I still remember the nerves and the piece that I read that day as I stood up in front of an audience for the first time. My piece, the twenty third psalm, *The Lord is my Shepherd*. I have had little fear of public speaking ever since after staring at the rows of sober, grim-faced, black-suited men and dark clothed ladies in St John's church: I have earned a useful living out of coaching, presenting and lecturing once I stopped *Contracting with the Devil* and real work; an ecumenical and life changing bonus I never understood when having to face the ritual piss take from the lads in the street every Sunday morning on the way to what I felt was a temple of doom.

School Assemblies and Hymns

Once I got old enough to face my father I decided to give up Church. He never objected. But we still had our fair share of religious instruction through school assemblies and class. Assemblies still bring back memories of standing still and quiet for what seemed hours in the morning assembly. Everyone lined in class rows and age. The music teacher played hymns and the Head teacher said prayers. Our school hymn was, *He Who Would Valiant Be* and I can still see a person fainting as it was sung. It is strange that standing still for a few minutes seemed to make people faint then. It was always blamed on having no breakfast.

I can never really remember having breakfast but I must have because today I had a bowl of my Lidl branded Frostie flakes and remembered something from all those years ago. Interestingly, the makers have a secret code stamped onto the inside plastic packet which if you can access and decipher their website you may win £500 if the code is the winning one on the site. I was attempting to read this illegible and inaccessible code without pouring all my flakes on the floor and into the waiting jaws of my Jorman hound when my dearest reminded me of how we used to have little toys and collectable cards in our cereal boxes. Those days we didn't wait till the box was empty to find the toy, we shook the box to try to get the toy to come to the top. Or when your mam wasn't looking, put your filthy hand in the cereal packet raking around to find the toy. It was such a disappointment if you already had the collectable and missed out on completing the set. I remember submarines that sank in the bath and a plastic scuba diver who did the same and strange plastic horses that I had no idea how to play with. The real joy was, if I remember correctly, and if it wasn't my kids' cereal box, were the *Thunderbird* models. Happy days indeed, we had a hearty breakfast and a pretty useless toy to play with but we loved it. It seems after my breakfast discovery this morning that to enjoy your free gift, you must have access to a laptop or smart phone and become IT literate and enter into the first throes of online gambling addiction to get your reward of 500 quid. I fear, like all us grumpy old folks would I'm sure, that this will lead our innocent youth astray. It's where it all starts folks, eating frosted flakes! This simple box of cereal could turn our kids to gambling online, and then drugs, pornography, cyber crime, grooming, trolling, suicides, Muslim jihad recruiting sites, Trump Proud Boys, and Daily Mail online. You name it and your kids might

58

get into it all because of a box of cereal tempting them. Bring back the sinking plastic submarines and save our kids I say.

Sadly, if you didn't eat your cereal, you might faint and anyone who fainted was mercilessly taunted afterwards as being soft. Not very Christian you may say, and yes you are correct; kids are horrible creatures. Maybe we should let them read The Mail on line?

Now as we live in a very different secular and multi-racial world to then and it is deemed not politically correct to point your children to a faith or have assemblies based on faith, I do ponder on what harm it ever did us. I know that most of the people I have known who had some form of religious instruction either be it as little as Sunday school or school assemblies did not subsequently enter into organised religion and now maintain a mainly agnostic, if not atheist, belief. They also live a very caring and forgiving life. Christmas Carols, Sunday school or assembly hymns did not turn us into raging, fundamental religious maniacs. In fact the real maniacs I have known had no faith-based grounding at all in good or bad morals, through Sunday schools, schools or anything - mind you they had little moral education in their own homes for the most part which is probably the real reason for their anti-social behaviour.

As a closing anecdote to this memory and the effect of hymns or Christmas carols on people, the lady Vicar of a church here was for a long time a Chaplain in Dartmoor the famously terrible male prison and she told me that her half empty prison chapel was always full at Christmas. She asked me, *What was the one carol they all wanted when I asked them individually?'* I said, 'I'm not sure, there are many.' She revealed that it was, *Away in a Manger* and the reason they each gave her was that it was the only song that they remembered their mothers ever singing to them.

As Joan Baez sang, *There but for fortune go you or I* or maybe, *There by the grace of God.* I leave you to ponder which.

NEW YEAR'S EVE
Boxing Day and Football
Christmas Day moved into Boxing Day and as kids we would all meet up outside on the street to play with each other's toys; those that had any - many didn't. For some families it was business as usual with little money or compassion from parents. For some of my neighbours Christmas was mainly for the men to get drunk and Boxing Day tended

to be the same, but not only for the difficult families, for most of us. Dad's went to the Club as usual and came home to yet another feast of a dinner with what was left over from Christmas Day yet again prepared by their loving wives, daughters or mothers.

Most Boxing Days many men and women had bets on horses and my dad would take me to the match at Roker Park. As I grew older nothing much changed; Boxing Day was for the drink, horses or football. I chuckle now when I think of all the people and friends I have found since these early days, some of whom on Boxing Day ride to fox hounds, shoot game birds, stalk deer, swim in freezing cold seas for charity, ride racing cycles and generally attend a sporty and affluent life style event on this hung over day. Sadly, in Shiney Row, we didn't.

It was a cold, grey day on the first Boxing Day football match that I remember attending. We got on the the Number 5 or 6 bus from Consett to Sunderland, Park Lane bus station. My father met his mates in the Park Lane pub and I sat outside with the other young kids. Dad brought me a glass of lemonade and a bag of crisps which was most of the kids would get too and he headed off back inside for a couple of hours solid drinking whilst we sat or wandered around the street, staring at each other as no one really knew anyone else. This happened most match days and sometimes I'd be allowed to buy a comic or a puzzle book at the newspaper shop if Dad had won on the horses or had a few more bob than he thought in his pocket. We walked through the town and over the bridge and through the closely packed terrace houses to Roker Park. There was snow piled around the sides of the pitch and stacks of straw which had been put on the pitch to stop it freezing. We as boys were put in the front of the massive Roker End, famous for the Roker Roar. I never understood the fact that small children were put at the front of a packed terrace which bordered on 20,000 people pushing down on you. But I loved it standing crushed among the straw in the dip, level with the pitch and trying to look over the bank of snow to actually see anything. I remember a player injured lying someway off towards the other goal, getting squashed against the front wall and straining to see what was happening over the snow and straw. It was 1962 and the day when Brian Clough suffered his career ending injury against Bury.

I loved those days at football with my father but Boxing Day at my wife's parents when we were courting was my worst nightmare. No drink. No football. No racing – only playing bloody Charades and some bizarre Yorkshire party games with her crazy, Selwyn Froggitt look-alike, Uncle Albert. My audible howls of pain and visible mental torture whilst being served up cream teas, and singing *The Holmfirth Anthem* or *On Ilkley Moor Bah Tat* whilst standing on a chair with a balloon between my legs did little for my impending marriage. And indeed my darling mother-in-law ended up banning me yet again from the house soon after - a cunning plan by me some of you who are cynical and conniving may think. I couldn't possibly say.

MR SNAITH
Coal Shovels and First Foot

We never had alcohol in the house. I guess we couldn't afford it and it was something that wasn't really done where we came from. I can't remember any house having beer or spirits in except at New Year's Eve. I never ever saw a bottle of wine anywhere until I started making my own at twelve years old. I never saw another bottle even when I started frequenting pubs as a fourteen or fifteen year old, and until my time at university, I never saw anyone drink wine. Wine was for rich folk or foreigners. Real women drank *Mackeson Stout* or *Pony's, Brandy and Babycham* or *Cherry B and Cider.* And men certainly didn't drink wine.

New Year was a magical time for us kids in the two streets because we could stay up as late as we liked and get pissed as newts. Every house in the streets was open those days for roving first footers to come in and have a drink with the folks who lived there all through the long cold night. Even the old ladies living on their own would have a bottle of sherry and a few bottles of beer for first footers to take a dram with them.

Our house was always one of the more open houses and full most of the night until New Year's Day early morning. Dad would save up to buy a bottle of whisky, port, sherry and a couple of crates of Federation Special from the Club. My brothers-in-law and sisters would buy much more and Mam would cook ham and pease pudding stotties. She also made non-alcoholic ginger wine for the odd teetotaller and supposedly for us kids to drink - foolish woman! She and I stayed in the house making up the table while my dad and sisters and their husbands went off to the Club for opening time till closing time at 10.30 p.m.

These days pubs and restaurants all have late licenses into the New Year morning and doormen as New Year has become a riotous, commercialised affair. Those days pubs closed at 10.30 pm.and people who didn't have their own homes to go to were thrown on the streets to go searching for houses that would be open and take them in. When my family returned from the Club, they usually had a lot of these homeless with them - friends, acquaintances and pure chancers looking for an open house. Everyone had to be in the house before the witching hour of twelve as Dad locked the door at 11.55 pm. This was because a few minutes after twelve, old Mr Snaith, Snack's (more of him later) dad, our first foot who lived three doors up would come and knock on the door. He had done this for many years and my father would let no one in after midnight before the old retired pitman arrived. He always carried a shovel of coal and when he knocked on the door my dad greeted him with a handshake and a silver coin plus a dram of whisky. Mr Snaith came into the small lounge full of drunken people and put the shovel of coal on the fire. Then he'd sit in Dad's chair by the fire (no one else ever sat in Dad's chair all year) and Dad would light him a tab. He would cough violently, as most of the older pitman did with their diseased, coal-blackened lungs, and we'd all sing and link arms for *Auld Lang Syne*. Only then could the family leave the house to their various other parties. Dad always insisted we were all in for twelve and then could do what we liked. I honoured this until he died.

Whilst the adults engaged in more drink, we kids sneaked into the kitchen and topped up the ginger wine with shots of any spirit we could steal a drink from. Most of the time the men would let us drink and even let us sample a bottle of their beer. Any mothers in the house tended to be a bit less compassionate with our road to eventual ruin and we would have to be careful they didn't catch us. We walked between houses and, depending on the how liberal or how incompetent and uncaring the parents in each house were, we'd get ever more tanked up on sherry, whisky and port. As you might guess we ended up either being sick or slumped in a corner until morning. It took me well into my late teens to be able to get out of bed next day and even face beer at the Club at the ritual afternoon session with the hardened male drinkers. New Year's Day always meant a hangover and sleep.

However, many older revellers would carry on through New Year's Eve and the following day with no sleep. Certain houses would still be open for first foots all through the morning and in the afternoon new parties would start in some houses.

The Club and pubs were only open 11 am to 3 pm (or in some cases 12 am to 2 pm) so for those who could stomach lots of beer time was limited. Those who sat with their head in hands staring at full pints were classed as 'soft' of course. But New Year's Day was a great time in the Club as most were still in good spirits, some nursing black eyes or burst noses after the odd fight here or there. Mostly it was older men enjoying a day off work again and playing dominoes, singing and telling tales of the drinking through the previous night. Younger lads talked about their prowess in drinking and if they had been capable (even if they weren't they'd never admit it) any sexual encounters they might have been lucky to experience with the lasses, who must have been half comatose to even think about it looking at the clip of most of the lads. I never saw a woman out in either a club or pub on this day, unlike nowadays - this year I noticed more women than men out enjoying the first day of the New Year. As Dylan almost sang during the good old days before the music died, *the times have indeed changed*.

Years later I was in the club in Whitburn, a mining village full of crazies who may end up in another book one day, but New Year's Day was always great craic there. The lads who had never been to bed kept an annual tradition alive and they stole a 'gallower' (pit pony) from the old colliery field and rode it through the streets and then past the old doormen at the Club door (they still had to 'weigh' in mind – this time as jockeys, not fighters) and into the bar, much to the amazement of non-locals and the amusement of the village nutters drinking there. They rode it around, knocking tables over while they whooped and howled. Great fun you may say or no wonder the male race will die out. It's your choice.

The Milky Bar Kid and Crime

I loved New Year right up to when my father died in 1975. After that it wasn't the same. We tried to keep the traditions, but Mr Snaith also died and I ended up first foot for my mother, but it simply wasn't the same without my dad. We started to get people coming in who only wanted trouble and petty thefts. Always remembered a lad called Milky, called that because he wore National Health round glasses the same as TV's *The Milky Bar Kid*. Anyone who wore these spectacles tended to be called Milky and relentlessly bullied and abused for their glasses.

Sadly many had these glasses with a sticking plaster over one eye for lazy eye syndrome or sticky plaster on the sides to keep the glasses frames stuck on the lenses. For those younger readers, *The Milky Bar Kid* was a young star who advertised - guess what? - *Milky Bars* - and the *Milky Bars were always on* him.

Curiously I was discussing The Milky Bar Kid in *The Jolly Sailor* in town today and remarked I hadn't seen any in the shops for ages and the only *Milky Bar* I ate now was the Easter egg that my precious buys me every year. A little time after this riveting conversation, Darren the landlord went shopping and kindly brought back to me a *Milky Bar.* On close observation of the bar's wrapper we couldn't help noticing that the whole thing was covered in information and warnings about healthy eating, environment, waste management, sustainable cows and fields, carbon emissions, the dangers of too much saturated fat, the horrors of sugar and of course the banning of fun . And worst of all there was no *Milky Bar Kid.* But wait...on folding back a flap of the cover there it was, hidden away, as if lost in a time warp, a tiny silhouette of a gender neutral *Milky Bar Kid*, without their dodgy, cheap, one eyed specs or their full cowboy outfit and Colt 45 six shooter. We decided there and then to campaign for the return in bold and full colour on every wrapper the male gender proper cowboy with his National Health specs and for sure, if the Milky Bars weren't on him then we'd kick his sorry, dodgy, NHS specked ass. You can't beat the good old days!

Back on Shiney Row, Milky had sneaked into Mrs Cain's open house and was drinking but when he dropped a whole stack of LP records from under his coat he got a bit more than he bargained for. Milky was a known rogue and tea leaf and not very bright as shown in the choice of house he picked to 'borrow' things from. He was duly battered by Patta and his three marginally less psychotic brothers and thrown out into a snow covered back yard. Here he disturbed Jocka Lawton who was lying comatose under two foot of snow, the only signs of life being two holes in the snow where the alcohol from his nose had melted it, and little snow crystals were blowing up like mini whale spouts. Jocka was an older man who had a propensity to get drunk as a newt any day, never mind New Year, and would wobble and stagger mortal down the street from the pub only to collapse comatose in a heap. He had done this an hour before and the snow had covered the hapless sleeping man. If a war-damaged Milky hadn't fallen on him, he'd probably have lain there all night and frozen to death. Schadenfreude - Shiney Row style. Happy New Year!

And sadly it all went sour for me. The final miner's strike seemed to eat the heart out of the area and people stopped the traditions after it ended. Also the slow and inexorable change from an inclusive, caring community culture towards crime, drugs, violence and apathy which caused many to stop opening houses as trouble always seemed to happen regularly. This drew our open nights for all to a very sad end and we were probably the last house in the two streets to close on New Year.

I guess the loss of my father and the passing of many of the old pitmen who kept these traditions going plus the massive social and economic changes post the 1984/85 miner's strike accelerated the inevitable loss of the unique community traditions and local culture in Shiny Row and other North East communities. These traditions and the life that my father stumbled upon in 1940 are what I return to next – the days when Mrs Thatcher was still selling apples in her Dad's corner shop and had not yet stolen our school milk, when Jean-Claude Juncker's mother was tending her Brussels sprouts patch and dreaming of a new version of a European sprout, whn Bill Gates was still a megabyte in his father's eye and Herr Schicklegrubber was bombing the hell out of Britain...

CHAPTER FIVE
FAMILY ROOTS

DAD
16th November 1940, Coventry, England

As the world war to end all wars finished my own father was born, in Shirland Road, Kilburn, London, in 1918. On the night of 16th of November 1940 it must have felt as if the next war would end all worlds. My father was twenty-two and working for Bristol Siddley Aero-engines, soon to be acquired by Rolls Royce. He was a machine setter and his job along with thousands more workers was to manufacture aircraft engines for the Royal Air Force in an attempt to stop Corporal Hitler's advance across the English Channel and the early introduction of *Vorsprung Durch Technike'* to the UK aero and car manufacturing sectors.

The problem was that he was trying to carry out his work whilst Goering's Luftwaffe were dumping on Coventry, England, the largest payload of high explosives ever seen in the history of warfare. He'd been bombed out of several places and lost good friends and family in London so was a little worried that Herr Goering seemed to have another fix on his arse.

Coventry was all but destroyed in the bombing, the famous cathedral emerging like a Phoenix from the ashes. Unlike the mythical half bird, my father emerged not from the ashes but from the public bomb shelter. Unhurt but dazed he was promptly transferred to a place even the Germans wouldn't know where to bomb: Birtley, County Durham, in the North East of England.

He had never been out of London and its environs in his life and the trip *Up North* was a new experience and hopefully a less dangerous one. It was to prove enlightening and lifelong and to lead to many a strange encounter with the natives, who were not necessarily hostile but insane most of the time.

My dad had grown up on the streets of London with a single father because his mother had died of a skin melanoma when he was young. He had three sisters and life was hard. He was a good footballer and a very good cricketer and joined Middlesex with Dennis Compton as a young teenager. Sadly he had to leave school at fourteen and go to work to help feed the family so his cricket career stalled. Dennis Compton was not under such financial and paternal pressure and went on to great things in the sporting worlds of cricket and football. My father ended up as an apprentice wood turner then a tool maker. I guess after his move to the frozen North he never thought he would end up living in a place that was used as the set from the movie *Deliverance*. Compton was a much a luckier gentleman because he never ended up in Shiney Row.

STRIPPER
Shiney Row and Lord Lambton

I never heard Dad say much about his courtship. Maybe there wasn't much to say. Men didn't talk about their relationships or feelings when I grew up. It wasn't done. When I was sent out into the wild world I did subsequently find people who seemed to have held deep meaningful conversations with their mother or father, but none that came from Shiney Row, the small County Durham mining hamlet my mother hailed from. My father met her while she was working as a barmaid in *The Barley Mow* pub in Birtley.

Shiney was in those days extremely small, a compact few streets of colliery and council houses with the odd street of private houses thrown in that the *posh folk* lived in. In those days we earned the odd pocket money from the posh folks by chopping sticks, carrying shopping, or at Christmas, carol singing for pennies. In the aftermath of the 1984 miner's strike and the devastation of the working lives of so many in the region, Shiney Row got the CB radio handle *Steel City* - remember Citizen Band radios and the classic song *Convoy* by C.W. McCall? - because of all the steel shutters that barricaded any shop, pub or house that could provide revenue for the rampaging criminal youth. Before this it was a close knit, caring but tough community of mainly mining families and it was in this wartime epoch that my father was invited to meet his potential in laws one fine spring evening.

My grandfather was a pitman (well, he was when he worked) down a mine called *The Dolly*. Most of the population of Shiney Row and surrounding villages worked in the many private mines that in those days were scattered across the landscape of County Durham or under the sea from the East Durham coast and they had their own culture which was a lot more bizarre than cosmopolitan Central London had been to *cockneys* like my dad.

Grandad was called Bob or *Stripper*. I never knew the whole truth of why he was called Stripper. However, one story that may be the source was that during the 1926 General Strike he was in the habit of poaching on Lord Lambton's vast country estate. On his nightly visits some weeks before the strike he had also found an open coal seam and with his brothers had been diligently plying his underground pit *yacking* skills to dig this new found proverbial gold mine to supply the local village with coal to keep their fires going during the strikes.

So, on this particular day he was hewing away at the coal seam with his brother when he was caught by Lord Lambton and his two gamekeepers who then tried to put them under citizens' arrest and to take them to the local police house for cautioning for trespass and theft. Stripper resisted, broke free, set his feet in fighting mode, clenched his fists and asked the belted Earl a quite pertinent question for an uneducated man: 'What right do you have to this land and this seam anyway and who says it's yours?'

The aristocrat took a few steps back and the keepers also, Grandad and Uncle Jim were known as good fighting men to the keepers and they cocked their shotguns in case. The Lord standing erect in his tweed coat and moleskin trousers feeling more confident now his keepers were poised with their guns spoke clearly loudly and pompously in his polished English: 'My ancestors fought for it many years ago.'

Stripper stared at him through his deep blue eyes and spoke softly but menacingly: 'Arlreet then: I'll fight thoo now for the bugger.'

He stripped off his coat, muffler and shirt, handed them to Uncle Jim and took up the boxer's stance again. The keepers pointed the guns at both men and told them both to back off. The aristocratic and sensible Lord decided that maybe they should leave the scene and let the police handle it which is what they did.

Grandad and Jim both served thirty days in Durham Jail for this as well as a little bit of sheep rustling to feed the starving masses for which they were also indicted. Jim told this tale to many down the Pit and in the Social Club for years after and I suspect that is where the name *Stripper* came from. He never did win the rights to Lambton's estate, mansions and castles: it would take another 1066 for that. He ended his days in a cold, damp colliery house coughing his guts up as a result of years of breathing in coal dust. Uncle Jim and Uncle Tom both blew their brains out with their shotguns some years later when I was a teenager before the dust took them the same way. Lambton and all his heirs died peacefully in their *Downton Abbey* beds. I guess that's *droite de seigneur* Shiney Row style.

As an aside there is a folk song that most of us sang when we were small at school which is still a local favourite; *The Lambton Worm*. It tells the tale of Stripper's opponent's ancestor, young John Lambton who after returning from the Crusades was asked to kill a huge River Wear dwelling worm that had terrorised local people and eaten all their sheep. The worm curled itself around a hill, Worm Hill at Fatfield on the River Wear. It is still there if you wish to visit it and you can see the marks around the hill where the worm curled around it. Lambton kills the worm with the help of a wise woman in Durham. Sadly, the wise woman told him he must kill the first thing he sees after killing the worm which happened to be his father, Lord Lambton. He refused and killed his dad's hunting dog instead. For ignoring her wishes, the wise woman cursed his family that nine generation's first born would die young with their boots on. And indeed, it appears that at least four generations of Lambtons died with 'their boots on'. If you fancy listening to the Lambton Worm song, look it up on YouTube. I'll sing you the chorus now though: Ready? Here we go....

> *Whisht! lads, haad yor gobs (Be quiet, boys, shut your mouths)*
> *An' aa'll tell ye aall an aaful story (And I'll tell you all an awful story)*
> *Whisht! lads, haad yor gobs*
> *An' Aa'll tel ye 'bootthe worm.*

Marvellous stuff....

Stripper was a tall man I remember, blonde to light brown hair (but grey when I knew him). All of his three brothers and his son, my uncle Ken, were six foot plus and well built, hard men. My relatives on Grandad and Nana's side had originated in Northumberland it seemed and they all had Northumberland Border Reiver names. So their penchant for sheep rustling may well have been from their ancestral roots.

NANA
Greyhounds and Idleness

My grandmother was a large, cheery, rotund woman called Bessie. When I was young and visited them she always sitting on a *cracket* - a wooden stool. Due to her large posterior the poor woman never looked very comfortable on the small hard wooden seat. The only armchair was reserved for my grandad who was always sitting in front of a coal fire burning in a black, cast iron Rayburn oven fireplace. He often warmed his feet on the iron griddles which were fixed to the oven and were used to place pans on for cooking. When I visited Stripper he very rarely left this seat. He was always dressed in his *Long Johns* (woollen long undergarments), his white silk muffler around his neck in winter and his flat cap on his head. In his older age my father told me he hibernated in winter like a dormouse. He gave up work and never got out of bed other than to sit by the fire smoking Woodbine cigarettes talking poaching and gambling with his brothers. My long suffering Grandmother would supply him with cigarettes (tabs) and food (bait) and tea to drink, she also used to light his tab for him, using the wooden spills that sat in a pot on the fireplace. He was so idle he couldn't be bothered to lean out of his chair and take a spill to light his own tab. The only other place that my grandmother might have had a to rest her big bum on was the two seater settee in front of the fire. Sadly she could never get on this because it was reserved for something that my grandad loved more than his poor wife - and indeed most pit village men I knew also loved more than their wives - their greyhounds.

Every time I visited their colliery-owned house, greyhounds were lying on the settee. Normally they were of the brindle-marked kind, but sometimes not – black, white or another shade entirely. You see greyhounds weren't pets; they were for racing and gambling, so if they were no good after a few races, Grandad or my uncle Ken, would sell them, or kill them by bashing them over the head with a five pound lump hammer. I never got to know any of the poor unfortunate canines as pets for long, nor did I ever get a seat! They were too important to be moved off the settee and I always sat on a chair pulled in from the kitchen. Grandkids and wife, it mattered not; dogs were more important, until they were no use. I guess my Nana and I were lucky not to have our brains bashed out. We must have retained some use to the men of the house.

UNCLE TOM
Broken Jaws and Vendettas

My father's first night meeting with his prospective relatives started in the Workings Men's Club (the club). He and his soon to be father-in-law and relatives were 'weighed in', (a reference to Shiney Row club where boxing among members was more common than drinking), my dad having to sign in, as he had not yet joined this Northern Gentlemen's club: a bastion of entertainment and culture. They were sitting at the small table drinking four pints of best beer - my grandfather, Dad, Uncle Tom and Uncle Jim. All of the men, except Dad, were carrying heavy walking sticks which my father found out later they used for beating for pheasant, all of them being unremitting poachers of Lord Lambton's land.

Tom, noticed a tall man come in, order a beer and remain standing at the bar. Tom turned to Stripper and said, 'It's that bastard Smithy.' He got out of his seat and Dad saw him go over and say a few words to the newcomer before he came back to his seat and picked up his pint.

Stripper leant over and asked Tom, 'What did you tell the bugga?'

'I told him he's got till 8 o'clock to apologise,' Tom answered, staring menacingly at the man at the bar. Dad said nothing, worrying what would happen at 8 o'clock. It was now 6.45 pm.

The four men played dominoes and chatted. Dad couldn't understand a lot of what was said as he still wasn't up to speed with the accents nor the craic about mining, dogs and poaching so he sat drinking and wishing he was on the bus back to his digs in Birtley. The man at the bar was never mentioned again and the night wore on. They finished another round of dominoes and Tom pulled his pocket watch out. Dad looked at his own watch and saw it was 8 pm. Tom said nothing but stood up and took his walking stick and walked to the bar. They saw Tom say something to the man at the bar. The man responded with something in response and was then promptly floored by a backhanded swipe of Tom's walking stick, teeth and blood rolling towards the rapidly drying stain of blood in the sawdust left over from the dental work of the beast slaughterer who masqueraded as a dentist.

Tom came back over to the table, drank his pint and said, 'He wouldn't apologise. Let's gan and have a pint in *The Odd Fellas*.' The three pitmen drank their pints, got up and left.

As my father hurriedly drank up and shuffled after them he looked back anxiously and saw the comatose man lying in the sawdust and blood. No one seemed to be bothered about administering aid to him or comfort. They were all carrying on drinking, playing dominoes and socialising as if the assault and battery had not happened and my father began to have serious reservations about his romancing of my mother.

71

The men said nothing about the assault on the short walk down the hill from the club to *The Odd Fellows' Arms*. This worried my father even more as they seemed completely at ease with the violence and retribution, over whatever slur or slander of Tom's character they never revealed. Instead they talked of how they would win money in *The Odd Fellas*, smiling to each other, speculating about the next prize they hoped to get.

UNCLE JIM
Guns and Ladies Toilets

Dad and the men walked into the pub. It was heaving by now and they struggled to get a place at the bar, but they managed to get pushed in and began talking and drinking with the customers, all of whom were known to the three men. One man walked over and posed a question to Uncle Jim. 'Well Jim, dee ya fancy ya chances the neet?'

'Why aye man,' Jim answered laughing and carrying on, 'put your money on the bar.'

The other man put a ten shilling note on the bar and Jim did the same. 'Nail the bugger up then,' Jim instructed his opponent.

My father by this time was yet again puzzled and confused by these odd men but stood quietly drinking his beer and observing. Jim's opponent went back to where he was and picked up a hammer that was lying on the window sill. He walked over the room and opened a bar door that lead into a corridor, at the end of which was a ladies toilet, The toilet was for ladies who might be taken out by their husbands once a year, maybe on a Saturday night, and they only sat in the Snug room - never the bar. He pulled out of his pocket a large six inch nail and hammered it into the toilet door. He then returned to the bar. He leant down by his bar stool and pulled up a rifle. Jim asked the bar owner to hand him his own rifle. To my father it seemed very strange to keep a loaded firearm in a public house, but when he looked around he realized at least four other men had some form of gun by their sides.

Jim then walked with his opponent to the end of the bar facing the Ladies toilet door down the long corridor. Dad now realized that this was a competition to see who could shoot the nail into the door. *Interesting* he thought, never having seen anything like this.

However, this was a test of skill and the opponent handed Jim the mirror that he had also brought from his seat and Jim put the gun onto his shoulder. Facing the opposite way the pointed the barrel at the toilet door; he was facing the stock of the gun. He took the mirror in his left hand and lined the mirror up along the stock of the gun, the reflection of the rifle barrel, gun sights, toilet door and nail in the mirror. He aimed through the mirror and fired. Bang! The crack of the rifle stopped the conversation for a moment and then a loud cheer arose as the bar's other punters saw that Jim had indeed driven the nail into and through the paneled door.

Jim turned and his opponent prepared to take his turn at shooting. Suddenly the toilet door flew open and a rather large old lady came flying out, clearly in distress, pulling up her baggy drawers and screaming obscenities at the men gathered to watch this epic shooting match. The nail and bullet had flown over her head as she sat on the toilet contemplating life and maybe another half of *Mackeson* stout.

The match was abandoned to the sound of fading obscenities from the woman as she retreated into the relative safety of the Snug to hoots of laughter from the drunken pitmen in the bar. The rest of the evening went by until 10 pm closing time without incident and my father left, walked the five minutes to Number 10 in the street of colliery houses, Barrack Row, to say goodnight to his new sweetheart and then off to catch the Number 5 bus to Chester-le-Street and the safety of his landlady and bed.

He never forgot his very first night in Shiney Row - his own Ben Stiller *Meet the Parents moment.*

MAM
Tin Baths and Coal Dust
Mam and Dad married in St Oswald's church, Shiney Row soon after meeting and gaining Stripper's permission I guess. They weren't given much of a reception - only sandwich and cakes at home and a few beers in the Club as this was still wartime, besides which Stripper only spent money on greyhounds, gun dogs and beer. They also had to live with Stripper and Nana plus Uncle Ken, my mother's younger brother. This was problematical as there were only two bedrooms in the two-up, two-down terraced colliery house. So Ken shared a bed with them both!

Over the years I have spoken with many from all over the world who have had similar experience of sharing rooms and beds when they were kids, but I haven't ever met anyone who had to share a marital bed with their brother-in-law.

I never dared ask my father about how normal married relationships could take place in that environment. You never spoke about those things but I have reflected upon it in my later life. I assume because Ken was a pitman (when he went) he would have been on the three shift system that meant some weeks he would have not been in the bed at night, others he would have left at 4 in the morning for first shift and I guess at weekends he would have been out at the dog racing, fighting or gambling, all he was good at. It seems likely my two sisters, Sheila and Margaret, must have been conceived during those absences.

Same sex bath times were also different compared to these socially compliant days. The tub was a tin bath that was hung up on the outside wall of Number 10 Barrack Row, when not in use. Nana or Mam would bring in it when the men were due back from work or getting up from a nap and put it in front of the fire. The bath was then filled with hot water boiled up from the back boiler of the fire or from a kettle. Baths were strictly in hierarchical order, Stripper first, then Ken. I'm not sure when Dad ever had his bath let alone when Mam or Nana had theirs. Recently during a normal afternoon debate and drinking session with my fellow inmates of Dom and Annemarie's great, but bizarre, Irish pub, I asked the same rhetorical question: 'When did your mother or Nana ever wash?' As none of us could remember seeing them in the tin bath and as the only place the full baths were sat was in front of the fire in the one room in full view of anyone, at the time of writing, we have no answer to that. If dear reader you can answer this world-shattering question which defies the great minds of the Mensa society in the pub, then I'll buy you a beer.

Indeed, none of us who talk about those days can remember ever seeing our parents anything but fully clothed. My dad only took off his shirt if the weather was sweltering and never in the house. Even then he still had his vest on in the garden and when on summer holiday fishing but most times he rolled up his long shirt sleeves in summer time. His only suntan was on his face and his arms: no money wasted on *Ambre Solaire* and *Nivea After Sun* by Dad, or indeed my mam, because I never saw her in anything but full dress and headscarf. We were a bit like an Islamic household when I think about it. I can't see what all the fuss is about these days about Burqas and Hijabs. In Shiney Row we were pioneers in ethnic dress and multi-cultural customs long before the *Global Villages* and *Arab Springs* of the future.

The Islamic female obligation thing was also very prevalent during bath times as my mother had to actually wash her father and her brother. My father said he could never really cope with this coming from a different world down South - watching his wife wash naked men but he must have suffered it until they could gain a council house themselves with a real bathroom.

The pitmen those days would never wash their backs during their working days as it was believed it weakened the back. Stripper and my Uncle Ken had my mother to wash their backs on weekend nights when they were going to the working men's club. She saw no issue with it as it was what she grew up with and was therefore *normal*. She had indeed had a difficult life.

In Service and Upstairs Downstairs

Mam left school at fourteen years old and had shown little interest in education at Shiney School. She was a petite, thin and very timid person most of her life and I guess she was a scared, timid and innocent fourteen year old when she was sent into service to a grand house in London (*Downton Abbey* or *Upstairs Downstairs* for those who enjoy watching poor people work in slavery for extremely privileged, filthy rich, bone idle people).

She told me that Stripper took her to the train. They walked down Station Road to Penshaw railway station. It was still there then, and I remember it as a child before it became a casualty along with Baron Beecham's 2000 mile axe to local railway routes. They took the twenty minute ride to Durham City to catch the East coast mainline railway which ran from Scotland to London. She said they never spoke, Stripper smoking his tabs and staring out of the window. They stood on the station at Durham silently waiting for the train.

My mother had never been outside Shiney Row's environs in her life and she said that she was shaking with fear and trepidation. She may well have seen the LNER *Flying Scotsman* shoot past as she took her first ever railway journey to the Deep South and the unknown. As the slower train came in from Newcastle, Stripper picked up her suitcase and opened the door for her, lifted her suitcase into the train as his teenage daughter climbed on board and waited at the open door. Stripper stood on the station with hands in the pockets of his grey coat. He was wearing his usual white muffler and flat pitman cap and looked at his trembling daughter with a frown on his face. My mother said he only spoke a few words. There was no kiss or hug or even a formal farewell handshake. 'Mind owt happening and yeah divn't come back yaem.' He shut the train door and went to the Station bar for a beer and to wait for the next train back to Penshaw.

My mother said she cried for ages while sitting on the train, no one taking much notice of a young, innocent girl off to a world she had no knowledge of and a life in service. She said it took her years in her innocence to learn what Stripper had actually meant with his farewell message of hope. This translated for people with a heart and compassion meant: *If you happen to have sexual relations with a man and you get pregnant don't expect any help, sympathy or support from me. You will stay in London on your own and never be allowed to come back home.*

Familial love: 1930's and Stripper style.

This was, despite being typical for such a hard man and hard area of the world, actually hypocritical as I later heard that my mother's older sister had been born out of wedlock but I guess he had little contrition or forgiveness in his hard heart.

It appears that my mother was very lucky with her allocated employers as she said she was treated very well by the owners of the Mayfair mansion. After a couple of years she developed an infected appendix and the lady of the house paid for the operation ordered by her Harley street doctors. However, she got complications and after more hospital treatment and care supplied free gratis from her kind aristocratic lady employer, she returned home to the bliss of Number 10 Barrack Row and Stripper's tender care. A year or so later she met my father in the Barley Mow and eventually married hoping to leave her parents' house for her own council house soon after.

ME AND MY SISTERS
Doodlebugs and the Last Rites

My sisters were born during the war and spent time in London as my father visited his sisters and his nephews there after the blitz. Their London cousins John and David were evacuated to Durham and they and Aunty Winn spent much time in the coal fields away from the main Blitz. When in London my sisters always remember lying under the kitchen table as the V1 Doodlebugs and V2 flying bombs came over crying, 'Mammy, fly bombs, fly bombs.' My father's aunty and cousin were in fact killed by one.

I came along twelve years later much to the consternation of my sisters I believe. Pushing babies in prams didn't give young teenage girls much street cred with the local Teddy boys in the Rock and Roll Fifties it seems. My mother had a difficult birth as I didn't want to leave the safety and comfort of her womb. Who could blame me for God's sake, knowing what I know now about Shiney Row and the lunatics I grew up with and dear Lord, the insane crazies I would eventually work with and the *Relentless Misery* of watching the football team I eventually followed. I must have had second sight of the horrors to come and tried to stay there for weeks over her due date but eventually I was reluctantly hauled out by an Obstetrician with pliers (I guess they call them forceps in hospitals, but the result was the same as if he'd used pliers). I wasn't dragged out screaming as I was almost dead it seems and was immediately whizzed off to intensive care. My head was swollen (some may say it never came down) and they believed I had suffered severe brain damage. I still carry the two indentations and lack of hair growth where the pliers gripped today.

My parents were advised that I would probably not live and were asked if they wanted me Christened. They said yes and the hospital brought a Catholic Priest, the only pastor around at that early hour. My parents were not religious but I think they were pleased that someone would give me a name and a blessing. The Irish Father gave me my two London cousin twin's names, and then gave me the last rites. It seemed he was premature as I clearly survived the pliers and the *howkin'* out of the safety of Mum's tum to write this epic. I guess, like in today's difficult times, I have to thank the NHS, the staff at the hospital and my Lord and Saviour for that, and I will: 'Thank you all.'

We lived at Princes Street, in Shiney Row. Mam and Dad had managed to leave Stripper's tiny colliery house for a pre-war, three bedroom, terraced council house with garden. Our estate was the older version of a couple more estates and was thought of as the more 'problematical one'; the others being less troublesome - more like Queens than Ramala or Birkenhead rather than The Wirral.

My first memories are of hens and chickens. Dad kept them in the front garden in a shed (a Cree in North East language) and pen. I can remember sitting with the hens as a toddler and Dad showing me young chickens hatched from their eggs which he incubated in the airing cupboard next to our coal fire and Rayburn oven. I guess my next memories are those of my mother cooking on this oven and also slapping 'cold cream' on my chapped and frozen red legs after warming them and my backside on the fire after coming in from playing outside. And talk of home cooking moves us onto Mam's food as an extremely important comfort to a young child before the growing pains of teenage youth took over.

CHAPTER SIX
MOTHER'S COOKING, SWEETS AND SCHOOL DINNERS

Dinner Money and Sago

Early days at Primary school we took our dinner money to school on Monday. It was a half a crown piece when I remember first doing it. Two shillings and sixpence for two courses of basic but very filling food, amazing value even in those inflation-free days. I was fortunate in that my dad worked and I never had to claim free school dinners. A lot of my friends did and for some of the shy, very poor kids it was used as yet one more reason to mock them by hurtful children.

I loved school dinners. Many didn't. But even I didn't like frog's eggs or frog's spawn. Tapioca had to be the worst food known to mortal man. Many years later I saw how they grow tapioca in Bali, Indonesia. It does not look like frog spawn at all so how the sadistic, sociopathic cooks of school dinners turned it into such glutinous little amphibian balls is a mystery of genetic engineering. Genetically engineering frog's spawn long before Dolly the Sheep! Wow, I have stumbled onto a secret as well kept as Area 51 or how Donald Trump's hair stays on. I may well corner the Balinese market in Tapioca before Biogenetics Inc. does.

I also didn't particularly like blancmange. I think I was sick one day after eating too much of it and from then on it didn't tick. But years later I grew to love *Angel Delight* which is a posher version of it I believe. What blancmange is I haven't a clue; maybe it is genetically engineered too from the Tapioca root.

Liver and Dolly the Sheep

I love liver. I love it fried with onions and lots of mashed spuds and with a tin of marrowfat processed peas. However, at school liver seemed to come from some completely different animal. Maybe this is another secret? Namely, those years ago animals were real. Now they are clones from Dolly the Sheep or some computer game that we are all living in. My point is that liver when I was at school always had pipes in it. Big horrible grey pipes that were as chewy as shoe leather if you unfortunately got one in your mouth. The liver itself was boiled or stewed until it was tough and solid and you could look through the pipes and see through the other side they were so wide and protruding...urgh!

Now when I cook liver there are no pipes; they have miraculously been naturally selected out of the mammalian anatomy or bound up in the eleven super-symmetric dimensions of String Theory. Liver has confounded Darwinian Theory and practice and has evolved into a completely different organ in only fifty years. Like girls learning to throw cricket balls - it's a miracle.

Cadbury's Smash and Steepy Peas

The mashed potatoes I now eat with my liver and onions do not seem as lumpy as school ones which also had a liberal dose of 'black and grey potatoes eyes' which they don't seem to have now. The best way to avoid any grief with mashed spuds is to use Cadbury's *Smash* instant potato powder. It has to be Cadbury's despite the imitations around purely because of the iconic advert with the Martian robot springy creatures with heads that look like giant Chinese woks and *Dr Who Dalek* voices: search for the YouTube video if you've never seen them. Herewith a description: Picking up a spud in his robot claw one of them decries the mashing of spuds process on earth: *Earthlings! They peel them and boil them for twenty minutes.* Then the creatures burst into insane robotic laughter. And the classic slogan at the end – *For mash get Smash.*

And indeed why not…..

Peas with liver is an essential, mine processed out of a tin, but my mother made what we all called *steepy peas* for Sunday dinner. I now know these were process dried peas which needed 'steeping' in water overnight on a Saturday with a small muslin *steepy pea bag*. The bag somehow softened the rock-hard peas. These were the only peas we really ate.

My mam also made *carlin peas* which were small little brown things. We ate them on Carlin Sunday which I always thought was Palm Sunday but today having used my Google again I now know must have been Passion Sunday which is two weeks before Easter. It seems the reason why we ate these in the North East was because of those bloody French. Isn't it always!

Legend says the French sailed a boat into the River Tyne on that day to feed the starving Royalist folks of Newcastle during the English Civil war. The English folk were besieged by wild Parliamentarian supporting Jocks. Instead of giving the Geordies decent bait like stotties and pease pudding, they threw them Maple peas. I guess the

80

natives must have looked at the hard brown pulses and said to their Gallic saviours: 'What the hell are these bonny lads. Howay man, weez canna ayte these buggers. Wor gobs and teeth aren't that hard man. Have youse nar got a canny French quiche or a patty afor grass or a git big wedge of Camembert, man.'

I guess the French replied practicing what De Gaulle said to us many times in the years to come - 'Non.'

So the French introduced another bit of their culture to us with Carlin Sunday.

And down the road in Hartlepool another misunderstanding took place a hundred and fifty or so years later when during the Napoleonic wars a French vessel was shipwrecked off the coast of that fine town. The ship's monkey, which was dressed in a uniform as small performing monkeys on shoulders are, was washed ashore alive. The good townsfolk of Hartlepool, who had never seen a Frenchman, took the unfortunate simian prisoner and duly hung it from a gibbet on the dock side as a Frenchman and a spy. Ever since then poor Hartlepudlians have been termed: *Monkey Hangers*. West Hartlepool rugby team always have a swinging monkey on their club tie. It's a tradition.

Many jokes of course arise from this. At one social charity event I sponsored at Hartlepool Association Football Club the comedian arrived on stage and he kept stamping the floor and looking around at his audience, 98% of them from Hartlepool. He did this two or three times and then took the mike for his opening gambit: 'Just checking for the trapdoor, the last time anyone was on this stage a monkey fell through it.'

No one laughed: except me. I escaped with my life simply because I was paying. I wouldn't recommend it otherwise.

Stew and Sweet Corn

Lots of people I speak to hated school dinners and especially the stewed vegetables, stews and things like *Spam*. I loved them. Annemarie the lovely Irish landlady in the pub is no fan of stew or anything with fatty meat in it. Purple Al agrees with her and after a debate of such riveting drama and torture on what a soup, a stew or a casserole are, his final conclusion is that the only liquid food stew, casserole or soup he eats is called Heinz.

Stewed veg was not only a school thing. My mother did the same. Cabbage was always watery and tasteless, only the gravy made it taste better. One vegetable we never ate was sweet corn. I can't ever remember having it at school dinner or home. Nor am I really bothered because sweet corn, as Stumpy so eloquently puts it in his Black Country accent: 'Is shoite. It's chicken food. That's oil it should be.'

Indeed, as he quoted this he explained his thesis he published in the Wolverhampton Hells Angels Journal of Nutrition on the, *Effects of Sweet Corn on the Human Digestive System*. It goes something like this. 'It doesn't matter in what form you eat sweet corn; you shoite it out whole. Even if you mash it will still come out the other end whole. I have elucidated that the anaerobic bacteria in the human gut treat mashed sweet corn as kids do with *'Leggo'* at Christmas. They use it to assemble whole sweet corn again.' This could be world breaking research from our one-legged Rasta biker. I am sending it to the World Health Organisation. He may be nominated for a Nobel Prize; President Obama got one, so why not Stumpy.

Black Bullets and Spangles

It is hard to list all the non-school dinner things we ate. Mainly we ate Sweets, *ket* to us, candy to the Yanks, Bonbons to les Francais; all were sugar and some were chocolate-covered - that is Cocoa, milk and sugar - marvellous stuff - a modern dentist's nightmare and a dietician's hell. So many sweets to remember, but why not, I'll have a bash, eh readers?

Black bullets were hard, minty sugar. Loved by school boys as you could get a sticky paper packet in your trouser pocket and try to prise one out without your mates hearing a rustle and demanding you gave them one. Greed was endemic with school children when it came to ket. Sadly ket has taken another meaning now with the advent of Ketamine, commonly called the horse slayer - no, not the Newcastle idiot who punched a horse in anger at losing to Sunderland yet again - but the veterinary anaesthetic product now serving as a potent narcotic agent for drug users.

Before ketamine, my wife who taught for years in Sunderland, used to think all children in push chairs and buggies pushed around the town were anaesthetised. This occurred in several stages of their development and was caused by objects permanently in their mouths. First a baby's dummy, Second sweets or ket, Third a Greggs' pasty and finally a tab (cigarette). 'Nowt wrang with that,' I'd tell her, 'did me nee harm!'

All hard sweets were the same; pineapple chunks, pear drops, aniseed balls, acid drops, bull's eyes, *Mintoes,* sherbet lemons…there were loads of them and all of them required careful extraction from the trouser pocket to avoid sharing or a teacher's wrath and confiscation. And the only way to buy them was to save up a farthing, half penny, three penny bit, or if you were in the Bill Gates league, a sixpence, commonly called a tanner. All sweets were bought in fractions of a pound weight. In fact I believe this was the only way most of my fellow schoolmates learned arithmetic was by buying ket. Sweets came in two ounces or if you were flush a quarter, four ounces.

Rectangular cubic packet sweets were more difficult to get out of our pockets without anyone hearing you as you had to tear the packet, and some were wrapped in plastic paper, which made a noise. I liked *Spangles,* hard, flat, coloured fruit sugar. I also loved *Tunes* which were the same but supposed to help your various upper respiratory tract diseases to breathe as they had some form of menthol supposedly in them. I did like Menthol and Eucalyptus sweets as well, even then as a young lad. I liked them more when I got older and mistakenly used to drink and drive as I believed they stopped the alcohol smell and the police would never know you swallowed more than the legal limit. They didn't work. I proved that. I suppose that *Trebor Extra Strong* mints may well have lost one hell of a market share as driving under the influence has rightly become social and legal anathema.

Fruit Salads and Black Jacks

Chewy sweets were always favourites. I loved *Fruit Salads* and *Black Jacks.* You could get four of them for half penny and eight for a penny if I remember correctly but it may have been four for a farthing and eight for half pence. They seemed to disappear, a bit like pipes in liver, as I grew older. It was the same with *Midget Gems,* small chewy wine gums really. However, they have miraculously reappeared in specialist sweet shops and as an interesting aside I first saw them again in a sweet shop in an old gold mining town, Arrowtown on South Island, New Zealand in 2006. Why there, only a cricket ball's throw away from the South Pole and mainly inhabited in the early days by migrant Chinese workers? I have no idea, but I bought myself (well, I said they were for my young kids) enough to last the whole holiday.

I never enjoyed the black *Midget Gems* for some reason but love Rowntrees' black *Wine Gums* or Rowntrees' *Fruit Gum* ones. I even like Rowntrees' black *Fruit Pastels*. I do not however like Bassetts *Jelly Babies*, even the black ones. Somehow I found biting the heads off small babies a bit macabre. I read recently that they were introduced in the 1900's to meet the demand for macabre and sadist pleasure to distract from the austere Victorian hold on society. They were commonly called *unwanted babies* and of course it was normal for Edwardians to laugh and enjoy biting the heads off poor unwanted children. Read Dickens, he had their Victorian parents all bang to rights long before this revelation.

I enjoyed Jelly Beans much more. Still do when I am allowed them. Something nice in your mouth, the slight crunch of the outer shell of a jelly bean - it's some form of narcotic fix to feel the slightly erotic resistance and then the ecstasy as you bite into the chewy outer centre. I should write commercials.

Pink Shrimps and Bubble Gum

The more sugary, softer, slightly chewy sweets like Bassett's *Liquorice Allsorts*, Dolly Mixtures, Peaches and Cream and Pink Shrimps were very nice. I liked the Pink Shrimps for some reason. Loved any Dolly Mixtures, but the brown ones were second choice. Still enjoy the pink and yellow liquorice Allsorts too.

All bubble gum was great but I especially loved the thin rectangular pink strip you got in packs of collectors' cards. To this day I haven't tasted anything quite like it. All collecting cards those days had a strip of bubble gum in them. It always had a coating of floury sugar on it too. Some was hard as rock and too *gone off* and broke into small bits which you had to accumulate in your mouth to get a decent taste and chunk to chew. The norm was to get flexible soft rectangles which chewed and dissolved the sugar beautifully.

Sherbet Dips and Liquorice Root

Two other sugary and sour things I loved were Bassett's *Sherbet Dips* and *Lucky Bags*. *Sherbet Dips* were cracking stuff. A big stick of hard liquorice and sherbet to dip it into so you could suck the fizzy tangy sherbet from the bag and when the sherbet was finished you sucked the liquorice until it was ready to chew. It left the gob tingling with the acid sherbet and your mouth and lips stained with black liquorice. Very difficult to tell your teacher you weren't eating any ket or your Mam that you hadn't eaten anything before dinner with black lips and tongue.

Another liquorice product was liquorice root. I mentioned liquorice root to people assembled in the pub other day and few knew about it or what is was. So what is liquorice root? I have no idea, but we bought it and chewed it when we were kids. It was like chewing a small branch of a tree without the green or sap. It tasted of liquorice and when you chewed it became a damp, soggy stringy thing that never seemed to dissolve or disappear. These days the bin men would fine you or you would be incarcerated with mass murderers if you put it in anywhere except the clearly marked nuclear waste bin as it is plainly not of biological origin. One day I will Google it and find out what it really is, but for now, I prefer to wonder at how we ate the stuff. Maybe it's meant to be smoked? I'll take some down for the David Bellamy Society to try in the Botanical gardens in the back of *The Teign* pub.

Lucky Bags were a bag that contained lucky things. Those days no one branded anything that required a brain wired to be capable of understanding a Picasso picture or a Bergman movie to choose their favourite sweets. It was quite simple. The lucky things were normally, toffee lollies on a plastic stick, *Flying Saucers*, which were what they said, soft material that melted in your mouth with Sherbet in the middle, *Refreshers*, which were hard suck sweets which turned into a lovely chewy thing or some weird chewy things. And if I am correct *Lucky Bags* also contained some strange useless toy similar to what you get out of cheap Christmas crackers. They were not really lucky but if you were given one by your mam you felt very lucky so maybe that was the whole point.

Crisps and Tiger Nuts

Potato in all its forms is great. I have to say that I prefer mince and mashed spud (mince and tatties to the Caledonian reader) to almost anything in the known culinary world. It's ambrosia to me but I also love crisps. Years ago we had Tudor crisps in the North East made in Peterlee I think. Long gone now, probably swallowed up in Gary Lineker's Walkers' Empire. Those days crisps were monochrome in flavour and salt came from a blue bag. The only other flavours next introduced were cheese and onion and salt and vinegar and then Oxo/beef if I recall. Not the choice we have now. Snacks such as

Quavers, Monster Munch, Hoola Hoops etcetera all have no potato so are in my mind inferior but great at absorbing gallons of beer.

Other subterranean vegetables I believe I ate were Tiger nuts. My mam loved them. You could only buy them at the vegetable shop near the market at Park Lane bus station in Sunderland. They were small, brown and furry and chewy, well most were; some cleverly cracked the rotten teeth I had as they had obviously been planted in the bag by Harry the dentist. Like liquorice root, I have no idea what the hell they were or where came from and like Tudor crisps, tortoises and *Champion The Wonder horse*, that great cowboy series, they have disappeared. It's a sad world.

Broth and Pease pudding

My mother made great food and she also made the best pease pudding (look the recipe up again if you are one of millions who has never enjoyed the delight of pease pudding) which is made from split yellow peas, with ham juice, salt and butter and should always be eaten with ham or boiled bacon. These days my wife cooks this with gammon, not bacon hock, because we are now posh and can afford it. My mother used to have no money but a few pennies housekeeping so her ham was always cut off bacon shanks that had been used to make broth. Ah broth! Yet one more past manna from heaven I adored.

Racing Pigeons and Pigeon Supper

Pease pudding reminds me of a cracking story and I will have to wiz on a bit from my school days. A group from Yorkshire who had problems with my mother's cuisine and pease pudding nectar of the God's were the pigeon lads from Barnsley. They had become regulars to our house in the 70's over two years as they were invited up by my brother-in-law, Mark Clark (not the American General, but a miner and pigeon man). This was a result of one of Mark's homing pigeons going missing one day after attempting to win the *over the water* race from France to Mark's pigeon loft (cree) on the Colliery Field allotments in Shiney Row. The tired and disoriented bird had landed in a gentleman called Brian's loft in Barnsley, which was over 120 miles away down South.

Brian was a head teacher from a school there and our Mark was in raptures that so eminent a professional would deem to help a mere miner. Brian had checked the ring on the bird's leg for registration and owner details and kindly drove all the way up to Shiney with the pigeon to give it back to Mark and a friendship had developed. So much so that Brian and three of his miner mates from the Social Club pigeon club attended the annual award giving piss up at Shiney Row Club for the Shiney Club pigeon club. This was *the Pigeon Supper*.

For two years running his mates had stayed at our house, sleeping in the spare room and on the lounge floor. Everyone got drunk at the pigeon supper and then we all returned to our house and to our mam's tender care - she had stayed in to make the supper (sadly Dad had died by this time). We bought crates of Federation Beer from the club and the odd Pony, Babycham, Cherry B for the lasses and returned to our house in Princes Street. Mam had always made Stotties, Ham and Pease pudding sandwiches and separate plated mince, corned beef and cheese and onion pies for supper. We all then got drunker still and partied into the night.

The three miners loved my mother. They always said they wanted to take her home to Yorkshire with them, get rid of their own wives and have Mam as a surrogate mother. Who wouldn't!

In the third year we were swallowing beer and listening to the dreadful Club singer again. They remarked that they were really looking forward to meeting my mam again and having a drink and some bait (food) with her and reiterated how much they thought of her. I thanked them.

'Cheers lads. She is a good un for sure. I'm starving mesel looking forward to those stottie cyeks and pies. Love owt like that me.'

They all looked at me with a worried frown and I could see they looked a bit anxious. One of the miners whispered something in the other's ear who then nodded and grabbed my arm to bring me close to them and he spoke above the horrible wailing of the singer howling out, *Do you know the way to Amarillo.*

'Eh up, Dave you know we think t' world of you and your mam and don't get wrong end of t'stick, but me and lads would like t'ask you to ask your mam to not spread t' chip fat from t'chip fat pan on t'stotty cyek this yor please.'

I looked puzzled and replied, 'Divn't know what you mean Bill? What chip fat?'

He looked at his mates anxiously again and continued. ' Dave, sorry but its t'yellow chip fat she spreads on t'stotties afor putting t'ham int' bun. Each year we eat stuff only to be polite but now we know you well, we think we should tell you t'truth. It's bloody horrible.'

I looked shocked and also puzzled and then it dawned on me I shouted above the raucous pub singer howling out, *Sweet Marie she's waiting for me there.*

'How man, that's not chip fat. It's pease pudding!'

Another Yorkie butted in. 'Sorry Dave, but we don't like t'bloody stuff.'

'OK,' I concluded. 'Let me get into kitchen before Mam puts it on the plates and I'll scrape it off and I'll eat the bugger. She'll never know.' And she never did.

She kept giving them the ham and pease pudding right up until they stopped coming and I kept scraping it off and eating it. Like the local Durham miners they enjoyed those pigeon supper nights until they lost their employment, their hopes and dreams after the 1984/'85 miner's strike. I often wonder how they got on in life without pease pudding to enliven their lives. If they or their families read this book, then look me up and if you fancy a treat I'll supply the ham and pease pudding sandwiches. You supply the Tetley's Ale.

My wife makes lovely pease pudding, although of course not as well as my mam. I told her this only once seconds before she maimed me with the bacon shank and I was removed to live with crazy Gus in his bus shed - but it's certainly very eatable. My wife does not make broth like my mam either, but it's passable. Also my German hound won't eat the leftovers. This I find strange as Stripper's dogs were fed broth and bread and I know many old lads who fed their dogs broth and they loved it. I remember dogs slavering and gobbling up broth in seconds. I guess my schnauzer Eva having Teutonic roots would prefer Sauerkraut and Bockworst to chopped vegetables and fatty bacon. No wonder they lost the war.

MAUREEN
Broth and Childbirth

Now then, a dog slavering over broth has brought back fond memories. I will explain. My dearest when she was very young and in the throes of young love with her Greek God worked as a new teacher. She was also stupid enough to move up from the relative sanity of Yorkshire to live with my mother and me in the madness of Shiney Row. She taught at a Nursery School and the class Teaching Assistant was a lovely local lady from Washington called Maureen.

Maureen was a typical North East mother with a wealth of tales which she told in the local vernacular. She mentored my darling wife as she was older and wiser and my wife was naïve in the ways of North East folks and the role of woman in this strange culture. One day they were talking about childbirth as my beloved was now pregnant with our first child. Maureen recalled her second child's birth in the Queen Elizabeth Hospital, Gateshead.

'Next to me was a young lass. She couldn't have been more than twenty and had two kids at home. We'd both given birth that morning and had two healthy babies. She had had a difficult time and had to have several stitches.'

My pregnant angel shivered as she thought of the horrors to come for her and her own delivery. Maureen continued. 'The poor lass was as skinny as a whippet, very timid and fragile. I tried to cheer her up and talk with her but she wasn't too bright either so the chat wasn't much. So I let her lie there looking dejected.'

She continued to tell the tale. 'As visiting time approached I thought I'd cheer her up and ask if her man was coming in to see her. She said she wasn't sure as he was always in the Club. Oh, I said, *Maybe he'll bring you something nice to eat and cheer you up. Doesn't he want to see the bairn?'*

'*Depends how much he's had to drink I suppose*, the poor lass said looking morose and a bit frightened.

Maureen continued again. 'Anyway, after this a scrawny looking bloke came in with the other visitors, saw the lass and headed over. His trousers were hanging off his backside and he wobbled a bit. Obviously he had been in the Club just as she'd thought .He brought no flowers or chocolates or any thank you. He went up to the bed, sat down and asked how the bairn was. The lass told him she was doing well, six pound in weight and black hair. He only nodded, saying nothing. He was a shifty looking bugger and kept looking around the ward, eyes and head moving like a shit house rat and he got out of his chair and started to close the screens around the bed.'

Maureen took a drink of her coffee and began again. 'I was worried - didn't like the bugger at all and so I pressed the button to call the nurse. Luckily I did because the next thing I heard was the lass screaming, *Get off me, you're pissed. I've had stitches, man. Get off, get off!'*

She took another sup of coffee and continued. 'At that moment the ward Sister arrived. She was a stern woman we were all scared of who ruled the ward with a rod of iron. She was also pretty large. She heard the screams and rushed to the bed and pulled the curtain screens back violently to reveal the man, trousers around his ankles, trying to have sex with the lass who was struggling to push him off. The sister took one look, picked him up by the scruff of his neck and the seat of his trousers and flung him like a rag doll onto the floor bashing his head on the cold floor tiles. She then grabbed him by his neck, picked him up and frog-marched him out the ward.'

My wife said that she stared at Maureen uncomprehendingly as she had no idea that such things could ever happen. She hadn't been long up here and never been to Gateshead so I guess this was understandable.

Maureen concluded the tale; 'Once he'd gone I spoke to the lass who had put her nightdress back down and pulled the bed clothes up. *You shouldn't be letting him do that to you pet. You've just had a bairn, man.* The lass turned over with a look of acceptance or sadness, Maureen couldn't tell which and she explained in her tortured way: *Ah kna that pet but what do you dee? He's a man and when he's never had it for a while and when he's been aarl day in the Club...he's like a dog at broth. I canna stop him, can I? Is yours not the same after arl neet in the club?'*

As I heard the tale I wondered if more romantic novelists than I would appreciate me educating them on the using the local Gateshead vernacular for *he made passionate love* or *he wooed her with an intensity that made her swoon* etcetera. But somehow I think *he was like a dog at broth* wouldn't catch on with female literary agents. I believe I'm better not writing in the romantic genre.

SCOTTISH ALEX
School Bus and Assault with a Deadly Weapon

I have to say I enjoy lots of broth as a main meal, as I do soup. I can never get away with ordering soup in restaurants as they bring a spoonful hardly covering the bottom of the bowl and think that's enough. My mam served broth in big, deep brown cake mixing bowls with plenty of home-baked, sliced bread. When she hadn't baked her own bread it would have been sliced *Wonderloaf* or *Homepride*. I miss that. Some people however were posher than us and ate broth as a starter for God's sake, Scottish Alex for one.

Alex went to Washington Grammar school with us in the late sixties. He was posh and Scottish. He lived in the posh houses in Penshaw and played the trumpet and bagpipes and wore a kilt. He also played rugby which was weird as everyone we knew played football. Rugby was only for posh people. One day we were sitting on the school bus coming home from Washington. There was Gary from Fatfield, scene of the Lambton worm slaying, and me seated together. Alex was sitting in front of us with his satchel and trumpet case. Gary mentioned that he was looking forward to having broth for tea as it was what his mother cooked every Wednesday when his father got in from the pit. I acknowledged this and said we'd have loads tomorrow. Alex turned around when he heard this and said: 'I like broth. My mother makes it as we had it in Scotland. We have it as hors d'oeuvres or a starter. Who on earth would eat it as their main course?' Gary said, 'We dee,' and hit him over the head with a stone pestle we had pinched from the Chemistry lab. We both had never eaten a starter or knew what the hell 'horse's douves' were. I guessed our mam's broth served in cake mixing bowls wasn't for posh Scots.

Stewed Vegetables and Nuked Meat.

It doesn't matter where you live or come from, most normal people remember their mother's cooking with affection even if tastes have changed through the years of posh TV cooks and epicurean critics telling us that it was shit. From the dominatrix Fanny Craddock and her four shades of grey victim husband Jonny, to MasterChef and the rotund cockney grocer and the evil Afrikaans, Monica, we've been told by millions of overpaid and over here cooks that the only way to eat meat is to get a vet to raise it up from the dead and that all vegetables must be al dente; that is - raw. This is not true. A false truth in today's perfidious, social media-dominated world. My mam knew nothing of gushing blood, saignant or bleu or what the Italian word was for raw - all meat was nuked and all vegetables boiled until they were mush - and it was delicious. To this day I still like my Brussels sprouts cooked as mush despite my dear daughter trying to serve them al dente, mixed with garlic, bacon, sautéed lightly. For God's sake leave me alone will you!

All stews were boiled for hours and casseroles spent from morning to night in the oven. Any vegetable was boiled for hours. It was never just steamed or lightly sautéed. And for God's sake nothing was ever covered in garlic, herbs and spices or sauces, only in water from the boiling or steaming pans. And of course, Vitamin C was for wimps.

Meat was roasted or fried and again cooked until it was black. If it was cooked in a liquid it was boiled or stewed. Mince was mince. Not the sweet, feminine stuff you put in mince pies at Christmas, not that steak tartar shit they serve uncooked in France with a raw egg on the bugger, where a good vet could bring both cow and the nascent chicken back to life, but boiled in a tatie pot or fried black in a frying pan.

HOGDKISS THE BUTCHER
Spotted Dick and Leek Pudding

As for exotic food? It didn't exist. My dad wouldn't touch anything but meat and two veg. Every day we had proper dinner. Fridays we would get fish and chips from the chip shop. Saturday night always mince or corned beef tatie pot in winter, nuked for hours in the coal oven in a huge baking tray. To this day it is still my favourite food and it is what I would have as my last meal. My dearest makes it for me when she knows I am distraught and psychologically disturbed, so almost always after a Sunderland football match. The best cure for hangovers is tatie pot. I even ate them in the 98 degree heat and 100% humidity of Singapore; my lovely wife cooking and sweating to death in the small kitchens with no air con. True love runs a rugged but unerring gastronomic course.

Meat was always the cheap cuts as that was all my mother and many others could afford to buy. Those days chicken was rare unless you ate your own as they were more expensive than the cholesterol loaded cheap red meat stuff we did have. Neck of lamb was one lump of cholesterol - really only bone, spinal cord and fat. I've tried it many times since and it reminds me of trying to eat chickens feet in Asia where all you're eating is gristle and cartilage. There is no nutritional value at all. Have you not wondered why the Chinese are so thin? Well it's bloody obvious; a diet of a bowl of rice, live invertebrates, chickens feet and Pomfret fish soup (recipe for this Pomfret delicacy - simply boil up the fish and green weeds in your child's goldfish bowl with tepid dishwater with lots of monosodium glutamate). These delicacies would make even Landburgher Gessler lose weight.

We also ate lap of lamb. This was what most people call breast of lamb. It was really mutton we ate, not lamb. Mutton seemed to be the meat of choice as it was cheap as chips relative to other meats. Lap was always cooked baked in the oven in a meat tray with lots of barley as a stew. I loved it. Pure fat of course and I have tried to make it these past years but can't get the taste of my mother's dish or indeed get over the pure fat that oozes across the plate when you serve it. I must have gone soft. These days I take statins to kill off the cholesterol. Those days we loved the full-bodied tangy taste of saturated fat and laughed in the face of rampant heart disease.

The saturated fat dish that we had each week was suet pudding for dinner and suet pudding for sweet (we didn't have pudding or dessert - it was called sweet. Lunch was dinner, and dinner was tea, while supper was, well, supper). Suet pudding for tea was normally meat and onions (meat being very cheap, fatty stewing steak) wrapped in a thick flexible layer of beet suet and flour and then steamed in a muslin cloth for yet again, like the veg or other stew, about twenty-four hours. Sometimes it would have kidney in it, other times not.

The real favourite suet pudding in the area was leek pudding. As everyone grew show pot leeks, the leeks used in pudding were the ones for eating not those cared like the Crown Jewels for nine months until the September show. Same method as sweet suet puddings but with a stuffing of leeks without sugar: Lovely stuff. Old Timmy Taylor, my brother in law's father, used to eat them constantly and his endearing wife, Lilly, had to get up at all hours to ensure he had one on his table when he came in at 4.30 am from back shift from the pit or with a full dinner for supper at 10.30 pm before back shift. Another dedicated North East lass. Sadly, I believe the art of making leek pudding has died out with the advent of more liberated, emancipated women who like to sleep these days rather than get up at 3 am to make their beloved his dinner and then do a full day's housework or go to work whilst also caring for the screaming kids. Sad days indeed.

Sweet suet puddings had sugar in them, lots of it. They had fruit replacing the meat or leeks. Most of us can remember them from school dinners as Spotted Dick mainly but we ate many puddings full of refined sugar and cholesterol and *Bird's* custard of course, which was pure sugar. We ate these at lunch for school dinner and ate them at 5 pm for tea (dinner in the real world). I refer back to my comments about rotting teeth and rampant coronary disease.

Amazingly most people were not massively obese - most were thin as rakes. Ladies who worked in the home never stopped with housework, cooking and little horrors to manage, and the men were almost all doing hard physical labour. We kids played outside day and night. It is my theory that it was the incessant smoking of tabs in conjunction with huge doses of cholesterol that caused the circulatory problems shown in many middle-aged people. Its tabs that kill you; I can't believe suet puddings do. Surely like beer, in moderation they must do you a lot of good. Well that's my theory; it'll take a good doctor, or funeral director, to disprove it. To conclude on suet puddings: the best I have eaten in the UK are in *The Smugglers Inn*, in Devon - the best in the world for sure.

Suet, like all the meat, was bought from Hodgkiss the butcher's shop on the front street. He had a farm at Penshaw and the slaughter house at the back of the shop so it was always fresh and hand-reared. He always had a huge slab of beef suet and beef lard on the counter.

As we all know chips are only to be eaten fried in lard. In my wife's home county, West Yorkshire, Tommy's were the best fish and chips I have eaten, except for maybe Minchella's at Seaburn, South Tyneside which I believe to be probably the best in the world. Many others compete but they fry in vegetable oil; heaven forbid - what next? Fish and chip shops are like heavy weight boxing titles - they all claim to be the best in the world. And don't get me into the argument between Cornwall and Devon over how to eat your cream scone. The Cornish believe that you must put jam on first then cream, Devonians the other way around of course. I spotted a car some time ago with a bumper sticker of the Cornish flag; white cross on a black background. The white cross had the words *JAM FIRST* written across it in bold red letters. With such divisions in the country over fish and chips, lard or oil, or jam or cream first, how the hell could we did we ever expect everyone to agree on Brexit for God's sake? Read *Footsteps on the Teign* if you want to know the truth about Brexit and also the real secret of which way jam should be put on scones. It makes *The Da Vinci Code* look like a Donald Trump tweet.

I have to say that Yorkshire puddings are also much better with lard as the cooking fat added to each little dish. My mam used nothing else and hers were perfect. My wife, coming from Yorkshire, turns out a canny Yorkshire pudding but she uses namby pamby vegetable oil so of course they can never beat my mother's. But please don't tell her I told you that - I really don't want to spend another night with Crazy Gus. She also tried to make dumplings with vegetable suet for a while in a valiant attempt to get my cholesterol down. Sod it! Now I take statins she has moved back to real suet. But she gets it from a box made by *Atora* not from a huge mountain of the stuff on the butcher's counter – despite this, it's passable. Hodgkiss the butcher would turn in his grave for he had the biggest mountain of lard and suet for sale in Durham on his Shiney Row counter. He kept it right next to the first portable defibrillator!

Fried Scotch Pies and Buckfast Wine

The crème de la crème of saturated fat gobblers must be Glaswegians. My great friend Kevin now lives there after being brought up in God's country by his mother and Nana who educated him in the ways of the world and fed suet to him in the same way as I describe in this culinary masterpiece. He still loves to eat real food, despite being an eminent surgeon. He has never forgotten his roots. He is an avid people watcher like me and has observed in that City of Culture they still fry in lard. They also love to fry their pies for a supper after guzzling umpteen gallons of lager and whisky.

A Scotch pie is a marvellous invention made of lamb fat and pastry as a circular object. It has a half inch lip all around its top providing an ideal receptacle for pouring peas, beans or more fat into. Frying it indubitably saturates it even more and probably makes the beans stick better to the indentation in the top. The Scots always were good engineers. Proven of course by the invention of the square sausage – a solid square lump of cholesterol that fits perfectly between two slices of Mother's Pride sliced bread or a square bun. Makes sense doesn't it folks, why have round sausages in square bread...clever buggers, the Scots.

Along with fried pies and square sausage they also deep fry Mars bars and pizzas in chip shop lard. They also smoke lots of tabs. Not surprisingly, they also have the world's highest rate of heart disease. My friend told me he heard of a hospital that treated an 18 year old man for a heart attack. His doctor asked his mother and father about his lifestyle. His mother explained that they had always fed him well even as a baby and didn't believe it was the food. The doctor asked what they fed him. The mother answered truthfully and innocently; 'When he could take solids we used tae put Scotch pies in the blender and mince them up and feed them tae him. He's ate them like that ever since. He likes them like that even now.' Apparently a diet of liquid Scotch pie since babyhood seems to be not very good for you.

Even more bizarrely they drink the whole production of a monk's small abbey in Buckfast in Devon. Buckfast wine, or *Buckie* to the Jocks, is a potent wine, possibly with some form of hallucinogenic effect. As it is prevalent as a fuel for the *Neds* in Scotland who are classified as violent hooligans, it is thought to be one of the causes of social violence up there. It is often quoted in pleas of mitigation after some Ned has maimed and scarred someone for life as the only reason he did such a heinous act was that *he was on the Buckie*. Given the level of violence in Glasgow over the centuries without the need to drink mild tonic water from the banks of the beautiful River Dart it would take a particular thick judge to believe that!

Frying everything wasn't just a Scottish thing. I didn't know any household when I was a lad that didn't have a chip pan permanently on the stove or fireside. Some people cooked and fried with a pan over the coal fire which was held on cast iron rings from the black Rayburn ovens; red hot fat, a few feet away from crawling bairns and rowdy young kids? A disaster of house fire and personal injury just waiting to happen and one day a neighbour's chip pan fell onto a six-year-old Davey Aire's head causing my young friend terrible injuries. You'd think we would learn, but, no – the chip pan remained an essential and permanent feature on fireplaces and in kitchens.

The pans were always burnt black on the sides where the red hot fat had spilled over. The fat was hardly ever changed for new fat; the well pure unadulterated lard, not the sunflower or palm oil like namby pamby stuff of these days. Everyone knows that new lard does not turn the chips that lovely brown colour so avoid it like the plague. What we never knew was that the tradition of keeping the same old burnt fat in the pan that your grandmother had handed down to your mother was killing us in a different way to that occasioned by cholesterol blocked arteries. We knew nothing of carcinogenic acrlyamides then. And frankly, I know nothing about them now. My mother's chip pan and her grandmother's fat is still knocking out great chips even as I type.

Tripe and Butter Mountains

Butter was cholesterol special and like suet it was piled up in mountains, this time in the Meadow Dairy in the Front Street, which these days would be classed as a delicatessen. The dairy had a huge cylinder of butter on the counter about one metre in diameter and one metre high. As kids we would be sent on *messages* to the street to get some shopping in for our mothers or neighbours who would offer a few pennies for doing it. I always remember going for butter and getting a half or a pound sliced off the mountain into grease-proof paper. The shop lasses would keep the message so that there was proof you actually went with the money and got the goods. I am certain though that in the Dairy and in the Co-op we had coupons and our mothers got some form of credit and then a dividend paid back on volume bought at the Co-op particularly. That was the *divi* and was essential to balance the family budget.

I guess my mother used lots of butter for baking as she baked most days, bread, stotties and cakes. Butter was spread liberally on warm stottie cakes for sure. The only sandwiches I really remember were the sugar and buttered bread ones which we ate when we came in for a break from playing. It was always sugar spread on buttered bread. My lovely landlady, Annemarie, tells me they ate the same in Ireland. I guess sugar and bread was the *Subway* or pancetta of the old days across the known world. God knows what the anti-sugar lobby would think now of that. I have to state that taxing sugar and bread sandwiches would be the final straw for me. With that and the increasing dental costs here I'd be thinking of crossing Hadrian's Wall to Nicola's new kingdom and getting hurled into fried Scotch pies with a nice hallucinogenic Buckie wine diluted with sugar loaded *Iron Bru* – still proudly made from *gurders*. Aye, the Scots know how to keep the National Health Service ticking.

Moving from sugar to savoury, my father's favourite teatime meal was tripe and onions. Urgh…I still feel sick at the memory of my first attempt to eat the horrible stuff. He loved it boiled in milk. He had a duodenal ulcer and always said that tripe and milk was good for the stomach. When he went into hospital, they gave him tripe and milk - something then even in my medical ignorance I saw as bizarre. And many years later I helped source a drug from a Japanese drug company, *Takeda*, which was called *Lanzoprazole*, a proton pump inhibitor for those medically inclined. Like *Losec*, *(Omneprazole)*, these drugs along with *Xantac*, revolutionised the treatment of ulcers after the discovery the that a bug, H. pylori, was a main cause of the excess acid in ulcers which could be treated with antibiotics. The tripe and milk they gave my father in hospital and prescribed every Wednesday for dinner never seemed to cure my dad's ulcer and it got worse. So as the years of eating the horrible stuff never seemed to mimic the results of a good antibiotic or proton pump inhibitor and made it worse, I believe I am correct in saying that tripe is bad for you. The medical profession have a lot to answer for.

I believe secretly my father knew it was horrible, as tripe was the only food my father allowed me not to eat. I was always told to eat anything that was put in front of me. *Children were starving around the world* and heaven forbid I ever thought about leaving food on a plate. But I must have held out against tripe as I was always given mince and onions on the Wednesdays when he ate it. My mother never ate it either. Also she never ate any rabbit or pheasant either; she was sick of skinning and gutting and eating the stuff when she lived with Stripper so we rarely ate our poached stuff - Dad gave most of it away to the posh folk. In true altruism my father used to give vegetables and dead furry things to the folk who lived in the posh houses in Hinsons Crescent or the new Leech builders *(Leechies)* private housing estate. He had two long strips of garden and he also planted and upkept the two next door neighbours' gardens, because they were too old to manage, so we had an allotment sized field of vegetables. This backed onto Chester Road, the road from Sunderland to Chester-le-Street and the posh folk walked up it to get their shopping in the Front Street. Dad often sat on the low wall that divided the footpath from the gardens and smoked his tabs. The posh ladies would always stop and admire his garden and they always ended up with a cabbage or lettuce, a few carrots etcetera. If they asked he'd give them the odd rabbit or pheasant I'd brought in hoping for a nice stew. I could never believe he did this and I wanted him to charge them as plainly being posh they had money and we didn't. But he always shook his head and said to me: 'Son it's better to give than receive. You have no idea if that lady has any money to feed her bairns because she lives in a posh house. We do alright son, and the day I can't give someone a cabbage is the day we won't be alright.'

A humble man and loving man - I love him for it. Sadly and forever my regret, I never told him so. Very soon after giving me his advice on doing small things with great love he wouldn't be around to sit on his wall anymore. And I never got to tell him that I loved him for it.

Tripe and Black Pudding in the Club

The only other time I attempted tripe was in the Club. Every Sunday, or on a special day like Leek Show Monday, the steward would put out tripe in small bowls on the bar. This was soaked in vinegar, like the pickled onions which were also on the bar. Along with cheese and those insipid round cheese biscuits these delights were open season for the hung-over men who piled into the bar on Sunday morning. I was in my teens by now and was tempted to try some tripe. None of us young uns ate it, and I think it was Jackie Tate, a miner with a huge furrowed brow and huge fists who practically threatened and shamed me and my mates to try some. I took a piece and looked at the furry, indented stomach that looked like a white brain and I could smell the insides of a newly dressed rabbit. I put it to my mouth and began to cockle. Of course everyone laughed which made it worse. Despite the imminent downgrade in my character to soft twat *(puff)*, I refused to swallow it and chucked the horrible thing to Tommy Cutts who gobbled it down as if it was his last meal...which it probably was. To this day I have never since eaten the stuff.

Dad used to boil pigs trotters and also make brawn as well with a pig's head; boiling the bloody thing up for days and stripping the meat and brains out to make the rough pate. I never touched that either or the whole oxtail he'd strip and boil and cut up. Now I love both...after writing this I may even try tripe. Our local peripatetic butcher, Yorkie, can probably get me some from his badger and other mammalian road kill menagerie; anyone else like some badger tripe?

Bloaters and Rag and Bone Men

On Thursdays the fish man would come around with his horse and cart. My mother would buy bloaters, kippers or roll mop herring depending on what we'd eaten the week before. Herring was the cheapest fish you could get. Dad and me used to fish for white fish at sea so that was the cost effective way to eat non-herring type fish. Once a month we ate fish and chips from the Anderson's chippie or the one around on Larkfield Crescent. Bloaters were whole smoked herring whilst kippers were gutted and splayed. Roll mop herring were filleted fresh herring rolled into cylinders and soused in vinegar. My mother used to bake roll mops in the oven and despite the bones I liked them. Bloaters I didn't eat much and preferred kippers, because the bones put me off as a kid but Dad made me persevere. Those days I didn't enjoy my dinner without tons of bread and butter to absorb the bones.

It seemed normal for horse and cart vendors to come around. The horse shit was a bonus as Dad always made me step out into the street with a bucket and spade to get it and put it into the sunken bucket of shit and animal detritus near his precious leek trench. This septic tank of putrid, decaying organic matter had dead cats, dogs, horseshit, you name it. If it had died or come out of an orifice he put it in there. I had the lovely task of dipping jam jars into the ooze and then feeding his prize leeks with the Quatermass-type liquid, pouring a jar down each of the two tubes either side of each leek in his special leek trench. More about leeks later:

The other horse and cart that came around was the rag and bone man. I can't recall if this was a travelling gypsy man or a local. But he'd take any old rags, rubbish, iron etcetera and give us wooden clothes pegs in return. I always thought that was where clothes pegs came from. It took years and marriage to know you could actually buy them. It isn't as much fun though - much better if bartered with a rag and bone man – and please, can we bring back the ice cream man and the pop man?

Fentimans Ginger Beer and Guidi's Ice Cream

The pop (soda) man came around on Fridays when Dad had been paid. The wagon would pull up at several stops in the street and sound his horn. They carried crates of glass pop bottles with screw tops.

Neds' pop was the first I remember. The factory was in Penshaw and must have provided some extra employment outside of what was only available at the pit. Young lads could get a job straight from school there in the pop works. Or they would deliver bottles around the area, hanging precariously by one hand off the back of the pop wagons. Some I know took delight in telling you they pissed in the pop in the factory. I was never sure if this was true but as by now you will realise there were some crazies around where I lived so I much preferred to drink *Fentimans'* ginger beer.

The *Fentimans* wagon came on Fridays too. Purple Al who lives here confirms that his pop man in Leicester came on Friday. He remembers *Corona* as the pop company - dear me, not a great brand name now for sure and maybe that's why he turned purple! His favourite was Dandelion and Burdock which curiously was mine, however, it hasn't made me purple like Al despite its deep colour.

Anyway *Fentimans'* ginger beer did not make you purple. It came in large stone jugs very much like the sour mash whiskey jugs that John Wayne would balance on one bent arm and then with the same arm pour gallons down his open mouth. Fentimans' jars had the pop factory's iconic logo on it, the head of a German shepherd hound. The ginger beer was still live - that is to say it was cloudy and partially fermenting. The jug had a cork like stopper on it and it was wise to keep it in the cold larder we all had then or outside in the coalhouse to slow the fermentation. Each week we returned the jug and got another full one. It was delicious.

We made our own ginger beer with a portion of the mystical ginger beer plant that was donated by Mrs Barlow who had one. It was of course mildly alcoholic and we loved it even though it didn't have the flavour of *Fentimans*. One day I will try to make it if I can ever find what a ginger beer plant is. Maybe there's one in the pub's botanical gardens that the lads haven't smoked yet. I'll go have a look today.

Fentimans pop disappeared in the sixties I'm sure. I now realise that it has revived, a bit like *Lucozade,* into a new and exciting brand. I have seen it in pubs which I have to say brings these amazing memories back but I can't bring myself to buy it as I know it won't be the same. And have you seen the price? It was pennies in my day!

The other motorised vendor was the ice cream men who habitually drove around the council estate ringing out their tunes from the van. We had several, and certainly we didn't see the ice cream wars of

Glasgow, so I am unsure why the one which seemed to come out victorious was *Guidi*. This ice cream was my favourite as it was brownish and really creamy. I have no idea who *Guidi* was or if they are still going but if they are, please let me know and I'll buy a few tubs for sure.

At the sound of the ice cream van's jingle parents would send the bairns out for a couple of 99's. 99's were a treat with a Cadbury's Flake squashed in them. Of course *Mr Whippy* is iconic and we all loved those too and I still do like them as I think this is the only ice cream that should be eaten at the seaside, with a *Flake* and of course, dripping in red *monkey's blood*. My youngest lad tried to get *monkey's blood* on his ice cream the other day in Paignton. They looked at him as if he was from Mars or the Amazon jungle. He had to explain he was born in South Shields, which to be fair is not a lot different from Mars, and every time he goes up North he eats ice cream with *monkey's blood* on it at *Notriani's* or *Minchella's* in Seaburn. As I type, my darling wife has told me that *Notriani's* has been voted the best ice cream in Britain. So go eat fish and chips next door at *Minchellas*, the best in the planet and finish off with a lovely ice cream at *Notriani's* - ask for *monkey's blood* - they will know what it is!

Vesta Beef Curry and Heinz Spaghetti

As described our meals were very basic and all our vegetables and salads were home grown. We only ever ate salad in summer and only when Dad grew it; unlike now where you get it all year round. And we never ate rabbit meat (rocket or any of that weird green and brown leaves). We picked rabbit meat in the fields and hedgerows and it was fed to our pet rabbits or missing tortoises and never eaten by normal people. And as for dressings? The only one we had, and frankly we really should still have, was *Heinz Salad Cream*. Mayonnaise? Vinagrette? Balsamic dressings? Come off it, man, none of that shite tastes as good as Heinz salad cream. Anyway real men don't eat salad or quiche it's a known fact.

Spices were unknown, salt and white pepper were it. I never saw a black pepper grinder until I was in my twenties. Dad was a conservative man when it came to food: 'Can't touch that foreign shite.' He never had eaten anything much but meat or fish with veg or chips. Then a momentous event happened, a cultural change as big as the first cultivation of wheat. They invented the *Vesta Beef Curry*. Even my dad tried it. He actually ate some. My mother and I enjoyed it so much that we bought a *Vesta* prawn one another weekend when she was flush. Dear me - prawns? I never had them except to eat as shrimps at the seaside. And then the pièce de résistance - the *Vesta Chicken Supreme* - a sauce with chicken! It had never been known - I had only ever eaten chicken with gravy. It also had rice as a side dish and not as a pudding. We had never eaten rice as anything but rice pudding. And long grain rice? What the hell was that! Rice with salt, sauce and curry and not sugar and milk - this was heresy to Dad.

Vesta Beef Curry was a packet of dried meat and dry flavouring and a packet of boil in the bag rice in a box. One had to rehydrate the curry and boiled the rice. To us, in days long before takeaway Chinese or Indians, it was an oriental delight. When Mam had any money we were treated to one between us on a Saturday night. Dad had tatie pot. Sadly they disappeared from my view for some 45-50 years, but joy of joy, last year I found a *Vesta Beef Curry* in the same box as all those years ago in the town cheap shop and tried it…I'll not spoil it for you, if you can't get one where you are let me know and I'll send you one from the cheap shop. All I will say is, perhaps living in Asia and eating their rich, delicious spicy foods has spoiled my taste buds - but to quote that iconic band *Family*, despite it's simple cardboard taste and purely for grumpy old age stubbornness, *Vesta* will remain the king of curries for me.

Another revolution in the house occurred the first time I tried to cook real spaghetti when I had returned from my first term at University and found out what it was myself for the first time.

'What the bloody hell is that muck!' my father shouted at me as he saw me putting the long strands of uncooked pasta into a pan of boiling water. My mother watching me was still shocked at what I'd paid for the hard tasteless raw pasta material and what the hell were green peppers? And telling her I was making Bolognese sauce which was not out of a Heinz tin. 'Are you alreet pet?' she kept asking.

My dad grumbled at the uncooked strands of dry spaghetti, 'Looks like bloody tab lighters. And what the hell are you putting into good mince. Smells like a tart's boudoir. Have you no Bisto?'

'I think they are herbs pet. David brought them all back from college. Looks lovely mind doesn't it,' my mother lovingly tried to assuage my father's angst at this new horror. She grabbed my arm and asked diplomatically, 'Would you like me to make you a cup of Bisto pet?'

As you can guess the only spaghetti we had ever seen (Dad had never eaten any at all) was *Heinz*. I had been educated by fellow students, posher than me, that pasta came in many disguises and not always from a tin. So I purchased some at a proper delicatessen in the great metropolis of Manchester, along with dried basil and oregano. I thought I'd treat my parents to an Italian delicacy on my return from three months of student exile. Once I had it served on the plates, I think you can guess the outcome. I watched as mam and dad tried to fork up the long strands of pasta with it slipping off the fork back onto the plate. I had showed them how to roll it onto the spoon first but after only one failed try to get the long strands into his mouth my father gave up the ghost. 'How the bloody hell can I eat this foreign stuff if it keeps falling of me bloody fork. And the mince tastes like those purple sweets you ate as a kid...parma violets weren't they? Not for me son, but thanks for cooking. It's foreign shite again, like that Vesta curry stuff, David. You can keep it down Manchester.'

And so ended our family experiment with Indian and Italian cuisine.

Mixed Grills and Posh Restaurants

I rarely ate in restaurants. I had never eaten to my knowledge in a restaurant with my parents. We only ever went to a restaurant once in a blue moon if my Aunty Rene and Uncle Hal came up on holiday to stay with us. Uncle Hal was a Geordie but had stayed in London, after leaving Newcastle *in a hurry* one day before the war. He was a bookmaker and was what you might call dodgy as he always seemed to have rolls of money and he took us out twice to a restaurant in Sunderland. I can't remember now what it was called but it was near Park Lane bus station. It might have been a precursor of *Elizabeth's*. But I do remember what we ate. Mixed grill.

Mixed grill was like eating caviar to us. We never had that much meat other than the cheap cuts and only one type at a time! So mixed grill was the first choice if someone else was paying; it was expensive and lots of it. Everything you would want if you were being treated to your first meal out. In fact for years I ate mixed grill everywhere I went as it was massive and therefore value for money. I knew nothing of quality or the nuances of haute cuisine or heaven forbid that abortion of a culinary trend, nouvelle cuisine.

When purgatory started, that is, I started working for a living and I used to entertain clients most nights. I ate in some of the best restaurants in Britain, Michelin stars, Egon Ronay you name it I ate there and they all served up bloody *Nouvelle Cuisine*. All paid for of course on expenses. Who the hell would pay for it out of their own money? A slither of meat, fish or seafood: A drop of sauce: A lettuce leaf or a raw carrot and a size of dessert that would have been the lickings left on one of my mam's cake mixing bowls. When I think of it I should have charged the company money for the takeaway Chinese, fish and chips and the tatie pots my dearest had to make me at 1 am after eating in these establishments.

And don't get me on about fish in restaurants. Who wants to eat fish raw or foreign weird stuff covered with cream or cheese for God's sake? I chuckle when I hear the fishermen here and read the Daily Brexit headlines on my Kindle about protecting our fish. Get real man! We don't eat fish! The Great British public eat meat, mainly in pies, pasties, pizzas and real British food like Chicken Madras and Sheish Kebab. We ship the fish and especially any invertebrate to the nasty foreigners in Brussels and the likes. My mate Eddy sums up fish for us all; 'I am not a lover of fish. But any fish we eat should come from gunboat-controlled, UK sovereign waters, be pure white, covered in batter and fried.'

These days it seems the menus are a lot better in posh restaurants than my days of novelle cuisine. Size matters. It seems the massively obese critics on *MasterChef* shun small portions and love loads of gravy (well sauce they call it and what the bloody hell is *jus*?) and the puddings need to stick to the stomach lining like my mother's did. What a job eh? Food critic! A lot better than pouring sand down a black hole all day. Get fattened up and pissed every day and treated like Lord Muck in every restaurant you turn up in. Then waffle on and on about the weird sea plants that no other animal eats except sea otters (I used seaweed from the rock pools to kill off wire worm in my spud beds, so how the hell can that be good for you!). Rave about slimy invertebrates that only the Chinese can stomach and horrible things that come from the gonads of sheep mixed in sauces with names that are now banned as we have left the iron rule of France and Jean Paul and his mates. I have to say *Eggs Scunthorpe* will sound less sexy than *Eggs Benedict* or *Lobster Mornay* switching its name to *Lobster Peterheed* might leave a bitter taste in the mouth for the Remain voting epicureans. But maybe these food critics may well be helping get real food back on the menus. So life is better than the nouvelle cuisine days.

But still avoid anything that has words like *Fusion* or *Flexitarian* or heaven forbid, Sushi or Quiche.

Quiche and Blue Nun Wine

No real man would eat Quiche. Why? Well you should read that iconic milestone of a book *Real Men Don't Eat Quiche*. In this book Flex Crush a nuclear waste driver declares this to be a known fact whilst eating a dinner plate full of fried steak, eggs, bacon, fries, hash browns and all things known to come from cholesterol making organs. It really can be summed up in a few clear mind-blowing observations and sociological and historical facts. I quote. 'How could John Wayne have wiped out the whole of the Red Indian nation and killed thousands of Japs at Iwo Jima on a diet of quiche and salad?'

The fact is he couldn't.

It is a known scientific fact that. 'Real men actually like the full bodied tangy taste of monosodium glutamate.' Flex offers another profound sociological and dietary lesson. 'Look at today's liberal world where people eat quiche. In *Kramer versus Kramer*, Dustin Hoffman and Meryl Street (clearly quiche eaters) fight each in court over custody of their son. John Wayne would have slapped the broad and shipped the kid off to military school. I rest my case.

Culinary trends come and go and certainly taste in wine for the average person has changed dramatically since babies started to boom. As I have written before, no one I knew drank wine. It took the seventies and the introduction of wine at posh meals out with your lass to start the trend. Wine offered then was always Blue Nun or Mateus Rosé. Blue Nun was considered posh and I believe the Nun was to appease those of us post-war babies who still saw anything coming from Germany as Satanic. To us it was lovely. As was Mateus Rosé that slight sparkling Portuguese delight in the unique bottle.

The Alsace and Rhine Valley *Hoch* wines like Liebfraumilch and Riesling were considered best in class to the average punter. Women loved them. I am amazed now how ladies have moved away to the more medium to dry wines of today's market. Blue Nun and Black Tower Leibfraumlich brands have virtually disappeared. As has the widespread sale of Chianti in the straw basket covered bottles that people made table lamps out of. That is a pity; they were useful weapons for an old employee of mine, *The Mule*.

Still have to say that a little bit of wine snobbery comes out in me when I hear barmen ask punters, who plainly have never seen a French person and think a terroir is their latest horrible little grandson (called Damien or Tyson) if they would they like a Chardonnay, a Merlot or a Sauvignon. And don't get me on about Prosecco; it's only posh Lambrusco man, which is price hiked to fool everyone that it's some sort of Dom Perignon. If you want proper real man or real woman's fizzy - drink good French Champagne for God's sake! Sauvignon, Merlot, dear me, in our day we asked for a red or white wine. No one would even have a clue or care if there was any difference in the original grape. It all tasted the same.

The real innovation of home drinking of cheaper wine those days was the introduction of two to three litre boxes of white, red or rosé wine. Real drinkers loved them and no one cared what grape or terroir they came from. Charlie told me that when shopping he asked his lovely wife Sue what type she wanted as he picked one up for her to look at. 'Give me it here,' she said and then juggled it in both hands. 'Bugger the type - just feel the weight.' No Merlot, Chardonnay or other grape preference those days, but pure specific gravity and volume. Women were real women then. Most were expert in squeeze technology and could take the silver bag that contained the wine out at the end and squeeze and squash it to extract the last glass of wine with the precision of a nuclear waste driver.

Bull's Milk and Diarrhoea

Moving on from alcohol to the softer drinks; I was discussing with my fellow inmates the other day the merits of Camp Coffee, no, not that drank by the whole cast of the *Carry On* movies, but the liquid coffee essence that came in bottles like Worcester sauce bottles. This essentially was for poor people. My mother bought it when she was skint and couldn't afford proper coffee by which I mean Instant coffee. We had never heard of Latte, Americano, let alone Cappuccino. Actual coffee beans would have been covered in tomato sauce and put on toast.

Camp coffee was horrible, end of... My mam and other mothers put *Bull's Milk* in it to try to make it taste ok. *Bull's Milk* to us was sterilised milk, not pasteurised; it came in long bottles with a narrow neck with a metal cap on it, much like a beer bottle and needed an opener to prise the top off. It was sweet and tasted so different that we termed it *Bull's Milk*. It was different to say the least. Can't say I have seen it since.

The other milk put in this coffee was condensed milk from tins. *Nestlé* made it and it was liquid sugar really, instant dental caries and obesity rolled into one can. Sweetest thing known to man: I had heard little of it until my dearest decided that Banoffee pie was the next best thing to heaven and made one. I believe it takes several cans of *Nestlé* condensed milk, several litres of full cream and a bag of brown sugar to make. The sugar tax on this would make you want to move to Lichtenstein. No wonder I struggle with wearing Lycra.

Tea? Coffee? I never drank any of the stuff; my liquid diet was fizzy pop, or maybe sometimes in summer, some form of diluted squash. *Robinsons Lemon Barley* water was a treat during Wimbledon; no one ever saw it again. But pop in all its forms was my refreshment, Sarsaparilla, Dandelion and Burdock, Cream Soda, Cherryade etcetera. hence my teeth rotted and I reached twenty stone.

Tea and coffee were for old people and it was only well into my late teens when I started to drink coffee: I drank tea only with whisky in it when I fished off Roker Pier in the depths of winter with Dad. I only started to drink coffee as it was the way to hopefully get into a girl's knickers when they *invited you in for coffee*. This was at University of course; in the North East before I left college girls couldn't invite you in anywhere, as they lived with drunken psychotic Dads who would beat you to an inch of your life purely for being with her late at night. Even girls didn't drink coffee. Well the girls I went out with didn't; they drank *Double Maxim or Brown Ale*.

The TV advert for *Nescafé Gold Blend* instant coffee became a classic. Even if it was later than our Paradise years it's worth a mention. Nescafé introduced a couple who were trying to have some sort of love affair - I know, I know, we don't really want to talk about lovey-dovey things like that but it gets better. The adverts went on forever. Each episode they got close to the nuptials but not quite and each episode she made him a nice steaming cup of coffee to enhance the ambience and romance for her. He being a man really should have preferred a beer but he was an actor I suppose. Anyway it went on for ages. Our lass loved it of course and the whole world did, women waiting to see if they finally *did it* and fell in love, men simply hoping he'd get his leg over and they could turn the telly over and watch *Match of The Day*.

Well, I can't remember what happened as by now I'd given up the will to live and was watching *Die Hard* on the bedroom telly . But what amused me immensely was a comedy sketch written to parody this nightmare of an advert. I have just tried modern cyber searching methods (that is, Google) and I can't find it. Maybe you can. But, it was a skit on the two lovers in the Nescafe ad…the couple have dinner and they eventually get back to her apartment and she asks him if he'd like a coffee. Sadly, he does not say, *I'd rather not* like my great friend Steed the Commercial manager par excellence in *A Turkey and One More Easter Egg* (or, like Michael Corleone in *Godfather Two*, when asked if *he'd like a banana daiquiri*, say - 'No!'). This poor man actually said, *'Yes please'*. His true love goes into the kitchen and all you hear is the sound of the coffee percolator *grr'ng, slavering, urghing'* with horrible squashing noises. After a short while she pops her head around the door. He looks up from reading some women's lovey- dovey magazine and says to her in some slavering romantic manner: 'Ah, Cappuccino?'

She looks puzzled and distressed at him and says: 'No: Diarrhoea'.

Well, it still makes me chuckle.

Gold Top Milk and Blue Tits

We all drank proper milk. Milk was delivered by the milkman every morning to your doorstep. How they did it in winter is still a mystery. As I type this we have suffered two lots of the worst snow since 1963. It lasted thirty-six hours two weeks ago and today it looks like a white wonderland after twenty-four hours of snow. It will go in a day or two but the whole place has shut down. There has been no milk, bread or bottled water for days due to panic buying and hoarding. Forget public transport and God knows how a milk man could deliver milk these days. But back then they did. And it was superb stuff. The whole top of a frozen milk bottle came out as a solid frozen chunk of pure cholesterol, lovely cream. It was common to see Blue Tits pecking at milk bottle tops to get at the cream. A sight gone forever I guess.

Everyone drank full cream milk. I do not recall there being anything else; certainly no skimmed or low fat - solely pure fat with silver metal tops. If there was any thin milk for strange people then I never saw it. All crates I delivered as a milk boy were silver or gold. The real crème de la crème, excuse the pun, was Gold Top milk. This was like caviar is to cod roe, *Chateau d'Yquem* to *Blue Nun* or *Dartmoor Jail Ale* to *Watneys Red Barrel*. In winter the frozen cream of a Gold Top bottle would rise two foot in the air. It was the ambrosia of the God's and to all the song birds. We should bring it back. It harmed no one. We all grew up normal. Didn't we?

Well, in Shiney Row some didn't, but I'll leave them to later. I move on to when we still drank Gold Top and school milk was still full of lovely creamy cholesterol and the highlight of the week was to get a comic to read while you drank it.

CHAPTER SEVEN
COMICS AND MOVIES

Japs and English

I've mentioned Mr Lister our junior school teacher who had been scarred by his time in the Far East and a lot of men in my schooldays which were only a decade or so after the war ended were scarred with their experiences in the war. My Uncle Joe Cassidy from Liverpool had been taken prisoner by the Japanese and suffered badly, but he was an amazingly pragmatic and forgiving man I thought. I never heard much vitriol and hatred from him; he only seemed to want to forget. Unlike Les's Dad, Jack, who hated the Japanese with a great passion, borne out of six years of their unique hospitality.

Jack lived over the street from us with his wife Anne and two kids. Les was older and always a bit more naughty I guess. As I grew up and got to know Les over many years I realized that from early childhood he lived his life perpetually trying to take the piss and humiliate people for fun. Jack could be a very funny man but he had obviously suffered badly in the prison camps. He told me of the horrors one day in *The Oddfellows Pub* and how he'd escaped the sinking of the ship on the Yellow River in China days before the war started. Jack got out of that engine room but the rest didn't - is my more culturally correct summary of how he ended the story. He then told of how he'd suffered four long years, culminating in him killing a Japanese officer at the end of the war when the camp was liberated and taking his samurai sword. From that day on he hated Japanese with a passion. His worst nightmare was when the Chinese takeaway opened in 1972 and he couldn't pass it without hurling abuse and spitting at it. No point in Les telling him they were Chinese not Japanese. He took to walking the long way home rather than pass it.

My point with Jack's story is that we were largely ignorant of the facts of the horrors and bestiality inflicted by the Japanese on prisoners of war when we were young. Mr Lister was a casualty of those times for sure but we never realised that then. I guess that wasn't taught and we had little access to any media but school books, comics and your parents' views on life. And definitely, no one wanted to be Japanese or a German when we played *Japs and English* outside in the streets and fields. They were universally stereotyped as evil. *Japs and English* (note the nationalistic lack of any other of our islands' countries mentioned) was a game where we basically used made up guns and weapons (sometimes real ones) to try to storm various imaginary military strategic positions. Only the younger lads or the softer lads were told to be Germans or Japs and then get their heads kicked him, or battered with catapults or hit with homemade bombs out of tin cans, paraffin and gunpowder from fireworks. However, curiously, some of the more lunatic among us who grew up to be raving and violent actually liked to be Japs and Germans so they could enact torture and violence back on us or their own little army. Another theory of sociopathic human behaviour I will add to my thesis.

We often used Jack's acquired samurai sword to play Japs and English with. I particularly enjoyed chopping Mr Lloyd's sunflower heads off in his garden. Gussy enjoyed cleaving small animals. The more psychotic, that is, those who went on to join the Army or the Hendon bike gang the Black Angels, enjoyed having a go at maiming the lads from Penshaw in the perpetual fights we had with them.

EEYORE ALAN
Comics and Retirement

Play acting in games like *Japs and English* came from the knowledge of war we gleaned from our parents who had experienced it first hand and from school masters like Mister Lister but mainly from the comics we read then which were very biased towards the macho hero. Of course I am referring to the boy comics, not the *Bunty* or *Valentine* which I guess had stories of horses and ponies in them. I never read girl's comics so sorry my female reader but I'm sure you all had similar stereotypes for the age as we boys did. *The Valiant, The Victor, Tiger, The Eagle* and others all had some iconic German and Japanese-bashing muscle man who won the war on his own.

The Valiant had Captain Hurricane, a hulk of a man with a lantern jaw, who spent the whole time riddling the enemy with machine guns, hand grenades or bashing and stamping on *Krauts Hun Japs Slanty Eyes* and *Eyties*. *'Take that you Kraut!'* Kappow! All great stuff to post war kids who knew nothing of racial stereotyping or inappropriate ethnic slurs.

There were also non-genocidal racists in the comics. *The Eagle* had Dan Dare: wow! 1950's Sci. Fi that was as real to us as Star Wars, Avatar and the animatronic wonders of today's youth - and long before Spock and Captain Kirk amazed us. *The Tiger* had *Roy of The Rovers* the iconic soccer wizard who could score goals with his boot lace, head the ball fifty metres into the top corner from the half way line and save the known world in his spare time, all long before Ronaldo and Messi. *The Dandy* had a cowboy hero, *Desperate Dan*, who was famous for eating cow pie. The pie dish was about a metre long and had two cow horns sticking out of it. His chin was made of granite with iron bristles that he used a blow torch to shave off. He was the toughest man in town - a proper cowboy.

Of course *The Beano* was everybody's favourite, along with *The Dandy*, *The Topper, and The Beezer*. There were characters in them for all, even girls. Naughty girl characters including the horrors *Beryl the Peril, Minnie the Minx,* and *Keyhole Kate.* Then there were *The Bash Street Kids, Dennis the Menace, Roger the Dodger, The Numbskulls*, etcetera, all iconic and long lasting friends of our childhood and also adulthood.

I have to admit I had *The Victor* and *The Beano* delivered to our flat every Saturday morning while I was at University in Manchester, a welcome break from Neurophysiology, Dr Foster's horrible statistics and Professor Scheiden's lectures on how to fool the police into believing you are a psychopath by eating tomatoes. Sadly, but probably truthfully, he seemed to think I'd need that pharmacological tip one day.

On Saturdays with the usual hangover I read *The Beano* and listened to Alan my roommate wail on about how he wished he was retired every time he woke up (he was twenty years old). He was, and still is, the manifestation of *Eeyore* from *Winnie the Pooh*. There was always a dark cloud that followed him over his head and his mantra was and still is, *'Ah just kna something terrible is gonna happen'*. He now wishes he was a student again after retiring from a life of trying to educate the starving masses of Tyneside in Algebra and Complex Numbers. The grass is always greener they say. Forty-four years later he was in his usual form texting me about *Strictly Come Dancing* and me winding him up about the constant appearance of his younger brother, on camera in what is after all a lasses dance show for God's sake! And him now a bastion of society; his Glaswegian grandfather would be spinning in his Keir Hardy dug grave. But even worse, much worse than all that, he was seen live on *Strictly* in the deep South on a Saturday when 'The Lads' were playing football at home that day. I texted back – 'he must have the *Strictly* curse.'

BURGLAR BOB
Alf Tupper: 'Oz' and Borstal Boy

On the subject of *Eeyore* Alan's desire to retire in those early days, Burglar Bob had some very wise words on the subject the other day in the Irish madhouse pub I live in. Bob was standing drinking with his jeans around his arse as usual. He burped loudly and coughed his day's paint fumes up, turned his head and looking over the top of his *one pound from the charity shop*, thick, black-rimmed glasses, he spoke these sagacious words. 'When I was at school in Nottingham the teacher asked me what I wanted to be when I grew up. I looked at him and told him I wanted to be a Lollipop man (a post normally held by retired elderly persons who saw children over the road on their journeys to and from school, stopping the traffic with a sign shaped like a lollipop).

'What on earth for boy?' the teacher enquired of the then youthful Bob.

'Coz I won't have to start work till I'm retired,' Bob answered truthfully and hopefully. Bob lamented, 'The bastard caned me for saying that too!'

In Bob's days children were expected to be seen and not heard or ever hope of better things than an early retirement, a lollipop person's job and the grave. In those happy days child beatings by teachers were the norm for anyone with acerbic wit and a perceptive brain.

In between being beaten half to death by teachers I loved reading comics, particularly *The Victor* and my favourite then and now, was *Alf Tupper, The Tough of the Track*. Alf was the original working class hero, long before John Lennon wrote the song, or maybe he wrote it about Alf. He was a top athlete for over fifty years, originally in *The Rover* and then *The Victor*. He only ate fish and chips. Note, like *The Duke* he didn't eat Quiche, and he never bought a pair of Nike running shoes, always his old spikes which he carried in a paper bag. He broke the four minute mile long before Rodger Bannister in these spikes and his old string Greystone Harriers' vest after welding a new jet engine together in his workshop under the Viaduct. He had not slept in twenty-four hours at that point and anyway his only bed was a mattress under the arches. He managed to get in a dinner of fish and chips wrapped in a newspaper on his way to the race. He loved to beat the runners from the posh athletic clubs or even the GB team. He used to stop regularly to fight toffs who took the piss out of his demeanour and his non-high tech, designer sports gear. *The Toffs* were tall, chiselchinned and with flowing blonde locks but Alf always knocked them out with a couple of punches.

Years later when I played and watched rugby there was an English wing-back called David Duckham and he could have played a part in an Alf Tupper movie. He looked and ran like the toffs in the old cartoon stories.

Alf also used to like to beat Yanks and of course any other Johnny foreigner of the usual stereotype. The Yanks were arrogant and boastful. Eastern Europeans were swarthy, moody and dark. And as for black athletes, they didn't exist. Except one day when Alf was running in a cross country race and he was miles ahead but he spotted some workers stuck up a church steeple, so he ran over and climbed up and rescued them. Then he ran back only to see *Zemba the Zulu*, the ebony-coloured, well-proportioned runner from somewhere like Birmingham well in front but in true Alf style he caught up with him and won. He finished it all off with another fish and chip supper. Those were the days before the dieticians got hold of sport and pasta and high energy drinks became the norm; Cod and chips and a few pints of bitter before a race, or indeed a fight, never did Alf any harm.

As I write and remember these publications it does cross my mind that we were indoctrinated by a John Bull type of media hype about England. Most of these *heroes* were English. Can't remember many other leading characters from other parts of the British Isles in the boy's comic strips and of course the foreigners were all despicable or shifty. Posh folk were also ridiculed, as were intelligent *soft lads*, who were simply beaten up. Cue the bespectacled, softie Walter, in *Dennis the Menace*. And as for people of colour? Well, I can't remember seeing any, except *Zemba* and Alf gave him a good thrashing. Lasses hardly existed in any of the boys' comics either and I'd be interested if boys existed in any of the lasses' comics. Maybe my female reader can let me know? As for all that gender stuff, well best not go there eh? I think the post war world of comics wasn't quite ready for that either.

Writing about comics, inclusiveness and all that, I am reminded that recently my son, who lives in a strange foreign place called London, has educated me into ways of being *woke,* something I am pleased he has done as I'm sure now that writing of those years ago, the post-war world wasn't ready for a *woke* comic. It took till 1967 and the comic/magazine *Oz* and a growing underground press to become *woke* and attempt to break the macho Anglophile establishment mould of our press and favourite comics. *Oz* was the sixties personified in an adult comic. Gay rights, civil protest, civil liberties, anti-religion, feminism, pacifism, racism, drug taking...you name it, *Oz* challenged everything in its pages. With its version of a more gender liberated *Rupert the Bear,* the school kids issue provoked arguably more controversy than *Lady Chatterley's Lover.* It was very heretical to those of us baby boomers used to perusing the *Rupert Bear Christmas Annual* or reading episodes of the cuddly ursine in the long running cartoon strip in the *Daily Brexit.* The *Oz* editors were charged with *Conspiracy to corrupt public morals* and the trial lasted six weeks amid massive publicity and support from the '70's progressive generation. As a young reader I loved it, as did most of my grammar school friends.

We loved any of this progressive, satirical protest stuff such as *Monty Python,* or Peter Cook and Dudley Moore as *Derek and Clive.* To quote Jim Anderson, the editor of *Oz,* 'Everything the establishment hated was in *Oz'.* I particularly remember a cartoon depicting a stoned hippy/zombie looking character, staring at his half empty beer glass, eyes staring out of his head and bloodshot, looking as rough as a badger's arse mumbling, *'Where's me Mandies?'*

Mandrax was a prescription drug often used with alcohol to get high. Another name was *Quaaludes* and the image in *Oz* was very like that of the great weirdo musician Frank Zappa, who sang of *Quaalude moonlight.* Even David Bowie, seemed to be looking for his *Mandies* in his song *Time* which referenced *Quaaludes and red wine.* Keith Richards, that iconic piss-head and druggie who defies mortality, medical or social logic, admitted possession of the drug. It provoked establishment controversy as did all drug-taking through the sixties and seventies. A Church of Scotland committee report on moral welfare reported: 'A further trend of misuse is mixing Mandrax and alcohol, with disastrous results.'

The Viz was the next comic to break the politically correct mould and arrived rather later than *Oz.* I guess characters like, *The Fat Slags, Sid the Sexist, Johnny Fart Pants, Biffa Bacon, The Modern Parents,* and *Cockney Wanker* all broke the mode in some way. The strip I thought was a masterpiece of legal and editorial jiggery-pokery was the edition where the magazine had to print an apology to the United Nations and the Romany Society of Great Britain for a cartoon strip published in a couple of previous editions, *Thieving Gypsy Bastards* portraying our Romany cousins as perpetrators of petty larceny around the towns and villages of Britain – a not uncommon allegation from many of non-Romanic culture in and around this country to this day.

Anyway, Viz, as part of a legal agreement had to apologise and printed their apology the next edition. They printed a full page apology with the title *THIEVING GYPSY BASTARDS* in massive print and the apology in very small print, and each time they referred to the original title in the text they printed it in large old type again *THIEVING GYPSY BASTARDS*. They also printed another comic strip called, *The Nice, Honest Gypsies* featuring a kindly Gypsy woman selling pegs door-to-door and helpfully returning forgotten change. A watershed for cross cultural awareness I guess.

They did try to break the politically correct mould for sure. I loved their advertisements. They advertised a set of the Queen Mother's Wooden False Teeth and I remember a full page advert for a Borstal Boy doll dressed in tracksuit and velour jacket and trainers with the statement, *Tilt him and he'll threaten legal action; also And he's so real, you think the **** has just climbed through your kitchen window.*

Sadly, I knew quite a few like our Borstal Doll as life moved on through the teenage and later years. Some I will introduce soon.

Cowboys and Indians and Wonderloaf
In 1969 my Aunty Winn's colour TV and heaven was watching the movies to me. I loved movies but I also loved *The High Chaparral.*

Cochise, the Apache leader in *The High Chaparal* always seemed to be available for sensible discussions with *Big John Cannon* or especially his brother-in-law, the Mexican, *Manolito*. He was the first Mexican I'd ever seen in cowboy films who wasn't portrayed as drooling guitar strumming idiot or an evil psychopathic rapist.

The ranchers always seemed to be meeting *Cochise* to discuss how to get *Big John's* beautiful Mexican wife *Victoria* back from her ritual and many kidnappings by *Cochise* and his mates, while *Blue Boy* cried and threw tantrums and *Uncle Buck* tried to kill everyone, like a good cowboy should. *Manolito* and *Big John* were always more passive and conciliatory with the great Apache Chief who spoke wise words, waved his war tomahawk a few times, smoked ganja with them in his peace pipe and allowed them all to leave unharmed. *Victoria* was never touched or harmed in any way, and seemed mildly flattered that such a good looking *Cochise* should constantly take such a fancy to her.

Having read much on the ways of Apaches after I grew older. I have to say that *Cochise, Mangas Colorado* and *Geronimo's* likely lads on their habitual raids of white settlers ranches were not known historically to treat the women so inclusively and ecumenically but maybe in the *High Chaparral* this was the turning point in American-Indian racial stereotyping. But to quote *The Duke* in *The Searchers*, 'That'll be the day'. Dee Brown's, *Bury My Heart At Wounded Knee'* was the book which first enlightened me to the racial issues and discrimination that still haunts America today and the movie *Soldier Blue*, which followed closely on from the book I believe changed many of us (well the less deranged) to question our own prejudices and monochrome histories we had been taught and viewed in popular television, comics and films.

Even before *Bury My Heart...* I liked Indians and I always bought plastic Indian figures to play Cowboys and Indians with. I loved the ones with big feathered headdresses, a bit like those that the Exeter Chiefs rugby team supporters wear now. Also I liked to buy Indian braves with tomahawks and bows and arrows in their hands. I bought these with the small amount of pocket money I had made from various ways of earning money or they were a special gift from my mam when she came back after Saturday shopping in the Town. Most of us bought these mainly from Woolworths or Josephs in Sunderland along with the plastic World War Two soldiers we also valued and played with a lot.

If anyone got a Western fort for a Christmas present, we'd enact battles with the other lads in the street, sometimes using the small cast metal cannons which we had for the World War soldiers. These cannons could fire a lethal barrage of used matchstick at rows of Indians or cowboys on the adobe fort battlements. Whoever shot and killed most won the game. We enacted scenes from the western TV shows at the time, like *Rawhide* or *Wagon Train*, and play-acted sometimes pretending to be the heroes we saw on the telly. Ominously, for the future in Shiney Row, it always ended up in a fight.

Wagon Train and Rowdy Yates

The first cowboy series on telly that I remember was *Wagon Train* with Ward Bond as wagon master. Then it was *Rawhide* and the cook, Wishbone who made soup every night for them, which was awful it seemed but when the cowboys complained about the soup he'd say, 'That's not soup, that's my soup.'

Of course *Rawhide* was famous as the start of Clint Eastwood's career. He played *Rowdy Yates* and we all wanted to be him. Clint moved on to star in Sergio Leone's spaghetti westerns and *A Fist Full of Dollars* was I think the first X-rated movie I ever sneaked into the cinema to watch as an underage viewer. But maybe it was James Bond in *Goldfinger*? I remember the opening scenes in the early James Bond movies, with silhouettes of naked ladies, particularly *Goldfinger* and *Thunderball,* which were in their day considered too risqué for the average eight year old boy. Just checked with that cyber genius Google and they were A certificates (under 12 kids must be accompanied by an adult). My dad must have taken me, but I am sure I watched *Thunderball* with the kids in the street because I remember talking at school about the naked ladies in the opening credits; first awakenings I guess.

I enjoyed the Bond movies, but I enjoyed Clint more and still think *The Outlaw Josey Wales* is the best Western ever made. Again it was very respectful to American Indians and Chief Dan George should have received an Oscar, as should have Clint. But I guess, 'That'll be the day.'

After *Josey Wales,* Clint made spitting baccy out of your mouth as a statement of hardness and disdain a fashion for macho males. Personally, I loved the shot of the 'God damned mangy red boned hound' after being covered in black baccy juice whining and then snarling at him. Also I still can't stop chuckling at Clint's line: 'What's it like with stains?' when he spits the baccy juice all over the snake oil salesman's white suit in a short but messy answer to the salesman peddling his stain remover. Disgusting, my dearest always tells me, but amusing to simple folk like me.

And, Clint spitting his baccy is my tenuous link into a pitman's life long gone now. I grew up with people chewing baccy and spitting it out. Pitmen couldn't smoke down the mines because of the risk of coal gas exploding, hence the use of Davy lamps after the Royal Society of Protection to Birds (RSPB) banned the use of pretty canaries to warn of impending death. Pitmen took *chewing baccy* down the mine with them to keep their nicotine addiction at bay until they could get back up in the cage and open up their five packs of *Woodbines, Capstan Full Strength, Senior Service, Embassy* and other carcinogenic, addictive weeds.

The pit was covered in baccy *hockel,* that is black spit which men crawled in as well as human faeces, as there were no toilets on the face and a long way back to the shaft through the tunnels, particularly if you were in the mines like the East Durham coast mines such as Westhoe, Wearmouth, Seaham Vane Tempest, Dawdon, Blackhall, Easington and the Northumbrian costal mines that went miles out under the sea.

Many men I knew still chewed baccy in the Club and in their house. Spittoons or sawdust on bar floors were still in use when I was young but no one seemed able to roll cigarettes with one hand while sitting on a gallower (pit pony) like the cowboys did. Cowboys always seemed to live on baccy, beans and coffee. They never seemed to eat much else. They also could roll a cigarette with one hand from the small baccy pouch they kept at their side. I debated this the other day in *The Teign's* botanic beer garden with some lovers of Jamaican tobacco and none of the smokers of roll your own Golden Virginoid and Rizlas can roll with one hand. Another lost art and skill and in this brave new *woke* world, like Rhett Butler and Scarlet O'Hara, it has gone with the wind.

However much we were indoctrinated in movies and television with macho cowboy types, it never seemed to work on me, I preferred my heroes to be more like *Captain Hurricane* in *The Dandy* and Stanley Baker in *Zulu*. Mind you we all loved watching the cowboy films on Saturday morning matinees at Houghton-le-Spring picture house. *Zorro* seemed to be everyone's favourite; I guess we liked the dark shadowy Latino type, with mask, black hat and sword better than frilly trousers and handkerchief cravats.

A trip to the movies in the fifties and sixties was always a treat, and of course an adventure because Houghton-le-Spring was two miles away or so and that was like going to Timbuktu for us. The natives were as strange as, and probably more hostile than, the African inhabitants of that far away land. We fought our way in and out. Nothing changed much as we grew into our teens, only the level of violence.

The big lads, or which village gang took over first, would sit upstairs and throw things over the edge at the young ones. Everyone used to sit excitedly waiting for the *Wonderloaf* advertisement and when the line and the *Wonderloaf* tune came up we shouted it out across the picture house. Why? I have no idea now; it's lost in time to me, but it amused us then.

Despite my angst about cowboys, I did enjoy the John Wayne movies. Loved all of them and I guess still do. I watched most at Houghton and at Sunderland Empire Theatre which showed movies then. *The Alamo* was my favourite but I also loved *The Comancheros, The*

Searchers and Tie a Yellow Ribbon. When and where I grew up politically correct meant you voted for the Labour Party so lines like the classic in *The Searchers* about the staying power of the indigenous folk of the USA I guess would be persona non grata these days:

BRAD: *They gotta stop sometime. If they're human men after all, they gotta stop.*

ETHAN: *No, a human being rides a horse until it dies, then goes on foot. A Comanche comes along, gets that horse up, rides him twenty more miles...then he eats him.*

I also loved *The Quiet Man* and wonder if that movie, like *The Searchers* would ever be made in these days of gender equality. The scene where Big John roughly drags Maureen O'Hara across the fields, streams and bogs of Ireland by her hand as she bashes off rocks, trees and drowns in streams, and then throws her onto his huge bed ready to ravish her, may be a bit too much these days. Especially when the Priest, who watches as they pass by him and she is dragged remorselessly to her fate, scolds her for not being a good wife and offers the big man *a stick to beat her with!* 'No', as my friend Charlie says, 'Davey, you just canna say or do those things these days'.

But maybe one day the Indians will get their day in the sun. Then they were portrayed as not human but as savages. This changed as time moved on through the sixties and seventies. I believe it was *The Lone Ranger* that began to portray Indians as intelligent and human. *Tonto*, the Lone Ranger's side kick, was always shown as a good guy and with knowledge and intellect and that was probably the first TV or movie Indian I saw who wasn't shown as a savage. It was sad when the Lone Ranger finally found out what Tonto always called him. It seemed that *Kemosahbee* meant *racist bastard* and the revelation ended a great friendship, or so the old joke went.

Talking about Cowboy and Indian jokes, I have to add this one. General Custer was riding into the Black Hills of Dakota looking for Crazy Horse and Sitting Bull. He asked his scout to come to see him. His scout came from Newcastle and was a Geordie and coincidently, called Geordie. Custer took a big draw on his cigar and said to the scout: *Geordie take some men and see if you can find where the Indians are camped.* Geordie said: *Wye aye general,* and rode off in the dust and the sun with three more ethnically-coloured scouts than our immigrant from Tyneside. Sometime later Geordie returns in a flurry of horses stamping and snorting with dust covering both him and his men. He rode up to Custer who was sitting on his grey horse surveying the Black Hills who asked him: *Did you see any Indians Geordie?* Geordie brushed the dust off his long coat and answered: *Nah, boss, but I heard lots of drums over the far hills towards the Little Big Horn River.* Custer took a drag of his cigar and looked concerned. He asked another question: *Were they war drums Geordie?'* Geordie looked at Custer with a puzzled look in his eyes but answered truthfully: *Nah, General, they were their drums.*

For those of you puzzled by the ending here is the translation - in Geordie dialect the plural pronoun *OUR* becomes *WOR* hence *WAR drums* is completely misunderstood by Geordie. To paraphrase *Basil Brush,* the long dead stuffed fox of TV renown...*Boom Boom!*

Blazing Saddles and Spielberg

The seventies saw much ground breaking in satire and general piss taking on accepted behaviours and rules of engagement and some wonderful movies helped reinforce that. Mel Brooks's *Blazing Saddles* remains one of my favourite movies as a masterpiece of black humour (not intentional) which illuminated the racist past of most cowboy movies and of racist American culture in general. The scene where the white cowboys ask the black guys to sing a slave song and they come up with the melodic *I get no kick from cocaine* and the rednecks crack up. *Hell that ain't no neegra song. How about 'the Camptown races?.*

Our black hero looks at his mate with a puzzled look and sarcastically says: *De camp down races, we aint heard that one.*

Rednecks: *Sure you have. It goes like this.* And they all start singing, whooping and slapping their thighs looking like the bigoted racist idiots they plainly are.

Great satire probably did more in our day to educate us racially ignorant folks to the fight against racism in all its forms than the horrors of *Roots* which was shown about the same time, or *Mississippi Burning* and *Twelve Years a Slave* has in much later times.

And of course *Blazing Saddles* has *Mongo,* the original horse puncher, our Newcastle horse-punching fan's hero I suspect. And who can forget the farting scene after a mammoth baked bean eating fest. It ends with a classic when all the baddies in the world turn up to fight the good guys - Nazis, Klu Klux Klan, Hells Angels, Mexicans of course (well Mr Trump's wall hadn't been built then) – ground-breaking stuff for those of us brought up on white heroes, Roy

Rodgers, Gary Cooper, John Wayne and Clint and the inherent racial stereotyping of such movies.

This era brought movies that remain classics today. It introduced Spielberg as the master of special effects and adventure with *Jaws* and *Close Encounters* followed by George Lucas and *Star Wars*. The girls loved the romantic slavery ones with Robert Redford, *The Great Gatsby* being one I was dragged along to watch, and oh my God, the hell of Ryan O' Neil in *Love Story*. I guess we lads also liked Redford in *The Sting* and *Butch Cassidy and the Sundance Kid* with Paul Newman.

Bruce Lee's *Enter the Dragon* prompted Ian King from school and me to seek out all the Kung Fu movies we could see in obscure picture houses across the region. We loved them. We even risked *The Stoll* in Newcastle, a renowned perverts' paradise to see *King Boxer*. As a result I took up karate at this time, taught at Herrington Burn YMCA. Unfortunately, I never did learn how to jump over houses like King Boxer could…disappointed me that. Ian kept on trying but I believe he only perfected the iron fist technique through grinding his hand in red hot coals. Very useful as he became a teacher in South Shields and would surely soon need it at White Lee comp those days.

This time also brought *The Godfather* with the cushion-filled mouth of Brando and the icy coldness of Al Pacino. De Niro hit the screens with the iconic but not greatly watched *Taxi Driver,* Jody Foster playing the under-age school girl prostitute causing a sensation from the right wing press and the 70's watchdog of all that might be corruptive to normal human beings, Mary Whitehouse.

Movies were a special treat when I was young because it needed hard earned money to go and spend time shouting at the screen about a slice of bread and I'm eternally grateful I was able to spend so much precious time with my father at the pictures. As I myself then went on to spend so many precious hours watching brilliant Disney, Dreamworks and Pixar movies with my own kids years after the happy days of my youth passed into the pages of this book.

As we couldn't afford these treats often we needed to keep busy doing something else we loved…playing outside.

CHAPTER EIGHT
FOOTBALL AND OTHER GAMES

MR. GRAHAM
Football and Coal Houses

We played outside from morning until night. If we weren't playing some form of killing game like *Japs and English* or *Dr Who,* we played football. Football in all its manifestations was the life blood of us boys. From a very early age we were kicking footballs in the street together. Throughout the 50's and 60' as kids, girls and boys, we played outside most days, sun, rain, snow, sleet, it didn't matter. As boys we almost always kicked or headed a football at some point in the day. Princes Street and The Crescent were separated by two paved paths and a Tarmac road and this was our football field. The goals were either the coal houses that we all had at the end of the small front garden which faced each other across the two streets or they were the wooden gates which lead to the houses.

We also used as a goal the openings for a path between two coal houses leading to the gardens and waste land at the back of The Crescent, *The Front.* The coal house lets were used as targets for heading or shooting practice. These lets were the hinged wooden openings into the coal houses about five feet from the ground into which the coal was thrown by the coalmen or by us penniless kids for pocket money from the older people after being dropped on the street by the local colliery coal wagon.

We normally picked sides and these could depend on which boys were around or who was into football. People like Gussie and Peter How who liked to collect or kill small creatures weren't really into football and rarely played at all and we never let the girls play - that would be soft and stupid of course.

Sometimes we kicked balls against the coal house, or lets, or openings or gates simply for fun and to attract friends from inside their houses because if they could hear the ball hammering against their gates or coal houses they'd persuade their mothers to let them out to play. Or we would play one to one *gates* where you defended your own garden gate against another player who defended their own and the winner was the one left standing after all the others were eliminated.

We rarely played on grass. The only grass we had was on the colliery field at the other side of the estate, where the pigeon crees and allotments were. The problem with the colliery field was it sloped and had inundations like waves in it so it wasn't flat but it did once have goal posts. Mainly if we played on grass it was at school or on a hillside over the main Chester-le-Street road which was cleverly named, the Hill. At play times we were on the School field or on the school concrete yard with coats or jumpers as goal posts. Knees were constantly scraped and cut from the concrete and also from the hard fields we played on in summer and the sheet-ice covered ones in winter.

Football Boots and Footballs

Shoes were used to play the game so I guess many pairs of shoes were worn out with football. There were no such thing as *trainers* - all we had were black gym shoes or *pumps* which belonged to and stayed at school in small wire-caged shoe racks next to the year group classrooms. They smelled perpetually of carbolic antiseptic which was sprayed in them to kill all known germs before they were handed to the next year's school child. I now wonder how long these gym shoes had lasted and how many children's feet they had covered before they were condemned by the World Health Organisation or used by Russia as a Novichok substitute to maim English football fans or ex-spies.

In summer some of us might have been given footwear called baseball boots. Of course no one had ever played baseball as it really it was for a girl's game, Rounders. We hated Rounders because we were forced to play it at school in the summer by teachers in an early attempt at gender equality and to be nice to the girls. Bah! Morris dancing, Rounders and American baseball shoes, you can keep them. Give me heavy, leather, wooden-studded football boots any day. Or the poor man's Doc Marten's - pit byuts (boots).

Football boots were precious objects and not to be used on concrete every day. Mine were always Christmas gifts from Santa and I still remember putting a new pair on my feet on a Christmas day and going out to play in heavy snow one year with lads from the street that had also been lucky enough to get their precious gift.

Football boots were of course, proper boots those days. It sounds a bit daft because now my sons' boots are more like the slippers you might wear in a Turkish brothel and Wayne Rooney got a poorly toe because of wearing those modern slippers to play football. Dear God, how would he have coped with some crazy psychopath grinding his foot to a pulp under two stone of leather and wooden sharpened studs. It beggars belief. And boots then were coloured black or brown, not pink or fluorescent yellow for God's sake! They were well rubbed with *Dubbin* before going out to play and laces were huge leather things that you wrapped around the boot several times. These boots also weighed more than Ronaldo's wage packet as they had wooden studs which you physically screwed into the sole of the boot. They were not shaped into the contours of your foot - they were real boots, with large toe caps (like pit boots) and some I'm sure were made of steel, particularly those from the boys' team at Bog Row (more later on Bog Row).

With such boots it wasn't as easy as it is now to curl the ball cunningly around a ten-man wall into the top corner or float it over the wall with a vicious spinning dip. They were meant for tackling and maiming your opposition and booting the ball as hard as you could at the boys standing in the wall, hoping you could emasculate them with a cunningly placed testicle height kick. Of course then the football weighed a similar weight to a shot putt, particularly when the rain had soaked into the uncovered leather and this made a lethal weapon at groin level. If you ever were mad enough to head the bloody thing you spent most of the rest of the game in a daze as the brain tried to recover from the severe concussion.

Footballs were like boots, precious objects which I only got at Christmas. They had an outside stitched leather cover inflated by inserting a red rubber bladder into the ball. The bladder had a rubber valve, or cock, though which you placed the bicycle pump flex and tied the cock tightly onto the flex whilst you pumped up the bladder. When the ball was hard enough you bent the rubber cock over and tied it off to stop the air coming out and pushed it into the leather case. Note; A football was called a *casey* then. You required a large steel needle like object to thread a leather lace through the casey. Each casey had several holes in it like a shoe where you would pull the lace through each holes and tie and seal the hole where the bladder and the cock went, like a leather shoe. Then you were ready to actually use the ball to play with but only after polishing the leather with Dubbin if you were fastidious enough to do this.

Heading a *casey* took bravery if not actual madness, because if you headed the lace part it was like heading a shot putt. It is increasingly well-documented now that many of the great soccer players of the past who were renowned headers of the ball have suffered almost the same brain damage as boxers. I do not doubt it.

The other madness when I look back is that we always played competitive football from the age of eight on a full-size pitch. Trying to kick a casey which had been soaked by the volumes of North East sleet, rain and snow was an act of sheer Sampson-like strength or amazing technique. Taking corner kicks and trying to get the ball into the penalty box when it weighed a ton and when you were only a couple of feet taller than the ball was pretty futile when I look back. Some lads managed it, many didn't.

I noted years afterwards that the foreign football teams never played on full size pitches until the players were in their teens. Maybe they were correct given the World Cups they have won. However, in those days they were just called *soft as shite* - not real footballers like Raich Carter, Jacky Millburn or Brian Clough.

School Football Teams and Shirts

To play for the school team was the height of ambition when I was a lad. Luckily enough I was a decent player so I played as a nine year old in the Shiney Row junior team and captained it at eleven. I have some pictures of our teams with great players in them you can view. You may spot a very young and tiny Alan Kennedy of England, Newcastle, Sunderland and who of course scored the goal that won Liverpool's first European Cup. I recently reminded him in the Irish madhouse over several beers that he was never as good as me or Terry!

Bringing your shirt back home and your Mam washing it and hanging it on the line was a badge of honour. Mothers those days did not have modern washing machines but hot tubs in which the clothes went and they bashed and stirred them in the hot water and soap using a large wooden stick which we called a *poss stick*. This stick could be used as great child beating weapon if they whinged on to the stressed out mother for their dinner or a sugar and bread sandwich. Mondays were washing days and after *possing* the clothes in the hot tub, I would help my mother by turning the mangle to help dry the clothes.

It was always a competition between mothers to see who had the cleanest nappies on the line. There were no *Pampers* then only flannel cotton nappies. It was instant isolation and eternal shame for a poor mother to put out on her line a nappy that wasn't clean and sparkling:

Poor bairns. Heaven knows what her house is like! whispering and gossiping between women leaning over each other's fences with their arms folded *Les Dawson* style. It was the same with carpets, which had to be taken out and put on the line and violently beaten with the flat, carpet beaters that seemed, if memory is correct, to be made out of bamboo strips.

Shiney School football teams then played in green and white, much like Hibernian's strip now. I loved it. Terry has it beautifully drawn on what I hope will be the back cover of this epic. It was always too big and was made of thick cotton. Like the boots and ball it weighed a ton when wet. It always had a long shirt tail which if it was left out of your shorts, as the more modern footballers like Nick Sharkey of Sunderland and George Best of Manchester United did later, it would trip you up as it hung almost down to your big boots. I remember to this day the green and white shirts hanging up in the washing lines in our two streets. Many of the boys I grew up with in the two streets and the other two council estates played for the team and their mother's proudly washed their strips every time.

My mother also came to watch me play after school in matches. Dad was always working; he only came when he was on night shifts and we were playing at home that week. Mam had no idea at all about football but she knew it was a loving thing to do and she could also gossip with the other head-scarf covered, burka-wearing ladies standing proudly in rain or shine gossiping about women's things and attempting to understand what their boys were playing.

We were in the Lambton and Hetton league and played schools with strange names like ours, Dubmire, Leamside and Bog Row. All had their peculiarities; Houghton R.C. pitch was on a fifty degree slope and had huge waves and furrows across the pitch which matched the North Sea only a few miles away. To win there you had to win the toss and choose to play downhill and score as many goals as you could first half by booting the ball down the pitch and hoping it would bounce over the keeper's head as it accelerated on the slope and hit the crest or slope of a wave. It normally could be relied on to fly in over the head and the reach of the dwarf keeper. The Roman Catholic schools had no significance to us in any sectarian or religious way; they were mates who went to a different school. However, their pitches always seemed better suited to left-footed players!

SHINEY ROW JUNIORS MID SIXTIES
With Mr Lister and Mr McInness - Spot a very young European Cup
Winner, a brilliant artist and a Booker Prize winner

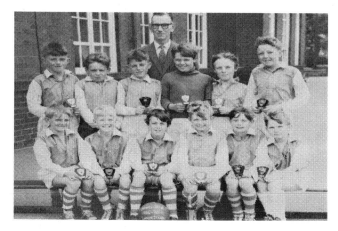

HERRINGTON BURN YMCA, MID 70'S
The lads grown up with hair

Author with Alan Kennedy in the mad Irish bar, grown up now, one a bit larger than the other but both still with hair. I could still cut him off at the knees like the old days if I could catch him.

An Earl and a Boxing Bishop: the author with his new 'marra', Ned Lambton, sixty years on from pinching his father's pheasants because all roads really do lead to where we stand.

Bog Row and Parent Hooliganism

We reached the final of the cup when I was playing for the juniors as a younger player and we played Bog Row. Now, I never really ever knew where Bog Row was - it was somewhere near Hetton-le-Hole, but as I never really ever knew where Hetton was in those days, it might as well have been in Namibia. I have *Googled* where Bog Row is to make sure that after all these years I wasn't suffering from my usual dementia after several beers and, yes, it still exists now, as a part of Hetton-le-Hole.

When I say we played Bog Row, I am mistaken as we mainly fought them. Not the eleven year old players, well, a little bit as always with boys, but we fought the parents! As we came out of the changing rooms we had to face a row of angry parents who proceeded to push, kick and boot us as we tried to run onto the pitch. I can't remember if we had any parents there. I doubt it as none had cars and most worked but our teacher ended up fighting them with us. The aggression went on all game and we were intimidated throughout and lost if I recall. Even afterwards the parents were abusive and aggressive, something we weren't used to then.

As I grew older and travelled outside the environs of Shiney I realised that this behaviour was quite normal for places like Hetton, Easington and Murton and turning the other cheek only lead to yet another kicking. We quickly learned these lessons in Shiney and I know that very few teams liked to visit the Secondary Modern for football matches because when the young lads who played with me had grown up, they, like Uncle Tom and Uncle Ken, had long memories and took their ultimate violent revenge.

Chester-le-Street Boys and Coaching

I went on the play football at many levels as I grew up but the one man who made a difference to me was Mister Graham, a Physics teacher from Usworth Comprehensive who coached the under fifteens. He saw something in me as a full back rather than the inside forward I played most of the time and he had a unique way of ensuring I became good at it – simply, he beat the shit out of me each Monday morning if I ever let a winger past me. Now of course these days, rampant physical abuse by your teacher is frowned upon and would have put him in jail and made him a pariah for life. But back then Mister Graham was my hero!

In the early seventies it was his advanced coaching techniques which lead to me playing representative football and being scouted by first division professional football teams. He used to walk into our house common room early Monday and select the members of his football team from the other kids and his particular motivation was to punch you repeatedly as hard as he could on your arm until you howled. At each punch he'd instruct you on the ways of playing soccer and the errors you'd made on Saturday. Then at practice sessions he'd make you do as many shuttle-runs, press ups, tackles, shots, corners, and set pieces you name it as the number of punches he'd inflicted on each us. Each training session fitted to an individual's Monday morning punch bag lesson!

He was a genius. We never lost a game for two years. Won every cup and league and most of us went on to play for Chester-le-Street boys and have trials for first division clubs. When we finally lost to Durham Johnston after eighteen months of winning, Mister Graham battered the ref who had plainly cheated us. I am not sure if the ref learned his lesson and improved like we all did after this novel coaching technique. To all of us players he was indeed a hero. Fergie and his hairdryer, Beckham crying over a boot hoyed in his face...bah humbug...all soft these days...

MRS LLOYD
Cricket and Dustbin Wickets

Before Grammar School as a child, I always seem to remember playing competitive football in winter; freezing, damp, ice and rain comes to mind. I hardly remember playing football in summer weather. Summer was for cricket or simply kicking footballs against coalhouses.

Cricket was never our favourite sport, that was always football, and heaven forbid if we ever picked up a tennis racket before or after Wimbledon. We only ever played tennis those two Wimbledon weeks and usually strung a rope across the main street between Princes and The Crescent tied to the gate posts on either. It wasn't until I was well in my thirties that I realised that there was any tennis other than Wimbledon because my son on the guidance of his adoring mother became a very good tennis player and I started watching tennis on TV.

Rackets were sourced from people who may at one time have been given them for some reason or they were pinched from Penshaw

Recreation where there were real tennis courts and you could hire the court and rackets.

We hit balls across the rope, blocking off the road and two footpaths for any very infrequent motorist or pedestrian. None of us were any good of course but it passed the time until we could go out killing small creatures again or kicking footballs off the coalhouse door.

Cricket was different; sometimes we would play as a whole street of boys, and surprisingly, we included the girls. The girls were mainly used to chase the balls and fetch them when we hit them over the fences into our parents' gardens. Sometimes if they were lucky they would get a chance to bat, never bowl, as girls couldn't throw or bowl - it was a known fact. Now I am astonished at how girls have learnt the noble art of throwing and actually bowling cricket balls. Ladies cricket and football is exciting to watch now. Something must have changed since we used girls as cricket ball chasers and goalposts for football. It is too short a time to be evolution so maybe it's a miracle? God works in mysterious ways for sure and one day She may allow ladies to control the TV remote control. I know, I know, you don't believe in divine intervention and it's highly unlikely for sure, but heh, who would have thought She could fix it that Claire Baldwin, and now Fiona Bruce, could present ten TV and radio programs simultaneously on every subject known to human experience. And how on earth could a woman beat men at the physically demanding, high-energy sport of darts if it wasn't through Her intervention. Dear me, girls learning to throw and kick balls properly, and the same distance as men? Yes folks, miracles do happen.

We used to like bowling the hard cork ball at the girls of course. Especially if they thought we were still bowling a soft spongy one. We called this proper red, leather-seamed cricket ball, *a corkie*. Of course it was ruined as soon as we bowled and hit it on the hard tarmac and concrete paths and we tried to save it for playing on the Colliery field, if and when we took actual stumps over there. The bins were too heavy to carry.

Bats were Len Hutton types and we did keep putting linseed oil on them to keep them supple and springy. Some lads played for the local clubs at Burnmoor or at Philadephia and my dad played well into his 50's at Sacriston in his later years. He played with Lance Gibbs, the famous West Indian spin bowler. He always wanted me to play professionally and I was a good cricketer in the street and in school games but sadly for me I could never stick it in the field for long due to really bad hay fever. All summer I suffered terribly from it. Those childhood days I was given no medication and had to suffer with swollen red eyes and streaming nose all the long hot summers. It was not until my middle teens in 1971 that I was ever prescribed any antihistamine and by that time I only played football.

The big cricket games had a wicket that was the middle of the sloping road; a dustbin was placed at the top of the slope and another at the bottom, the regulation one chain's length apart. Obviously the bowler bowling downhill had the advantage but we changed ends regularly. The main danger from this was hitting the ball over the fences and into the windows of the council houses or hitting old or dangerously psychopathic neighbours (of which there were many). If we hit a ball over the fences it was classed as, *six and out'* You had to walk off the road and sit on your dustbin when losing your wicket. If we hit the ball off a coalhouse and someone caught it with one hand, we were also out with *one hand off the wall.*

One day Les decided to blast the ball (he always said he didn't do it on purpose, but given his propensity for causing mayhem and nuisance, I never believed him) over the fence straight at Mrs Lloyds' toilet window. It went straight through shattering the opaque glass into many fragments. Some moments later poor old Mrs Lloyd ran out pulling up her drawers, covered in glass with blood streaming down her forehead, screaming obscenities at us. She was shortly followed by her elderly husband holding a chopping axe howling at Les who was pointing and laughing at the unfortunate old lady and still holding his bat. 'You young bastard. I'll howk the lot of you!'

We could all run faster than a seventy year old, lung-ravaged, ex-pitman and senior citizen and scuttled off down the street towards the relative safety of the Battery path. Days later we all had to cough up our pennies to pay for the window.

Staka Laka, Split the Kipper and Bays

The other games we played were very inclusive; we actually let lasses play these. *Staka Laka* was a game played at night under the translucent yellow street lights. It seemed to be a team game involving running around the streets touching each lamp post in some form of relay. If I remember the smallest lads and lasses seemed to be fastest. Sadly, running was never my favourite activity.

132

Bays were what most people in my part of the world would call Hopscotch. We found old plaster board, or new board pinched from the building sites, which we'd break open for the chalk and then chalk the bays on the road or path in the street. We used an old *Cherry Blossom* shoe polish tin to throw to each bay and then hop to the bay, doing a double hop when you reached two side by side bays. Great stuff...well it was for girls.

Skipping was also a game for girls. Normally the skipping rope was pinched from some poor mother's washing line. We only took it up as boys when we were told that boxers used it to get fit. Anything that helped us fight each other better had to be a good game.

This was the same with *split the kipper* a game where two kids faced each other, with a long bladed hunting knife, bone handled normally, and the game was to throw the knife to each side of your opponents legs and stick it in the ground. The opponent then had to stretch their leg to the where the knife stuck. They would then take the knife if they could without falling over and throw it in a similar objective to their opponent's side. The objective was to get the legs so far apart that your opponent would fall over. If I remember you still had to put the knife then between their legs to win; given the accuracy of throwing or the homicidal and malicious natures of most of my fellow street lads, this always worried me even at my pre-pubescent age.

It seemed everyone then had a knife, a catapult, air rifle and in some cases a shotgun. We didn't however seem to kill each other as regularly as we now see on our streets. Maim batter and torture each other but rampant knife crime? Well - no.

Mars Attacks and Flick

We also played marbles a lot in the dirt gardens, digging out holes to shoot the marble into or using the outside drain cover indented handles which were used as holes. Marbles were normal glass ones but the best were the steel *bots* or ball bearings or Bulls eyes that some lads could get their Dads to pinch from the pit or the *Philli Yard*. These steel bots destroyed the gaggle of marbles which had been placed in a circle. They were flicked by the thumb into the circle where the object was to smash marbles out of the outer ring and you could then claim them as your own. Those with bull's eyes always smashed a whole circle out of the ring. The lucky blighters!

The game cards we collected had moved on from the footballer cards that we collected from packets of *Rington's Tea*. Now they came in packs with chewing gum in them bought from the newsagents. They depicted more modern things than ancient footballers and gave more sixties street cred I guess, than Stanley Mathews or Ivor Broadchurch. My favourite card collection was *Mars Attacks*. I loved these. We stole, borrowed, worked and threatened money with menaces to get enough money to buy these at the newspaper shops. We got three or four cards to a pack if I remember and a strip of bubble gum. Everyone was looking to get the set. I still remember lying in what today would be called social isolation in my parents bed, sick with what was probably 'the Mumps, when Ian Fasham who lived over the road with his grandparents and isolating with the same disease came in with the one card I was missing – *Smashing the Martians* – this was a picture of obviously American GIs bashing the brains in of glass bubble-helmeted Martians with the stocks of· their automatic rifles and their brains splattering all over. As an aside - why do all aliens land in America when there is a whole world to visit and maim and conquer? In many other places the locals would probably greet them with nice Fried Rice, a Curry or Greek Salad rather than the world's greatest military arsenal and a President who can fly supersonic jet fighters and practices Kung Fu in between ruling the known world. Anyway, rant over, back to cards. Ian had two missing cards and wanted to swop. Swopping was what we did to get rid of cards you had accumulated duplicates of. The other way to accumulate cards was to play *Flick*. *Flick* was a game we played where one player flicked one of his cards, preferably at a wall of some sort. Once it had landed and settled the object was to flick one of yours so that it landed on the other card. Even slightly touching was accepted. The goal was to win as many cards as possible and if someone flicked a card that you did not have in your collection you tried valiantly try to get your card flicked onto it. Riveting stuff for us kids in the 60's long before *X Box* and *Playstation*.

I gave my Mars Attack card collection, and the other two I really loved, *The American Civil War* and *The Second World War*, to my nephew Hedgie. I have regretted it ever since as I missed them over many years. I used to bore to death disinterested non-*Mars Attack* fans in bars across the world about the cards and the pictures of smashed Martians and their evil machines of war for years. No one I ever met had collected them or even heard of them. But then one day not so long ago I watched a movie called *Mars Attacks*. It is an absolute parody of the cards. The Martians are the same, exactly the same form and with bubble heads, their weapons the same, the green gunge that comes out of their heads when smashed by actor Jim Brown, the heavy weight champion of the world, the same - everything is, even the huge mechanical robots they use to kill everyone. I love it.

Herself thinks it's daft, as do my kids. But I am really delighted someone has preserved the cards in some visual epic movie. How can it be bad with Jack Nicholson, Rod Steiger, Glenn Close, Pierce Brosnan, Sarah Jessica Parker, Natalie Portman, Michael J Fox and of course the geriatric Welsh crooner, Tom Jones in the cast. If you, like my family think it's daft, well simply fast forward to the end scene where Tom Jones has saved the world and stands strutting his hips and an American eagle lands on his arm, two Bambis come and lick his man parts, and squirrels and birds come to listen to him singing as he bursts out into, *It's not unusual to be loved by anyone...* This has to be the most bizarre ending I have ever seen in a movie. Even John Wayne's line in *The Greatest Story Ever Told* spoken in real all-American hero cowboy dialect, *Shirley this man is the son of Gaad* can't beat it. It's bloody brilliant boyo!

CHAPTER NINE
POCKET MONEY AND WORK

Pocket Money and Returning Bottles

The money we had as young kids came from a variety of sources.

Some had milk rounds which paid slave wages for getting up before dawn and delivering milk bottles to our fellow citizens. Others had paper rounds, similarly paid for delivering newspapers. Some stole scrap and sold it over at Cuslow's scrap yard.

Favourite scrap was the lead pipes that were all over houses those days. We'd either get the lead from old demolition sites or from new build houses in the posh areas but some sawed off the lead waste pipes which we all had coming through the kitchen walls of the terraced houses. Of course, the real bad lads pinched the lead off the church at the top of the road.

Taking empty beer bottles back to the pubs was the favourite of most as it avoided juvenile court and a good thrashing off the local policeman and then as a consequence a further hiding from your father when he dragged you back home to him. Many a slap I got off the local polis with his massive leather gloves and a warning: *If I catch you again, I'll take you to your fatha and he'll give worse than this.* And then another whack across the cheeks with the glove of iron and sent on your way with a kick up the backside with a size 14. They counsel you these days.

The pubs gave you a penny or half penny a bottle returned.

We got wise to this and would climb over the back of *The Oddfellows* wall into the back yard where they stored the empty bottles for the brewery and then pinch them. We'd then take them around the front of the pub into the off beer sales next to the men's bar. The landlord or bar lady would open up the hatch and take the bottles from you and hand you the pennies. Cue; the boys heading back around the back of the pub and pinching the same bottles. The pub owners all caught on in the end.

It was at the hatch that I fell in love with the smell of pubs.

When the bar lady opened the hatch once you were tall enough you could see over the counter and see all the men in the bar, standing drinking pints and smoking. The smell of beer and tobacco was a wonderful aroma to most of us, and sadly most of us continued a life later much like that of our parents who inhabited those bars.

Potato Picking and Blackberry Week

As this lockdown socially isolated summer has moved on to the end of August and towards autumn I notice there are hardly any blackberries left and my garden produce is all but harvested. Here in the Deep South everything grows much sooner and faster than back in the frozen North but this year it seems to have gone even faster. This prompted me to turn from my laptop and editing this story to ask my darling partner if she remembers *tatie picking* and blackberry week in the days before Mrs T. She remembered blackberry week as October half term but couldn't remember *tatie picking* at all. I do remember it and I guess it must have been half term in the North East because whole families from the two streets used to go by the farmer's open wagon for a week into the fields to pick the farmer's potatoes for a pittance in wages. I remember Mrs Cain used to be always troubled with a terrible back ache every time but this was a source of real money for our parents and for some us pocket money to help the community though Christmas. I believe potato picking has long gone into autumn history unless our friends from across the channel are fulfilling that role - maybe after Brexit and Covid it will return for all us.

GAS MASK GUS
Work and Lumley Brickworks

As we grew up and moved from newspaper rounds, milk rounds, bottle stealing and picking vegetables as a source of pocket money, most of my school friends from Shiney Row primary school eventually left school at sixteen and joined places like Philli Yard, the pit, and the shipyards or became apprentices on the buildings. They were in full time work now and didn't need pocket money or part-time casual work.

I stayed on at school, maybe because I have a fear and rabid dislike of repetitive, unending tasks. I think it is deep-seated in my consciousness from the days at school trying to clean my arse with Izal medicated toilet paper. I guess some, and most of my past bosses, would say my phobia of work is called bone idleness. However, to survive I had to do part-time work. I never enjoyed it, especially manual work that never seemed to have any point. I was meant for a different life, maybe not of this world, as I seem to have spent most of it with the cast of *Star Wars* in bars.

My long lasting experience of a job which was probably the most mind numbingly inane thing a person should be asked to do was to try to fill up a hole with sand that had no bottom to it. I'll explain.

Whilst at Washington Grammar School in the early seventies, some years after leaving the loving music, poetry and care of Mrs Rodgerson and the Morris dances of Mr Telford at Shiney Row Junior School, I started a summer vacation work for real money at Lumley Brickworks; a forbidding place about two miles from Shiney Row. Again like in the absolute zero bathroom, and the poor folks in the movie *The Alien,* at the brick works no one could hear you scream.

My first job was to work in the sand hoppers. This was an elevated loft type structure above the brick making machines below. There were three huge metal hoppers which held masses of tonnes of sand that came from a quarry about five hundred metres away on Lord Lambton's land. The sand was passed along a huge rickety conveyor belt from the quarry and was dumped in each hopper. The hoppers were about ten foot high and were conical shaped with a hole at the bottom through which the sand was drawn by the brick making machine. It reminded me of the *glumpter, glumpter machine* into which cartoon character *Bash Brannigan* (Jack Lemmon) dropped his wife in the movie *How To Murder Your Wife.*

I was in charge of one hopper and my job was to wait until the sand had been dropped by the conveyor and then climb down into the hopper and keep digging the sand from the sides to the middle and make sure the sand flowed freely into the hole. It was a dangerous task as you never knew when the conveyor would begin to drop more sand. The only warning I'd get was a rattling noise from the stanchions and rollers that held the belt which meant it was being started up again half a mile away. I had to quickly climb up the ladder and try to get out before the thing started dumping thousands of tonnes of sand on me.

My supervisor, who was supposed to warn me of impending burial alive, was called Gus and he worked in one of the other hoppers too. The problem with his warning shout was that he wore a full World War Two gas mask and had no teeth. So his slurred shouts above the noise and through his gas mask were incomprehensible. I had a 3M paper mask to wear when the sand and dust particles were pouring and saturating the whole room and hopper. It was choking and no doubt toxic to my young and then fit set of pristine lungs but Health and

Safety Management was in its infancy in the early 70's at the Brickworks.

This day of torture began at 7.00 am with one fifteen minute break at 9.15 am and thirty minutes for lunch at 12.00 am and then finished at 5.00 pm without any afternoon break. I decided I wanted to live long enough to write this book so I took to introducing some clever process engineering.

The next day when the first sand arrived I climbed into the death pit and worked like hell to dig all the sand from around the walls into some gigantic pyramid. I then climbed out of the hopper and sat on the bench above the rim and watched the pyramid slowly reduce over an hour or so until the next load of sand began to arrive. I repeated the exercise, working like hell to shovel up the sand into the Great Pyramid of Giza and then climbed out and sat on my bench, reading a nice book and nibbling the ham and pease pudding stotties my mam had made me for my bait.

I thought I'd cracked it. A bit of hard exercise to keep me fit for the football, a nice relaxing hour reading and eating stotty cake and chilling out waiting for the next set of aerobic exercise. I had forgotten about Gus.

After a couple of hours he decided to leave his pit where he and the other lad in the other hopper stood all the time all day long shovelling a small bit of sand every minute into the middle of the pile and watching it go down the hole. He shouted something at me, gesticulating with his arms as I sat on my bench enjoying *Catch 22* or *The Ascent of Man*. I shouted back: 'What's the problem Gus?'

'Urgh, urgh..ug ug…' He was trying to communicate something through the gas mask and without his teeth but I couldn't understand a word.

So I tried again. 'Sorry Gus, what are you saying mate?'

He flung his arms in the air and pointed at me and tried to speak: 'Ug, urgh, ug…******** ug…****, urgh…'

I did get the swear words through the toothless mouth and thick rubber mask but nothing else, so I shrugged my shoulders and got back into my book. This seemed to send him into an apoplexy. He hurried over to me with his arms flaying about mumbling and shouting something that sounded like Urdu or Inuit expletives. As he approached he took off his mask and tried to talk, obviously angry. Given he had no teeth and had a thick accent and was also thick of

139

mind I only got a general understanding. He was fuming that I wasn't working and doing in his words, **** *all*.

'No I'm not. The sand is still in there. It's still going down the bloody hole and it has done all morning. I don't need to stand in that death trap for ten hours man. There's no need. It works.'

'Yes, you do it's your ******** job you lazy sod,' Gus shouted.

I was starting to understand him, which was a worry as he was slobbering out of toothless gums and still almost incomprehensible.

'No I don't. The job is to get sand into the machines and I am doing that. A lot more safely than you!'

'I'm off to get Mr Wise. He'll sort you out,' Gus howled apoplectically.

I guessed Mr Wise must be the boss and sure enough he was. He came and he took me off on one side and told me the ways of the working world. That is, either do what Gus says or bugger off back to school. Given that I needed the money and my dad would have never forgiven me for being such a twat, I acquiesced and returned to the monotony and certain death of shovelling one shovel of sand every minute into a hole for ten hours a day.

I was I guess the talk of the place at lunch. Gus obviously had me down for a soft school boy and swot and bone idle and my rampant socialism and nascent struggle for workers' rights didn't enamour me to my fellow workers who only wanted to get through the day, get paid and then get pissed in the Club. A lesson I learned on human motivation and never forgot. I therefore shut my mouth and decided to follow the herd. But before returning to the hell of the hopper I asked a decent bloke who seemed to want to talk to me at the lunch break a question which I thought was worth asking. 'Heh mate, any idea why Gus doesn't put his bloody teeth in when he's here? It's bad enough he wears that gas mask all day but I can't understand a word he says.'

'Aye, he never wears them during the day only at night,' he answered.

'Why?' I asked again.

'Because can you see the old bloke over there taking his cup to the sink?'

'Aye,' I replied looking at an old man smiling with a lovely pearly white set of huge gnashers at the lass who washed up the dishes.

'Well son that's his dad. His dad wears the teeth during the day as he doesn't go out to the Club after work in the week; he stays in with his lass. Gus puts his dad's teeth in at night when he goes on the hoy and chasing lasses at the Club dance. They share them at weekends. His dad wears them Sunday afternoon at the club and Sunday night when he takes Gus's mother out. Gus wears them on Saturdays at the football and the disco on a night.'

My education in the real world was beginning.

MISS LAWSON
Latin and Vestal Virgins

In my absolute depression standing in that hopper watching sand go down a hole for ten hours a day I did finally realise that a Latin education could one day be some use and support. In my dark hours in the pit of death, I remembered Miss Lawson, our Grammar School Latin teacher, and her indoctrination of Latin grammar, pluperfect tenses, subjunctive clauses, Caesar's Gallic wars and Horace, Catullus and Ovid's poetry. I had learned Catullus's *Hypermnestra* for my Latin GCSE O level a couple of weeks before. Never did I think I'd ever see any point in learning it despite Miss Lawson's propaganda that *We would see all life in 'the Classics.* But as I stood watching my life pour away down the hole I quoted out loud to no one but myself the poem and chuckled to myself in my despair. The tale is told of the vestal virgins who having succumbed to sexual pleasures of the flesh are condemned for eternity to fill up a jar of water which has a hole in the bottom and can never fill. Exactly like the sand in my pit of death.

Let Lyde hear of the maiden's crime and punishment, well known, and of the vessel ever empty of water vanishing through the bottom.

Thanks Miss Lawson and Catullus; you saw me through the pain.

GREG THE MINER
Pit Boots and Apprentices

Still on the subject of first work experiences, I was grateful that I didn't have to keep pouring sand down a hole in the brickworks for a living. I was moved on from that to relentlessly lifting bricks off a conveyor belt continuously for ten hours a day and then joy of joy, moved on to kiln cleaning. The best job in the brickworks was kiln drawing. These guys were fit (well they were then, I suspect once the fumes and toxic chemicals got them, they didn't last too long) as they started early morning at 6 am and once the kiln was broken, they began to draw the hot bricks out of the kiln and stack them ready for transport. It was very hard work and the kiln was searing and red hot

141

with the glowing ash, dust and fumes of the bake surrounding them. They were on a *job and knock* deal - that is, as soon as they had drawn all the bricks they could leave and head to the Club for many beers to quench their thirsts. They strove to finish as soon as possible and it was normally sometime around midday to 1 pm they finished after losing gallons of sweat and headed off to swallow more gallons of beer, much to the dismay of those of us who had to stay until 5 pm.

As they worked, we had to clean the kiln, our only protection from instant lung cancer a paper mask. We sweated heaps and toiled shovelling up the red hot ash and dust breathing in the fumes. Sadly we were not as exalted as the kiln drawing men and we had to keep cleaning until 5 pm, no early louse and gallons of beer for us. After these experiences I realised that real work was not for me and neither was an apprenticeship after hearing about what happens to them.

Apprentices all over the world are remorselessly tortured I have found out, not only manual workers, but young office and knowledge workers. In many ways this would quite rightly have now been called harassment, bullying, sexism or racism. Those days it was the norm. Greg the Miner is a man I met in Singapore but he actually came from Seaham, a pit village and coal port on the East Durham coast, a couple of miles from Shiney Row. He had been a miner in his former life before he gained ten university degrees and a very well paid job in Pharmaceuticals; a far cry from hewing coal under the North Sea. He had many tales of his former life and one which amused me as its effect was staring me in the face all those years later after it occurred. I will use it as an example of apprentice torture – there are many others for sure.

When he was a young man at the pit in the Seventies like all pitmen he wore pit boots (or pit byuts; in the Durham pitmatic vernacular). These were heavy protective leather boots with large steel toe caps and segs (steel pegs in the sole). He was sitting on a bench in the pit yard one day eating his bait with the men around chatting about life over their break time. When he stood up to go back to work he tried to take a step but he couldn't make headway, his legs were stuck together, he tumbled and he fell face downwards like a tree, flat and face first into the concrete breaking his nose and front teeth. Despite his injuries the lads all broke out into hysterical laughter at this - as you do! It seems that as he was eating and talking, one of the lads had crawled under the bench and spot welded his two steel toe caps together.

Greg still carries the broken nose today. Great craic some of you may say; or some of the more liberal minded, that Greg should have hounded the National Coal Board for discriminatory abuse in the workplace before Lady Margaret in her undoubted vision of compassion for workforce bullying kindly shut it. We all see things differently I guess. Greg may well see it another way; a lot of ladies in Asia said his smashed crooked nose makes him look majestic, and with his fat wallet in his back pocket, almost like Robert Redford. So why would he complain eh?

Cobbles and Crabs

In the mid-seventies my insane brother-in-law, Timmy, gave up eating my father's pedigree leeks, maiming pedigree dogs with chimney pots and terrifying house owners in his building business to become a fisherman. My sister married Timmy in the sixties when I was about eight and in the seventies he employed me and a lot of the Club lads like Mason and Con on welfare fiddle jobs in his building business. His overriding corporate governance statement was; 'Davey, that taxman is a canny lad. Got him pissed on a bottle of whisky but that ******* VAT man he disn't drink - the bastard.' When he, or the VAT man, closed his building business he took up fishing and he *employed* the same lads. Everyone was terrified of working for him. Simple reason was he was quite mad. He, like his father, was ginger-haired and had a similar temper to him. Curiously, his father was also called Timmy. Actually, our Timmy was named John but everyone called him after his dad, who was also mad. Neither had a psychotic illness I must clarify, they were simply crazy sons of bitches as my old American Dixieland mates in *A Turkey and One MoreEaster Egg* would have called them.

Old Timmy was my father's friend and he worked as a Deputy and then Overman down the pit. Deputies were men of esteem and needed to command respect from the hard men they oversaw. The Deputy's stick was something most pitmen were feared of. Some of the biggest pitmen I knew just cringed when you mentioned owld Timmy, as he was known to fly off the handle at the smallest thing and heaven help anyone, big or small who got in his way. Young Timmy once told me: 'If me fatha iver gans for yeah, let him punch yeah. Coz if he gets his hands on yaeh neck, it'll snap.' And this was from his son who was one of the strongest men I knew. Both of them had hands like vices and could rive and tear most things up with ease.

143

Young Timmy had a fearsome reputation for laying bricks. He burnt out many a hod carrier, not just with incessant non-stop work, but with incessant non-stop drinking the night before. Few could stay with him in the drinking stakes. He saw off fellow bricklayers and from the adopted names that Timmy gave them you may gather the result of nights and days of heavy drink. Fred Dowsett was *electric legs* and Ray Allison *chocolate legs*. Mind you Ray could drink and smoke most under the table. Like most bricklayers he was small, wiry and thin but with a propensity to drink in vast quantities - all bricklayers defy the calorific theory of obesity; that is, they drink excessively, eat bait that is massively high in calories and saturated fat, yet stay thin as rakes.

Some building folk were crazier than Timmy. Cappy from Penshaw, the hod carrier used to torture my friends Davey and Stan when they were apprentice plumbers on the site and on the bus home from sites every Friday afternoon after a session in the pub. All building sites finished at 12.30 pm those days and every one piled into the pubs to get blooted. Cappy was one who liked a good punch up and to batter the young apprentices on the bus every Friday. He had a grizzly face that Davey said, *someone must have been chopping firewood on with an axe.* But one day retribution must come you might say. And it did. Not by the poor tortured apprentice plumbers but from his wife. At bait time Cappy used to eat the sandwiches made by his wife in the bait cabin and for many weeks he'd said they tasted different. Then one day after a particular chewy corned beef sandwich he opened it up and there was ground glass sprinkled amongst the *Fray Bentos* and *HP* sauce. The tortured Davey told me years after his apprenticeship ended, 'It nivva bothered the horrible bastard and more importantly it nivva harmed the twat.' I gather he may still be alive and well, which says his wife's cooking must not have been too bad after all.

My father knew that Timmy was crazy. He asked my sister in the wedding car to the church if she really knew what she was doing and that it wasn't too late to turn around. But she loved him I guess, and I suspect still does, despite the divorce and years of separation. As teenagers when they married they were in the era of rock and roll and Timmy was a Teddy boy of course. My dad struggled with his antics perpetually in those early years, particularly his habit of getting pissed and sitting in his garden eating his prize vegetables.

I had worked as a hod carrier and labourer for him during my school holidays and can vouch for his insanity and now he had bought a coble, which is an historic North East open boat, similar to one that was used by Grace Darling, the heroine of the sea who with her father rescued many sailors from the shipwrecked SS Forfarshire off Bamburgh. He kept this at Seaham Harbour.

In those days Seaham was quite run down as its history as a coal port had long gone - described in that most excellent football book *The Far Corner* as the set for *Alien Three*. Now I am told that it has become the Riviera of the North with beautiful beaches, marina and chic bars and restaurants. I don't believe it.

Timmy, his dad and me started his first fishing venture in the summer of 1972. For me it was yet another work experience whilst at school which made me realise that 'You can keep real work, I'm off to be a perpetual student' (I failed). It was a nightmare of *Elm Street* proportions that haunts me today. Both men were clearly insane, so that didn't help and when stuck in an open boat on a raging sea - dear God, the memory terrifies me still. Health and Safety? Risk Assessments? Maritime Law or sanity? None of this existed then in Timmy's coble. Timmy sailed out of the harbour in any weather, even when the coastguards forbade him. He cared not one jot; neither did his crazy, bad-tempered, red-haired father. Early days all we had was one fleet of twelve crab and lobster pots and a huge long line of hundreds of hooks. It was my job to haul the pots up by hand as he had no mechanical hauler then and also let out and pull in the long line of hooks. All of this in seas the size Francis Magellan faced sailing around Cape Horn. We had no lifejackets, radios or flares or nowt, only the two Timmys howling at me if I failed to pull anything up or got a hook jammed.

The final straw for all of us was when the long line got tangled. Now if the hooks get into you, and the sinking weight on the lines and motion of the boat pulls you over the side, you are dragged to the bottomless depths and die - a simple fact. Young Timmy was on the tiller and Owld Timmy was trying to untangle hundreds of hooks while hopefully not being pulled over and down fifty fathoms to Davey's locker and I was baiting up. All the time they were howling and screaming at each other and me to untie the hooks, I'm trying in vain to save my life. Young Timmy leaves the tiller and the coble starts swinging beam onto the huge waves rolling into the Dawdon coal blast beaches and jumps in between his dad and the tangled lines pushing his father out of the way. Owld Timmy clouts him with a pot that we were using to bail water out. I watch the boat swing perilously beam on and start to pray. They start fighting and swearing and pushing each other. I realise the only way to save myself is to get between them and do something constructive, so I crawl under the fighting screaming ginger banshees and loosen two hooks which were causing the jam. The line begins to rush out again, just as a massive swell turns us in a 180 degree spin. Timmy comes to his senses and leaps back across the engine and takes up the tiller and with all his huge strength he turns the flooding boat back bow on to the huge swells. Timmy's Dad spoke gently, as if nothing had happened. 'Great that, Davey: now get hauling the pots son.'

Young Timmy started singing the song from *Jaws* and whistling away as he stood facing the howling North East gale kept the boat into the huge swells. I shook my head in despair, listened to my pulse slowly slowing down and began hauling the pots.

Of course it didn't last - with the cast of *Mad Max* on the boat that would be impossible. I had pulled about two pots up and we had caught *bluey's* and crabs in everyone when the rope stuck. I pulled and heaved, feet on the stanchions, getting soaked by the waves that broke over the bow, my hands frozen with the cold. Young Timmy howled at me *to pull the bastard up*. His father howling at him to *Shut the **** up and let me do it* - both red faced and howling at the moon. *Oh shit* I thought *he's leaving the tiller again* and sure enough he leapt over leaving the boat swinging in the seas. As he passed his father, his father hit him with a crab pot which nearly knocked me over the side. Young Timmy ignored it and pushed me out of the way, grabbed the rope, set his feet and pulled. The boat swung ominously and with suicidal menace beam on again into the massive swells. I said a small prayer yet again. But as I've already clarified, Timmy had the strength of a bull and he freed a entire fleet of twelve pots with one huge pull. Luckily his father didn't brain him with a lead weight or the only oar we had and he leapt past his screaming dad to take the tiller back and we were safe again.

After some heated discussion once safe back on shore, and I had sold the crabs by the road side, it was decided that as Olwd Timmy had retired now from the pit maybe he should stay onshore and do what he was very good at, fix things mechanically. I persuaded Timmy that we should buy a mechanical hauler like every other boat known to man and we expanded the number of fleets of pots, got proper nets and sold the produce on the road side at Seaham or at Hendon docks. I moved on to slightly less life-threatening things like summer work at the hell of the brickworks sand pit of death and then a life of relative safety and debauchery at University. Timmy grew his empire and, like Roy Scheider had pleaded with Robert Shaw in *Jaws*, he got a bigger boat.

He gave the dole and criminal lads the likes of Mason and Con *guvvie* jobs on the boat to supplement their benefit money. None lasted. Con and Mason came back to the club after their one and only day helping on the boat with the inevitable and predictable assessment of Captain Timmy. 'He's ******* mad.'

They had been sea sick from the moment they passed the harbour bar. Timmy of course had set sail on a cold, pitch-black December with storm force gale warnings cracking around his radio and the coastguards valiantly trying to stop him. As they lay in the boat pleading to turn back, Timmy laughed insanely and informed them that it was only 5 am and they would be out there till 5 pm at least. He then passed them a bucket to be sick in. As they reached for the bucket they smelt and saw the contents - fresh crap, which was the morning's waste products from Timmy and Joe, his mentally challenged and deranged sidekick. Up came the stomach again retching at the smell. Con was distraught and weary as he concluded. 'Davey, once we thought we were feeling all right the bastard would start cooking bacon and eggs and offer it to us. We'd just hoy up all over again. Next time he'd give us the shit bucket again. We wor the awnly boat out there man. No one else is daft enough. He's loopy, the bastard. Nivver agyen.'

And he turned to shout at the club steward, 'Giz another pint Ralphie.'

Princess Anne and Washington New Town

I worked for Washington Development Corporation planting a million trees and cutting grass across the new town during my sixth form school holidays. Washington now is a virtual forest with more trees than the once pristine Amazon rain forest. Those days in the Seventies it was a brand new; a product like Milton Keynes of a baby booming government's New Town expansions.

Curiously our area was where some of the first future Americans had ventured across the Atlantic to found the New World. Philadelphia, Pennsylvania, home of the Liberty Bell, was named that by those who came from the village where my sledge was made. I went to grammar

147

school in Washington, County Durham, where General George came from and Jimmy Carter visited in 1977 and planted a tree. The main street and houses in Washington was called Concorde, the famous first big engagement in the American War of Independence. It was here that I met Princess Anne as we lined up, spades at our sides, to shake her hand as she came to open up the New Town in 1974. Close up she was very stunning, which was surprising as I'd always thought on the telly she looked like one of her horses. She was also very polite and not haughty or stuck up. Funny enough yesterday in the bar during one of my increasingly grumpier and more frequent rants about political life in Boris's new United England, even Burglar Bob, right wing of the Proud Boys, agreed with me that she is the best hanger-on of the lot. I guess the President of the United States and one of the best British Royals was in exalted company in the real Washington those days.

This budding New Town was a massive lost world for anyone who stupidly came to visit or deliver goods there. The place is built of a series of villages on a circular wheel that are linked to a centre hub, the town centre. Each village district, was given a name and number. On many road signs only the number was displayed. It drove cockney and brummie van drivers mental. Every day as I strimmed away at the newly planted African savannahs around districts 1 to 2000 divided by pi and planted tree after tree on their highways, van drivers would stop and hurl abuse at me.

'Heh mate, where the **** is district 12. I've been driving around this shithole for days now and what the **** are you planting trees for you daft Geordie twat. You should be putting up ******* road signs with real names on them.'

This ritual abuse was met with subtle retribution and I'd send them off towards the A19 and a nice trip to meet the crazed lunatics that I eventually managed in the beautiful chemically devastated landscape and eternal smog of Middlesbrough, twenty miles away. However, unlike these truck drivers, I did not send her majesty the mercurial Princess Anne on the *Road to Hell* to meet Chris Rea when she visited.

STAN
Cockney Rebel and First Airplane Flight

In 1976 I headed to the Isle of Man to work for the summer in the bars there with, my mate Stan. He was yet again one the characters I seem to have attracted all my life. When at school he became obsessed by De Niro in *Taxi Driver* and shaved his head Mohican like him and bought the same green army jacket. He could quote the movie and would often frighten total strangers with his portrayal of the character. He'd walk up to anyone in Newcastle on a Friday night and stare at them with his shaved Mohican and whisper, quote, 'All the animals come out at night', to the bewildered revellers – he was mad as the March Hare; but heh, what the hell, so was the Taxi Driver.

Stan then moved off Robert De Niro to mimic James Dean, with his white tee shirt and jeans and very soon he was Steve Harley from *Cockney Rebel*. He had a run in with the polis outside *The Gardeners Club* in Washington one night when he was acting up as usual and collapsed worse for a few beers and mandies in front of a polis. The policeman kept trying to help him up but Stan kept brushing him off and singing the line from *Come up and See me and Make me Smile* he always quoted to anyone friend or foe, namely, 'Away, away, and don't say maybe you'll try'. Needless to say, the polis was not a *Cockney Rebel* fan – result, another night in the cells.

When Stan came out of his apprenticeship he decided to throw his plumber's tools off the Tyne Bridge and take a gap few years to find himself. He got to Heathrow and tried Bermuda but couldn't get a visa. He then tried South Africa - for some reason he couldn't get there. So he turned back and went to the Isle of Man with me for a summer season of work for me and fun for Stan.

We went via Blackpool. Stan had his apprentice savings tucked down his socks and after a huge drinking session with some mad lunatic Glaswegian axmen who attacked a few bouncers with their favourite weapons while we did a quiet flit around the corner, he realised he'd lost it all. So he too needed to get more funds. We actually flew to the Isle of Man from Blackpool. My first ever flight. We flew into another piece of 70's culture - terrorism and into the arms of Special Branch or MI5, I never found out which.

Isle of Man and the IRA

We both looked like normal seventies people. Me, long curly hair, beard, jeans, moon boots and combat jacket; Stan, looking like his new alter ego, Bryan Ferry from *Roxy Music,* slicked back greased hair, white tee-shirt and a leather jacket. We did not really look like Irish terrorists or freedom fighters (your choice) but when we landed in the Isle of Man we were pulled into a room by two men in suits. Foolishly I pointed out to one man as he held my arm taking me away from freedom that the man with suitcase and briefcase walking through arrivals was more likely to be a terrorist than me. 'I might look like Ché Guevara but are you that thick and stupid enough to think a real terrorist would dress like this. And we speak like Geordies man not from the bloody Bogside.'

This did not impress them. Six hours later they let us out. Welcome to the Isle of Man in the time of *the Troubles*.

We had no idea why they were so vigilant towards visitors to the Isle of Man then. The Isle of Man was a virtual offshore Blackpool and thousands of Irish, Scousers, Jocks and Geordies used to descend on it. We didn't have any knowledge of the Irish troubles those days as we had no experience except from village and old school lads who were in the army or from television and that of course was heavily biased. Sometime later we were to come to terms with what it meant for many in Ireland.

We settled down working in a bar in Douglas. In the early seventies Douglas was the Benidorm of the UK with girls, night life and booze but without sun. *Summerland* was a complex of fun built to attract the young and old accordingly offering something for all. When Stan and I arrived it had burnt down, so the island was in the throes of trying to re-establish itself as a hedonistic paradise. And like that other hedonistic paradise, Singapore, there was little crime, despite a mix of all that should have caused major mayhem - Jocks, Irish, Scousers and Geordies all pissed and looking for fun. Why no crime? Simple, if you did anything wrong the Manx police beat you to death with long sticks, like they do regularly in Singapore. Deterrents worked in those days.

It was a few days later on our day off when we were drinking that horrible Manx brewed stuff *Ockells Ale* - well it was to my palate, weaned on *Fed Special, Newcastle Exhibition, Boddingtons, Robinsons and Marston's Pedigree* and in the Seaton Inn, Seaham - *Theakston's Old Peculiar* - that we got drinking with some Northern Irish folks, mainly because we both had met their daughters each night after work. To this day I can't remember what side of the divide they were on as it all meant little to us - we knew virtually nothing of the sectarian divides of the Green Isle. Stan's latest girlfriend's father, a large bald headed man, was vociferous in his hatred of his alter-religious denominations and as he befriended us and we were both English I must assume he was of Loyalist persuasion.

150

He tried to educate us in the reasons for his hatred and venom but I am sorry to say we were more interested in his daughter and her friend's romantic favours and assets, not their loyalties or politics. He got quite annoyed and in the end drew a revolver from the small haversack he had with him and started telling us to listen to him or we might go the way of the objects of his own vitriolic hatred. I still remember his twisted face, dribble down his chin and the blue barrel of that revolver but what frightened me was that his daughter and her mates laughed as if this was normal behaviour. I vowed then to try to get back with my old love from school, her coal house leaping, ninja father was a pussycat compared to these psychopaths.

I guess that was why the security services were so vigilant at the airport, but we both still wondered how they could let this maniac through with his gun yet torture us innocent travellers and seekers after transcendental pleasure. A few years later working in Belfast and fishing in Ireland I was to meet much more of this tragic behaviour from both sides and not too long after this Isle of Man meeting my best friend Paul joined the Paras. Soon he was lying in gardens on surveillance in Anderson Town, and barracked up in Borucki Sangar, Crossmaglen, wondering how he went from a school lad in a Durham pit village to this madness. Two years later he was killed.

Thankfully, Stan and I were more interested in drink and girls than sectarian hatred and the fight for a united Ireland, so despite the revolver and the spittle we continued our courting of Irish girls from all sides of the Troubles. As they were all looking for a good time and they seemed to like the *When the boat comes in* accent as much as posh English girls did, we did ok with our Irish cousins. Then I met a Scottish lass who stopped my attempts at Anglo-Irish reconciliation in their tracks. She was a student too and working the summer there and we became great friends during that long scorching summer of 1976. When she left we vowed to keep up the relationship but like a lot in those halcyon days of youth it never lasted.

The 1976 summer was the hottest ever. We saw little of it as we worked at night, slept during the day and in between we drank a lot. We tried to stay there right up to the time I'd have to return to University but we were running short of funds. We agreed to stay to watch the last bike-racing of the season, the GP for amateurs. Pure madness, how anyone can drive around that island like they did and sober? They were *leet in the heed* as my old friend Jack Kelly would have

151

said. I had to return to University and funds were approaching zero but I'd heard that if you were destitute the police have to get you off the island so I took Stan and me off to the local nick and told them we were skint. Sure enough the rumour was correct. As in Singapore, dossers were not allowed on the Isle of Man. We were deported and they paid for the ferry. What we didn't expect was that they took us to the ferry as if we were felons with linked arms to a policeman but thankfully no cuffs. Holiday makers looked on in disgust at these bedraggled youths with the two police escorts, moving their children away from us, pointing and telling them to take heed because this is what happened if you didn't eat your crusts and if you grew your hair long, probably all thinking we had just been birched as well. I was sure I saw the two Special Branch men at the ferry, one of them nodding to his partner and saying, *'I told you so'*.

I have never tried to go back - they may want the ferry fare back.

Yes, vacation and part time work had its ups and downs in trying to earn your pocket money or keep as you got older. It was much better to play than work and as young kids we certainly did a lot of that, mainly outside and at the edge of nature, red in tooth and claw and it's that outside play which I return to next.

CHAPTER TEN
EASTER, BIRDS NESTING, POACHING AND HUNTING

Easter Eggs and Birds Nesting

In the sixties when not sliding, sledging, playing football, eating Mam's food or working for pocket money we looked forward to the end of winter and to start pinching bird's eggs. Easter was the start of spring and the laying of birds eggs was important to us. In reality those days the only religious significance Easter had to me was that we sang Easter songs in assembly. Easter was also when my Aunty Winn who lived in London, and compared to us had by now become rich as she had her own house and a car, would send me a postal order for ten shillings. She sent a small leather bound bible one year which I still have to this day. That day I wished she'd sent the ten bob!

The whole *new life* message must have been engrained in my mother and father somewhere as I can vaguely remember as a young lad being given new clothes for Easter. It seems this has been a tradition in most normal places and families. I guess for us it wasn't so important or financially viable and only a few families around made any effort to follow the traditions.

My father did however follow the *new life tradition* by hard-boiling our chicken eggs and dyeing them vivid colours using vegetable dye and with better chemical dyes he'd sourced from those 'in the know.' He did this as there was a financial benefit to be had. He was trying to win the Club's dyed egg show. This was held every Easter Sunday and was a precursor to the main event in the autumn, the Leek Show, without the angst and the financial reward of the vegetable show. He hoped to win a few pints as best egg. I believe he did one year as he came home absolutely mortal and struggled to eat his dinner as he'd stuffed many hard-boiled eggs down his gullet as a bet, à la Paul Newman in *Cool Hand Luke*. He was also leading a Billy goat by its tether rope - he'd acquired it from Hodgkiss's field and thought it might be a canny pet for us. Only time I remember my mam howling at him or swearing. 'Tak the bloody thing back you drunken bugger.' Which he duly did, but not before he'd shouted over to Ernie Cain to pass him the football we were kicking around the street. Ernie did and me fatha blasted it at the coal house goal but sadly he was as accurate as the Toon's Joelinton, or that other prolific Sunderland goal scorer Jozi Altidore, and he smashed it straight through Mrs Lloyd's toilet window yet again. Cue Dad, running up the street with the Billy goat in tow chased by a crazed mad seventy year old Mr Lloyd. Les, in pure mischievousness, remembering his own cricket ball terrors of the old axeman, tripped the poor man up. Laughing, he did a runner with Dad and the kidnapped goat up the street as the demented senior citizen rolled around in agony with a suspected broken hip. Dad paid up next day for the window and a bottle of whisky for his dear neighbour to ease the pain as he lay on his settee with strained ligaments. Les just laughed; as I told you, as he does...

We also tried to dye eggs and then we'd take them to Penshaw Hill to roll them down in our own kids' competition. I can't ever remember my egg getting further than the hole in which, I was told by Johnny Watters, the great Scottish goalkeeper and sixties physiotherapist for SAFC, Jim Baxter, the iconic Scottish footballer, used to hide his vodka bottles during pre-season training - or it was lost in one of Gussy's mole-catching holes. I tried to do it with my kids years later and was still hopeless at it. As I looked around at the scene of our childhood games with Baxter long gone and Gussy's moles gone to that great mole hill in the sky, it was a sad return for me. I much preferred eating Milky Bar chocolate eggs to rolling boiled ones anyway.

At Easter we waited for the nesting season to arrive with unrestrained joy. Most of us had birds' egg collections which we stored in boxes, the blown eggs nestled carefully in individual indentations of soft sand. It was an art to blow a bird's egg, especially rare ones or dippy eggs. Dippy eggs then were not what my children grew up asking for, that is a boiled hen's egg that you dip toast fingers into. In our day they were eggs that had either gone off or had live chicks in them. I can't imagine what my two sons would do if they ever had to crack open a hen's egg and be greeted by a mini T Rex. They are not, can I say, countrified or lovers of slimy things like worms, maggots or slugs. Unlike my dear daughter whose favourite animal still remains a slug! These days it is rare indeed to get a fertilised egg served up to you. In days before the British lion was stamped on our eggs I distinctly remember opening up boiled eggs to see small embryos in them. Or am I still in the throes of cerebral flashback after watching *Alien* last night?

Back to blowing eggs. We used to use a thorn from a hawthorn tree, pierce each end, make one end slightly larger, put the thinner end into our mouth and gently blow, hoping to push out the yolk and albumen and leave a clean empty shell.

Curiously, and I now know hypocritically, in our closed and personal world of environmental protection, it was considered not *the done thing*, bad sportsmanship, and truly you were, excuse the pun, *a bad egg*, if you took dippy eggs from the nest. You could tell if they were dippy by *hockling* (spitting) into the palm of your hand and standing the egg up in the hockle. If it tipped over then it might well be dippy. Sadly if the bird's egg was one that was rare or one that you had not collected yet, then a few boys would still take it and hope to be able to blow it without smashing the whole shell if it had an embryo in it.

This inverted moral code was also extended to the number of eggs you could take from a warm nest - a warm nest being one where the eggs were still warm, so the bird was still nesting them (well hopefully they'd carry on after we'd stolen one or two). The code stated that you should only take one or two depending on the number in there. However, it wasn't like the Royal and Ancient rules of golf and this code was not prescriptive, or indeed followed by everybody, so many nests were taken without thought for the survival of our sport or the poor creatures' existence.

It was the same with *huggying* the nest. This was our term for destroying the actual nest itself after taking the eggs. The art of reaching in to a nest and extracting a single egg without disturbing the rest or indeed frightening the birds off sitting on the nest again was what many of us practiced but some didn't. Some tore the nest out the tree. Some because they were hanging perilously off high branches and didn't want to risk falling or others because they were simply nasty, psychotic, horrible little bastards. We had our share in Shiney as I've already told you. This again confirms my theory that these same kids who never went to bed, never went to Sunday school, got caned continually, were never called in to bed by their mams and loved kicking the hell out of people for no reason were normally the ones who tortured animals and *huggied* the birds' nests. And of course they ended up in Durham nick.

Recently, that Shiney Row stalwart and great artist and architect Terry 'Tosh' Greenwell who painted this book's cover, visited me in my exile and told me over a beer and a world beating *Smuggler's Inn* steak and kidney pudding of another inhabitant of that asylum and proof of my behavioural theory. The subject of his angst was prone to mischievous japes like strangling or thumping the smaller boys. A bit of a loner and recluse but when he socialised it was normally to cause some mayhem. This day he had heard that Tosh had found a Curlew's egg and he knocked on his door to ask if Tosh would like to swop it with a rare egg as he had pinched the lot and had a spare. This egg was a prize that Tosh would have given more than his rare Curlew's egg as it was a Garganey duck's egg: rare as anything and no one in the gang had one, except the man standing at his door. Tosh took the egg and examined it and checked yet again in the bible, *The Observer's Book of Birds Eggs* and confirmed it had indeed the size and markings of the rare duck egg. They duly swopped the eggs. As the egg giver left, he asked to see the Garganey egg one last time. Tosh gave it to him and he placed it on his palm and spat on it and began rubbing off the brown marking much to Terry's distress. He gave Tosh it back. He pocketed his Curlew egg and grimaced in his attempt at a smile (he rarely smiled or laughed or showed any form of emotion) and seemed to take some sadistic pleasure in informing the diminutive Terry 'It's a hen's egg I dyed with brown byut polish you daft twat.' And turned and left with Terry's prize egg.

Terry said to me over his steak and kidney pud. 'The big bastard could have kept quiet as I'd never have known but he had to torture me. The cruel bugger nivva changed.'

I took a long sup of my beer and sympathetically asked the egg collector still grieving 56 years after the event. 'Is he deed now?'

'I hope so,' was his laconic reply full of hope for divine retribution.

Like most of us, who didn't huggy birds nests and end up in Durham nick, Terry developed a conscience over his egg collecting days and now is an avid bird watcher and RSPB conservation supporter. One can only hope Terry's nemesis developed the same conscience; people do change I am told. Indeed, Terry texted me the other day to remind me of someone named after pineapple chunks, another stalwart of Shiney Row peculiarity, with the illuminating diagnosis, that, 'He wasn't a real psychopath - just a marginal one'. Freud could have gained another doctorate if he'd studied at the University of Shiney.

Finding nests was an art. Some had the gift, other didn't. Of course Gussy and Peter Howe were good, as they spent most of their lives out in the woods, fields and streams and were real nature boys. We roamed miles to look for eggs. We became experts at climbing trees, some much better than others for sure. Some fell and broke arms or legs and poor David Gartry fell badly while after conkers. He nearly died but survived to become one of the country's leading ophthalmic surgeons, now heading up The Wimpole Eye Clinic. Which proves that not all who spent their waking hours hunting and foraging ended up at Lumley Brick works or Borstal or writing books.

The real danger was climbing the rocky outcrops up near Herrington Hill where the sparrow hawks nested. One day Gussy who lived across from me climbed up and got a live chick. Gussy wasn't too environmentally clued those days. Many boys were badly injured or killed going after the seabirds' eggs at Marsden cliffs although we managed to get a fair collection without killing ourselves.

All of this was purely to see who could beat the next boy and to secure the whole collection of eggs in the book of *Observers Book of Birds Eggs*, which was our bible. Most of us knew that book better than any school times' tables or maths textbook. I reflect on this and can see certain old school friends now in my mind's eye who were, shall I say, a bit compromised in the learning scale, sitting discussing how to tell the difference between the eggs of the Corvus genus or the location, nature and size of the tree creeper's nest. Maybe we should introduce bird's nesting again in the National School Curriculum? Only a suggestion folks...

Pets and Tortoises

We roamed constantly across farmlands, woodland, rivers, and agricultural fields and collected what we could from them, either for fun or for food. We had little thought for who owned it or if it would wipe out an indigenous species or flora or fauna. We would collect what animals we could, frogs, newts, toads, and catch whatever we could in ponds and streams. There seemed to be so many sticklebacks and minnows in our burn those days and we spent hours trying to catch them with jam jars. Newts seemed to be everywhere. Now I hardly ever see one (except in Nick the Hat's garden pond but given his reputation for espionage as revealed in *Footsteps on the Teign,* I believe they could be MI5 remote listening devices). But really we were all competing with each other as to how many animals you could catch and keep alive at your house. Sadly most died, only Gussy and Peter Howe mastering the art of maintaining a viable Zoological garden on council-owned property.

I loved my toads and frogs and we used to have long jumping competitions in the street with them – I still remember watching Bob Beamon's record breaking leap at the Mexico Olympics in 1968 on our black and white TV but my frogs could leap proportionally further. The art is to tickle the backside of your amphibian and coerce it into leaping into the air. I had a particularly good toad which I kept in a box in my bedroom some nights, feeding it chopped up garden Lumbricus terrestris and flies. My sister Margaret still has nightmares today from when she was sat on the one toilet we had inside the house and no lock on the door. She was sitting doing what we must do, singing away to herself a song from the latest new band she liked, The Beatles, when I sneaked up the stairs and put the toad down at the slightly ajar door. I opened it further and tickled the toad's arse. It leapt up onto her lap. Cue huge screaming and cursing and exit me through the front door. I got a real telling off from my dad and she never spoke to me again until she left to get married.

I have no idea what happened to Toady; she wouldn't ever touch it, so I live in hope she never stamped on him and he managed to swim down the toilet back to Fencehouses' sewage works. These sewage works were excellent hunting grounds, and, as well as toads, there were hundreds of condoms we used to find flushed there. We would fill them with water and throw them at the lasses. Urgh ! The thought of what we were touching...and this was the good old days!

We kept many species of animal as surrogate pets but the one that most of us had was the tortoise. Now I guess keeping tortoises, as with bird's nesting, collecting great crested newts and rare raptors, shooting water voles and skinning moles is not politically correct anymore and could result in joining my old mates in Durham Jail. Now in my adult enlightenment I'd agree with you but there was something quite soothing and certainly mysterious and exciting about keeping tortoises. They did absolute nowt but gnaw at lettuce, sleep and potter around their hutch or the garden but they left a legacy, a mystery as deep as the Bermuda triangle, and one which no one has yet solved. Where did they all go? Every tortoise I or my mates ever had just disappeared. Apart from the ones who were squashed by cars in the street or like Stumpy Tony the Wolverhampton Rasta biker's, eaten by rats when hibernating. Where did they all go? Everyone came to school and said the same thing. 'My tortoise has disappeared'.

Maybe they were abducted by some reptilian alien species that took pity on them for living in a frozen North East wasteland with only stale lettuce to eat and moved them off to where they should be - in tropical paradises. Maybe the Chinese takeaway shops took them? There were many racist rumours going around those days that they stole dogs and that what we had in our *Number 56* with rice could be anything they could catch. Tinker the landlord was convinced they took tortoises and used them in the Sweet and Sour. Whatever the answer, I liked my tortoise and liked my toad and I sincerely hope they are both enjoying life in whatever Paradise they escaped to.

GUSSY
Shooting and Dogs

Food we often poached from Lord Lambton's estates or stole from gardens or sourced from the environment around us. Some were much better hunters than others and some were closer to nature in all its forms than the rest of us. Hunting, foraging and just having fun was really an extension of playing games for most of us. Some took it more seriously and others took a vicious sadistic pleasure in it. We were to say the least a microcosm of country life in all its redness of tooth and claw.

Gussy was my older friend who lived ten steps away opposite me in Hunter Street. He loved hunting and he taught me how to catch moles, mainly on Penshaw Hill. The Hill was covered in mole hills as well as gorse and Gussy showed me one day how to catch the subterranean mammals by placing a milk bottle over their hole. The next day I'd pick up the bottles with the moles in them. They were trapped as they sought to explore above ground in the dark.

Gussy had a penchant for catching and keeping animals. He caught many different species and showed me as the younger kid many ways to catch mammals, reptiles and birds. His favourites were Tawny Owls, which he had stolen as fledglings from their nest and a Sparrow Hawk chick he had also stolen from its nest. I helped him feed both from the insides of starlings and sparrows that he shot everyday with an air rifle. I watched them fascinated as they grew into birds large enough to be freed back into the wild. We also caught live field voles and shrews and fed these to the birds. These small rodents lived under any old wood or carpet or any refuse lying on the uncultivated ground surrounded by the many pigeon crees on part of the Front. This seemed very natural back then and we saw no harm in it.

Gussy's complex of crees (sheds to keep racing pigeons in) and huts in his back garden was situated on The Front, the stretch of the land at the back of his house which was used by the tenants of The Crescent - the circle of council houses surrounding this land. Gussy's complex kept all known species of creature that inhabited the ecosystem of Shiney Row and its environs. Up from this zoo, there was another nature resort - Peter Howe's complex. Peter was older than Gussy, a single man living with his parents three doors up the Crescent from Gussy. He was the David Attenborough of wild life catching and keeping and Gussy was in awe of the great man.

Gussy read the *Exchange and Mart* avidly, searching for exotic animals for his zoo. He bought a snake once but I cannot recall what happened to it. Maybe there are colonies of Black Mambas roaming the gardens in Shiney Row to this day. I pity them if they bite the natives – they are much more dangerous than the poor reptiles. He bought two chipmunks I remember but sadly his father stood on one wearing his heavy pit boots. I think Rinty his mongrel dog, which was the nemesis of all rodents, savaged the other.

Peter and Gussy and many of the lads from the Street would take their dogs and either a 4/10 shotgun or 0.22 air rifle off on a hunt. Gussy and Les with their two mangy hounds Rinty and Sandy spent hours hunting in and around the local pit stream, *the burn* or *the beck* depending on your fancy. The burn was the small stream that was sourced from an underground water source from Herrington Pit and flowed through East Herrington, Herrington Burn and on towards the sewage works at Fence Houses. We searched for small rodents and birds to hunt, shoot or capture for Gussy and Peter's zoos. *The burn* was a regular playground for all of us from the village, both girls and boys. Competitions for jumping across the burn were called *Dickers* and many a time we ended up soaked coming home to yet another scolding from angry mothers. We also caught sticklebacks, toads, frogs, newts and minnows in the stream. Sadly, you may say it's not surprising given our activities, that all of these are so rare now in local ponds, streams and burns.

Rinty and Sandy were real mongrel hunting hounds and had a nose for rooting out water rats in the banks of the burn which they chased up and down the burn until they caught and savaged them, or Gussy shot them. We had no appreciation of the need for conservation then. We assumed that the environment that we lived in would go on forever, unchanging. We had no real knowledge of the outside world really, or of David Attenborough and other pre-global warming naturalists. *Zoo Quest* was on television but most of us didn't watch such things. Indeed most of us didn't have a telly or if we did see a TV the only water rat we watched was in *Tales from the River Bank* on *Watch with Mother* and he was cute and called Ratty. If he'd lived on our little river bank the only *River Bank* tale I could tell you was that Rinty mauled him or Gussy plugged him with an air rifle slug.

The sewage works tended to have more brown and black rats than water voles. Rats, no one loved, but my daughter does for God's sake and she slugs too. I am pleased that thankfully David Attenborough has made his remarkable conservation and environmental protection mark on future generations like my beautiful, caring daughter. However, despite my belated adult enlightenment of loving and protecting all living things, I am still not keen on rats and co-incidentally recently one ran up my arm and over my shoulder when I was cleaning the chicken hutch out. Sadly my Jorman hound is not as vicious or skilled at riving rodents to death as Rinty or Sandy and I'm sure the rat turned and laughed at both of us before it buggered off under the fence with a mouth full of my chickens' *Layer pellets*. It wouldn't have done this all those years ago when it was open season on poor rodents by most of the natives. The dogs loved savaging them and Peter annihilated many with his shotgun. Peter's Jack Russell killed many in the surrounding farms and barns at the behest of the farmers and years later the lads would have bets on how many each dog could kill. I believe Simpa's Jack Russell won and killed up to fifty in one quick session at Cuslow's Farm.

Killing for fun I guess was what this was as there was no financial, basic food need or countryside benefit to justify what we did. Sadly, it's what a lot did in my deranged world. Gussy even shot a swan one day at the sewage works. Sorry Queen Bess but where we lived your protected species was treacherously just another target. Gussy is long dead so no point in prosecuting him for treason and chopping his head off. He was taken early when he fell from high cliffs in Northumberland fishing for cod; well so it is said. I believe he would more likely have been hunting sea birds' eggs if he was that high up the cliffs, as we always did at Marsden Cliffs near South Shields. Mind you, this time, like the empire in the *Star Wars* the animals may have struck back.

We actually ate the swan back at Gussy's surrogate zoo on the Front. Basically we lived there most of time in crees or underground in camps which we dug out and roofed. These underground camps had fires and chimneys but they were not that efficient at removing carbon emissions and we were covered with smoke most days and nights.

Those days before global warming we knew nothing of carbon footprints or indeed ozone; we'd burn anything and everything. We lit these fires with mineral felt which we had ripped off our father's and neighbour's pigeon or hen crees and kept them going with any wood, coal or linoleum we could steal or forage. It was on one of these fires this example of the Queen's protected avian species was roasted. Tasted tough and fishy if I remember - not something I'd recommend with nice chilled Chablis; you'd be better off with a nice brace of North Yorkshire grouse and a good claret.

We stank most nights of smoke. Our clothes, hair and bodies and hands and faces were covered with black soot, dirt or the remains of dead, roasted endangered creatures. Every night our mothers tried to get us into the house for a bath and bed and I can almost hear my devoted mam calling my name across the two neon lit streets as I type. Most mothers shouted out their kids name at some period in the evening and we returned to the inevitable wash and a carbolic soap scrub to take off the day's muck from the body, and then finally bed. It was a pecking order, a rite of passage when I look back, on who was called first and on how late you could stay out. Sadly, my parents were strict on this as Dad liked to have a chat to me before he went to work on nightshift. He cared I guess and liked to discuss school and the world with me. Also I was more compliant than some kids. I respected my parents a lot and actually obeyed them; well sometimes. Other kids were less obedient and some of their parents just didn't care. So I used to watch them from my bedroom window, still playing in the street, kicking the ubiquitous football, sitting on dustbins and hanging out or playing the various street games we all played and getting into mischief.

I believe there must be a provable correlation between actually getting hauled into your house to get supper, bath and early bed with your future life prospects. Most of the kids and young adults that stayed up late, and their parents didn't bother about calling them in for bed, ended up in petty and violent crime, and in some cases prison.

Worth someone getting a PHD in sociology or criminology with that hypothesis and the findings I quote in this masterpiece on human behaviour.

Poaching and the Polis

Nature is indeed red in tooth and claw and poaching for food had been a family tradition in my mother's family. Stripper and his brothers were very good at it; indeed so good they used to feed the local polis (police). My dad was in Barrack Row one day when the local copper knocked on the door. He came to mention to my grandad and his brothers that they were 'Staking out Lord Lambton's 3rd gill (wood)' that night and if, by any strange chance poachers were thinking of going there, it would be wise if they went hunting somewhere else. The polis then went on to enjoy a nice pheasant casserole from my nana for his lunch and a piece of her game pie for his bait. It is called symbiosis in biology where two species benefit from sharing between each other or looking after your own people in the real world. For us poaching was endemic and the local polis mainly turned a blind eye, if not a hungry stomach.

The poachers didn't only use four-ten shotguns, rifles or snares. Stripper showed me how to soak grain and raisins in alcohol and then sprinkle them around the forest floor during the afternoon for the pheasants to eat. They roost early evening and at dusk go back to their trees. After a meal of booze-soaked raisins they were so pissed they fell off their perches.

Rabbit catching was not really necessary on the Lord's land as there were plenty of places the furry creatures lived in the warrens in the fields, copses, hills around the village. The villagers mainly used terriers, ferrets and nets to catch them or the younger kids would shoot them with air rifles or 0.22 rifles if they could borrow one from John Alison or the like. John lived with his mother all his life across and down the street, never seemed to work but was in the pub drinking eight pints every day. He lived entirely on game. I wasn't sure if he ever ate vegetables or fruit but he always had rabbits, hares, pigeons, pheasant, partridge deer and anything else that he could shoot. He was a beater on the esteemed Lambton's estate during the season and knew the various gills and woods like the back of his hand for his own purposes. A useful source of poaching information was John, but I guess not a man for working hard for a living.

Most of the lads had some form of hunting and killing dog. These were either for rats and water voles or anything furry that moved. Many had terriers for putting down holes to get rabbits or rats. Sadly some lads went for badgers and dug them out for their more fierce dogs to attack. Most of these people were of course not normal *in the heed*. They were violent psychopaths or introverted potential serial killers and prove my theory that not going to Sunday school, staying up late, perpetual canings and similar behaviours are useful predictors for who would turn out bad. Badger baiters are among that list.

As I said we spent most of life underground in our camps roasting vegetables we'd *scrumped* or mammals and birds we'd poached. We also lived in these camps during the most important time of the year - Bonfire night

CHAPTER ELEVEN
BONFIRE NIGHT AND GANGS

DAVEY
Bonfire Night and Arson

November the fifth was bonfire night to us. We had learned of Guy Fawkes at school and how he'd tried to burn down the Houses of Parliament but we knew little of politics or religious freedom. It really wasn't until I was living in Singapore that it occurred to me there was any harm in it when my Scottish Irish friend Pat told me that no one in Ireland or Catholic Glasgow did Guy Fawkes Night. It seems that Catholics feel that a plot that failed to get a Catholic King on the throne and that the consequent torture and burning of true Catholic patriots should not be celebrated. I guess the Celts always were a bit fussy with their history. Anyway, we knew nothing of these geopolitical things as kids in the baby boomer generation. Bonfire night was when we burned each other, Catholic or Protestant it mattered not, with fireworks, committed arson attacks on anybody's bonfires or materials and generally wreaked havoc around the area.

Our two streets mainly had the bonfire around The Front next to Gussy's Zoo. Some who were not really in the gang had theirs in their own back gardens. Silly really because all we did was raid the garden and steal the wood and trees they had collected. One stubborn small bunch on the other side of the Crescent on the Front didn't join us so Davey and me bought some pink paraffin from Mr Cairns' shop and made two petrol bombs which we put on long flexible sticks we'd chopped of Mrs Davidson's lilac bush with Les's dad's samurai sword. We lit the bombs and threw them using the sticks as hand held catapults, hiding some way away behind a pigeon cree. One bomb hit the fence and exploded setting it alight and the other bounced off the trees on the bonfire and smashed against the house, the fuel spilling over the walls and igniting. The fire brigade were called but the fire was doused by a very angry council house owner who searched up and down The Front for the culprits.

THE GARGETTS
Mantraps and Catherine Wheels

Davey and me were safely hidden from the wrath of both house owner and the police as we ran to hide in the deep pits below our own bonfire which we had dug out to live in. These pits contained all the necessary essentials for life and to protect our own bonfire from attack; water, air rifles, catapults, knives, pop, sweets, and an underground fire so we were perpetually covered in smoke. As most families were perpetually covered in nicotine and cigarette smoke I guess we all smelled similar to our families, teachers and friends. Surrounding the *bonny* were man traps we'd dug - deep pits with stakes and broken glass bottles in them, the hole covered over with cleverly concealed grass or twig mats. We had an intricate pattern of high-tech early warning devices surrounding the bonfire to rival the apocalyptical white nuclear war warning domes on Fylingdales Moor - tins with strings on them.

Long before bonfire night we'd go searching for wood and cutting trees. We kept most of the bonfire separate to stop wholesale burning by other gangs and in the large circle in the middle we placed old sofas to sit on and take turns on guard duty above the pits underground where the reserve *soldiers* lived. We hid lots of wood and trees in each other's gardens. We only started putting all the bits together near bonfire night. All of this was an attempt to stop anyone coming and raiding your *bonny* or worse setting it alight. The main culprits were the Gargett gang who emanated from the other end of the council estate, Maple Terrace, Lowerson Avenue and Hunter Street. There were several Gargetts in the family ranging through the ages but all older than me. Some were normal, well as normal as you can be coming from there, others crackers. And they had the Olivers with them too, a bit like the Sioux joining forces with the Apache - extreme violence wasn't too far away from any raid. Hence we carried knives, rifles and bows and arrows. We also made traps with exploding fireworks, mainly from the many types of *bangers* and *cannons* which we'd buy then from any shop. In those halcyon days any kid could buy almost anything from the shops, cigarettes, knives, air rifles, bullets fireworks, petrol, paraffin, matches - you name it, if it could main or kill, we could buy or steal it.

And then Dicky Lop was sadly maimed one day.

Dicky was so named because his head had a propensity to crawl with small bugs - if he had only had nits he would have been Dicky Nit. Nits were the eggs of head lice. Lops were the crawling larvae of nits...end of entomology lesson number one and I hope this story brings back to you happy memories of the school *nit nurse* and the *nit comb* for you all. Dicky Lop had broken several firework cannons and bangers up and tried to light the resulting pile of gunpowder with his cigarette tab. He put his head right down to the gunpowder in order to blow the tab end to make it redder and the whole thing exploded in a flash of light and smoke with Dickie rolling around the ground holding his head with third degree burns to his *fyess* (face). How we laughed (kids are awful, I've repeatedly said so) but the positive for our unfortunate premature Guy Fawkes, it cured his lops - well for a few days.

The Gargett gang controlled the Indian passes to The Burn and the Colliery field, like the *Comancheros* did in the Wild West in that other great John Wayne classic. The passes led to good hunting grounds for live trees and also random wood for the *bonny*. We made periodic raids on the encampment but they had similar traps, warnings and weapons so both sides engaged in fierce and deadly guerrilla warfare. Ho Chi Minh, eat your heart out son; we kids invented jungle warfare not you.

Foraging for fuel for the *bonny* was always fun. We used bogies to carry large railway sleepers we pinched from the coke works and rail lines. Sometimes we rolled big ones or big tree trunks using logs or cans as rollers underneath, like we'd seen the Israelites do building the pyramids in the film *The Ten Commandments* or in our school history books about the stone age people building Stonehenge. Anyone's trees were fair game if we could chop bits off them. The same with abandoned sheds or pigeon crees - they were taken, especially the mineral felt which burned so well.

Bonfire night always seemed to be wet and miserable but the *bonny* always got burned with a replica Guy Fawkes on top. We wheeled our *Guy* around the village in an old pram or sometimes on a bogie and tried to get money for fireworks with the old *Penny for the Guy mister or missus* plea. Most paid something and it went towards the purchase of anything that went bang or could be thrown fizzing or jumping at old people.

Bangers were the favourites of course. They were put through old people's letter boxes to frighten them, the more psychotic inserted them in frogs' bottoms, tied them to Askeys (newts), put them in bottles to try to produce bombs, slipped them into trouser pockets and generally caused mayhem for the ambulance service and police.

Crackerjacks were great fun - long strings of explosive all scrunched up in a snake-like firework. Once lit it jumped and fizzed everywhere, banging and exploding and frightening the hell out of any innocent in the dark. These did serious damage through letter boxes. I guess in the end as safety and child protection improved dramatically in society the sale of such weapons had to be banned for everyone's safety. Pity though because they gave us nights of endless fun in late autumn.

Catherine wheels seemed to go on forever nailed into gateposts. I notice they fizz out quick now. It's the same with Roman candles and rockets, only a few seconds of pleasure. Before Mrs T, the rockets seemed to reach the moon and the bombs that flew out of the candles went into the stratosphere. *Standard* and *Brock* fireworks are those I remember and you could buy only one or enough to destroy an Old People's Home, depending on your wealth.

After the *bonny* died down a bit we threw spuds in to roast. The potatoes were pinched from Smithy the farmer's field near the school, as were the turnips. We'd stay up as late as possible watching the embers burn down eating black and burnt spuds before being called in to bed. Our faces were black as were our teeth. Excitedly, if all had survived the fireworks and the fire, the next day we'd search the area on the way to school for rockets that had landed. The smell of the still smouldering *bonny* and the gunpowder from fireworks always pervaded the air on the walk for the whole way to school. I remember it as if it was yesterday.

The Sandy Banks and Penshaw Hill

We always seemed to be in some form of gang, whether it be to protect our *bonny*, play street games or to wage war we tended to stick together. Penshaw was our neighbouring village to the North East of us. We knew many Penshaw lads but in the sixties we also used to fight with them over a territory called the Sandy Banks

I remember the walks to Penshaw Hill as only happening in summertime. It always seemed to be red hot and a very long journey. We probably stopped off at many places on the way doing what small boys do but what I always remember was blazing sun and thirst. I also remember we knocked on people's door and politely asked for a drink of water. I can never remember being refused one and sometimes we'd get Pop (Soda) and a few biscuits. On the way we would play on the Sandy Banks, a high escarpment of sandstone surrounded by allotments and fields. The new Shiney Row Working Men's club was built on them 10 years after. We used to fight like the South Wales Borderers at Rorke's Drift against the Zulu warriors of Penshaw to gain a colonial hold on the territory in the 60's.

When these pre-arranged fights were held, we younger boys were summoned by the older teenage lads to craft weapons for the fight. I would carve spears out of branches and tie knives or six inch nails to the end of bamboo canes with the shot wire used to pass the electric charge to the explosives used in the pit. We also used shot wire to build catapults from the Y of a tree branch and strong elastic. We either had to buy the elastic from Cairn's hardware shop, or steal from the old snooker tables we found breaking into a closed old miners welfare club on Bunker Hill. The elastic was always tied to the old leather eyes from Dad's braces which were then attached to the Y with shot wire. The pouch for the stone or ball bearing was usually also cut from the leather of the braces or the tongue of an old shoe and again tied with colliery shot wire. We used ball bearings that were stolen from Philadelphia Yard or the Pit, or taken out of any scrap machinery wheel which had bearings and balls. We also used to get iron *bots* from the railway lines near the Lambton Coke Works where they seemed to be forged in the red-hot ovens. These were lethal, particularly to Penshaw lads, and also to the local birdlife and rodents.

Once the tribe was armed we would be rounded up by the big lads. I remember Russell Dixon (he had been in a Borstal detention centre.) was one of leaders and we would march up to the Sandy Banks to retake the hill from the Penshaw lads. The kids like me would be kept in reserve firing catapults and throwing spears at the entrenched enemy while the older lads stormed the hill. Once ground had been taken, big boy heads had been bashed and eyes been blacked, the kids would run up to fight those the same age if they hadn't run off or we'd whoop with joy. I was hit in the head during one of these assaults and still have the scar across my brow today of the spear which buried itself in my forehead, luckily not in my eye.

During one of these assaults on the Sandys one boy was killed, thrown off or pushed off the high escarpment I believe. It's a bit faded now the memory but I think that put an end to that era as we never seemed to carry this on into my teenage years. The Sandys were bulldozed down for construction of The Club and they are now a private housing estate.

Penshaw Hill didn't see such a war like the Sandys. Later on in teenage years it was the scene of fights with the lads from Pennywell, a part of Sunderland and the next place on from Penshaw. It developed a reputation as the worst area in Sunderland for car theft, violence and various criminal activities. At one time I believe Sunderland was the worst place in Europe for *twocking* and *ram raiding*.

As an aside I was imbibing beer with Loud Pete and Deaf Dave and showing them the lovely article that the Sunderland Echo had published on my latest masterpiece 'Relentless Misery.' Dave, who is an ex-squaddie, hence his deafness, and also ex-Old Bill, told me of the time he was sent by Devon and Cornwall's men in blue with three other undercover traffic police to support Northumbria's finest poliss in catching the horrible scroats who were nicking so many cars. They drove up in their new super charged unmarked motors and were booked into the Mowbray Park Hotel, Sunderland. What a life you may say, sent from the English Riviera for a jolly holiday in the world's worst car crime and ram raiding city and put up in a hotel than wouldn't go amiss on the shores of Beirut. The cars were secured in a separate cage and locked compound. On waking after several beers in the cocktail bar they enjoyed a hearty tax payer funded breakfast and they walked out to patrol the beautiful landscape and ambience of the largest council housing estates in Europe in their souped up police cars. 'The bastards had nicked our cars. They had used a car jock to prise open the cage; a skinny charver crawled through, wired one car and drove it through the cage doors. They then drove all six police cars around Sunderland all night chased by six local traffic old bill. *How do you Northern idiots sleep at night?* We had to get the train back to Cornwall,' was all that the distraught man could say about his one and only trip to Sunderland.

We were also never aligned with townies. Sunderland was different to us. It was the big town. They spoke different to us and acted different or so we thought in our earlydays and tight pit village culture. I guess we were a bit like The Wirral thinks of Liverpool when I look back. But we in Shiney Row were nothing like the Wirral - more like The Gorbals, so you can guess what Pennywell was like.

And as we grew older the threat of violence was never far away

Pit Boots and Butcher's Coats

Life was always problematical as a lad anywhere those days as fighting seemed to be the way of the world. In school there were always playground fights with a ring of boys around watching two lads scrap. It was seldom a fair fight because it was normally one psychotic lad who wanted to fight and another boy trying to survive.

Pit byuts were famous those days as a cheap version of *Dr Martens*, the boots made infamous by the skinheads of the late sixties and early seventies. Whereas most skinheads wore their Martens with pride and with polish and care, as with their *Levi Sta press*, *Harrington* jackets, *Crombie* coats, *Ben Sherman* shirts and butchers coats, the lads I knew liked to wear pit byuts with the toe caps polished or buffed with blood, it didn't seem to matter with which to many. It was a low cost way to kick someone's head in I guess.

One of my fellow street urchins wore pit byuts as did most of the daft lads. He came from a family of seven and was the craziest of them I'd say. To sum my mate up and for you to understand our world in that place at that time, he was discharged from the Army a few years later for, *being too violent*. Too violent for the army but allowed to roam the streets of Shiney...uhm?

Every weekend it was mayhem outside the Chinese takeaway. They resembled a war zone every Friday and Saturday night after the Club shut.

Chinese Takeaways and Mother Goose

In a lovely anecdote to the Chinese takeaway war zone comparison, we normal lads used to chuckle at the thought of strangers who passed through the village who might have thought: *By isn't that a quaint little Chinese restaurant. Let's stop and sample the cuisine.* And we'd speculate what their reaction would be once the Club poured out and the cast of *A Clockwork Orange* piled out, heading towards the Chinese takeaway, which those days doubled up as a cage fighters' ring. One night our dreams came true when a couple of amateur actors decided to do exactly what we used to chuckle about. Jackie Wanless's brother was there and he recalled it for posterity and this book as he told me the story.

'I left the club early and was standing in the Chinese on my own when in popped two characters, one dressed as Mother Goose and the other as Widow Twanky. I couldn't believe my eyes. One of them almost skipped to the counter and looked at menu on the wall with open eyes. He turned to his mate, the Goose, and asked him. *What do you want from the menu?* His mate, Mother Goose said, *Oh look Clive; they've got the Duck with Spring Onions you love. Aren't you pleased we stopped off here before we got to the hotel in Durham?'*

171

Jacky then said that Clive waddled over and pointed at the menu. *Looks delightful James, lets treat us to Banana Fritters too.'*

Jackie said that he stared at the two and looked at the clock on the wall behind the counter which showed 10.35 pm. He looked expectantly at the Chinese lady who always served there and now had a local accent as she also looked at the clock. She looked worried. Widow Twanky continued and started to order - 'Can *we have the...'*

He was interrupted by a gesticulating, irate Chinese girl pointing to the door. *'No. Go! Pliss go now...out of the shop. Go! pliss...'*

'What's wrong? Please what have we done wrong?' the two strangers asked in unison.

The Chinese lady pointed at the clock and shouted: *'Hoh!...It is Club closing time. Five minutes...daft lads will be here. Go! NOW!'*

Jackie said: 'The two thespians looked at me. I shrugged me shoulders and told them the cold facts of life in Shiney Row. *She's reet lads. Better bugger off quick; once the daft lads get here from the Club they are gonna love you two knackers.'*

I gather the two made a hasty exit to their car and probably room service at their hotel. I often wonder if they ever went back to thank the Chinese lady for saving them from *the daft lads.*

One of the more violent daft lads, was street fighting specialist, Digger, who had long hair and if he decided he was going to kick off with anyone he'd tie it nonchalantly back in a ponytail with an elastic band he kept perpetually tied around his wrist for such eventualities before violently head-butting the unfortunate victim, or, in many cases, victims, several times, before kicking them unconscious. Something those of us in the know always watched out for if we saw imminent impending violence; was if Digger went for the elastic band, well, there'd be claret.

One icon of violence really only asked one question. He didn't speak much. That question was always: *'Who are yeah looking at?'* This would be seconds before the puzzled observer of non-psychotic things would be head-butted and kicked half to death. It was his and many others' only warning to any stranger, or indeed friend if the schizophrenic mood took, that he was going to get assaulted. One became quickly street wise to this tactic.

Viz was to immortalise this rhetorical social bonding questioning in their cartoon psychotic character, *Biffa Bacon.* With the other classic line, *You calling my pint a puff?* Long before Biffa was published I used to talk about my deranged old school chums to people I met in more normal areas of the country and that their first words to their mothers or fathers in their prams would not have been *Ga, ga,* or *Mummy,* but: *Who are yeah looking at?* Viz published their own take on this some years later when *Mutha, Biffa's* mam, gave birth to a son and *Biffa* looked into the cot at his new brother and the baby said, 'Who are yeah looking at' and stuck a nut on *Biffa.* I am certain I defined this behaviour first with my observations of life in Shiney long before Viz and *Biffa Bacon.*

Shot Putts and Head Cases

The Number 39 bus stop in Shiney was a scene of mayhem most nights as it was where strangers got on or off the bus from various local villages along the bus routes. The main targets were normally lads from Washington or Houghton, Hetton-le Hole, and Easington. The Number 5, 6 and 7 had their moments for lads from Sunderland, Lumley, and Chester-Le-Street too. This was reciprocated at the 39 bus stops in all those same places by the same level of violence by people who looked very similar in dress.

Washington was particularly problematic for me as I went to school there and spent most of my social life there so I had to use the bus stops at both ends of my journeys. I was always being sussed out by the gangs but luckily for me I always knew one or two of the ring leaders as I either grew up with them or played football with them. One Christmas Eve I was saved from harm, not by Clarence the guardian angel who saved Jimmy Stewart in *It's Wonderful Life,* but by playing football. Big Trev was with me but as he was a 400 metre sprinter he managed to avoid the pending disaster.

Big Trev was called that not because he was big in massive bulk or could run like the rugby player and athletics champion he was, but because of his classic spoken line to us as we sat in Usworth comprehensive school 6th form common room during a Humanities lesson from that wonderful head of sixth form, Mr Purvis.

Having recently arrived into the madness that was the North East, Mr Purvis was delightfully naive about the colloquial ways and sayings of his pupils. His role as Humanities teacher was a pastoral one - to reach out and try to educate his late adolescent cherubs in the ways of the real world. Part of his role was to offer us guidance on out of school activities and hobbies and keep us from harmful things like early pregnancy, drugs, gangs and crime. In one lesson he asked the question, what did we do at weekend?

Big Trev was sprawled in his chair almost horizontal and his lanky legs were split across the low level table. He was scratching his nether regions, as boys do, and he shouted out: 'We gan to the clurrb man!'

Mr Purvis was puzzled with this answer and the idiomatic speech and asked a perfectly logical question. 'Which club?'

'Which clurrb! Which...clurrb man!' the astonished lad shouted out across the quietly chuckling audience, clearly disturbed at his teacher's lack of understanding. He tried to clarify the situation: 'There's anwly one clurrrb!' Fully expecting his humanities' coach to understand there was only one club in most of his audience's world.

'The tennis club?' the still to be enlightened man asked hopefully.

Big Trev nearly had apoplexy; he shuffled his long legs of the table and sat upright, dropped his head, put boney fingers to his face and ran his hand up his brow through his hair before howling at the poor man: 'What the ****! Neebody plays tennis around here man. Ah've twold yeah, we gan teh the clurrb - Shiney Clurrb!'

'Shiny?..Is it a pottery school club?' asked the teacher innocently.

'Pottery? How man, is thoo daft or what? It's the clurbb! The clurrb. Dee yeah not have clurrbs where yeah come from, man?

'How, Sir. I think he means, he goes to the Working Men's Social Club,' interrupted Linda Cruddas, saving the poor man from even more ridicule from his tennis and ceramics protégés.

'That's reet pet. She's reet sor, the Clurrb man,' Big Trev uttered, his hand still running through his hair.

'Oh!' said the teacher understanding at last. 'What do you do in the Social Club?'

Big Trev stroked his head and head one more time and stretched his legs again wide open across the table and blared out:

'We get pissed man. What else would yeah dee in the clurrb?'

'As it's a Social club I'd assume you chat, dance, meet girls and generally play games or music?' our naive educator rhetorically suggested.

Big Trev, now visibly shocked, sat upright and with one last stroke of his hair he stopped the conversation in its tracks. 'Why nor man, we divn't dee that man. We get pissed with oor fathas and grandfathas and oor mates. Then we tap up the lasses after the band has been on and we might get lucky around the back of the clurbb. Yeah kna what I mean?'

And this being a 'Humanities' lesson it led to a debate about more romantic and normal sexual courtship rather than making love to our potential partners *round the back of the clurrb*. It moved on to contraception, sexually transmitted disease and, for some reason I can't now remember, the male penis. This conversation was stopped in its tracks by another Big Trev utterance. He stroked his hand through his hair, spread his long lanky legs across his coffee table and lolled across the comfy chair and looked up at the teacher, his hair and head thrown back. He paused for a moment clearly about to make a profound statement and quoted his line that made me name him Big Trev. 'How Sor,' he drawled, 'it's not the length of mine, it's the thickness: Its huge man.'

It stopped Mr Purvis in his tracks again as it would most normal human beings. However, some of us just nodded and shook our heads at the great lad's profound statement as this utterance was not unknown to some of us. It had first been told to us one night in Shiney Row Club by his much older vivacious girlfriend who told an astonished and sexually naive couple of teenage boys and girls that she had an operation for a vaginal stretch to supposedly take his huge organ. She was a lot older than our girlfriends and wise in the ways of the flesh, unlike us. She talked a lot about things which our girlfriends had only read about in *Lady Chatterley* at O level. Her body was as endowed with assets as much as Trev's pants professed to be and she loved to show them, top and bottom, much to the angst of the lads and the annoyance of our girlfriends, who looked visibly distressed at the mention of *vaginal stretches*. Most of our girls had yet to try or master using tampons never mind some huge tunnelling or boring device that would widen and pave the way for Big Trev and his mythical organ. Nights in the Club with Big Trev's lass were special, if not always sexually accurate.

And that's why he was named Big Trev so let's go back to the story of maniacs at bus stops. Trev and I were drinking in the *Washington Arms* in Washington Village that Christmas Eve and were pretty drunk. I was under age, Trev, a bit older, was just eighteen. The *Arms* was our school local from our time at the Grammar school up the road and they were pretty lenient with school kids who looked like sixth formers. Unfortunately we got spotted by a gang of lunatics who were annoyed that Big Trev was pinching the lights off their village Christmas tree while I wandered off innocently to the bus stop. Cue Big Trev legging it off down the road and me being caught in maelstrom of fists and boots. I was only saved from the joys Christmas in A &E because one of my assailants recognised me from playing football with him. And football helped in similar circumstances not long after.

I had gone with a lad from Shiney called Eddie Emms to Sunderland town centre for a few beers and hopefully to track down some female company. I was still well under eighteen, and Eddie two years older, well-dressed in his skin head apparel - his *Sta Press* trousers, *Ben Sherman*, brown brogues and a *Harrington* jacket. What I didn't notice was that he was also wearing a small Newcastle United football badge in his *Harrington* collar. This was to prove a little problematical.

We ended up after a couple in *The Bee Hive* and *Borough* pubs around Park Lane bus station and then in the pub called *The Upper Deck*. There were the usual lads standing around drinking and looking for bother, mostly skin heads of some sort. I needed to go to the toilet so I went, off leaving Eddie trying to encourage two young girls with very short miniskirts to share our stimulating company. I was zipping up when this very large, shaven-headed lad came in, closed the door and staring at me aggressively asked what two Mags (Newcastle supporters) were doing in his town. I thought, *here we go again, another night of joy and lost teeth*. Almost as quickly I wondered why he thought we were Newcastle United fans. Rather than try to get the first blow in, which experience had taught me was often the only course left to you in these circumstances, I thought the better part of valour was to maybe talk my way out of this and I asked aggressively, why he thought that and he then drew my attention to the badge on Eddie's Harrington.

Now I knew Eddie was indeed a Magpie but I had never thought he'd be stupid enough to wear a badge on a Saturday night in Sunderland. *This is going to take some talking our way out of, the stupid bastard* I thought. Maybe the good Lord took some pity on me or maybe I'm just a lucky bugger for this huge hulk of a lad looked at me clearly puzzled and he asked, 'I've met yeah before haven't I? A couple of weeks ago in Durham? At the Athletics wasn't it?'

I looked at his large ginger shaved head and staring eyes and I too remembered the moment we'd met. It was difficult to forget and I've never seen anyone do what this mad man did then or ever again. I was throwing the javelin and discus at Durham Athletics Schools championship and was standing with my fellow team mate, a shot putter, Paul Stangrome, from Fatfield, a very large, fit boy who played centre half with me in the Chester Boys football team. Up walked a similarly girthed but squatter boy with a ginger shaven head with a shot putt clenched in one hand. He came right up to Paul and stared him in the face threateningly. He and Paul stared at each other for a few seconds and the other lad stepped back and then threw the shot put into the air. As it followed Newton's law of gravity and started to fall to earth he launched his huge neck forward and head butted the 7.2 kg (16 lb) steel ball which, following Newton's first law of motion and with much more inertia than a human skull, continued falling to make a large dint in the muddy earth. The boy's head understandably stopped dead where it had impacted the ball with a dull cracking sound of bone crunching and yet the skinhead glared at Paul with no look of particular pain or fear on his face, twisted his mouth and spoke. 'I'm from Sun'lund and I'm hard and I'm gonna win this shot putt: **** yeah.'

He walked away swaggering, from arrogance, madness or brain damage - I never could tell which. He did win too! I think Paul had decided that football was safer. I was pleased he didn't compete in my events and throw either discus or javelin.

And now here he was again: in the Upper Deck toilets about to throw his shot putt honed head-butt at my new shining teeth. I faked an aggressive stance, trying not to look worried and said: 'Aye I remember you now. You were the shot putt champion.' And hoping a bit of flattery might help, I continued: 'You did great to win that marra, a massive hoy.'

He looked pleased. *Maybe it's worked*, I thought.

He grunted. 'Beat that big mate of yours didn't I. So, are you a Sun'lund lad then?

'Aye,' I confirmed, hoping this would end well.

'Ah weel, that's alreet then, just tak your mag mate out and tell him he's lucky we're not gonna knack him. I'm called The Bear. Everybody kna's me in the town. Mention my name and yeah'll be alreet.'

I have often wondered if heading shot putts left him with some form of altruistic, forgiving centre in the limbic system of his brain. He certainly showed me some that night.

Anyway there was always trouble at the Chinese takeaway, which was a nuisance, because their food was so new and different and I would have enjoyed it more if you didn't have to fight the cast of *Greenstreet*

Hooligans every bloody night. But when we did get it home it was magic so I move on to food again and its wonders.

CHAPTER TWELVE
CHINESE AND INDIAN TAKEAWAYS

The opening of the Chinese takeaway in 1972 changed everyone. It was another cultural revolution in line with Mao's Little Red Book, except here the rules were the various takeaway menu options that you could order, given as Numbers 1 to 72. It changed everything as people who had never ever experienced foreign food could now easily eat it - well a Cantonese version of it. As a groundbreaking social consequence of the era, it also virtually wiped out the late night fights outside the chippy, simply because they moved to the Chinese takeaway. Fish and chip sales were decimated too for awhile but after a brief flirtation with spicier, exotic food, most of us settled down to curry and chips, Chicken Maryland and pineapple rings and sometimes a beef curry and chips. I rarely saw anyone order much else especially late at night.

The lovely lass behind the counter always put salt and vinegar on whatever you got with chips as she obviously thought everyone wanted salt and vinegar on their chips. She'd get the meal from the cook through the hatch and take the salt and vinegar bottles in two hands, always saying: 'Hoh!.Sall an vinnega?' She never waited for an answer and immediately shook both hands simultaneously and threw tonnes of the stuff onto the silver aluminium container full of food and bag of chips And indeed everyone took it anyway, even if they didn't want *sal and vinnega*. But one night being mischievous as he was Les said he was going to have a laugh. She poured the contents of the two bottles of condiments on his chips and curry sauce, looked up at Les and said the habitual, 'Hoh! Sall an vinnega?'

Les waited until she'd piled loads on and then said: 'Nah.'

The poor Chinese girl looked aghast; the two bottles still in each hand and then with big brown eyes looking pleadingly at the nuisance, enquired softly: 'Noh, sal an vinnega?'

'Nah: I hate it.'

Then a bit more angrily our Chinese lass pleaded again: 'Hoh: you take food now?'

'Nah: I want another one.'

The lady looked so sad and put both bottles down. She turned dejected and passed the food through the hatch and shouted something through the window (probably Cantonese for, *Put some saliva and whatever other detritus you have available in his curry please*).

Les smiled at her and waited for his new food. As I said he could be a nuisance at times.

YORKIE
Peking and Bombay Duck

I never ever sat in a Chinese restaurant until the late seventies and that probably was in Stowell Street, Newcastle in Chinatown. I guess that was the first time I ever had Peking duck. Living in Asia you get used to calling it Beijing duck or Duck with plum sauce, but it is still Peking duck to me.

As a result of eating good Chinese food, the arrival of Indian cuisine and living in the big city of Manchester, I decided to ask Santa for a book on Asian food for my lovely new wife. Santa duly obliged and she made exotic dishes from places I'd only dream of going to as a young man but eventually actually lived in years later, like Indonesia, Burma, Vietnam, Thailand and obviously China. One New Year's Eve she decided to make Peking duck with her own homemade pancakes for a New Year celebratory dinner with her parents who were coming from British West Yorkshire to visit us in God's country.

The risk of doing this was very high as her father Derek was quite xenophobic those days, very like my own dear departed father, in that he thought all foreign food was *shite*. He thought that indeed all foreigners should not actually be foreigners in this country but should have *stayed in their own bloody country*. Her parents actually thought the same about me of course as anyone who didn't come from West Yorkshire was a soft Southern foreigner. They were displeased that their darling daughter had become involved with anyone not from their bellicose and stubborn county. I had pointed out a geo-cultural fact to my now dearest mother-in-law during one of our early meltdowns that I actually came from farther North than she did, resulting in being banned and thrown out the house; sadly it became a habitual event for me with my extremely tenuous early relationship with my now darling Yorkshire mother-in-law.

However, by the time of the Peking duck story she had calmed somewhat and adopted me as a token Yorkshireman and they both seemed to like their trips to the beautiful North East. Nevertheless, I feared every trip, because Derek, a very Yorkshire man, loved to come out with me to Fulwell Road or South Shields to buy fish and chips, go to Hendon or Seaham docks to get crabs and even take in the odd half of beer in the local nuthouse pubs. This was strange for me in that he didn't drink. I knew no one from home who didn't drink but Derek was Derek and I liked him enormously and enjoyed his company - well I did until he caused the next War of the Roses every time he met anyone up here. It was always the fish and chip shop where the most awkward moments came. You see, Tommy's fish and chips in Heckmondwicke, British West Yorkshire were by far the best in the world to Derek, and indeed he wasn't far wrong. But the problem was he loved to tell the local chip shop man in Fulwell that Tommy's were the best every time he came up.

'Bloody hell David, have you seen t'price of t'fish in t'ere lad. Bloody daylight robbery up here in this place. In t'Tommy's in t'Yorkshire they are half'd t' bloody price'

He would shout this out whilst we were stranding in a big queue of large men who had left a long afternoon drinking and extremely large tattooed women who had been sent out by their drunken men to get supper. The large shaven-headed and tattooed owner looked up and glowered at me with a look that said that I was about to get a slap with a large fillet of cod. I'd try to talk about non-controversial things like gardening or his small granddaughter, avoiding any mention at all of football, which would have been instant death in the deep-fat fryer given his obvious lack of tact as you may gather. He supported Leeds.

'Bloody hell David!' He exclaimed to all in the shop, pointing to the chip shop man who was draping diligently each fresh cod fillet through the white batter mix. 'Look at t' daft bugger's batter! It's bloody thin as bugger it. Tommy's ist thicker than that. In t'Yorkshire he'd not get away with that son.'

More mumbles of 'Bugger off back there then' and worse from the assembled masses.

The myth that the North East is a quaint friendly, jolly jape, cuddly place for strangers is just that – a myth. Like all Scousers are curly-haired jovial comedians or Cockneys are cheeky, chirpy, and salt of the earth. Ask any football supporter who's tried to bond ecumenically and culturally with these mythical Mother Theresas if I'm correct. The chip shop owner I suspect had little humour because he looked up and glared ominously at Derek and then worryingly at me. He dipped each fish into his hot fat then picked up a huge knife and waved it threateningly as he cut up two half slices of Mother's Pride white sliced cardboard bread. And then when he added the chips from a plastic bucket into the oil pan it sizzled and spat and my dear dad-in-law pointed out another error of his ways. 'Bloody hell David! Look at t'oil. It's that bloody margarine stuff.'

'It's vegetable oil, Derek. Everybody uses it now,' I said looking around nervously at the shuffling, mumbling and increasingly hostile audience.

'In t' bloody Yorkshire we don't. In t' Tommy's he uses real lard. These chips will be bloody nowt like Tommy's if this daft bugger uses that bloody stuff.'

The chip shop man took the next pile of filleted fish out of his back room on a plate and begin to dip them into the batter to begin a another fry. Derek pointed at the man and loudly said: 'Well bugger me David, look! He's not taken t'skin off t'bloody fish. In t' Yorkshire Tommy always takes t' skin off t' fish.'

A small neatly dressed, grey-haired old lady holding her shopping bag in one hand and in the other she holding her pretty curly-haired granddaughter was waiting hungrily to take their suppers back home. 'Well **** off back to Tommy's then, you Yorkshire bastard,' she said.

'What did't owld lass say David?'

'Nowt Derek; it's only that she wouldn't mind trying Tommy's herself if she ever goes to Yorkshire.'

The large fat man standing behind us in the queue heard it all and whispered diplomatically to me. 'Son, you are some canny bullshitter but I'd keep the bugger quiet if I were you.'

I whispered back: 'Aye: for sure mate. His disn't understand man. He's foreign. He's from Yorkshire.'

The dear little old lady who had heard this said: 'For ****'s sake the whole shop kna's that man.'

To return to my wife's New Year plans, given past history I was not hopeful of Derek enjoying a Peking duck. I took some pork chops out of the freezer just in case but didn't tell my lovely cook. I was proved correct and my pork chop contingency plan was very prudent. The recipe for Peking duck required a whole duck to be dried outside for some time. As we didn't realise this until about lunchtime the only option was to hang the duck upside down off the hook that normally held a flower basket on the wall of the house about 6 feet up the wall which faced the freezing cold icy wind of the North Sea. The skin started to dry nicely. At about 4 pm my in-laws arrived from a long drive up the A1 from Yorkshire. They parked at the front of the house and walked around the garage into the back garden to enter via the patio doors which looked over the garden and the sea. We greeted them warmly outside the door and I took their suitcase off them. They both swivelled to admired the view and take in the bracing sea air and I noticed that the duck was swinging above Derek's head in the bracing North East wind and wondered if now was the time to tell them of their daughter's long day of cooking a very special Chinese meal for them.

I didn't have to because Derek spotted the duck above his head. He shouted out: 'What t' bloody hell is that!'

My mother-in-law stared at it in absolute horror. I decided the better part of valour would be to let my darling cook tell him.

'It's a duck, Dad. We are having a special Chinese tonight. It's called Peking duck and I've got to dry the duck first by hanging it outside.'

I looked at his face and knew that this wasn't going to go well.

'I'm not eating that bloody thing. Only bloody t' foreigners hangs their bloody food outside. Foreign muck and hanging the muck t'outside. It's what them black buggers in t' Bradford do and I'm not eating that.' And then, he turned to his beloved daughter: 'Bloody hell lass I thought we'd brought thee up better than that.'

And then he walked into the house and kitchen still speaking to his devoted daughter: 'Put t'kettle on't lass. I hope thee's got Yorkshire tea bags.'

So ended the great Peking duck fest.

Another Yorkshire man whose accent is even more unintelligible than Derek is Yorkie. Strangely he inhabits the same bars I do and as no one but me understands him. I still have to concentrate intensely to do so though despite being happily married to Yorkshire folk. He is a wealth of funny tales if and when you can understand him. Many tales are recalled by his alter ego in *Footsteps on the Teign*. In this epic they relate to the new foreign food that arrived for us epicurean philistines in the 1970's

Indian takeaway food came to Shiney much later than the Chinese. It was greeted initially with massive suspicion as most had deep-seated worries about people from Pakistan and the possible take over of the known world by them. They had little knowledge of the geopolitical and religious divisions of the Indian sub-continent. For some reason the Chinese were never seen in this way, as threat or as foreign. I now know they experienced racism in many places and the stereotype of slanty-eyed, yellow, criminal Fu Man Chu types was common then.

The Chinese brought a revolution in food to a post-war rationed Britain. Few ate out in restaurants and even fewer had tasted anything but rationed, bland, basic food. The first Chinese restaurants were a success across Britain and massively outshone the Italian, Greek or Indian restaurants. The takeaways then spread this food to the masses and most people I knew liked the Chinese people in them. They kept themselves to themselves, bothered no one and were simply just there. There were sceptics who worried about what was in the food and also what they did in their shops and flats, as they never seemed to mix much in the community. As a comedian once said at a boxing match I was sponsoring. 'Have you ever seen a Chinese funeral? Ever seen a hearse leave a Chinese takeaway?' Well, I ask you dear reader, *Have you?* No one I know has. I will leave you to ponder that. The comedian's reason why we haven't is far too culturally incorrect for this book. But be careful when you eat a Number 35.

So *having an Indian* took a while to catch on as a routine addition to British culture but once it had everyone seemed to thrive on them and the Indians, who were actually from Bangladesh in the main, were well accepted. It was some time before I ate a sit down Indian and like the Chinese restaurant in Stowell Street it was not in Shiney Row but in Manchester. I had never eaten Bombay Duck in a restaurant either, but Yorkie had. He explained to me how his first taste of Bombay duck, came about although I've had to translate it into English.

Some years ago, before he left British West Yorkshire in a hurry as a young and handsome lad, Yorkie's dad was a scrap man and a pub landlord of some wealth and Yorkie followed him into the scrap trade, and then into butchery. Given some of the tales Yorkie has told it seems they were both, shall we say, *Jack the lads* in those days and sailed close to the winds of the law. Anyway, Yorkie's dad suggested that his young entrepreneur should move up in society and try to get involved with the rich doctor's daughter who lived in their small town. She must have been either deaf or had grown up with the same accent as apparently she understood and accepted his invitation to dinner.

Yorkie explained that he really thought he'd made it as she was really good looking and more importantly rich. So he booked a table in the top restaurant in the area, The Regent. He dresses well now so I guess he dressed even smarter as a young man. She was dressed in typical

70's attire - a tight suede skirt and suede jacket, leather boots and loose shirt that showed off her obvious assets. She was some looker and very sexy and she seemed really impressed that he'd flashed the wallet and invited her to the poshest place in town. They seemed to get on well over a pre-dinner drink and sat down to order. There was a string quartet playing in the restaurant and the ambience was heavenly.

The menus were bigger than Yorkie's money belt and as he peered through the large embossed card he noticed they did a dish called Bombay Duck. Now he'd never had Bombay Duck but he loved duck. *Champion* he thought *I'll have that* and he ordered it with gusto. His partner ordered her dish and he settled down to woo her with his dulcet accent and charm. The waiter brought the dishes and placed the Bombay duck in front of our hopeful lover. He was aghast. In front of him were two small pieces of what looked like dried shoe leather. He was horrified. As the waiter said 'Enjoy your meal' and turned to walk away he grabbed his arm and shouted loudly so that a few around on separate tables looked over at the pair with disdain. 'Heh up lad. What bloody hell ist this! I ordered t'duck.'

The waiter brushed his hand away and looked pompously at the distraught Yorkshire scrap man and clarified his action: 'I have brought you the duck sir. It's the Bombay duck you ordered?'

Yorkie was unamused. 'Aye you daft pillick it wor duck what I ordered but this bugger smells like bloody rotten t'fish and it's not battered either.'

'Bombay duck is fish, Sir. It's fish that has been dried.'

Yorkie looked at the waiter, and then looked at the disgusted people staring at him and then at his lovely date, who had lowered her head and was staring at her plate plainly embarrassed. He decided that if he had any chance at all of wooing his potential fiancé he had better get on with eating it and try to win back some self-respect. 'Heh up, ah nivva knew that. You bugger's ayte sum't reet weird stuff. Are t'you bringing t'chips with it?'

The waiter stuck his nose in the air and, plainly distressed, he answered the disappointed man: 'No Sir, it comes with a green Mango salad and Balsamic dressing. We don't *do* chips in this establishment.'

Yorkie being an intelligent man knew he was beaten and shrugged his shoulders, looking at his girl who was silently pleading for him to shut the hell up and settle down to try the fishy duck. 'Well bugger it. Ah've paid for t'duck and ah'll ayte the bugger. Thanks lad.' He took his fork and picked at the insipid looking dried fish and hoping to break the ice he spoke to his sexy partner. 'Next time ah'll have t' steak eh love?'

She never replied and watched him as he struggled to put one piece of the 'duck' into his mouth and chew it. But being a true Yorkshire man, he told me: 'Ah'd paid for the muck so ah ayte the muck. It wor bloody horrible Dave. And I never even got me hand away from lass in't car. She just buggered off into her fatha's door and ah never saw hor agen. Heh up, that's romance for yeah Davey.'

This was the last thing our gay Lothario said to me before drinking up his half a cider and walking off to place another winning bet and skin another badger.

Chinese Mushrooms and Yorkshire Cunning

Sit down Chinese restaurants were always a bit easier to find those days than Indians and Yorkie also took his new wife on her birthday to a really posh Chinese restaurant as a birthday treat, *The Mandarin* in Huddersfield. He'd had a good win on the horses so he was flush and thought he'd be good to her. When they arrived and he had looked at the menu he wanted to change his mind as the prices were not what he expected but his lovely wife was so happy that he thought he'd have to think of a way out of it. Where gaining or not losing money is of prime importance Yorkie makes *Del Boy* of *Only Fools and Horses* an amateur. He decided he'd scam paying for the meal and this is how he did it. You should try it yourself when you take your partner out next.

He had formulated his plan whilst his lovely wife was ordering her expensive Chinese dishes. He too ordered the best on the menu and also a portion of Chinese mushrooms as a side dish. He always carried his Benson and Hedges cigarettes in his trouser hip pocket and he eased out one without his wife or anyone seeing him and pulled off the tip and a small portion of the cigarette. When the waiter brought all the dishes they tucked in. As his wife was eating he managed to slip the cigarette end into the mushrooms and mash it up in the dish. They ate most of the meat dishes and rice and when Yorkie went to try his mushrooms he spat them out and shouted:

'Heh up! Tha's summit horrible in t' this bugger.'

Everybody turned to look at the irate and clearly disturbed man. He shouted for the waiter who came over hurriedly. Yorkie took his fork and drew out the offensive object.

'Look at this bugger, it's a cigarette. I thowt ah tasted baccy. Go and get ya boss young man.'

The young Chinese waiter went into the kitchen and came out with an elderly Chinese man who took the offensive item off Yorkie on a napkin and examined it with a chop stick. He smelled the object and picked it up with two chopsticks looking at it for a few seconds and then tasted it. He smiled and gave his oriental judgement on the offending item: 'Hoh! It is mushroom root.'

Yorkie pretending to be severely hurt and distressed with this slur on his judgement shouted out: 'Like bugger it is. It's tobacco lad. Ah'm no bugger's fool.'

'Hoh! Sir, no one smoke in my kitchen. My kitchen is clean, Sir. Pliss, come and look.'

Yorkie took up the invitation and left his new wife clearly embarrassed at the scene and trying to keep a low profile from the stares and whisperings of the other customers. The kitchen was indeed spotless and the owner asked everyone to turn out their pockets and no tobacco product was found. He smiled at Yorkie and tried to appease the *Del boy of 'Uddersfield*.

'See Sir, it was mushroom root.'

Yorkie took the man aside and told him the reality. 'It wor nay a mushroom root lad. You know it and ah know it. Ah aint paying for t'dinner and ah'll mek such a fuss out there in t'restaurant. But maybe we can compromise eh? It'll be a mushroom root if you can see t' giving us free meal. Yeh knows what ah mean lad?'

'Hoh! So you will say mushroom root and no trouble for me or kitchen?' the owner said and then cottoning on. 'I think what happened, the waiter put dish down on another table with cigarette on and it got squashed onto the bottom of the dish and when he picked it up and carried next to the mushroom dish it fell off into mushrooms Sir. You agree, my kitchen is velly, velly clean. It is waiter fault not my restaurant?'

Yorkie smiled at the oriental face that looked hopefully at him. 'Aye lad that sounds about reet and what happened: It wor definitely a mushroom root.'

'Velly Good: Pliss have the meal on me and I buy you drinks after.'

'Thank thee lad. Thank thee very kindly. Make mine a large whisky.'

And so the great mushroom root debate was ended, fairly and equitably. Yorkie and their lass enjoyed a lovely meal and a couple of after dinner drinks free gratis for a smiling friendly owner. When they went outside Yorkie took his packet of Benson and Hedges out to light up a cigarette. His wife saw the one sticking out of the packet with the end pulled off and realised what her crafty husband had perpetrated.

'You bloody villain you. Why did you do that?'

'Ah were skint lass,' lying through his back teeth: as he felt the *monkey* of the bookie's crisp new tenners in the money clip in his trouser pocket.

His wife was pleased he'd thought to take her out even when skint. 'Oh that wor kind of you love. But ah'd have paid as it wor my birthday. You didn't need to put yourself through that worry in there.'

'Eh lass, Ah'd dee owt to mek thee happy you know that love.'

And he lit his cigarette and wondered if he could pull the same scam on the Indians!

The Manchester Plaza and Meat Cleavers

The Plaza Cafe on Upper Brook Street in Manchester was my favourite eating house of all time when a student in that waterlogged city. The Plaza was a greasy spoon/Indian/who knows what curry house. Charlie, or that was the name we knew him by, ran it. I was never sure what nationality he was as he was darker than most Indians and his staff were very West African looking. All he really ever served was Chicken Biryani or liver and onions which I adored and ate if I ever went there in the daytime for food. However, most of the time we went late at night, mortal drunk, as were 99% of all his customers. The place was iconic to those who lived in Manchester in the seventies. The main entertainment was to sit and watch through the serving hatch the staff chop whole chickens into pieces with large meat cleavers and then rive them to bits with bare, unprotected hands with blood dripping off onto their white coats. Charlie's coat was particularly caked with blood and detritus. He always looked more like a butcher or a Rwandan genocidal maniac than the owner and patron of a Michelin star greasy spoon emporium. Needless to say, the odd raging gastroenteritis episodes after a curry didn't put us off. *(Editor's note: Charlie's real name is believed to be Adam and he was Somalian).*

The choice of curry was simple; there was only one - Chicken Byriani. It consisted of raw bits of the mutilated chickens, a pile of yellow coloured rice and either a mild, medium, hot, killer or suicide sauce. Many drunken machos bet each other on who could drink a tub

188

of suicide sauce fastest. Most ended up in the Manchester Royal Infirmary (curiously it was not far from the Plaza; ideal for those needing oesophageal transplants and stomach pumps, also with a great bacteriology department). Accident and Emergency (A&E) was also useful as it would kick off now and then. A & E was for the customers after Charlie and the boys had set upon them with various kitchen implements.

Indeed, one night after attending the Hofbrauhaus, with my mate, we were both absolutely legless and staggered into the Plaza and then for some crazy reason decided to do a runner and not pay. We managed about a hundred yards and rounded a corner where we sat down knackered thinking we had done well. Seconds later around the corner came two cooks (well - chicken mutilators) one waving a meat cleaver, the other a huge boning knife which he waved in my face threatening various dismemberments. A few seconds later Charlie came jogging around and shouted to his mass murderers to stop.

'Davey why you do this to me? We are friends man. What are you thinking?' he asked. All the time the man with the boning knife was jiggling it and his own body in some ritual Zulu war dance.

'Tell him to **** off. I'm not paying,' my mate said, still sitting on the wall pissed, on another planet, knackered and not really worrying too much about the cleaver waving above his head. I ignored him as ending up as a portion of the following night's Biryani was not an option I favoured.

'Sorry Charlie. We're pissed man. Didn't kna what we were deeing. Sorry mate. Here tak the money.' I paid him what if I remember was 40 pence a meal then and he called off Shaka the Zulu and the dogs of war.

'My friend, do not do this again. You are a good customer, we like you. Next time you leave the boys a bonus for their trouble or we might not like you anymore. You know what I mean don't you,' he said and turning to his assassins. 'Come on back to the kitchen.'

I knew what he meant and made a mental note to tip the boys next time. We walked home with no money. It had been a tough day at the football and another close shave at the takeaway. Maybe if we had had a girlfriend with us this might never have happened. Sadly, they never seemed to stay long those days.

And that brings me back to sex.

Menu

```
CHICKEN,CURRY.HALF RICE HALF CHIPS. . .  3.80p.
CHICKEN,CURRY,&,RICE. . . . . . . . . .  3.60p.
MEAT,CURRY,&,RICE. . . . . . . . . . . . 3.80p.
MEAT,BIRYANI.FULL. . . . . . . . . . . . 3.95p.
MEAT,BIRYANI.HALF. . . . . . . . . . . . 2.95p.
CHICKEN,BIRYANI.FULL. . . . . . . . . .  3.80p.
CHICKEN,BIRYANI.HALF. . . . . . . . . .  2.40p.
VEGETABLE,CURRY. . . . . . . . . . . . . 2.30p.
EGG CURRY. . . . . . . . . . . . . . . . 2.10p.
CHUTNEY. . . . . . . . . . . . . . . . .  .25p.
ONION'S. . . . . . . . . . . . . . . . .  .25p.
POPADOMS . . . . . . . . . . . . . . . .  .20p.
```

ENGLISH DISHES

ALL.MEALS.SERVED.WITH.CHIPS.OR.BOILED.POTATOES

```
ROAST CHICKEN. . . . . . . . . . . . . . 2.75p.
SIRLOIN STEAK. . . . . . . . . . . . . .
EGG. . . . . . . . . . . . . . . . . . . 1.20p.
BEEFBURGER . . . . . . . . . . . . . . . 1.50p.
LIVER.&.ONIONS . . . . . . . . . . . . . 1.95p.
MIXED GRILL. . . . . . . . . . . . . . . 4.50p.
SAUSAGE. . . . . . . . . . . . . . . . . 1.40p.
SAUSAGE.&.EGG. . . . . . . . . . . . . . 1.70p.
CHICKEN OMELETT. . . . . . . . . . . . . 2.40p.
LAMB CHOPS. . . . . . . . . . . . . . . .2.60p.
STEW STEAK. . . . . . . . . . . . . . . .3.00p.
```

```
SANDWICHES.                      DRINKS.
CHICKEN.....65p.           TEA. . . .35p.
SAUSAGE....55p.            COFFEE. . 30p.
EGG.......55p.
```

ALL.CUSTOMERS.PLEASE.PAY.ON.BEING.SERVED.
THANK YOU.COME AGAIN

Plaza Café Menu mid-1970s

CHAPTER THIRTEEN
SEX EDUCATION AND LOVE

I loved Christine when I was in the junior school. She lived in Maple Terrace, a couple of streets away in The Gargett and Oliver gang territory(*the hood* in today's terms and as violent albeit without the automatic weapons) so we only went there in the Autumn to burn their bonfires down. I could only see Christine at school never in Gargett territory. Of course I told no one and especially her. Only soft lads spoke to, or played with girls, but she was my first love and I believe I was hers because she volunteered to embroider my name on my school towel bag, a major sign of young love long before *sexting* and the like destroyed the romance.

I remember being secretly chuffed when she picked me to dance with and also sat next to me on a bus all the way to Close House, a residential house where we spent a couple of nights on an outward bound course. On the radio was *Silence is Golden* by The Tremeloes. How you indelibly associate special times with certain music still amazes me to this day. Sadly, it was an unrequited love. She blossomed into a vivacious and intelligent young girl and I always wanted to get the courage to ask her if she'd go out with me as I never lost that first young love feeling but as that would have been too soft, I never did. I was told many years after leaving school by her great friends that she carried that flame for me well into the Grammar school. And now I have lost the towel bag after fifty years of treasuring it. Lost romance and such hidden angst...there is a book in this romantic story somewhere which female literary agents may well for once like...I must try harder to satisfy the ladies with the next book.

As we grew into our teens we got more curious about the differences between us. Sadly for us, in our budding realisation that girls were more useful than chasing cricket balls, they also got wiser than in the early days of initial exploration and love, and so did their parents. In Junior school earlier initial forays into what our various private parts looked like or might be used for, apart from normal waste removal, took place around the Front and over The Hill, sometimes on Penshaw Hill. We played *Doctors and Nurses* and *You show me yours and I'll show you mine*.

Mister Fasham caught me and Davey Aire one night over the Hill with his daughter and gave us both a real clip around the ears and boot up the arse. But this didn't frighten me as much as when Tucker

Anderson and I were invited to see a female classmate's assets in the woods behind the big house over the road from Cosses' off licence. I believe we were ten or eleven as was our female friend from school who having seen our hairless boyhoods took off her knickers to show us a huge hairy thing that growled and then unbuttoned her shirt to show us things we'd only seen in movies like Zulu. None of the other lasses I'd looked at were much different to us, hairless and white. I was never the same again!

The frightening episode in the woods put paid to my explorative sex for some years I have to say. Football, brewing home-made beer, music and wine and fishing took preference. I guess we tried in our own ways to look attractive to girls for some reason with some bizarre behaviour.

School Dinners and Bra Straps

When we moved from Washington Grammar school to the brand new sparkling Usworth comprehensive school, school dinners changed from a central kitchen and food hall to individual house blocks with kitchens where food was served on individual tables and by the students themselves. We were deemed mature and capable enough to act like good team players and world citizens and share out food equitably and without prejudice – the fools.

On our table were three girls, Barbara, Glenda and Sylvia. The girls we called *The Prattletons*, after a mind-numbingly boring and incomprehensible Chaucer or Shakespeare lesson where this Middle Ages term was used to describe incessant, inane chatter. All girls did this of course.

The boys took it in turns to serve. There was a pecking order, like chickens I suppose. All of us got what we asked for and then the girls were given what was left. It was rarely very much. They were girls and they were fussy anyway so they didn't need much to eat. Well that's what we told the Headmaster before he caned us all.

Strangely, we always seemed to be with these prattletons. We sat behind them in the same form class. By now we were starting to get some urges beyond using girls for goal posts. And the girls were by now pretty much in the throes of blooming. Our courting methods were not very refined though and these days would probably get us banged up in a social media penitentiary of disgrace. But those were different times.

The girls all wore white shirts as a school uniform requirement so their bra straps showed through the back. Brian and I had a wonderful courting technique of betting with a Black Bullet or a Pineapple Chunk sweet who could pull the strap as far back and twang it without the girl howling enough for the teacher to come over and clout us with a board rubber or Samurai sword.

Another courting game was to see who could tie the girls' hair to the back of their chairs without them knowing and we'd howl with laughter when they got up to write on the blackboard and the chair came up with their hair tied to it. Even though we did this as a nuisance, secretly in our naivety and ignorance, we hoped this would show that we had an interest in them, but we would never let on to our mates, or indeed the girl. We didn't need sexting or emojis then to show a girl you loved her!

The other game which was a bit more erotic for a young teenage boy was to see who could drop a pencil, rubber, ruler or anything under the girls' desks without them knowing and then slipping down your chair and under the girl's desk to retrieve it. The whole object being to get a chance to look up their skirts and see what colour knickers they had on. I know…I know, it would constitute abuse or harassment now, and always was I understand, but then we thought it was fun. Girls those days wore very short miniskirts so it wasn't difficult. Not as short as they did outside of school as Miss Dot Lawson, the Head of Girls, measured the length of any skirt above the knee. If her hawk eye spotted anyone who didn't have a skirt the regulation six inches above the knee they were sent home. This annoyed both girls and boys for different reasons.

Strangely, none of our own brand of romantic wooing seemed to work with our three girls – starving them, physical assaulting them or sexual harassment by up-skirting didn't seem to make us any more attractive to them. However, it must have done something because one night the three invited three of us to come to Glenda's house to listen to the first Black Sabbath LP. Sitting in the darkness and hearing that church bell ring out for the first time, the hiss of the rain falling and then the deep guitar and bass and finally the haunting voice of Ozzy: *'What is this that stands before me…'*

The skin shivered, hairs on my arms stood up with the dark satanic ambience and one of the girls cuddled up really close in teenage fear, hoping for a comforting hug. I gave a tentative hug, hoping no one could see me in the dark and received a long-awaited first kiss. To this day it was still a memorable night for a fourteen year old boy. Thank you Glenda:

I think they loved us really!

Cherry B and Cider and the Birds and the Bees

It was mid- teens when I resurrected my loins again and fell in the throes of first love. I was fifteen when I realised I had found my first real girlfriend. I'd gone out with a couple of others, had few clumsy gropes and cuddles after dances but the first time I took a girl home to see my parents I knew this must be it. She was fifteen like me and at my school. We were I guess in love then and we explored the ways of teenage couples in ignorance and the pleasure that comes with uncertainty and a little guilt. I had had no education or grounding in sex or contraception. Even Biology then was limited to what Phyla an Aardvark was classified in and how amoebae reproduced by tearing themselves in two. It seemed a frightening prospect for an eleven year old boy! We could only learn by practice and exploration and of course the consent of a willing partner getting which for a teenage boy those days was like scaling Everest. The only time I ever had any sex education was when my father faced me in the garden as I was digging his leek trench out. My girlfriend had stayed over the night before in the spare room and I guess he thought it was time to talk to his innocent son.

'Oh,' he said. 'Son, do you know about the birds and the bees now? How our hens mate and get chicks?' We had gone recently into business with our Mark keeping hens at his pigeon allotment and selling eggs.

'I think I do Dad,' I answered.

'Oh,' he said looking surprised at my knowledge of the ways of the world and he continued, 'That's ok then. So you know to be careful then son.' And obviously happy he'd educated me, pointed to the leek trench and said. 'Can you make sure you hoy the dead cat I got off the street in there before you fill it in. I'm off to the Club.'

And that was the only *off the job* sex education I ever had.

My partner loved Cherry B mixed with Cider. So did all the girls then and so did the boys who called them *knicker droppers* because we were in perpetual hope of the drink making that mysterious event happen. However, much to our annoyance it didn't work as the older boys told us it would but we carried on trying and we drank in those pubs that let us in as we were only fifteen then and well under the legal age. Some knew our age, others didn't

Very sadly my girl and I broke up just before we entered sixth form. Why? I never really ever knew. Maybe we grew up. Possibly, she pointed out some years later, the fact that in temper I'd stabbed her finger with my pocketknife one day when she innocently pointed out with the said digit the question that I had missed out a vital section of my Physics O level paper made her wonder about my sanity. This memory was recalled a few years later when she gave up on getting married and came to Manchester to study teaching in my final year there. It seems despite the digit assault with a deadly weapon, she still loved me! I met her one night in *The Red Lion* in Withington. She was with a lovely, smiling, bubbly, curly-haired girl with the most beautiful brown eyes I'd ever seen and whom I was one day to wed. But that night my old flame and I were reunited. We tried to relive the past but it didn't work. She reminded me of this reunion some thirty years later on via cyber media and how, not long after reuniting, I'd done a runner out of the back door and left her to pay the bill in the restaurant in Manchester. She also reminded me of other various other crazy stunts and that she was amazed that I was still alive or not in prison. It wasn't long after that conversation I asked the same question myself, and received an answer I never expected.

As I sit here writing near the end of the great Bard's *Seven Ages of Man* I am remembering last night and watching the film *La Vie en Rose*, an absolutely brilliant biographical drama film about Edith Piaf with the Oscar winning Marion Cotillard playing the great singer. Maybe Shakespeare should have added one more 'sans' for an age to be added, *sans regrettes*. However, *Je ne regrette rien* is not strictly true for me; there are many things I regret doing. But Piaff is singing that she regrets nothing as she has been given a new start, because her life begins with her newfound love. I guess if my old flame had not met me that night in Manchester and I hadn't been such a stupid idiot with her yet again, then I wouldn't have found my guardian angel, my friend, my wife. God works in mysterious ways.

One of the joys of that early schooldays relationship that still lives on was the trip we both did to Sunderland one night to see Jethro Tull live at *The Rink* in 1972. This was totally unscheduled and only advertised that afternoon in the Sunderland Echo. Ian Anderson did it for a friend

I gather who was invested in the place. But it was a magical night with very few there. I am sure Ian Anderson told the audience that this was the first time they played *Thick as a Brick* live.

Home or Hospital

I went out with another young love for some time while in sixth form. She is famous for her father. I'm sure she is famous for many other things now she is a grandmother and successful woman but to me and to other traumatised men - her father lives on.

She decided to have an eighteenth birthday party at her home near Shiney and invited several school friends around. I was worried as she said her dad would attend but would try to keep out of the way. Now, I had a good relationship with her dad. Why I don't know but he seemed to like and trust me with his daughter (fool). I think it was because we came from very similar backgrounds. He was a pitman and knew most of my family. He was also very protective of his daughter, to a level possibly of psychotic compulsion as a few of her past boyfriends had found out. He was a black belt judo champion, very lean and tall and mean from days and nights hewing coal down the pit - not someone to tussle with. I bravely humoured him whenever I could and never did anything but pat her on the head affectionately in his presence. Sadly, before my courtship a lad from school two years older than me decided to take her out. He went on to tell me and the other football lads in the dressing room on a Saturday morning of the terror he endured the night before.

'I took her to the Washington Arms and tried to get a few drinks in her. She wouldn't budge as she said she had to be home as her dad was waiting. So we took the bus to her place and I walked her home. As we got to the coalhouse I tried to kiss her and get a bit more. You know what I mean?'

We all nodded as by now we did know what he meant and were very jealous if he did get more than a kiss. She was a pretty and sexy girl and my age too. *This old bugger shouldn't be trying, I should*, was my jealous thought.

'Anyway, she's not letting me go further than a kiss when the next thing I know this body leaps from the top of the coal house, all dressed in black and lands between me and her. The body picks me up in some weird hold and throws me right over its shoulder. I land with a smash and think, *This is it; I'm a goner* and then it leaps down on me and gets

196

me in a Japanese strangle hold. As I begin to lose consciousness I hear her voice dimly. 'Dad leave him alone please. He was only walking me home.' I felt the grip lighten on my throat and the body got off me and stood up. It pulled its balaclava off and I saw the grizzled face of what I assumed was her old man. He growled at me, grabbed my arm, yanked me up and pushed me down the street. 'Get your dirty backside to whatever rat hole you live in. If you can't behave with my daughter I'll beat you to an inch of your life. Now bugger off!'

The lad took off his shirt and showed us the bruises. I saw a few other lads who also fancied her grimace, look afraid, very afraid and shake their heads. I thought well that's them out of the competition. For some unearthly reason I thought I would woo and win her and her dad. And I did; and I was host of her 18 year birthday party that night whilst her dad and mam retired upstairs to the bedroom supposedly to leave us in piece.

Sometime after it started a few likely lads arrived. One I knew from school football was a younger lad. He was a big lad though and a good centre half. He and his two mates had been drinking and they wanted to get in. I told them they couldn't and a bit of an altercation started. The next thing I knew her dad arrived behind me. *He must have ears like bats* I thought *or a listening device.* I hoped in belated optimism that he didn't have one in his daughter's bedroom!

'What's up Davey?' he growled through his narrow lips and stuck out his chiselled chin.

'Nowt I can't handle,' I confidently answered, and frankly it wasn't.

'We awnly want to get in man. Nee one can stop us; she invited us,' so said one of the drunken lads.

'No she didn't so just **** off,' I said.

The lads stepped back. Then, I was pushed aside by my possible future father-in- law who stood towering on the doorstep facing off against the three of them. He said three key words after which they slunk away as fast as their pride would take them. I cherish his words to this day. He said to them slowly, deliberately and quietly, opening and closing his shovel-like hands and tilting his head sideways in a deliberate questioning, 'Think very carefully about the choice I'm offering' mode: home? or...hospital?'

They wisely ran off, tails between legs and my possible future dad-in-law grunted, put a hand on my shoulder and calmly said. 'Time the bairn was in hor beed son. You be finishing up and kicking the rest oot and then get yeam to your mam; yeah can see hor at school on Monday.' And wisely, I did.

The big lad met me at school on the Monday and after apologising for the minor bother he said: 'Davey are you insane or something? *Home or Hospital*, he meant it man. Ganning oot with hor is life threatening man.'

'The course of true love runs deep mate,' I replied smiling. I feared not the wrath of the pitman ninja warrior. I had love on my side. But sadly, like most of my first loves, we didn't last and she consequently met and married her own true love. Sadly her father has passed, greatly missed. Rest in peace my old Ninja was finally called Home instead of Hospital.

Thankfully I have had no real run-ins with my potential father-in-laws. Unlike my own dear daughter, whose father has been less than welcoming for some, mine seem to have been in the main ok. Given there is only one real reason men bother with the hassle of girlfriends when they could be playing football or in the bar, it is very understandable to me now as a loving Dad that fathers of daughters should be so very wary of men.

Dom the engaging, frantic and dynamic landlord of his Irish imbibing asylum told me of his encounter with his future father-in-law when he spent the night at his dear Annemarie's house in Cork in Ireland. 'He took me out to the pub and we came in to the house after swallowing a few Guinnesses. When Anne Marie had gone up to bed, the owld fella pointed to the settee and told me I'd be sleeping on there tonight. He then started to walk up the stairs. Half way up he turned and said: 'And now son let me be telling you in case you have any other ideas now. There will be the only one pair of balls going up these stairs tonight and those are mine. Do you understand me now son?'

'Yes Sir, I surely do,' Dom replied, feeling his testicles shrink a little at the thought. 'My future father in law then said,' 'God bless you son and make sure you'll be having a good sleep now.'

The owld fella went to a peaceful night's rest. Dom didn't.

Contraception and Motherly Love

The first thing I ever knew about contraception, or sex I guess was when the older boys would fish strange looking balloons out of the burn as it ran into the sewage works near Fencehouses. These they called *johnnies* or *blobs* or these days they're more correctly called condoms. They took great delight at throwing them at the younger kids, especially the lasses. I had no idea what they were for even though the older boys thought they did and told us in their own peculiar way. When I was much older and a teenager in the throes of first loves I thought it wise not to go fishing in the burn for these strange things that were supposed to stop babies arriving but seek them elsewhere. The Chemist was of course out of bounds, remembering the measure story and girls who worked there. Geordie Corn the barber was also out of bounds as the older men would rip the piss out of you and may tell your fatha in the club one night. So that left the *blob machine* in the Shoulder of Mutton. First problem was to get the money; they cost more than my pocket money for Christ sake. Next to sneak into the toilet without anyone seeing you from the bar and pray no one would come in for a pee. If the machine didn't work it was a nightmare, as I daren't go into the bar and ask Jimmy Elder for my money back as he and the lads would destroy me with the piss take. That would also risk being one more number in a growing statistic of being the potential father of an illegitimate child. There were no more machines in Shiney and no more money in my pocket. No wonder the Sunderland area ended up the highest illegitimate under age birth region in Europe. I believe the car stealing crown of Europe they earned was a vain and criminal attempt to drive around the area's pubs trying to find a *blob machine* that worked!

Buying a condom was never easy. Even as I grew older, lads still took the piss out of anyone putting money in to buy their evening's entertainment. It was not unusual to see lads waiting in the various *netties* across the region as if they were washing hands or combing their hair when really they were waiting until the *netty* was empty and they could safely buy their safe sex (days before AIDS safe sex meant buying a condom without anyone taking the piss).

And as for girls things? Well we knew nothing. All we were told was that they were on their *rags* when they were having their monthly period. What that meant and why blood was involved I had no idea for years. Sanitary towels were de rigueur when I was young I gathered and tampons and the like were still in their infancy. I had no idea how they all worked. The other night fifty plus years after learning of these things I finally found out why the sanitary process was termed *on the rags*. I am now an avid watcher of period dramas (well not the BBC socially engineered woke ones) but ones where the ruling class were white, privileged, bone idle, extremely thick, Tory, Anglo Saxon protestants. Why? I have no idea but I like them. So when I watched *Belgravia*, ITV's adaption of Julian Fellowes' books and the lady's maid said to her mistress, 'You are two days late marm. I have already torn your rags for you', I stirred in amazement at what I had heard and woke up from my few hours doze after a really good session in the Teign Brewery and a stone of Sunday dinner and thankfully missing the Strictly results show yet again. *Ah* I thought, *so this was the origin of the term, rags.* Ladies must have worn rags during their menstruation in the old days. This promoted me to ask my dearest if she'd heard of that as it seems to me that poor people like us could not afford to tear up clothes every month like the posh Belgravia folks could. However, it seems even in the sixties and seventies this practice still actually happened because when she was a teenager her Aunty used to keep her cousin in the house and give her rags during her time which she diligently washed after her period every month. She didn't have a lady's maid to do it either.

Mothers I guess were only trying to help and even in the sixties and early seventies in darkest Yorkshire they tried to keep up the old ways, superstitions and practices, even if they might be archaic but were given with great love. And a lot of North Eastern women in this modern day still practice quaint old customs many of which show their men folk they love them in a special way, an example of which I recall now as it fits into this sex education section in quite clever way, don't you think?

Food and Marriage Vows

The best young wife I ever met was married to a friend I found some years on. I had actually taught her at a Northumberland school when I had taken leave of my senses and worked briefly trying to educate our young teenage cherubs in Northumberland around 1980. This was many moons before I met her husband at real work and was reunited with his now grown-up wife at a client dinner. I had taught her sex education when she was fifteen and her husband always jokingly said: 'Yeah, could have done a better job!' I tried to point out that Biology lessons were not instructions in the Karma Sutra, but failed. Understandable I guess - he is from Ashington. I failed badly at this teaching sex lark as I seemed to struggle to get over to a couple of the more developed girls at the back of the class the concept of safe sex.

'No Wendy, it's not all right if he pulls it out before he comes.'

Prompting a reply from the mini-skirted, full-bosomed fifteen-year-old: 'But he arlways diz.'

When I returned after Easter she was missing. I asked where she was getting a reply from several of my little cherubs in the class: 'She's up the stick Sor.'

I pointed out to my little angels that this confirmed that he may not have *pulled it oot* quick enough.

My colleague introduced their lass to me and my dearest plus two clients and their wives over dinner one night. She had grown up somewhat from the giggling innocent fourteen-year-old girl sitting with the others being taught in my class. I had taken my clients salmon fishing over on the river Nith in Dumfries and Galloway. We were staying in a lovely hotel on the river called Friars Carse. Gerry Marsden, he of Gerry and the Pacemakers and *Ferry Across the Mersey* fame, was staying as he always took a week fishing there. Nice guy, but sadly passed away now.

A lovely evening evolved and the talk was of many things. His dear wife was quite shy as she had not been exposed to business and entertaining evenings and was finding her feet. Both were very broad Northumbrian and loved country life. Both came from pit families and the ways of pitmen and their mother's cooking and service to her family was ingrained in them. Talk moved towards killing things as it always does with my country friend. The other ladies were not too impressed with talk about slaying deer, lamping foxes or catching cod fish and tried to move the conversation onto women's things like shopping in the Metro Centre, dresses, or knitting. She steadfastly stuck to talking about her husband's prowess (not thankfully in what I had taught her) but in killing things and she excitedly and lovingly told everyone in her broad Northumberland twang of her love of the evenings when he had been cod fishing off Druridge Bay.

'Ah just lerve it when he cumbes yeam from fishin. He's cawld and I always waarm uoop a hert bath for him. He hoys the fresh cerd intae the kitchen sink and ah tell him to gan and taek his bath. I then lerv to gut his fish for him and then ah fillet it. I maek his bait for his worck the morn. When I've cleaned and weshed up I gan into beed and ah wait for him to combe in. When he combes in he jumps intae beed and then...' she paused momentarily and smiled lovingly at her husband before turning back to the dinner guests, '…ah let him waarm his frossen feet on me arse!'

The men nodded warmly and understandingly and also with a hint of jealousy and each thought *What a great lass*. Her husband, as he finished his last piece of venison en crûte, looked delighted with his lass's contribution to the discussion and pleased she described her love for him so adoringly and descriptively. The other wives were visibly shocked and aghast. *Heresy* they thought and looked gloweringly at their respective husbands. Each miming, *'don't think I'm going to clean your bloody fish and let you warm your frozen feet on my backside.'*

Keith's very prim and attractive middle-aged wife broke the ice. 'Bonny lass, why don't the women retire to the lounge and let the lads play snooker. Let's you and us have a little chat about men eh?'

Luckily this lovely woman never changed her adoration for her spouse and her charming Northumbrian way. I know that's true as a couple of years after I stayed with her and her husband, his mother and father in a cottage on the Nith. When I arrived from work early evening the men were sat in front of the fire drinking whisky and the girls were in the kitchen cooking dinner. I was greeted and sat down and given a beer in my hand by the lovely mother. I talked all things fishing with my friend's dad and he and we drank a few more drams while lovely aromatic smells came out of the kitchen. I noticed that the table was set with almost a full silver service and cutlery laid out as if we were in the cast of *Downtown Abbey*. I asked the dad, 'What was so special about tonight?'

'Nowt son: We eat like this ivry neet.' And so it was. The lasses had cooked a five course dinner and then they got up at 3.30 am to cook us a full breakfast before we went fishing including kippers and porridge. Later in the ghillie's hut drinking whisky I told the men that I had to leave soon cutting my break short as there had been an emergency at work. 'So please apologise to the girls as I can't make dinner tonight.'

'That's a pity. They were going to put something *special* tonight on for yeah but nivva mind, Fatha and me will eat it anyway.'

Yes: they still do make women like my mam.

I often relate the fact that if I walked in the house any time of day or night and had told my devoted mother that I had killed my wife and kids, all she would have said was, *'Oh dear pet, never mind, you'll need some bait'* and then she'd have gone to make me a tattie pot – all North East mothers were the same by the way. To illustrate this, one day my mother opened the front door to the sound of a heavy knocking. *That has to be the polis* I thought as I lay on the small settee and sure enough it was.

'Regional Crime Squad. We've come to interview your son. Is he in?'

'Aye, come in.' She said without questioning and brought them through to the room and they immediately came out with an astounding claim: 'We've come to interview you as we've had a call that you are the Yorkshire Ripper'

My mother showed little shock or emotion but said: 'Oh, well you'll arl need a nice cup of tea and I'll just make some meat paste sandwiches for the bairn. He'll be missing his tea if you tak him away.'

My mother's only concern was that I might be hungry after that news.

The fact that I fit the profile, because I was medical, worked in Manchester, travelled back forwards across the M62 over to Bradford area each weekend to see my newly engaged dearest and was a *Geordie*, had alerted some grass at my work that I must indeed be the Ripper. The fact I was doing an A level Physics paper, couldn't drive and had never been South of Seaton Carew when he committed his second murder didn't seem to deter our old bill sleuths interviewing me but after taking a sample of my handwriting, taking a look at my wellies and my teeth and then frightening my fiancé by phoning her to confirm I was with her at my engagement party the night the horrible bastard murdered another poor lass, they left me with a comforting thought; 'We know exactly what he looks like,' they told me. 'And you aren't a match, so you should be ok.'

When he was finally caught years later, I was in fact his spitting image.

And that leads me onto the subject of crime and punishment

CHAPTER FOURTEEN
CRIME AND PUNISHMENT

'SNACK'
Doormen and 'The Club'

When not eating tripe and onions or drinking *bull's milk*, gambling or chasing furry creatures most of the men I grew up with were either working or drinking in the Club. Some played sport, some kept pigeons, some dug allotments, others were petty criminals and many fought each other. Shiney Row club when I was a lad in the 70's had a reputation for being a bit *lively*. The various comedians used to love to talk about how dangerous it was; one always used to start his act by saying: 'I see it's harder to get past your doorman here than to break out of Durham jail', referring to the fact that every working man's club had older, normally retired pitmen who monitored those who wished to enter the club and check that you had your official affiliated CIU (The Working Men's Club and Institute Union) club cards with you. If you didn't own a set of fully paid up CIU cards you had to sign in as a visitor and pay a few pennies which paid the doormen in kind a few pints for their dedication. The doormen were known across the region to impose this check and charge visitors diligently and in many cases forcefully. The comedian carried on about Shiney Row club. 'I didn't sign in here. I weighed in…' This was a reference to the *weighing in* of boxers prior to a fight.

Usually fights would regularly break out either in or outside the club, Shiney not being very ecumenical towards strangers and xenophobic to all but the few hundred who lived in the village and even then it depended which street you came from to decide if you were safe from a battering. Strangers were always a target for the local hard lads and even the comedians and singers were not immune!

My father told me of one fine Saturday night in the club during his first years in that peculiar village when the comedian was unfortunately dismissed early from his show. The club always had a concert secretary, a man who was paid by the club committee to make sure the acts on a Saturday night were booked and who made introductions on the stage and close outs at the end of each session of the act. He also paid the act afterwards…that is he paid them off. This particular Saturday night my father was sitting with my mother and friends watching a particularly poor comedian and the audience were getting restless with his performance. The committee decided to terminate the man's show early at the first break and spoke to the concert secretary, Jack Snaith, and asked him to 'Pay the man off when intermission before the bingo and his next act came'.

Jack, or *Snack*, as he was known, was a giant of man. He had shoulders that made Clint and John Wayne look small and fists the size of meat plates. He was known as a very hard man and from what I heard the best fighter in and around the pit villages and towns of Durham in his prime.

Education had passed him by and his days in Shiney Row Modern School were spent fighting and not studying, similar to 90% of the lads who went there. After leaving school he hewed coal all day, his massive frame jammed in a coal face only two foot six inches high, laid on his back under a mile of rock and he was happy to carry out his clear instructions and *pay the turn* off.

As the comedian was finishing his last joke, Snack walked on stage and over to the man. Without saying a word he punched him with a right hander to the jaw. The hapless comedian fell like the proverbial sack of manure and lay sparked out unconscious on the stage. Snack grabbed one leg with his bear-like hand and dragged him across the stage into the recess at the side of the stage. He then walked back on stage took the microphone and told the audience: 'The turn has been paid off and the bingo will start now'. He then had two of his burly henchmen carry the sleeping, horizontal raconteur down the aisle to throw him out into the street. As they walked past the seated club customers my father noticed that no one seemed to care at all about what had happened; everyone was drinking and talking as normal as they would on any given Saturday night in the club. He told me that this was the worrying thing, as he was still relatively new in this zoo, no one gave a second thought to this event; it was quite normal behavior in this bizarre part of our Lord's beautiful world.

It was a simple misunderstanding that caused the comedian's early bedtime and broken jaw. Snack being a simple man had heard his Secretary of the Committee say: *'pay him off.'* At the time of this event and when I grew up in that strange place, most inhabitants had not heard of Doctor Johnson and were devoid of the Oxford English Dictionary: the verb *to payoff* in the North East also meant: *to thump someone senseless.* This verb in this backwater of English grammar was rarely used to remunerate someone for their labour as the committee chairman had expected. English grammar and cross cultural communication were lost on Snack and the alumni of Shiney Row Modern School....and also on comedians.

OUR KEN
Fighting and The Easy Six
Most of the time my Uncle Ken seemed involved in crime and violence. In his youth he was a great friend of Snack. Snack had actually lived at my grandad's house when younger because he'd been thrown out of his own for various youthful misdemeanors. His mother had flattened his nose with a flat iron one day for him being a naughty boy as they say. His nose bore that shape for ever and it was only my family that knew it was not the result of his usual scraps and assault and batteries. As to where Snack slept when my mother, Dad, Ken and he had only one room, I never asked, and it's too late to now, but it beggars belief.

Snack grew very good at fighting and one night five men came from Washington to give him a good hiding. They got off a bus at Herrington Burn and were met by Snack. He promptly knocked them all out and left a couple in the burn and the rest lying in the road and he headed back up the bank towards *The Travellers Rest* pub. Ken who was leaving the pub bumped into Dolphie who was nervously excited and trying to push past him into the bar.

'What's up man?' Ken said to Dolphie as he tried to push past.

'For ****'s sake Ken, lets tilt, get your arse into the bar man, Snack just paid off five lads down The Burn and he's up for the easy six.'

The easy six being the tote double gambling game in the pub where you won if you had six numbers. I gather when Snack was on heat he wasn't too bothered whom he hit next!

Safe Cracking and Golf
In the early days both he and Ken were also inclined to try larceny to supplement their pit yacka's wages so they decided to rob the Golf club at Chester-le-Street and managed to break into the lightly secured club house one fine summer night. They decided that the safe in the secretary's office might reveal better takings than the meagre amount in the bar till. However, not being skilled in the noble art of safe cracking and without access to *jelly* (gelignite), unlike that other famous North East safe cracker, the former Darlington Football Club owner, George

206

Reynolds, they thought they'd steal the whole safe and break it open outside the clubhouse.

Both men were large and strong from hewing coal underground for years and carried the small safe out of the club towards the woods towards the bank of the river Wear where they thought they'd break it open by smashing the combination lock with half bricks. Sadly, the lock and the safe were tougher than the bricks - made only one mile away at Lumley brick works, my first place of purgatory - so they sat down on the bank and had to rethink.

Now as you may gather both men were not blessed with higher intellect - huge fists and lantern jaws but limited cerebral dexterity. Snack told Ken that he was getting sick of bashing the safe so, given his renowned temper, he decided to pick the thing up and hurl it down a slope onto a large Oak tree in the hope of breaking it open. Sadly his aim was a bit askew and they both stood and watched the safe miss the target tree, or any other tree, and roll, with a loud splash, into the flowing dark waters which held The Lambton Worm. I believe grand larceny was given up after that in favour of normal, if extreme, violence and gambling with menaces.

Our Ken used to laugh – a bellowing guffaw - every time he told this story in the Club, normally over a pint of Federation Special beer, dressed like a big-time gangster.

'David, the safe is still there lying in Chester river son. One day we'll have to gan back and try to raise it from the deed. Every bugger at the golf club, the polis and the newspapers thowt it was a professional gang from Newcastle that had pulled off a major heist. It was awnly a couple of daft pit lads and arl we got was thirty bob from the till and Snack ate all the cauld pies left on the bar. Ha. Ha. Ha.'

'Sweet Sixteen' and Pub Singing

Uncle Ken was the youngest of Stripper's family and the only boy. He was a tall, well-built man, with striking blond hair. He had gone down the pit with his father and uncles after leaving school at fourteen. With a body honed on hewing coal and a nature very like his father by the time my father joined the household, he had built a reputation as a fighter, character and hard young man. He also had a wonderful voice and spent a lot of time in the pubs and clubs in the village and surrounding pit villages singing for pleasure or money.

When I was a young lad singing in working men's clubs was still the norm up in the North East. Monday afternoons were the time I enjoyed going to the various clubs around East Durham with the welfare (dole) lads, miners, shipyard and building lads. Our outright criminal friends who had never hewed anything but safes, car locks and post office doors also came along in their *twocked* cars for the drink and the fun. Few worked on Mondays and then they would also take a Friday sick day. As I was told many times by *working men* who took a couple of days off without pay: *You can't make a good week out of a bad one.* Maybe this was why Lady Margaret decided that buying Polish coal, Indian steel and Korean ships would be a better deal for the economy? It's only a thought, folks.

The working men's clubs were full on Mondays for the domino handicap and singing competition. If you won the domino competition it was possible to win enough money to keep you in beer for a few more days and forgo actual work. If you won the singing one too that was a veritable license for a whole week off. My friend Eddy reminded me today that once we won the domino card in Usworth Club when we were in the sixth form and won a pound. We believed we'd won the lottery and promptly started buying umpteen vodka and limes and had a great night in Tiffs nightclub in Sunderland. A pound was the equivalent of ten pints of best beer. Now in most places that is nearer fifty quid; how people survive now I'll never know.

And God knows how I survived the singing. How many times I listened to Tommy Mason, Sean Mooney et al trying to sing: *Riders on the Storm* and *Yippee Aye Yay*: the hell of *Tie A Yellow Ribbon Around that bloody old oak tree*: the absolute murdering of *San Quentin, you've been living hell to me* and *Ring of Fire* and for God's sake that bloody mangy hound, *Old Shep*. Sadly, The Doc's counselling years later in Singapore never cured those memories.

Croker's dad, Cecil Crawford, was more animated than any of them as he looked, and shaped, like Jimmy Cagney and he could mimic the iconic gangster's actions and voice. It took no encouragement to get on the stage and sing. He was a bus conductor and sometimes he'd sing in his full uniform - rather bizarre to see Jimmy Cagney with a Northern Bus uniform and I still have flashbacks now seeing and hearing him sing: *I'm a Yankee Doodle Dandy* pouting and strutting with all the Cagney stage actions but mingling Geordie and American accents, with all the drunken pitmen, villains and dole *wallahs* cheering him on in the beer-fumed, smoke-filled rooms. And remember this was only 1 pm on a Monday afternoon! This memory returns me to Mrs Thatcher's economic model of monetarism, productivity and market forces versus fun and drunkenness. Well, let's not go there, eh?

I loved Mondays. Lately, in our old age, various illnesses and Covid incarceration, Eddy and I have been reminiscing on that cyber lifesaver *Whats App* video about how good life was before we got our pension. He reminded me of a day in Usworth Club when a few men were talking about which was their favourite drinking session. Most said Friday night because they'd finished work and were out in town with their mates, others Saturday night out with their lass and a good Chinese on the way home. Others loved Sunday dinner time and the strippers and the bands on at the club. I supposedly said nowt and one of them asked: 'Davey, you've nivva said what yeah like?'

'I love Monda dinnertime,' I said.

'Why Monday man? It's a shite day,' one lad shouted over.

'Coz everybody is at work and I'm not; same any other afternoon session. I love it.'

I'd forgotten that great philosophical statement but sadly the behaviour it drives has followed me most of my life. Work you can keep it. Give me an afternoon session with crazy people any day.

Safety Advice Notice: Kids, please don't do this at home. You may end up harming your BMI, marriage and career prospects and your liberty.

Yes, Monday afternoons were great and one event was the highlight of the session but only rarely happened. Everyone tried to get our Ken to sing but he was a man of his own ways who took little notice of anyone else. He was a stubborn, hard man and a loner in many things. He would sing only when something deep in his troubled mind or heart said it was time and that was very rare. But when he sang he quieted the whole singing end and grown men cried. His special songs were always for his own mother, or his sister, my mother, the only person he had loved he told me years after. The songs were: John McCormack's *Silver Threads Among The Gold,* the haunting *Danny Boy* and his iconic song *Sweet Sixteen.* I saw and witnessed hard men crying at his voice.

When he was a young man he was spotted by a talent agent or someone like that, I really don't know who, but he was asked to go to London to sing in a nationwide talent contest. I guess this was a post-war X Factor or American Idol equivalent but without bloody Simon Cowell: heaven it must have been. Ken won the competition and was offered the chance to make two vinyl, long playing records (LPs for the historically challenged). He cut *Sweet Sixteen* and *Danny Boy*. He won a hundred pounds, in those days a fortune, and received an offer to go to London for voice training and a potential career in music. He returned with his records a proud man but to a morose welcome from Stripper who took money off him for his board and for the greyhounds keep. He told him he would not support his costs or life in London if he left and he'd physically stop him as the house needed Ken's board and lodging money. By now though Ken was quite capable of fighting Stripper man to man so this threat was an idle one but Ken had more pressing matters on his mind than bettering himself.

Sadly, Ken was similar to his father and was more interested in spending the money on the greyhounds and beer, which he duly did. He threw away most of his winnings within weeks on the dogs, racehorses and also girls in the nightclubs of Newcastle after the race meetings. He went back down the pit, penniless and never took the wonderful opportunity he was given to make a life outside of his comfort zone. He carried on in that couldn't care less manner on the fringes of the organised crime world for as long as I knew him.

After being banned yet again from the North East's dog tracks for *stopping* dogs and fleecing the bookies Ken took up a consultancy role advising the bookies on which dogs had been stopped, switched, drugged, painted, or dyed and taking a cut of the book. He also worked for Joe Lyle, a well-known bookmaker advising on both dogs and horses. Through these activities and his regular nightclub and fighting activities he was always on the periphery of Newcastle's underworld.

He spent time at nightclubs across the North East and was involved in some way with the underworld characters in them. I never ever found out what he was up to as he never talked about whatever work he did. He was certainly involved with the fruit machine mafia at the time and he always said he knew more about the murder of Angus Sibbet, the fruit machine oligarch, found shot in a car at Hetton-le-Hole, and the other players in that story, Luvaglio and Stafford. It has gone to the grave with him though.

Money Belts and Tinned Salmon
Our Ken was always well dressed. He came over to our house every Sunday for his dinner after he moved to Newcastle when Auntie Babs left him. The day she left he had the door locks changed. Dad tried to

reconcile them but Ken had little reconciliation in him and he never saw her again. He had a hard heart as I've said. In the seventies, my cousin became really depressed when his wife left him. Ken's new wife had gone around to see him and had found him lying in the house with the gas switched on. She saved him.

'The daft bastard; He gets lucky and the wife leaves him and he still tried to top himself. How lucky can you get? She ****s off and you then gas yourself. He should have been on the hoy celebrating. I told our lass she should have left the stupid bugger in the oven.' Ken said this whilst swallowing a pint to an assembled audience of other dole wallahs, thieves and vagabonds in the Club who howled with laughter. This was his sister's son he was talking about.

Ken always brought my mam several tins of ham and salmon every week as a thank you for his dinner. Tinned salmon those days was a massive luxury. My Mother used to keep them in the bedroom wardrobe. I never knew why she didn't keep them in the pantry. It wasn't until the seventies I realised that he knocked them off the local supermarkets. It was the same with his suits, shoes, shirts and Crombie coats. He used to go in with an old suit on and take the new stuff into the dressing room and then walk out fully suited and booted. His favourite shops were *Joblings* and *Binns* in *Sunderland* and *Fenwicks* in Newcastle. Everyone thought he was minted and spent hundreds on his dress. I knew different.

Every Sunday he'd ask me to write his love letters. He would bring the latest cutting from the Personal Column of the *Newcastle Chronicle* and show me the advertisements from women who had written into the paper seeking soul mates. I wrote his replies as he could hardly read and write apart from betting odds and betting slips.

'Davey, look at this one man. She lives in Gosforth; that means she's posh and must be minted. She will have hor own hoose. Write a letter back for me son. Tell hor that I'm a single man, have a hoose, car and work as a bookmaker. I'll take hor to the pictures in Newcastle.' Or: 'David read this one son', and he'd give me a letter that some other unfortunate woman had replied to my previous week's love letter.

'Bloody hell man I've struck lucky here man. She lives in Jesmond, works as a chemist and has hor own car and hoose. Bloody great and she's given me a phone number. I'll carl hor when I get back yaem from the pub.'

And so it was, he'd meet these women and some would actually stay with him past the first date and then I'd ask how as it all going when he came for his Sunday dinner. Inevitably, they didn't last. Whether they realised his ways or he realised they didn't have enough money, I never knew. He did marry one however, hoping that her parents would pass quickly as they lived in a very expensive posh house in Cleadon Village. To his eternal grief, they outlasted his marriage!

He kept seeking his holy grail of a partner that would fund his lifestyle right into his seventies. Supermarkets were his favourite hunting ground and he'd pick up likely ladies trapping them with his looks, dress and lies. And one day he seemed to have found his perfect partner. We'd been to a Saturday match and after the game I'd popped into a pub outside Vaux brewery in Sunderland, *The Brewery Tap,* with Les and Eddy. Sadly both the brewery and the pub have been knocked down now. I saw our Ken sitting with a lady at which point I had not spoken to him for about four years. Sometimes he took the huff for the slightest offence with anyone and when the family had upset him he simply disappeared from view. I did hear that he had done some time in Durham Jail for using a knuckle duster on a man from the same family that Uncle Tom had the feud with in the club which my father witnessed all those years ago. Vendettas with Ken were never forgotten.

That night he greeted us and asked us over. He gave me a fiver from his false newspaper roll of notes and told me to get all the beers in. Then he introduced us to his latest true love, a rather large, elderly lady, not one of the usual well-dressed, smart and slim ladies he had shown me in the past. Over a few beers we see he's cuddling his lady, or prey, all the time. This was also unusual as he'd never shown any love or physical affection in him before.

After another drink they explained the story of their romantic meeting. The lady had come up to Sunderland on holiday from Somerset (I know, I know - you Southerners are thinking who the hell would come to Sunderland from Somerset, but the beaches and the craic actually are marvellous - as we say here; it's lush! Try YouTube: *Visit Sunderland Today*) and Ken had trapped her in his favourite hunting ground, Morrison's supermarket at Seaburn. He had noticed at the checkout that she had a bank book and large purse in her handbag and when he had invited her to a slap-up lunch, she had paid for the round of drinks and bags of crisps in Whitburn club. After this

212

wonderful romantic first date she had come up to Roker a few times and now they had decided to get married. Ken sold his old marital two–up, two–down, ex-council house home and was moving down to Somerset. This was amazing. As she stood to go off to the bathroom, Ken placed his arm around her and gave her a peck, whispering gently to his wife to be: 'Divn't be too long pet. Ah'll miss yeah.'

I looked at Eddy, aghast at this behaviour. *Bloody hell he's turned soft* I thought. Eddy shook his head in sorrow at the thought and took a long sup of his *Double Maxim* in consolation. Maybe he'd found love at last. But we should have known better

Ken waited till she had closed the toilet door, leaned over to us and grabbed her handbag. He opened it and took out a building society book and a bank book. 'How man lads, look at how much she's got in here man. Five grand in one and ten in another and that's awnly two byuks. She's got wedge all ower the place and she's got a mansion in Somerset. She norsed an owld millionaire and he's left hor all the money and the hoose man. I've made it lads, moving down South and a life of luxury.'

Well, well, I thought *he may well have done it this time.* His next wife-to-be came back and he gave her a huge cuddle as she sat down.

I turned to whisper to Eddy, 'Bloody hell, Eddy, I've never seen Ken cuddle anyone. It must be love.'

Eddy took a large swallow of his beer and shook his head, looking at me as if I was daft in head. 'Davey man, get ******** real. He's not cuddling hor man, he's checking for hor money belt!'

And so it was Ken sold up and left the area for the first time since he'd left for London all those years ago to win the singing contest. I never heard from him for three months. Then one day I went into the Club and there he was suited up, buying drinks for Con and Mason and the other patrons of the Star Wars bar, laughing and enjoying himself. It took a while to ask why he was back before he told us his sad story.

It seems that when he went down to the mansion his new wife had a couple of sons who quickly sussed him out. It also seemed that his new partner was cannier than he'd realised because the family of the millionaire she had nursed were challenging the validity of her legacy. The sons were also very *Ken-like* and did not want someone else capitalising on their new-found wealth. After a month of hell, with no club, no pub and a woman he had married only for her wealth, 'I looked at hor drunk lying on the beed in hor basque and thowt, *I'll strangle the bugger and picked up me tie.* But then I tossed my head back, threw me tie away and laughed, *Ha..ha..ha,what a daft twat I've been.* So I packed my bags ordered a taxi, stole her purse and headed back. I'm staying at Ernie's house in the town. I've nee house, nee money and nee job…ha. ha, what a daft bugger.'

And pulling his last tenner off his newspaper bank roll: 'Here, get the beers in Con! Let's gan to the canteen at the Yard after and I'll buy youse arl dinner.'

And we all laughed and the merry go round started all over again.

Nut and Byut and Robbery without Violence

As I may have mentioned Ken was what you would call these days a wind up merchant. He loved to play jokes on his mates. His favourite was to treat to a good meal the likes of *Nut and Byut,* Con and Mason, Sean the Mackem gypsy, none of whom ever had any money except what they'd acquired through the dole or other non-legal means.

Ken was always dressed like a gangster with smartly cut, fitted suits, camel hair Crombie coat, leather shoes. He also carried a roll of money that would choke a gallower or cuddy (pit pony) which he would pull out and peel off five pound notes to buy the rounds of beer. The dole and villain lads' eyes would be like organ stops at the size of it. Only I knew it was all rolled up newspapers with a couple of fivers on the outside.

After a session in the Club our Ken would invite the lads down to the Philadelphia Engine works canteen and buy them all a slap up grill. Half way through eating his, he'd go off to the toilet, calmly walk out the back door and jump on a bus to go for more drinking in Sunderland or Newcastle leaving the impecunious lads to argue with the canteen's staff as to why they couldn't pay. He had done this several times but the lads had never learned. One time he offered to take the newly released *Nut and Byut* to Sunderland on a recent freedom from Durham Jail celebratory piss up. 'I paid for the daft bugger most of the afternoon in a few bars. We met my mate Ernie Berwick and old Tommy the other boxer in *The Railway Club* and did a few horses. *Nut and Byut* was pissed by now and skint of course. So as we walked up past the Jewellers in Fawcett Street back to *The Bee Hive,* I told *Nyut and Byut* why not gan in and try and pinch a ring we could sell in *The Borough.* I stood outside. He went in and asked to see the tray of gold and diamond rings in the window as he said he'd seen one he liked.

214

The stupid shop assistant opened the window and brought the tray with the rings on to the counter. *Nut and Byut* said could he have a closer look, so the lad handed the bugger the tray. He then turned and ran out the door. He passed me and shouted, *Haway Ken let's tilt* as he ran up the street. I thought *bugger that* and stood looking through the window as if I was shopping. The shop assistant came running out shouting and screaming, but *Nut and Byut* was way gone by then.'

Ken laughed and laughed and then chuckled, saying, 'Who the hell would give *Nut and Byut* a pile of gold rings for ****'s sake. The clip of him! Ha....Ha....Ha...Bet that daft sales bloke gets fired for that. Ha. Ha. Ha.'

Indeed, the lad couldn't have been particularly street wise for sure. *Nut and Byut* had a shaved cropped head, an unshaven chin, broken nose, few teeth and dressed like a tramp; he also smelled of several hours of Vaux and Newcastle ales down his neck. Without stereotyping our disadvantaged felon, only a fool would give someone like our *Nut and Byut* a tray of precious gems and metal worth thousands.

Sadly, *Nut and Byut's* battered, misshapen, ugly old lag's face was well known to the local old bill and he was lifted late on trying to pay a taxi driver with a ring which brought his brief period of freedom well and truly to an end. So the sales lad may well have survived this lesson. I do hope so. We all have to learn. And I believe Paul my friend did.

EDDY KELLY
Amon Düül II and Heart Attacks

Paul was a school friend from Penshaw who was a character and he was also famous for nearly giving a Penshaw man a heart attack with his art and with the music from the weird and progressive German rock band *Amon Düül II*.

One night he climbed up a tree in Penshaw village graveyard, next to *The Ship* pub. He took a tape recorder and a macabre and terribly frightening dummy he'd made with its twisted ghoulish face painted with luminous paint. He waited for a person to come out of the pub, probably pissed and wandering their weary way home through the graveyard. Unfortunately the first man who wandered his weary way home was old and of dodgy cardiovascular health. So when Paul switched on the weird, ghostly droning of our German progressive band, *Amon Düül II* (probably the album *Phallus Dei* for music afficionados) the man became frightened and catatonic. When Paul

215

dropped the dummy down from the tree with his torch on the luminous ghoul's face, the old man collapsed. Luckily, someone came through the graveyard and revived our poor unfortunate geriatric but Paul was summonsed to appear before the magistrates.

Eddy Kelly was the chairman of the bench that day. Eddy was a great family friend and was to become a mentor in ways to me when my father died. Eddy liked a drink and he also liked to drive. It was a bit incongruous that Eddy would sentence people for drink driving after a few whiskies on his cornflakes and then drive back to the Club for quite a few more. But heh folks - that was some time before social enlightenment.

The afternoon after he had sentenced Paul, he arrived in Philadelphia Comrades Club about 1 pm. I was in the lounge with a couple of mates. Eddy ordered a whisky and a half of Federation Best Bitter and sat down with us young lads.

'David, that friend of yours has been up in front of me today. The curly-haired one we met a few weeks ago,' he began. I had introduced him to Paul over a few beers some weeks before his visit to the beak. Not legally compliant you may say, but Eddy knew most of the villains he sentenced personally anyway. I hoped he could help Paul and prevent him getting sent down if things went bad.

'Dear me! How we laughed in the retiring room after the case. Luckily I didn't have the ladies from the shires with me but a couple of the old lads.'

Eddy always referred to Conservative party members on the bench with him as *the ladies from the shires*. Eddy was a Labour party man. He was a councillor and soon to be Vice Chairman of Tyne and Wear County council. He was in line to become our next Member of Parliament. He was of Irish parents, a strong Catholic and defender of the working class. He was not too keen on Tory ladies from the shires.

'Bloody hell David, that Paul is some artist. The effigy was so real. When the clerk hung it up we nearly had a heart attack looking at it. Poor Bob the victim and the witness shivered in the court and staggered a bit even then, months after at the memory. I thought he was going to have a heart attack again. And what the hell that music was..it was something like out of Dante's Inferno.'

He took a long drink of his beer. 'We retired and laughed. I told the other magistrates we can't do much to the lad as he has no form and what the hell, he might end up a famous artist or in movies or something. So we agreed to bind him over with a three pound fine. When we came back I gave him the fiercest bollocking I could.'

And he quoted it. 'You are guilty of frightening an old man almost to his grave who had fought for his country. You are facing a prison sentence and a life of ruin for a future. However, we feel you are truly sorry and understand the wrong you have done to this poor man and only because of your contrition; we are going to bind over to keep the peace for one year with a three pound fine. Now leave the court and pursue your artistic talents to a more profitable and compassionate end. You are dismissed.'

Eddy used to sentence compassionately in many cases, especially if he knew the circumstances of the perpetrator, which a lot of the time he did as he lived in a Fence Houses council estate amongst the local populace in work and play. He knew and was known in most clubs and pubs around the County, especially the Fencehouses and Houghton-le-Spring Clubs. With most juvenile crime he knew the lads' fathers and sometimes used that in his decisions on sentence. One time after a morning session at the magistrate's court he told me over a few whiskies of a lad from Rainton whom *the ladies from the shire* wished to fine over hundred pounds for some petty crime.

'David, I told them, what is the point. I know the family has no money. He will have to go and steal it and then probably end up in youth detention and then probably jail. I told them I know his dad, a good hard working miner and I'd see him in the club and put the fear of death into him. Tell him that he will have to pay up personally and that his lad will end up in Durham next time.' He drank his whisky and picked up his half of beer. 'So we fined him five pounds and bound him over. I saw his dad that night in Houghton Club. He was pleased I'd helped his lad and bought me a beer and promised to sort him out. Sure enough he did by giving him a clout and fixing him up labouring with his bricklaying mate. The lad has never been up in front of us since.'

JACK KELLY

Not long after this episode it was Christmas Eve afternoon and I was in the Comrades' Club at Philadelphia with a few friends and Eddy's older brother Jack; a wonderful man; but even as a small, wiry, diminutive seventy-year-old he had a tendency to extreme temper and occasional violence. Jack had worked down the pit all his life and had

217

cared for his disabled, wheelchair-bound, wife for over forty-five years as she had had a stroke only a few days after their wedding. He stuck to his caring routine hell or high water. When I knew him he'd retired but up till then had never missed a day's work or a session in the club. Every night after caring for Norah, he'd leave at 7.30 pm and arrive at 7.45 pm, leaving the Club lounge promptly at 9.30 pm. Weekends it was 11.00 am leaving home on Saturday and returning 12.45 pm while on Sundays it was 11.45 till 1.00 pm. He also never missed a Mass or Holy day and a most conservative man (with a small *c* of course) in his manners and clothes. He always wore suit and tie and a flat cap. But he was rabid Labour in his politics and needless to say in later years Mrs Thatcher was the subject of Jack's considerable angst as was his own brother most days. It was hard to tell who he wanted to wage war on the most, our Lady T. or his brother.

The brothers were very different in their characters, Eddy had been in the Army from 1939 to 1946, having spent the year after VJ day in Palestine. He had moved on in life through politics, was widely travelled and read, and could be very pompous and officious when he wanted to be to some people. Jack was simply a down to earth pitman who never left Norah's side or the village. So many times their personalities clashed and with the Irish in them it often came to blows. When Jack, about seventy years old then, tried to *bottle* Eddy one night in the club, they were both barred. This was a bit of a problem as Eddy was Chairman and Jack a Committee member so they actually had to bar themselves. Who needs the United Nations - peace and democracy. Clubs and Committees were much more important than the legal fraternity or judiciary in my day and Banty Bailey was the Lord Chancellor of this Supreme Court and we'll come to him shortly.

Anyway when Jack died Eddy was still overcome with grief despite his near exsanguination by his brother with a broken Fed Special bottle but he chuckled throughout the drunken wake at Jack's final legacy to us all. During his funeral mass, Jack's personal request to the priest was that his wish to be carried out of the church to his burial place to the song, *The Lord of the Dance*. Given his ultra-conservative Catholicism and rabid hatred of popular songs and culture, this was his final throw of the *well you never knew me and you'll never get the better of me ya bugger* to his brother. We all drank a bottle or two of whisky to the cantankerous old bugger who on his final farewell did not *look back in anger* but was called home in dancing joy.

Club Committees and The Dole

I was enthralled with the politics of the Club, the social hub of the area in the seventies. These were the heady days of the Edward Heath government, the first miners' strikes, power cuts, the Red Brigade, PLO, and OPEC. The Committee in the sixties and seventies seemed to have more power than any union, political organisation, terrorist group or my even my old mate, the judge Ted Kelly. They could suspend you, ban you *sine die*, arrange loans for the Club and seemed to have unlimited beer tokens (cash) to spend. None of them ever seemed to work even though it was an unpaid, voluntary, elected position. They also seemed to be in the Club and on the piss as much as that other bunch of renowned non workers - the dole wallahs and villains. It was an economic mystery to me to rival quantitative easing or furlough payments.

Banty Bailey was the club secretary of the Philadelphia Comrades Club. He always dressed in a suit and tie and had a tab stuck in his mouth twenty four hours a day. Sometimes he wore a flat cap betraying his pitman roots but his days of hard, dangerous work were long past; as Club Secretary he was much safer and certainly more solvent than a yacker of coal. Poor Ralphie, the steward, unlike some of the bigger club's stewards didn't have a posh car or a horse or holiday anywhere because Banty controlled the club with a hand like a vice. The more observant of us noticed that when Banty paid for his beer, which seemed to be rare, he paid in sixpences. His pockets bulged with sixpences.

Now some less trusting than me wondered if this could be the result of always being in first and being the only holder of the keys to open the sixpence-fed one-arm bandits. Surely not? A club secretary and the Committee using club funds for their beer? Never! I say, some people just don't appreciate self-sacrifice.

BOB SNAITH
Balance Sheets and Annual General Meetings

Shiney club those days had Bob Snaith as its steward, Snack's brother. Bob was as large as Snack but less violent. Unlike the Philadephia steward he did well; it was a paid job with a declared salary. And he drove a BMW, holidayed in Spain and kept horses for his lasses (proper ones not gallowers). This was a conundrum to many members who couldn't afford to back a horse never mind own one and whilst Shiney Club in the seventies could command full houses of 1500 people every weekend for the bands and turns they put on, his salary in the annual accounts seemed to be less than his members earned.

This was a perpetual issue at most clubs. The members always assumed the committee was taking a lot more than they gave and especially the paid staff like the steward. This should have come to a head at the Annual General meeting where members were invited to discuss the annual report. Everyone ground their gums prior to the meeting over what was in the balance sheet. Now, no one understood basic accounting, never mind the intricacies of double entry book keeping or off balance sheet financing: all they were interested in was the salary of the steward and the expenses of the Secretary. I was asked as I grew older to explain this for many a man in the bar prior to the meeting. I knew as much about accounting practice as them probably, but I had *my tickets* (I could read and write and had passed O levels) therefore I must *kna aboot money*. Every AGM the vexatious members decided to challenge the committee and steward at the meeting over their expenses but come the day no one did for one simple reason; they were all too drunk! This was logical because at every meeting free beer was given to members who turned up early before the meeting and in reality that was the reason anyone bothered turning up. Everyone got pissed prior to the meeting and throughout the actual meeting beer flowed. Feeling happy now and not wanting to miss opening time at 12 pm no one ever actually challenged anything and voted them all back into power. I learned a valuable lesson and the other great lesson was that club secretaries were cleverer than most Labour politicians are these days.

Incompetent Burglars and Paint

It was a Christmas Eve when I was educated on how not to pursue a career in crime.

I have mentioned Con before, an icon of sloth and with a magical ability to survive on the dole, as a lot of the lads in the Club did. Con was a family friend who had worked down the pit originally until certain criminal traits were rewarded with periods of borstal and then jail. He had sired six sons who were following in Dad's footsteps. One morning Con who was sitting in his usual place in the bar, his feet eroding the vinyl tiles and etching his eternal fossil footprints in the floor. He took his two year grandson on his knee and bounced him up and down. He looked at me and said proudly: 'Look Davey! Another Borstal boy on the way; the little bastard is following in his Granda's footsteps.' So you can guess the career paths for the family were not those of the classic English ruling class – the eldest son ran the estate, the second son joined the army, the cleverest the clergy and the fourth and thickest, was sent to the colonies. Here on the fringes of Lord Lambton's estates, the choices for Con's lads were - the pit, the dole or her Majesty's pleasure.

Anyway, this Christmas Eve Con had been up before Eddy at the Magistrates Court in Houghton-le-Spring that morning along with his fellow partner in crime, Tommy Mason. Tommy had been in and out of jail and never seemed to be very good at the profession he'd chosen as he always seemed to get caught. He stole the blind box one night from the Club. As he was the only one in the bar at the time, it didn't take *Columbo* to find the culprit. However, this time they were in front of the magistrates for breaking into the Co-op in Shiney. They were now in the bar drinking heavily and celebrating so we all thought they must have got off. Eddy came into the lounge and ordered his usual half pint of Federation Special and large whisky and sat down with us.

'I see Con and Mason are having a good time in the bar, Eddy. I thought they were banged to rights?' I asked him.

'They bloody well were. Do you know what they did?' he replied.

'Aye, they pinched a ton of paint from the Co-op.'

'Aye that's correct. But did you know how the police caught them?' the slightly pissed judge asked with a smile.

'Assumed the coppers knew who it would be; it normally is them,' I said.

Eddy laughed, picked up his beer, took a drink and put it down. 'Yes, it usually is them or their bairns. But this time the police didn't even have to think. The two daft buggers pinched a wheelbarrow as well and they wheeled all the paint back to Con's house in a few trips. What they didn't notice was that they had knocked the lid off one and it leaked. So when the police were called all they did was to follow the trail of paint spots on the pavement straight to Con's house.'

Everyone howled at the poor lads' incompetence. Eddy continued: 'They had no option but to plead guilty. They will go down for this given their record. Anyway, as it's Christmas, I thought I can't send the lads down yet. Let them have the festive season in the Club. I couldn't let the bairns not have a Christmas.'

We all looked shocked; *the bairns* would get very little festive joy at the rate the two were drinking already. And a few of their offspring were already spending time *inside* anyway. As an aside, my dad used to give Con my old toys to give to the boys to help him out over Christmas. I leave you to guess whose car never got stolen or house burgled when both we were growing up. Coincidence or brotherly love, it mattered not. It was a good swap.

Eddy continued. 'So I met with the ladies from the shires in the retiring room and insisted that I needed social reports on them both before sentence. They played hell and referred to their record of a life of crime and that there was no need for reports; they were habitual criminals. But I won the day. So the clerk advised we could bind them over to keep the peace over the Christmas break and sentence them once the reports were written.' He looked into the bar at the revelry, took a large sup of his whisky and concluded the case. 'We came back in and I looked at the two standing in the dock. I told them - *You are the most incompetent burglars in Christendom. You should expect to serve a jail sentence for this stupidity but I will defer sentence subject to social reports. You are bound over until January the 5th when you will return to this court for sentence. During the festive season and at the time, we celebrate our Lord's coming I expect you to reflect on the life of crime you have chosen to follow and realise that you are not very good at it and you should consider giving up your incompetent transgressions and following His path to redemption. Reflect on your lives and spend time with your families at this happy time. Do not break the terms of your bail or I will deal severely with you. You are dismissed until January the 5th.'*

We all looked at the lads in the bar celebrating and Mason singing his awful rendition of *Tie A Yellow Ribbon* for their brief return to freedom and thought that there was little chance of *reflection on their transgressions*, redemption or much time in the family home. Ralph the steward waved Eddy over to the lounge hatch bar and gave him two large whiskys. 'Con and Tommy have bought you them, Ted,' he said.

Eddy raised a glass to the two incorrigible villains and they returned the compliment with two huge grins. Eddy returned to his seat laughing and shaking his head saying: 'The most incompetent burglars in Christendom - one of my better ones that.'

Asbestosis and Compensation

My life has been full of characters, most from Clubs and bars from around the world. Some will say I should deduce something meaningful from that, but in *The Comrades* club there were more than any place - except *Tinkers* in Shiney and *The Down Under Bar* in Singapore of course. Tommy Mason was one character. Like *Nut and Byut*, Tommy was looking for the big steal all his life, and finally he made it, albeit a legal but Pyrrhic victory.

Tommy spent his life when I knew him on welfare or in jail. However, he had worked once. I knew that because he always told me he had a cough from working in Newalls' factory on the River Wear where they made asbestos. He was hoping that he could get some compensation one day for this as the world was now beginning to realise the deadly effects of asbestos and the liability the companies held. Years of idleness and incarceration in various borstals and jails had gone by since then and one fine day I walked into the club to see Tom and the other welfare lads sitting as usual watching the telly and playing dominos. Con, the other master criminal and lay-about, shouted over: 'Heh, Dave, you just missed a good horror film on the telly.'

I replied naively: 'Aye, what was that?'

'Where The Jobs Are!' he shouted to all who were listening as a burst of laughter from the smoke-filled corner containing the North East's finest reluctant workforce.

To explain; those days there used to be a program on Tyne Tees regional television after the local news every lunchtime which sought to show our reluctant hewers of stone and drawers of water where to apply for a job. Indeed, a horror movie to all of them.

Con continued once the laughter had died down: 'Haway man, come and sit down Davey and read this for Tommy will yah? He might need a sick note.'

As I was currently employed in working for my PHD in medical research all of my erstwhile idle-handed or itinerantly working dole-fiddling friends and acquaintances thought I could write sick notes, or medical certificates of sickness. This was the ticket to paradise for them as they hoped I would be able write dodgy sick notes and allow them to take time off work and drink excessively or claim for some form of industrial injury or past compensation from the dole office. It was pointless trying to explain that I had no clinical practice license, so I used to humour them.

This time Tommy only wanted me to read his new letter for him - few could read or write and those that could didn't understand the medical terms and legal things. *The wonders of a Borstal education* I thought. I was their unpaid peripatetic solicitor and doctor. I should have known then where my career would end up.

Tom's letter was indeed bad news it seemed to me. He was diagnosed as suffering from asbestosis and was requested to attend a further medical examination and compensation hearing. I told him and his drunken mates what it contained. Tom was ecstatic, if he'd had money he would have bought a round of drinks, but as usual he hadn't, so I bought him a beer.

I was confused. Asbestosis was a death sentence in its worst cases for many but Tom wasn't bothered at all about the pathology or prognosis - only the thought of money.

Many months later I went to the club again to find Tommy, Con and his Fagen clan all drunk and celebrating. Tommy called out to me: 'How man, Davey, come and sit down and have a drink on me, bloody good news man.'

'What's happened?' I asked, sitting down and taking my first ever management consultation fee, a free pint of Federation Special Ale, from the normally impecunious rogue.

'I've been diagnosed as a bad case and they are going to award us thirty grand.'

Bloody hell I thought, *30k for Tom, that should see him ok for years*.

'What do they say about being a bad case?' I foolishly asked, concerned about the prognosis.

'****** if I kna Davey but I'm ower the moon coz it's bad enough for them to give me thirty grand. Have another beer. Ralphie - get them all in!'

So they all celebrated his certain death.

It was bizarre, but I was young and knew little of any other culture but my own where this behaviour was quite normal in those with Tommy and his like's morality and values. Where he got the money to pay at this stage was a mystery but the post office had been raided the night before and Con's young boys, who allegedly were following diligently in the old man's steps, were also in drinking and smoking and sticking first class post stamps on postcards to their mates in Borstal and Franklin Jail.

Tommy was awarded his *compen* (compensation) and duly began a spending spree. He set up a bank account for the first time. He and his wife both had cash cards and credit cards long before the banks would give anyone with a pulse unsustainable credit facilities and the world would face the consequences. Given Tommy had never worked more than a couple of years and had a criminal record longer than an Aardvark's face, it still amazed me he'd get a credit card and still does to this day. They went on holiday to Spain and when his son got out of jail they proceeded to spend what he could get his horrible hands on and Tom spent every day in the clubs and pubs buying drinks for his new found friends. He died within the year destitute again, money exhausted, landlords richer by far, friends gone and his son back in the tender arms of the law...but he had had his time on the stage, his Andy Warhol hero moment.

I was off to attend the funeral and told my PA that I would not be back to the office after lunch as it would be a good piss up with all the vagabonds in the area that unfortunately I knew too well. She asked who had died; I told her a friend of sorts. She asked what his problem was and I told her he'd had terminal asbestosis.

'Oh dear,' she said, compassionately. 'My uncle died of that. He suffered badly in the last six months. I hope your friend didn't suffer that much?'

I answered confidently: 'No pet, he didn't suffer too much, the asbestos didn't kill him, it was the eight pints and bottle and half of whisky and forty cigarettes a day that killed him. He had another couple of years to go with his lungs but his liver and heart ran out.'

Philadelphia Comrades Club and Ativan

One day I entered Philadelphia Comrades Club to be greeted in the bar by all the vagabonds sat around the corner. Con the master Fagin of them all was sitting in his usual place opposite the bar. Con was well over twenty-two stone and usually came into the bar every morning as Ralph the Steward opened up. Con liked a beer or twenty every day and then after closing time and taking a couple of Ativan tablets (as prescribed by the friendly Doctor for the stress and anxiety of a life doing nothing but drink and sleep) he'd sleep until morning and the pubs opened again. Con had been in his seat as usual from the moment

Ralph opened up before legal opening time which in those days was 11 am. He usually drank the slops that Ralph pulled through the beer pipes when he was cleaning the lines. These came to about one gallon and were in a large galvanised metal bucket and mixed no doubt with cleaning fluid but Con supped the lot. Tin and cleaning fluid had no fear for Con if his *Federation Special* came free and gratis.

Con never left his seat until closing time at 3.00 pm. He drank probably fifteen pints at least a day, most of it free from a couple of his lads if they had been night-creeping the night before and from daft people like me who took pity on him and his other partners in crime. His kidneys and bladder seemed to absorb urine. It is a fact that the floor lino below Con's habitual seat was permanently worn into the shape of his two size 11 shoes. Banty Bailey the Club Secretary used to whine on about having to spend money one day to replace the lino with the footprints. We all insisted that the floor stay as it was as it was a living legacy to sloth, indolence and obesity.

That morning Tossa was sitting with Con and the other old lags looking morose and puzzled. He was a thin, pallid man who never looked well when I knew him and was usually pissed. He had a speech impediment too which was worse in drink resulting in slurred incomprehensible *pit-matic*. Tossa was actually an engaging and simple type of pitman with a kind heart and helpful nature and I really would like to record him in history, for outside of Trigger in *Only Fools and Horses*, no one could beat him for simplicity of character. One day he had issues with rats in his pigeon cree so he asked our Mark in the Club what to do about it. Our Mark kindly answered: 'Borrow Dowsie's Jack Russell terrier and put him in and he'll sort the buggers.'

So Tossa diligently did so. Next day on Sunday lunchtime he came in to the Club looking crestfallen. He always did mind; he had one of those faces that looked perpetually puzzled, as if the strain of being alive with a brain that works as slow as tortoise on Mogadon was just too much.

'What's wrang Tossa?' our Mark asked.

'It's that bloody dog man. Bloody thing ate me pigeons!'

It seems Tossa had thrown the dog into his pigeon cree on its own when he got back pissed as usual from the Club and locked the door and went to bed. Jack Russells are a bit like Tossa but with psychotic tendencies and do not differentiate between small mammals or avian prize winning homing creatures if left to their own natural killing instincts. So Tossa lost his whole flight of birds in one night. The rats feasted on their bloody winged carcasses.

One day someone stole the television from the Club during a period when no one was in the bar. Tossa's response to the Committee man who was telling of the heinous crime to the assembled pit lads at the bar one day was: 'Well it will teach you lot on the Committee for putting it where people can see it.'

So I guess you now understand that Tossa wasn't going to win the Nobel Prize soon but that day in the club he looked very worried. Sean Moody the itinerant Mackem gypsy shouted across the assembled cast of Dickens's *Oliver*. 'How Davey man. Tossa's had some bad news at the Doctors. You kna aboot that stuff. Mebbie yeah can help him?'

Sean was a peripatetic Sunderland townie, now called a Mackem, who turned up now and then and loved to take the piss out of unfortunate members of the gang. He was as dodgy as the Artful Dodger and could be as violent as Bill Sykes, without the bulldog. And he loved to poison Tommy Cutts.

Tommy was an elderly man, an ex-pitman, who lived in a colliery terraced house next to the Club. The house was perpetually without electricity or water as he never paid the bills. He was emaciated normally as he spent his money on beer and tabs and couldn't cook as he had no power. Sean always brought him some sandwiches which Tommy gobbled down as if they were his last meal, which indeed they well might have been. I thought this compassion and hospitality from Mother Mooney was his natural Irish background hospitality coming out of him. Sadly it wasn't of course.

I am told, especially by Purple Al, that I try to see good in too many people, and I suffer because of it, and to prove Grumpy Al's character assassination correct, this time with Mother Mooney I was wrong yet again.

Once Tommy had gone off to his lonely seat at the other end of the bar, Sean laughed and chuckled and told us that the sandwiches were made with *Kit-e-kat,* a cheap cat food. He continued that sometimes he'd use tinned dog food; all shoplifted of course. As Tommy seemed to flourish on his pet fodder, Sean took to putting small ground-up glass to test his latest theory that Tommy could eat anything. Indeed, Tommy seemed to flourish on that as well; so who needs Muesli and Quiche when *Kit-e-kat* and ground glass can keep you subtle and with regular bowel movements. Mind you Tommy didn't live as long as Con, so maybe there is a twisted lesson somewhere.

Back to Tossa's problem:

'What's wrong Tossa?' I asked reluctantly hoping I'd understand him and wishing I'd gone to *The Lambton Castle* up the road instead.

'It's not me Davey, it's the bairns man. Our lass sez their teacher sez we have to tak them tee the Docs as they are nivva iva well man. So we took them the morn.'

Sean with a mischievous Irish gypsy glint in his blue eyes prompted Tossa. 'Tell Davey what the Doc reckons is wrang with the bairns, Tossa.'

Tossa looked puzzled and lost and tried to explain his Doctor's diagnosis. 'He reckons they've got that...what's it called lads?' He scratched his floppy, lank hair and continued his sentence, '...erh...mal...erh...mal...malnutrish, malutrish-eon.'

'Oh,' I exclaimed. 'Malnutrition; that's not good news Tossa is it?'

'Divvn't kna, Davey: We're gonna keep the bairns in the house though. Divvn't want them to play oot with the other bairns.'

I responded to this with surprise. Surely the Doc had suggested nutritious supplements and I wondered what the social workers who would soon descend upon the Tossa household would say about his solution to the child's illness. 'Why? What good will that do Tossa?'

'How man,' he uttered through his slur, 'ah divvn't kna who they caught it from dee ah. They might catch it again.'

Sadly, everyone laughed at the latest Tossa misfortune, drinking, smoking and oblivious to his bairns' circumstances. It was not unusual for this neglect in some families and I guess we accepted that some were just skint and in difficult times and not particularly clued up about life. We grew up with those events all around us. It was the craic that seemed to matter more. Tossa was a good man trying his best and certainly was not an abusive or cruel father by any means; he was, well, not over bright. That's why we need social services.

And by now after meeting these characters you probably fancy a break. And so did I - I actually had to live with them! But in those happy days we couldn't afford holidays...but we did enjoy boiling Hot Summers...

CHAPTER FIFTEEN
HOT SUMMERS AND HOLIDAYS

Jubblies and Camping out

Just as winters all seemed to be cold and icy, summers were always hot and humid. We spent days lounging around the two streets sitting on dustbins just chilling out after playing football or cricket in the heat. The favourite food was sugar and bread and our favourite drink was to suck on orange *Jubblies*. These were frozen orange and water sold in a green and orange twisted pyramid carton. For the mathematically inclined these cartons were tetrahedron shaped. I believe the richest man in the world may well have pinched our beloved *Jubbly* shape for his *Tetra Pak* Empire. I hope he enjoyed sucking them as much as I did. The objective when sucking them was to make yours last longer than anyone elses. So sucking was an art. As also was the art of pouring the dregs of ice cold water down the back of the lasses' necks. God, we were romantic in those days.

Another nutritious thing we did was to eat the tar that was melting on the tarmac road in the sun's heat and to pop the bubbles that formed. Solid new tar used for roofs or fixing roads was a particular favourite. We'd also eat the chewing chum that was stuck to the road as some form of macho girl or boy thing. Black teeth were de rigour then, as was peritonitis of the bowels.

Summer was the start of camping out in each other's back garden; no glamping with blow-up beds, portable toilets, electric ovens and the like that people expect now. Then we had only a single small tent with no fixed groundsheet. It was held up by two poles at each edge. Even in summer we froze. Not that we slept much. Most the night was spent raiding our neighbour's gardens for vegetables and fruit. Scrumping is a polite name - stealing was what we did really. Prized among vegetables were peas and turnips (*nagers*). Fruit was strawberries, raspberries and gooseberries and of course apples and pears. Very few people in the council houses had exotic stuff like raspberries and strawberries and none had apples as that was just an invitation for the local kids to destroy your prize vegetables, like leeks. We would have to prowl the streets at night to raid the posh folks' houses for the more exotic stuff.

I got my arse bitten badly in the Boundary House garden one night when the owner set a bulldog on Paul Stoker and me and he got over the wall quicker.

We brought our spoils back to the tent to dish them out, eating raw peas, carrots - you name it, we ate it. I loved raw *nagers* (or *neeps* in bonny Scotland). I have loved raw turnip ever since. Not this horrible bland insipid coloured stuff that purports to come from Sweden, but orange, crunchy British turnip.

Sometimes we'd shoot the odd rabbit or two to make a stew up and boil it on a camp fire and Les would tell ghost stories to try to frighten the younger lads, so sleep didn't happen. We were all knackered the next day and thirsty so we pinched and drank the odd bottle of milk that had just been left on the folks' steps by the early morning milk man. We would never let our parents know we were tired in case we were never let out to roam and pillage again.

The Club Trip and Egg, Tomato and Sand Butties

Camping out in someone's garden or a field was a holiday for most of us. As a family we never really had exotic holidays. Dad tried to take us away every few years but due to lack of money we took the public bus and went to a caravan at Crimdon Dene, near Hartlepool for a week. For me it might as well have been Benidorm or Dawlish Warren, as I had no idea where Crimdon Dene was until I was well into my twenties and went fishing there. We took the bus as we never had a car. I assume we got the bus from Sunderland.

Some years we'd also take a bus but go to London to my Aunty Winn or Aunty Rene in Paddington. Then one year in 1966 we went to Pontins Holiday camp in Lytham St Annes. This was luxury and something wonderful. I loved it all. The swimming pools, the games, the shows and most of all Dad spent a lot of time with me in the pool and playing snooker and other games. Back home we only fished or walked the beaches talking about nature and the war, so it was so good to share active sports with him. And we watched England win the World Cup there. I will always remember the smoky, beer-smelling room with the huge projected TV screen that I'd never seen before. And who knows one day it will *come home again* before this writer's seven ages of man run out.

Most summers we looked forward to the Club trip. We also had the Sunday school trip which was similar but without the pissed-up fathers.

The Club trip was when men and women and kids would head off on a hired bus to the seaside resorts of the North East to spend a day at the beach paid for by the Club. Well, the mothers and kids went to the beach; the Dad's spent it in the pub or Club. We always ate egg and tomato sandwiches with diluted orange squash and our mothers had Thermos flasks of tea. The sandwiches always had sand in them. Even now when we have picnics anywhere I ask my darling wife to add the obligatory sand to my egg and tomato sandwiches - tasteless without sand.

Mothers always got rented large canvas tents to share between them. It was necessary as the North East Coast was always freezing with the wind howling in. If the wind and rain didn't freeze your bollocks off the sea certainly did. We went to exotic places like Whitley Bay, Cullercoats and Tynemouth which were located up country over the Tyne Bridge a few miles away and seemed another country from us. It took hearing Dire Straits years later playing their iconic song *Tunnel of Love* about young love and the White City at Whitley Bay to finally learn where the hell Whitley Bay was. Another weird place I had thought must be down South somewhere was Seaton Carew. It is *down South* I found out - a few miles away in Hartlepool.

Most of these resorts had fairgrounds for which we all got a few free tickets out of the Club trip fund to spend on rides or games. Even today everyone loves to go to fairground and have a bash at winning that Goldfish or picking up that Teddy bear with the metal grab. The one arm bandits were proper ones then (not the ones now you need a degree in electronic engineering to understand) that you put a sixpence or penny in and tried to get three bells, three cherries, three gold bars etcetera. I also loved the horse racing one where you bet on jockeys…and I still remember the old ones, Scobie Breasely, Lester Piggot, Joe Mercer and Pat Eddery.

Memories of days at the beach either on the Club or the church Sunday School trip or on days out to Roker and Seaburn, always seem to revolve around freezing cold sea and sunburnt skin with *Calamine Lotion* put on by my mother at night. I find this strange as I remember our mothers in tents or deck chairs with more clothes on than a fully *cammed up* Arab lady. They never seemed to be sunbathing. Dad like all the men wore a suit, shirt and tie and flat cap because they went to the Club, never the beach. So I guess us kids must have been left half-naked to the risk of exposure from the sea and third degree burns from the sun. Indeed, happy days for sure, despite the sunburnt sleepless, sweaty lotioned nights in soaked bed sheets with shrivelled gonads that still hadn't recovered from the icy waters of the North Sea.

I once asked Mrs Cain, a rotund cheery lady who lived in perpetual hardship opposite us with her seven kids if she was going away on holiday. She replied, 'Davey I'm dreaming of taking a slow boat to China.' For ages in my naivety and ignorance I told everyone that Mrs Cain was going to China for her holiday. When she, my mam and a few other ladies took all us kids from the streets on the Number 5 bus to Chester-le- Street River (the Wear) four miles away for the day as our one and only summer holiday treat, I realised that her dreams of China, were just that, dreams. And sadly would always be so for that poor but cheery lovely mother when she passed away had never got to holiday past Roker Pier, never mind the South China Sea.

As the years rolled on and I reached my teenage years I had no holidays as I worked the summers for badly needed money and they were not as much fun as when a kid just earning a bob or two pocket money. As I have described working with my brother-in-law, Timmy, either carrying his plastering hod or hauling his crab pots or with Mad Gus in the brickwork sand pit of hell these jobs were a hell of a lot more stressful that the halcyon summers of youth.

Leeks and Broth Monday

Leeks were more important than anything then and all summer they were tended with the care of a loving mother by our fathers. My father won Shiney Row Leek Show the year my sister Sheila married Mark. He had no money for a real present but the leek show provided a brand new bedroom suite. It was the same when Margaret married Timmy; he came third and won a dining table and chairs. Real bonuses for someone who could not have bought anything like that for his beautiful daughters on his wages.

Once I grew bigger I had to dig his leek trench. The trench would be about eight feet long and three foot wide and about three feet deep. In the bottom was thrown anything that had carbon, phosphorous and nitrogen in it - dead cats and dogs, birds that Gussy had shot, rabbit guts my mother had cleaned, horse manure from the rag and bone man - if it could rot and supply nitrogen it was hoyed in.

He also had a water barrel sunk into the ground which was the like of something from a Zombie film. It contained all the rotting detritus that he or I could collect from road kill or shot creatures all dissolving in a mass of stinking, putrid horse faeces. I expected life not as we know it to evolve any moment from the primeval soup. It was my job to take an old tin can and dip it into the seething mass and then use it to feed the leeks by pouring it down the plastic tubes he had each side of individual leeks. You try and get the kids to do that now!

In September the Leek Show was a mammoth event in the calendar of the North East. Two leeks were benched with all the other entrants and many other vegetables in the concert hall of the Club. Each leek could be no more than six inches long and with no tear or bursting of the white part and its green flags intact. The winner was the pair with the largest total cubic inches of the white leek bottoms. The prizes were, in relation to wages, very substantial and the leeks were protected throughout the growing season by many means from devious and criminal acts. Leek slashers were as reviled as paedophiles. These slashers were people who would come at night and cut the bottoms of the leeks, hence destroying any chance of winning. My father used to ask us street lads to camp out in the garden with air rifles to *shoot the buggers if they try to do mine*. We'd get a tanner or a shilling for the work we spent on chocolate smoking kits or the like.

The Monday after the Leek Show, the Clubs would put a broth made from the leeks and the other vegetables shown on for anyone who came in the afternoon. As usual it was packed, with the usual domino handicap's and club singing competitions. They were marvellous times.

Rex the Dog and Barley Wine Ice lollies

My father was actually more worried about his son-in-law Timmy eating his leeks than the threat of slashers. This raw vegetable eating habit, after getting massively drunk after work every night and turning in late, did little for my sister's humour or eventually her marriage. Sometimes Timmy drank a lot of *Barley Wine*, a drink you hardly see these days, but it was like a dense Belgium beer if I recall, massively potent in small doses. In the summer months my mother would get up in the morning to find that Timmy had made *Barley Wine* ice lollies in her fridge the night before which he'd suck on the way to another day laying bricks. A novel way to actually drink and drive to relieve the hangover.

My sister hoped getting a dog might help him - and her. Sadly the dog was as crazy as Timmy. It was called Rex and was a cross between a Border collie and a crocodile. It was squat as a Scottie but with huge jaws like a croc. It was the best football player I ever played against as you couldn't beat it - it mercilessly savaged the ball, your ankles and legs if you tried to dribble past it. Mind you it savaged anyone's legs particularly rent collectors or tallymen who turned up at Margaret's door. She once told me of a very lucky insurance man who sat down to talk to her in the kitchen and she looked down and Rex had crawled under the table silently and slowly put his jaws around the man's ankle ready to strike. '*Rex no!*' she howled. The reptilian canine slowly drew his gaping jaws away from the leg as the man, startled by her cry looked down, screamed and jumped up, papers flying everywhere.

'What the hell was that!'

'Don't worry, its only Rex. Would you like a cup of tea?' He left, hurriedly.

The dog was as crazy as Timmy, mainly because he fed it several bottles of *Barley Wine* every night in Jimmy Elder's *The Shoulder of Mutton*. It was as pissed as him when they walked home to the bus stop to take the bus to Burnmoor where they lived. It was also mad, because one night Timmy was so pissed he forgot to ring the bell for the bus to stop so he leapt up with dog on the lead and threw himself off the bus as it flew past his stop. He hit the bus stop, and the dog, in a scene from a *Deputy Dawg* cartoon, was swung several times around the bus stop by its lead until it finally wound all the way around and stopped only when it hit the post. Both dog and man were hors de combat, Timmy with a broken nose and two black eyes and the dog half a jaw missing. The schizophrenic behaviour of Rex worsened after this much to the amusement of Timmy and the lads as the poor hound would do his crocodile impression with leg chewing results on any unsuspecting customer in the *The Shoulder*. No one dared complain or get the police and Timmy always bought them a round of drinks after the chewing to kill their pain.

Sadly Rex got worse and started biting anyone he met and I had to take him to the PDSA to be put down. No one else would, even my extremely hard brothers-in-laws couldn't face the trauma. It was a tough lesson for me as a young teenager I must say. I liked Rex.

Durham Big Meeting and Punch Up's

My other brother- in-law, Mark Clark, was less manic than Timmy, but a hard, small, stocky pitman. A very good boxer - he learned in National Service - he was the only man I know to have knocked Snack down. He habitually fought at the summer Durham Big Meeting, the annual miner's gala, where all the pits of the region gathered every summer in July for an immense piss up and to listen to the famous labour politicians of the time speak. Great days following the banner from the Miners Welfare in Herrington or from the Club, where drinking commenced very early till late. Every year the gypsies, travellers and old pugs would challenge the lads to boxing matches for money. Every year men like our Mark thought they could win. It normally ended in a free-for-all with everyone from the pit fighting with the gypsies, with everyone comparing black eyes and thick lugs back home in the Club at night.

Recently, I listened to *The Miner's Lifeguard* at a great local Sea Shanty Festival where that wonderful man Steve and his daughter Katherine from CASK also sang our *Frog on the Teign* pirate song from my *Footsteps* epic published for my wife's children's charity, AIMS. It brought back so many happy memories of the summer and the Durham Big Meeting and also my early life in the pit communities with our struggles to support families in the face of so many adversities. As I listened to the song I could see in my mind the lasses skipping and dancing in front of the banners, the jazz bands with the drum majorettes, the songs and the speeches at The County Hotel and the Showground.

Afterwards, I watched a few YouTube videos of past Big Meetings. Some of my family and friends who danced in those videos had lain squeezed under thousands of tonnes of rock hewing coal out of seams some of which were only two foot high. Some had been killed and lamed in rock falls and the farewell salutation I often still use, *Keep your timmer in* – a colloquial *Look after yourself*, meant make sure your wooden pit props are well hammered in as they were the only thing to save you from rock falls and cave in. It was dangerous, unhygienic and life reducing with the dust and the exhausting manual work even when, by the time of my teenage awaking to the horrors of it all, the face workers had the use of massive shearing machines and the pit ponies had been put out to grass.

Those YouTube videos brought me to tears because watching these old videos of the lads and lasses at the Big Meetings reminded me of the one day everyone forgot their life struggles and joined in a short period of joy. It was also a statement of pride, comradeship and unity from hundreds of thousands of people and a reflection in a mirror of a culture soon to be thrown into the dustbin of history.

And for sure, the year-long 1984 fight to keep their employment and self esteem which saw such hardship and suffering for many families may seem incongruous to many who have said to me that people should not have to work under those conditions and we should have been glad to move on to better jobs. And yes, you are absolutely correct. No mother or father I knew ever wanted their kids to go down the pit or willingly starve them for a politically motivated strike. They all wanted safer, cleaner, better paying work. The pit was a shackle that bound them to early deaths and low wage slavery. If the chains could have been broken by the closure of the pits and a safer, brighter future secured no mother or father I knew would have cried. But in 1984 they had no other choice of work and there were not millions of existential Norman Tebbit bikes to allow them *to get off their arses* and cycle to sunny Torquay to claim the dole or work as dishwasher in *Fawlty Towers* or to open a Greengrocer's shop in Grantham. So they were led blindly, many unwillingly, into a politically motivated war they couldn't win by archaic and politically corrupt union leaders who like mice following a modern Pied Spider of Grantham fell into the vengeful spider's web that she had cruelly designed and so carefully spun.

The result of all this hardship, violence and anger in the coalfields, shipbuilding and steel-making towns was the end of industry as we had known it and the cultures that thrived upon it. The unions were far too powerful and the work was never good; nor was it well paid and in retrospect, despite the devastation left behind and hardship many decent hard working people lived through after the closures, we should be pleased to have moved on from working in these environments. For me, the fact that the elected government of the time planned it all, used all the powers of the State to enforce a revengeful political and party doctrine and had no plan or seemingly desire, except *market forces*, to help the millions of this country's people left behind - those who in the main didn't vote for them - is what I struggle to forgive them, or her, for.

However, it is time we moved on to happier things and I know in my heart it's time I did forgive. Obviously many people in the North don't remember or care, or quite logically and passionately believe that Labour and Westminster has consistently failed them over many years and believe it is time to move on and give the modern Conservative politicians an opportunity to prove their *one nation* rhetoric. They seem a lot more compassionate today about supporting people who are suffering financially from viral forces than they ever were about supporting their electorate who were suffering financially and devastated by fictional, pre planned and corrupt market forces, union dogma and the absolute incompetence of British management. I sincerely hope after Covid, we are not left with the financial and social horrors and individual hopelessness that many proud people of this country, who only wished to work safely and with financial dignity, suffered after Thatcher. Today, I will forget, and I will forgive: Tomorrow? Well, I refer you again back to Mark Antony, let's see if he comes to praise the new Caesar or bury him.

Sorry, but I had to get some that off my chest. Memories of old Durham Big Meetings, the drink and the devil and good protest songs do that to you. One woman's terrorist is another woman's freedom fighter and all that.

I listen to *Desert Island Discs* and the lovely Lauren Laverne so maybe that's why I cry sometimes; Ian Wright, Samantha Morton even Kier Starma and as I finally finish, Tom Daley this week, sad stories but triumph in the end. I have to confess that I even felt a lump for Mrs T last night in the final episode of Neflix's epic, *The Crown,* when the Queen pinned the order of merit on her after the jackals had fallen upon her and the bottle-less, grey-haired men in her party turfed her out. Men who had followed her without question for their own gain until the Ides of March saw her brutally slain. Who can forget the old *Spitting Images* of her and her obsequious cabinet in the 80's?

She is served her lunch by the minions in the Cabinet Office and the waiter asks: 'What would you like maarm?'

'I'd like the steak please.'

'And the vegetables?' the waiter asks.

The camera pans to the puppets of her Cabinet and their wobbling heads and blah, blah, blahing, sitting with their knives and forks in their hands. Lady M turns to the waiter and drones in her affected voice. 'They'll have the same.'

I loved it. But I must have *torned soft* as I told Eddy this morning on the phone of the lump in my throat for her ladyship. He was shocked and then he corrected me. I have to say maybe I have gone soft - I'll be holding our lass's hand next when we stroll along on the prom. Eddy's reply was succinct and unwavering after forty years of reflecting on forgiveness. 'The Queen should have stuck the pin through the black-hearted bitch's heart. If she could find the bastard, that is.'

And he reminded me of another old *Spitting Image* clip portraying her speech at the Conservative Party Conference in which he didn't find the sarcasm and sardonic humour as funny as I did at the time: 'And as for the miners? We should burn the bastards. Use them as coal...'

As I said, it's time to forgive. The Queen seemed to think, as I do now after years of reflection, that things had to be done but did not support the way the spider did it and with no plan or compassion for what she'd left behind. The Queen/Palace leaked her thoughts to the press which severely hurt our Shelob's reputation and party position. However, I believe she was correct after Mrs T. was betrayed to thank her for her dedication and leadership of the country. Few of her party have shown those qualities since; she had much more integrity, honesty and balls than the latest *Spitting Image* puppets. So yes, though it hurts me to say, but after leaving my admittedly biased pit village roots and years of listening to the other side of the Mrs T argument from more conservative friends and bar acquaintances, history will show she changed industrial relations and British management eventually for the good of most of us and that had to happen to move on with public health, social mobility and eventual economic freedoms.

However, the latest faux pas in Scotland of all places from the tousle haired buffoon puppet leader of the Conservative and 'Unionist' party saying that they should be grateful to Thatcher for her insight in closing their pits to prevent global warming, well that makes my piss boil again and start thinking Eddy is correct and they'll never change. Sadly, the opposition never seem to change either – it's the media and the people who decide which type of government and who they want to lead them not the party activists. The great British public is nothing but conservative and contrary – likeable buffoons they will elect, but not *woke*-thinking, weird looking ideological Marxists – strange that isn't it.

Rant over again, and I'm sober as well, so maybe it's time we moved on from old wounds and puppets and get back to the fun we had during those boiling hot summer days when we danced in the streets of Durham and played at weekends in the towns of Sunderland and Newcastle with great music thrown in so we'll move on to when the music was definitely not dead.

CHAPTER SIXTEEN
MUSIC, BARS AND PLATFORM HEELS

Under Age Drinking and Progressive Music

Most of us went to see bands play live then. Many became world famous but at that time were unknown, new and exciting, part of a new wave of progressive music coming out.

I didn't have to travel far for great live music. My favourite venue was *The Bay Hotel* adjacent to Whitburn beach. It was a small, cosy and atmospheric. I saw *Family* there for the first time and also *Tyrannosaurus Rex*, when Bolan and Finn bashed out tunes on classical guitar and bongos before they went electric and morphed into *T Rex*.

Polly was a friend from Penshaw. He was unusual those days as he was a rabid Newcastle United supporter. Pre-Kevin Keegan most of the area I inhabited was about 75% Sunderland AFC. Polly was also unusual as he liked all progressive and blues bands and that no one had ever heard of, like *Amon Düül II, Captain Beefheart, Frank Zappa, Pretty Things, John Mayall,* and *Miles Davis. He* shunned anything popular.

Polly and I watched *Pretty Things* and *Ten Years After* there with Polly approving greatly of such avant garde stuff, me wishing it was *Black Sabbath.*

The Newcastle City Hall and the Mecca, soon to be Tiffs, in Sunderland were the venues to see many bands, *Jethro Tull, Free, Deep Purple, Zeppelin, Groundhogs, Black Sabbath* and many more. I guess all these had some influence and memory of first love and heartaches and also young growing friendships between a similar band of brothers. Girls were always part of this by now - if we could remain sober to pick them up.

Drink, music and girls all went together wonderfully when we were teenagers in the sixties and seventies, as I guess they always have and will. I was never into drugs - Brown Ale was hallucinogenic enough for me - and frankly neither were 95% of my mates, even at College. I guess Ian Dury's, *Sex & Drugs & Rock & Roll* wouldn't have had the same ring about it for me and my friends if he'd called it, *Rampant & Federation Special & Captain Beefhart.*

My sisters loved the rock and roll icons like *Elvis, Chuck Berry, Richie Valens,* and *Buddy Holly.* My father was a great fan of opera, and loved *Caruso* and *Mario Lanza* and the pub singers of the day. It was their era, along with the coming of *The Beatles, The Stones, Dylan, Hendrix, Aretha,* and *Motown*. My taste was more from the middle of the sixties and progressive rock to punk and glam rock which held the romantic and youthful innocence memories.

We always tried to take our budding girlfriends into a pub but as we were only fourteen or fifteen it was problematical. Tinker in Shiney allowed *the boys* in the back room but his favourite trick was to wait until everyone had a full drink and rush back in shouting 'The polis are on the way' so we'd all rush out of the back way past the outside toilet. Tinker then picked up all the drinks and gave them to the real lads in the bar, laughing his head off and tapping his pipe on the bar. The old bugger!

The Ship Inn at Penshaw Village was the first pub I ever went in on my own to drink at fourteen years old. 'You boys in there', was the landlord's instruction to us to go into a back room away from the bar, which I found full of my school mates.

The Coach and Horses pub next to our school in Washington also let us in. I used to drink there at lunchtimes in my school uniform with the dole wallahs and old men. I had given up school meals and used the new decimal coin dinner money for beer: 12p for a pint of Newcastle Exhibition.

A couple of years later our head of Sixth form and Humanities teacher caught me in there on a Wednesday afternoon after lunch. Our leader was livid and insisted I follow him to school. I told him he couldn't make me do that as I was eighteen and had a full pint. Weirdly he had to agree. I agreed to meet him in his office after I'd supped up. Needless to say nothing much happened; he was a Humanity teacher after all! Different if he'd been a woodwork teacher I'd have been beaten half to death. And thank God it wasn't Mister Curtis the Head. He had reputation as good - or as bad depending on your persuasion or politics - as Attila the Hun. A fearsome man: with a head like a medicine ball. He reminded me of Colonel Cathcart in *Catch Twenty Two*, a face so awesomely horrible that no one dared speak to him. He used to terrify the school at assembly with his loud voice and insane threats of beatings and torture whilst perversely singing, *The King of Love our Saviour is*. When we reached the sixth form we went along to sit in the balcony above the hall just to see the small kids crying and shaking with fear at his lectures on what would happen to them if they dropped a sweet paper in the playgrounds. Despite his ferociousness and his malicious intent and persistence, he never did get me expelled. I forgive you Mr Curtis, hope you could have forgiven me. The boy didn't do badly after all.

Home Brew and Deep Purple

Mostly because of lack of money I drank a lot of home brew beer and wine which was becoming popular in the late sixties/seventies. The beer came from a shop on Vine Street in Sunderland which sold all sorts of brewing equipment and weird stuff like lentils, smelly things, and yeasts. I loved the smell of the hops - they sold lots of different ones - and also tins of malt. I made two or three types and a Stout, but settled on one particular brew. It was bottled off in old beer bottles and I had metal tops to hammer on with a device that crimped the serrated edges around the tops like real beer. I also put them in screw top pop bottles to save money on tops.

My mother's airing cupboard usually had a few clothes drying in it but mainly it was full of beer brewing in large black bins and wine popping away in one gallon, glass demi-johns. These shared shelf space with incubating chicken eggs too. I was never sure if Mark and Dad's chickens became alcoholics from pre-nascent life in the alcohol fumed airing cupboard womb but whatever their exposure to beer fumes they laid cracking eggs.

Gussy and me both brewed beer and we drank it in his shed in the front garden. He had a small portable tape recorder (remember cassette tapes!) and also a moped that he used to get to work as a trainee gamekeeper (what else) on Lord Lambton's land. He was two years older than me so had left *Glebe* school in Washington at sixteen. We listened to homemade tapes at night with the flashing lights of the moped indicators as surrogate live lights for shows featuring tracks recorded through a microphone from BBC radio. We also taped TV shows like *Top of the Pops*. This programme drove my father crazy with the weird, long-haired tramps performing, but secretly he always seemed to watch it. I now suspect it was because of Pan's People; in those days I wouldn't have even dreamed that my father would fancy women; he was old for God's sake!

Another favourite TV show to tape was *The Old Grey Whistle Test* with Whispering Bob Harris. How I wish affordable video tape recorders were around those early days. So many now iconic bands had their TV debut on there.

The favourite show on radio to tape was John Peel's show because he played all the new progressive rock bands. Sunday I'd tape the Top Twenty show while lying in the habitual Sunday night bath. As I grew into an older teen, I'd listen to the top twenty in the bath after waking up after a Sunday afternoon snooze, induced by a late Saturday night, Sunday lunch time in the Club and one of my mother's monster Sunday dinners. I never heard the top 4 or 5 records each week as I had to quickly get dressed and head out up the Street to be sure to get to the Club for 7 pm opening time. It is a long gone scene, never to be seen again, the hordes of North East men and women walking up the close packed terraces of houses at 6 50 pm every Sunday towards their ultimate *Frankie Goes to Hollywood* pleasure dome - the Club. Liberal licensing laws, the end of working men's clubs and their unique culture has seen an end to those experiences.

One special day in our lives Gussy acquired an extension lead and a record player for our beer hut and as a consequence we could play actual LP records and singles rather than dodgy sounding tape recordings from the TV or radio. Those days they were vinyl of course and the album covers were surreal to us, each one more bizarre than the other, giving you instant street cred as owners of cover sleeve art for the weirdest bands. Sadly as we used candles for light sometimes the albums and covers got caked in grease. A real pity as many have now become iconic, sought after and valuable.

One great Saturday night Gussy bought something new - *Deep Purple in Rock*. He'd been paid at work and bought it that very afternoon. Then one disastrous night he got Sheila Vlaming, a very pretty girl from up our street, to listen to it. She was semi posh - she still lived in our council house street but her Dad had a car and seemed to have a job which was not hewing coal, humping bricks or welding things. He also didn't drink with our dad's in the Club, so that made them by definition, posh.

My life changed that night listening to, *Sweet Child in Time* in the candlelight because my old friend had found girls and henceforth abandoned catching and killing small mammals and birds while I was relegated to drinking alone in the shed listening to John Lennon - *Working Class Hero* - and Fleetwood Mac - *Green Manalishi* - while Gussy pursued his first true love, never to be the same again. Bloody girls!

GARY
Neil Young and Tyrannosaurus Rex

Having lost my friend to the charms of the fairer sex, I moved from the shed to my own back room and set up the bar there. Friends, who still thought of girls as a nuisance, came from school in Washington to play snooker and drink home-brewed beer.

Gary was my great friend from Fatfield. He brewed the same beer and we'd explore different brews and bottling techniques and play snooker and drink it to the latest progressive sounds and bootleg albums we could afford and source. Gary always seemed to have a few more bob than me, his dad was a fitter at the pit with better wages and his grandmother had some real money which she donated to her grandson, so he bought more with his pocket money than most of us. He bought the first LPs from such bands as *Ten Years After* and the great *Albert Lee, Man, Taste* and *Rory Gallagher*, the original *Tyrannosaurus Rex* LP, *Neil Young* bootlegs and the iconic *After The Gold Rush*. Can anyone remember Tony Blackburn crying on the radio to the song *Only Love Can Break Your Heart* from *After the Gold Rush*? It was all during his very public break up with his wife Tessa if I recall.

The first album I could afford was by *Free, Tons of Sobs*. I loved *Paul Kossoff* on guitar and of course the gravel voice of *Paul Rodgers*. The girls loved him more of course. As they did *Robert Plant* from *Led Zeppelin* the pouting and trouser bursting lead singer that heaved a thousand bosoms and the Seventies next thing up from the sixties *Mick Jagger*. The next album I bought was *Stand Up* by *Jethro Tull*, rapidly followed by their first, *This Was*. I was a Tull freak, loved *Ian Anderson* and his one-legge, flute-playing , bearded tramp persona. My dad hated him with a passion. 'What the bloody hell is that!' he exploded when he saw Anderson, grunting, slavering, scratching his balls and moaning as if in pain or ecstasy whilst singing *Witches Promise* on Top of the Pops. 'He's a bloody tramp. Dirty bugger - can he not get a bloody wash and a haircut and a new bloody coat?' And then when Pan's People came on. 'Can lasses these days not wear decent length skirts? Bloody dressed like tarts showing their knickers like that.'

The joys of teenage parents in the early seventies: But I guess nowt will change there while teenagers' rebel and their parents forever grow old, grumpy and weary anywhere in the world.

Windows of Newcastle and Frank Zappa

Gary and I played lots of music and drank lots of beer. So many bands and so much great music then, it's impossible to put into a short story the times and events and also the heartaches we all had throughout our school lives in the late sixties and seventies. But some need putting down for posterity. One was *Windows* in Newcastle.

I often headed off on the World Challenge trek to the lost world of Newcastle on the Number 39 bus to Worswick Street bus station and then off to Central Arcade and into *Window's* music store. Here I could ask to listen to any album and they allocated you a sound proofed booth to listen to it before you bought it. Here I heard so many bands for the first time and finally bought some iconic and memorable albums that still live on today. *Family; Jimi Hendrix, Zeppelin, Deep Purple, Black Sabbath, Wishbone Ash, Groundhogs, Roxy Music; Lindesfarne, Crosby, Stills, Nash and Young, Yes, Bruce Springsteen,* I could go on, but…

Gary's cousin, Polly had the weirdest taste in music that I had met up till then and probably since, except Paul at University and Stumpy Tony here in the Irish madhouse. I was reminiscing with Tony the other day over a gallon of Scrumpy about *Zappa* and *Captain Beefheart.* We both agreed that there was some great merit in their work, *Trout Mask Replica* being Beefheart*'s* best along with Zappa's *Weasels Rip My Flesh*, both classic albums with amazing covers. In a fit of progressive rock nostalgia, Stumpy lent me *Weasels.* I listened to it writing this masterpiece and I am still traumatised. Nostalgia sometimes comes with a kick in the teeth. It's still bloody horrible!

DAVEY DITCHBURN
Lucas Tyson and Strippers

As we gained our CIU working men's club cards and realised that girls may have some use, we moved into the clubs of the North East to do our courting and listen to music, in between the mass fights of course. In the seventies the big clubs like Shiney and Usworth, Downhill and all across the whole North East put strippers on Sunday lunchtime. Long past their Methodist roots you may say, and you are correct. But they brought in the people and the money on the door. As did the comedians that played with them and some weekends the local rock bands played Sunday lunchtime too. The North East produced some great music those days and in many a way launched a few icons of music. Everyone knows about *The Animals* and *Eric Burdon* and *Chas*

Chandler, *Alan Price*, *Roxy Music* and *Brian Ferry* who went to Washington Grammar by the way and his first gig was in County Durham's answer to Nashville, Shiney Row, and in that Hall of Fame for all budding megastar musicians - *Mac's café* - *Lindisfarne* and *Ray Jackson* and *Alan Hull* and later on *The Police* and *Sting* and *Dire Straits* and *Mark Knopfler*, *The Eurythmics* and *Dave Stewart*. And just to prove I'm not just old and grumpy, here's a couple for my millennium son, *Kenike* with the lovely *Lauren Lavrene* and *Little Mix*.

The Clubs in the area also were the scene of many very good imitation and own brand musicians and bands and all for a ten pence cover charge and beer at ten pence a pint. You can't beat that! Mind you, we had to fight your way home past the Chinese takeaway after the gigs but what the hell, the music was great.

I saw *Brian Johnson* of *AC/DC* fame in Shiney Row club long before he was famous. He was with a band called *Geordie* (no surprise there then). Everyone loved the band, no football rivalry or Mackem and Geordie nonsense then, we were all proud to be from the region.

I saw *John Miles* play one Friday night and also *Goldie* with their one hit *Making up Again*. But my favourite was *Lucas Tyson*. I loved the guitar of *Pete Barclay* with his wailing *wow wow* pedal and the howling noise that came from his *Stratocaster* echoing around the smoke filled club. I can still see him now stood there, long greasy hair, reminding me now of *Rick Parfitt* from *Status Quo*, except Pete was no beauty queen as his nose looked as if our own *Biffa* had met him in the toilets before the band went on stage. His versions of *Split Part Two* and *Cherry Red* as recorded by *The Groundhogs* were immaculate. I went to see the band in clubs across the region and also the big venues like the Mecca in Sunderland and the Mayfair in Newcastle. I was there when they put the microphone through Usworth Club roof, causing a meltdown from the concert chairman and the inevitable mass brawl.

Brass Alley I guess were the most famous and most booked band around then. Lead by the *Robert Plant/Paul Rodgers* clone, *Davey Ditchburn*, they wooed the lasses and Davey's *Free* songs and Paul Rodger's imitations were almost perfect. The girls at our school loved *Paul Rodgers* the lead singer of *Free*. We lads couldn't see why as they had much more gorgeous long haired lads around them all day anyway, without the broken teeth. I guess he was like *Robert Plant* and maybe it was the tight, large bulge-included trousers that attracted them. Sadly for the lads, Davey was similar looking and endowed and the girls would go mental and actually get up and dance at his last song, the epic, *The Hunter*' After treating our girlfriends and wives to a night of Davey Ditchburn, *a* Cherry B and cider and then curry and chips from the Chinese on the way home and they were anybody's! Oh the romance and nostalgia of passionate requited love in an idyllic pit village you may correctly say. Maybe, I really should write romantic novels. You can read much more about these musicians and many more on my publisher's website and buy the discographies. Very good stuff. Music page – www.andrewsparke.com

The Bigg Market and the Match

Most weekends in the seventies as we grew towards legal drinking we headed into the towns for entertainment. Really we were only going to get drunk and hope by some insane chance a girl would throw their scantily clad bodies at us. Friday nights if not at the Club we would be in Newcastle, which then, like today on a weekend, was a thriving metropolis of beer, barnies and big purple legged lasses.

We started off in *Penshaw Catholic Club* at 5.30 pm because beer was cheap, they opened early and they had Keg Newcastle Exhibition which was stronger than normal we believed. Next we'd take the Number 39 bus to Worswick Street Bus station. There we went straight to the *Manors Working Men's Club'* minutes behind the bus station where beer was cheap and it too was *Newcastle Exhibition*.

I'd meet Eddy in there who had become a great friend. He was two years older than me but I'd got to know him as I played football for the under 18s and outside clubs as a sixteen year old and he was in the teams. Sadly he led me astray into pubs - the terrible man. He lived in Washington and never seemed to be at school much. I realised that this was because he worked in the local bookies and as a barman at Usworth Top Club. A- Levels were something he would worry about when it happened. When he was at school he was mainly playing cards and fleecing his fellow students or stealing the tuck shop money. As a penance for being caught, Mr Curtis, the *Shrek*-looking, terrifying Headmaster told him he'd have to act in the school play. The cruel, heartless bastard! This was an absolute nightmare of a punishment which the head knew very well. Six strokes of the cane would have been less punishment.

However, Eddy got his revenge as the part he played involved him drinking a glass of sarsaparilla pop. Eddy substituted the sarsaparilla for

Brown Ale and when he cracked the bottle open and poured it slowly and deliberately into his glass he smiled knowingly up at the sixth form sat in the gallery clapping. Mr Curtis's huge awesome head blew up!

Eddy was over the moon one day when he showed me the new shoes he'd won from a daft lad in *The Stella Maris* club in Albany, Washington who didn't know the Three Card Brag dealing fiddle that Eddy had perfected with the ease of the Grade 1 A-Level maths student he clearly wasn't. But he could count cards and odds.

He worked at both the RCA record factory and Timex watch factory in Washington and soon realised that security needed a revamp as a consequence and a welcome bonus he spent most of his time selling watches and new LP's. A marvellous role model for a young man you may say. Indeed, my famous eye surgeon school chum, Professor Gartry of The Wimpole Clinic, also worked at RCA but he was more interested in listening to the free RCA reject John Denver albums than pursing a life of felony. Eddy perfected the surgical technique of extracting money from his school mates' pockets rather than perfecting corneal transplants. Children - if you are reading this book – stick in at school like Professor Gartry because sadly, Three Card Brag and selling dodgy records and timepieces in the Club will only make you like Del Boy and, unlike becoming a famous eye surgeon, you will have to wait until next year to become a millionaire.

Eddy somehow stayed out of jail and became very famous as an educator of those young people who were a bit special, a lot like him; a great friend who will step into this play later.

Gay Troopers and Viv the Puff

In Newcastle, after hurtling as much cheap beer as we could down our throats, we moved off up Worswick Street, across Northumberland Street into *The Adelphi,* then walked down to *The Turks Head, The George and Dragon, The Man in the Moon* and into *The Pineapple.* Curiously, I remember a bar called *The Gay Trooper* it seemed to be under a shopping centre near the Big Market. Doubt it was LGBT; those days LGBT was a badge you had on the back of your Ford Cortina car. It took me many years to realise that Newcastle had quite a large LGBT scene based around Pink Lane, funnily enough. The first and last time I went there I fought my way down Bath Lane through Pink Lane and finally the Central Station after beating Newcastle 1-4 in '79. It was like Rorke's Drift and frankly to quote Stanley Baker in *Zulu*, 'Who would want to go through that hell twice?'. The only LGBT scene I had experienced in my youth was when we went to Big Viv the puff's bar - I think at the *Duke of Wellington*, near the High Bridge. Viv was always very pleasant and quite funny but I saw him kick off with some lads who thought they'd come in and take the piss - a very hard person. He met a tragic end, stabbed to death outside his pub the *Asia Blue* in Gateshead.

Mercifully in those days I didn't have to employ or mix with the real hard men - that would occur later in purgatory when I went *Contracting with the Devil* - so I tried to avoid them. However, that was not always possible as the Big Market kicked off every night then. The police used to be in massive numbers with huge dogs and the lads thought it fun to attack them and of course mayhem resulted. Now Newcastle has rightly gained a fabulous reputation for its inclusive nightlife but those days it was a tough old *toon*.

We avoided the bars in the Big Market (*Blackie Boy/Groat/Coffy Johnnys/Dobsons*) and walked down to the Quayside and drank in *The Red House* and then into the nightclub *Julie's* on the quay. Some Fridays we'd get pissed in the *Manors* and head straight down to the *Hofbrauhaus*, the German Bierkellar. They were the rage in the seventies. Why? Maybe it was the new liberated sixties culture where everyone tried to love each other and even the mind blowing, boring Jorman culture was classed as *far out, man*. I still can't get away with German culture. Who the hell would like men in leather shorts and hats with feathers in them and girls that act like Eskimo Nell, *with a squeeze of her thigh*... I won't finish the line as this is a family book, but please, apart from *Marlene Dietrich* and *The Scorpions, Can, Faust* and *Neu* what have the Germans ever done for us?

It was mayhem in the *Hofbrauhaus*. Bus loads from all over the area turned in every weekend, everyone drinking huge steins of lager and drinking schnapps, umpah bands playing, lads and lasses fighting. Eddy and me and the lads would be pissed already and wait till people got up dancing and then pinch their steins, swallow as much of their beer as possible and put them back before they noticed. Everyone was so drunk it didn't matter. This was the only place we really tried with girls. In the seventies, unlike later and now, there weren't that many ladies out in the pubs those days. Nightclubs were where you met lasses then such as *Scamps*, near *Hofs* or *Maddisons, Tiffanies* and all before the *Tuxedo Junction* and *Tuxedo Princess*, onshore and offshore started.

DAVEY
The Vestry and Platform Heels

Nightclubs were where we hoped to find a girl but more often you found a fight. In Sunderland we would head off to *The Rink* in early days and as we got older to *Tiffs*. *The Vestry* was another great pub/club and relatively free of lunatics, unlike the other two. *Annabel's* was for the more sophisticated girls and poser boys. I can't really remember leaving *Tiffs* without either being in some altercation or watching mass brawls. Eddy and I often stood drunkenly waiting for the last dance and then try to *tap up* a lass at the last dance; but more often than not you were fending off punches rather than the girls trying to fend off you. Sunderland seemed to be always dafter than Newcastle; fights seemed to occur everywhere, pubs, bus stops, buses, taxi ranks or clubs. However, *La Dolce Vita* was to be an exception to my peaceful Newcastle wooing. Here I ended up getting kicked all the way down their stairs by bouncers who took exception to me head-butting the lad who had glassed my mate Davey. Out with a few bruises from the bouncers the real problem was that I had lost the heel off my four inch platform shoes and had to walk all the six miles to Washington with one shoe. I finally climbed wearily into Davey's bedroom window in his parents' bungalow to doss down with Tabatha the tabby cat. The platform shoes, not the usual violence, being the point of the story as I can now recall the weird clothes we all wore before the milk went.

PETER THE TAILOR
Loons and Pom Poms

My parents could never afford to buy clothes in the main department stores in the sixties or early seventies so a man called Peter the Tailor used to call on us and Mam and Dad would buy a range of clothes he'd sell; all on tick. This didn't bother me too much in the sixties until I went to Grammar school and met kids with richer parents and especially as I got into fashion. I could never afford to buy the latest *Levis*, *Staypress*, or *Ben Sherman's*. I would have to wear *cross bot* jeans, the humiliation a nightmare for a teenager. It's like giving a youngster now a pay phone card instead of an Apple smart phone. Slowly I'd save up money to get the latest, but only one pair or one shirt unlike other boys who had all the gear.

Before that in the Fifties and Sixties my mother knitted most of the stuff. These woollen jumpers are now in fashion again - I should have kept them. Don from Carlisle, still wears them. Mind you most of the lads there in Cumbria still do, especially sleeveless jumpers, tank tops, with intricate patterns. They are quite special people in Cumbria as you may guess. You may read more about Football and supporters and claw hammer knit jumpers in my epic *Relentless Misery*...a must for anyone who supports a football team which has won bugger all in their lifetime.

Moving from knitted jumpers back to platform heels, I was reminded of the type of shoes that were all the rage around that time by Stumpy the Wolverhampton Hells Angel - shoes which had animal footprints on the sole and a compass embedded in the heel. As if most kids in the Black Country would be like Bear Grylls or a Comanche Indian, tracking deer, badgers, foxes and whatever other animal through the dark forests and prairies of Dudley. Moon and desert boots came out too, but no one I knew had walked on the moon or tramped the Kalahari. The same with Baseball boots; no one played that. *Doc Martens* were once the pharmaceutical tablets the vet gave you for exterminating your cats' lops, not the boots that skinheads bought in their thousands to exterminate normal human beings. Fashion I guess moves on and as the seventies crept on so did the clothes. Flares, loon pants, kipper ties, round collars, velvet jackets, platform shoes, and afghan coats. Many used Army and Navy stores to buy haversacks to carry their school books and football gear and we painted the names of our favourite rock band on the back. We also bought Army Great War coats and jungle jackets from them. Skinheads as I've noted before had their own culture and gear. *Harrington's, Ben Sherman's, Sta-prest* and *Doc Martens* and also had brogues with *segs* (metal studs) in the soles.

As I earned pocket money and worked I could buy *Levi* jeans and get my mother to sow patches on and wear them until they were dying on their feet. Tartan patches too. My dad cracked up with my patched jeans, couldn't believe I had saved money to then patch jeans *like a bloody tramp*. The Bay City Rollers had a lot to answer for. Tartan patches on cut off jeans above *Doc Martens*, tartan scarfs tied to wrists and the like and at football matches of all places for God's sake; never did see a tartan butchers coat mind. Most bikers and greasers' jeans were condemned by the World Heath Authority and stank of greasers' favourite type of *Old Spice* - patchouli oil.

250

As the seventies ended and Eddy got married, as his best man I wore a suit I'd bought on tick in Burton's Newcastle. The wedding photograph probably summed up the seventies fashion for the non-fashionable man. The suit was cream, with round collars. My shirt was brown with round collars and the tie cream and I had four inch platforms on. I guess I was always a natty dresser.

Our Ken was also a natty dresser but as I told you, most of his gear was nicked. Still he always looked the part when fleecing the bookies across the Region and some days he brought me along as his stool pigeon.. As you will read shortly, I never learned…

CHAPTER SEVENTEEN
GAMBLING AND FISHING

Pitch and Toss, Greyhounds and Whippets

Our Ken was what you called those days a *dog man*. He'd been brought up with greyhounds and whippets in the home and racing and gambling were his life from a child. Pitmen would gamble on anything. *Pitch and Toss* was still prevalent around the villages, pubs and clubs when I was a young boy in the 50's and early 60's, having been played there since the 1700's. Locals also called it *The Hoy*. The North East verb to hoy is translated by normal people as to throw.

It was a man's game and played with a ring of men in a field or large yard betting on the outcome of *hoying* two pennies in the air. Gambling being illegal it was held in supposed secret with look-outs (scouts) for the police. If caught, fines were imposed and even jail for the more recalcitrant men. Bets were placed on the possible outcomes and men could lose lot of money.

I was told one day in the Philadelphia Comrades' club of a well-known *hoyer* and gambler, Cecil Towers, innovative way of winning an indoor successor game to pitch and toss. Cecil was a large man; his lungs shattered by coal dust and on his hands and face the blue coal dust-tinted scars that all pitmen had. This new game was to bet on who would be the first person to have a bluebottle fly land on his coin. They laid out pennies on the ground or the bar and waited to see whose coin the fly would land on first. Cecil Towers was the one who always seemed to win the money. People were curious why until someone spotted him with his hands down the back of his baggy trousers and underpants and rubbing his penny up the crack of his backside. Despite the unpredictability of Quantum Theory and the Heisenberg's Uncertainty Principle, Darwin's Theory always wins. Flies do like shite. Nature beats chance anytime. Einstein was correct; 'God does not play dice', or indeed, *the hoy*.

The stereotype of the Northern man with his flat cap, muffler and whippet is well-known and frankly when I grew up it was true except whilst some had whippets most had greyhounds. Ken was a known *flapping track man* when I was young. That is, he was an expert at racing dogs at the small and sometimes unlicensed tracks across the North East. He was also barred from most of them for illegal race-fixing and subsequently earned a living from bookies telling them which dogs had been *knobbled* or *stopped*.

Ken's mate, a pitman from Shiney Row, *Dolfie Smith* told of one classic day in the 50's when Ken was asked to take Stripper's dog to the Houghton-le-Spring track. This dog was the favorite to win but Stripper's cousin from Fencehouses had a dog in the same race that they both knew could only get near to Grandad's dog if Stripper's dog was running slow. So Ken was told by his father to stop his dog and put his dad's crisp new white five pound note (a week's wages) on his cousin's dog which should have much better odds than his father's, which would be the favourite.

Now, stopping dogs was a black art. Many methods were used; food, excess water, drugs, physical injury but in those days the method commonly used by Stripper and Ken was over-feeding. My nana cooked several meat pies made from the pheasant and rabbits poached from Lord Lambton. These were wrapped and given to Ken to feed the dog just before the race. They were laced with salt to make the unfortunate canine drink loads of water too. Ken and Dolphie then set off to walk the dog the three miles to Houghton-le-Spring in order to tire the dog. Stripper's last words to Ken were. 'Mind yeah put that fiver on Jimmy's dog and divn't drink any of the winnings or I'll belt yah.'

Ken and Dolphie set off to walk along the battery which was a long raised mound at the bottom and parallel to our council housing estate and to follow this across the small burn, past Cuslow's scrap yard and on through Sunnyside to Houghton. They had only got about half a mile when Ken said: 'Let's sit down, Dolphie and get the pies out.'

Dolphie duly opened up the pie bag and began to feed one to the dog. Ken grabbed the pie and said: 'Bugger that, give it to me man!'

Ken proceeded to eat the pie in two swallows (he was a big lad). The poor dog sat slavering at the mouth while Ken proceeded to eat every last pie. He never offered Dolphie one either; something Dolphie never forgot or forgave even twenty years later when he told me the story.

Once at the track, because no one trusted Ken when he turned up at a track with his own dog, word had got around that Ken was stopping his father's dog. As a result the starting price rose from favourite to 3 to 1 and his cousin's dog went to favourite. Ken then placed the five pound note on his father's dog, not the one he had been told to.

Grandad's dog romped home as it was always going too unless it had a stone of meat pies in his stomach. This dog was hungry and also duly rested after been carried by a wasted Dolphie the last mile.

The dog was desperate for its dinner and Dolphie was starving but Ken with a stomach choc-a-bloc with pies and grinning from ear to ear didn't care; he'd picked up fifteen pounds. They both ended up drunk after drinking all night and when Ken went home he lied and told his father that he had done what he'd been asked and stopped his father's dog with the meat pies and water and placed the fiver on the other dog. He couldn't understand how his father's dog had won. He kept his winnings himself. From this you may gather the morality of a man who would even cheat his own father.

I experienced some of this amorality in person. In the late seventies I was studying for my PhD and as I was actually salaried as a medical research assistant and University lecturer. I had purchased my first car, an old dilapidated green Mini 1000. Ken was pleased because he asked me to help take him to Wolsingham, a small town up the River Wear valley in County Durham. There he was racing a dog at the local flapping races that were set up in a field every year to celebrate a summer festival. I was happy to take the day off.

I picked Ken up at his flat and on the way he told me that the race was fixed and he couldn't lose. He had bribed the race starter (the man who sets the field: that is the one who chooses which dogs were in each race) to ensure all six dogs were Ken's. Five of them had been stopped including the favourite and only one of the six was free of all drugs and noxious compounds and that was a fast dog he had sourced from another dodgy dog man. He always laughed that loud raucous laugh of his he used whenever he had conned or buggered someone up. 'We canna loose David. Mugs the whole lot of them, I'm hoping to get a couple of grand on before they suss me: watch and lorn son.'

This was indeed good news to me as I was needing money desperately in my postgraduate poverty so I suggested I'd pull over at the bank in Shiney and get my last couple of quid out to put on the dog. Ken grabbed my arm and replied forcefully: 'Divn't dee that David, I'll put some money for you and see you alright.'

'Ok Ken. But I need some money for petrol, it's nearly empty.'

'Arlreet pull ower and put a quid's worth in.'

And taking a pound out of his pocket he handed it to me. The petrol man put the pound's worth in and as I handed him the pound through the driver's window he said: 'Have a nice day.'

I wound up the window and began to drive away. Ken burst out laughing. 'Have a nice day? We bloody well will, you daft bugger. Ha, ha, ha!'

We arrived at Wolsingham at lunchtime, a lovely place if you ever go, but I fear the dog racing has now passed into the realms of history and maybe this book is the only record of that day. Ken introduced me to a man with a van in which was a brindle greyhound bitch. This dog was the favourite and was well fancied as it had won several races. It was owned by Ken; the man had brought it to the races and was falsely down as the registered owner. It had been given a dose of *Largactil (Chlorpromazine)*, a powerful sedative normally used on schizophrenics and was quite sleepy. Ken told me to walk the dog past the Vet and the starter and bookies and make sure I kept its head up so it didn't fall asleep or collapse. He also gave me a collar to put on its neck and leash. I picked up the collar and it weighed a tonne.

'What the hell is this made off for God's sake?' I exclaimed.

'Lead,' Ken replied, laughing raucously yet again.

I lamented, 'Poor dog,' feeling sorry for the poor thing.

Ken had no such conscience. 'Just put the bugger on yah soft twat and remember to keep its bloody head up. I bunged the Starter a fiver so he is bent but not the bloody Vet - he's honest, so keep it walking and head straight.'

I took the collar and put it on the unfortunate hound's neck. Her eyes were glazed over and she seemed in another world. As soon as the collar was on her neck her head sank to her chest. I attached the leash and reluctantly pulled her head up.

Ken encouraged me. 'That's it; keep her head up all the time. It'll be ok once she's in the traps. Tom here will walk with you to the Vet and the course. I'm off to sort the other four out.'

Ken had another four friends who had brought his dogs, all of them dosed up and fed pies. I believe mine, as she was by far the best dog, was the only one who had a lead collar as well. The ringer dog was in perfect health, the one that was going to win with all the rest doped, was taken by yet another friend.

Ken went off to begin his *Sting* operation. He didn't bet as he was too well known and any bookie's observing him placing big money would immediately stop taking bets on the dog and he could be reported before the race. So his friends placed small money separately with the eight bookmakers in multi bets on the only dog in the race not drugged. Eventually the bookmakers rumbled that something was not quite kosher and they struck the dog off their books and took no more bets. Its odds had fallen from a starting price of 5-1 to 1-3. I was unaware of this at the time as I was worrying too much about being hauled off by the police for race fixing.

Ken of course had never told me that I was to walk the favourite in with her heavy metal encumbered neck brace and sleepy head. I nervously walked her around the field in front of the Vet and others, keeping her head up as asked with my wrist hurting from the effort, trying to look innocent but feeling guilty as hell. *It's only a matter of time* I kept thinking *before they handcuff me and it's off to Durham Jail.*

Amazingly no one seemed to bother and I, along with the five other dogs and their walkers, took the dogs to the starter traps into which they were placed facing the track. The inevitable rabbit would soon be dragged on the wire past them seconds before the trap doors opened and they could hurtle or fall out of the traps. I worried that my sedated lady would curl up and sleep in the trap but that wasn't my problem now. It was Ken's and his gambling buddies.

I found Ken standing on some raised ground near the finishing line. He was as always immaculately dressed in his expensive suit, shirt, tie and *Crombie* camel hair overcoat and polished leather shoes. He was smiling. I asked if he had got his money on. He replied that not all of it had gone on as the bookies struck the odds after about five hundred pounds had been placed (at these tracks bookies and gamblers weren't taking massive bets. I asked if he'd put a bet on for me. 'Aye', was his answer and I thought great maybe twenty to thirty pound win, a King's ransom for me then.

The race began. The rabbit set off and passed the traps and the hounds were released. I prayed that mine would at least run out and not fall asleep and sure enough she did. In fact she raced out well ahead of the others who frankly jogged out and gave up. Fearfully mine, despite the cocktail of sedatives, was actually well ahead of the ringer and I turned to Ken and said: 'Bloody hell Ken, she might win this. What the hell is going on?'

He looked straight ahead, standing erect and confident and smiled knowingly. 'Divn't worry son. There's time yet.'

And sure enough he was correct. My dog after about a hundred yards dropped its weary head, yawned a bit and slowed into a gentle walk while the ringer whizzed past and on to the finish line.

Ken turned to me laughing, still chuckling at the Shiney Row garage man's advice. 'Have a nice day? We bloody well have...ha, ha, ha!'

We took an enjoyable ride back down the Wear valley towards Durham and home. Ken keep chuckling, 'Have a nice day'.

As I dropped him off at his flat, I asked if he had my winnings. 'David, I paid for the petrol and a beer didn't I? But here's another pound to get you to your work tomorrow. I told your dad I wouldn't get you into gambling son. Divn't get started deeing what I dee. It'll get yeah neewhere. Stick in at college, get yah tickets and remember - have a nice day...ha, ha, ha!'

He got out of the car still laughing.

I did a few other similar stings with Ken, one at a more famous track in Newcastle, where the dog was actually dyed a different colour to hide the fact that it was far better than those it was racing against and hence much better odds and a guaranteed win. By the time I grew out of this behaviour our Ken was barred from racing dogs or placing bets on almost all the dog tracks in the North East.

Dominoes and Magic

Another *sporty* character who inhabited the Club was an ex-pitman Pop Burell. Pop spent his time doing magic shows in the Clubs around County Durham at night. He could pull razor blades out of his mouth all strung along a long cord with Union Jack flags also tied to it. He could pull rabbits from his pocket or hamsters from oranges. You name it, he could magic it. He could also cheat at cards and dominoes pretty well, which was not a wise thing to try if your opponent had seen your turn at the Club the night before as a magician. However, that never bothered Pop much but it did our Ken.

Ken told me many stories about accompanying Pop as a minder in an attempt to stop him getting battered from his cheated punters. They used to travel the trains from Newcastle to the race meetings in the North and play cards with the punters. Pop always lost for the first few stations and then slowly started getting lucky with prials of three, royal flushes. They used to earn more on the trains than they ever did at the horses. They also did the same with dominoes and travelled the region playing in the handicaps that were organised in almost every club and bar in the area on Monday afternoons. Ken was his bouncer as he was not in the same league, even fairly, as a domino player like Pop. He told me about one day in Gateshead.

'Davey, we went ower for the handicap. Pop deliberately lost in the semi-final and then played the best players for money after. He lost more than he won and scammed it so that just afor closing time that dinner time he lost a lot of higher value bets. We said we'd come back that night to try to get our money back. The locals loved it as they thowt Pop was nee use and daft enough to hoy his money away. So that night at six we came back and started playing again. Pop lost ower fifty in the first hour and a half and then doubled up the bets again. As usual he slowly started winning a few and dragged them nicely in. As it got nearer nine, he started winning ivry game and the suckers kept doubling up and putting each other's money on his opponents. Finally he cleaned them all out. And remember these games were played out of the bag.'

To explain: dominoes can be played by shuffling the tiles on the domino board, one person shuffles and his opponent then picks up his seven tiles first. Those who know how to cheat will mark the tiles with a spot of grease or dust to ensure they get all or most of one number, which means they will have a large percentage chance of winning, especially if they pick all seven of the sixes, blanks, etcetera. Pop was expert at this, as were many others I knew. To try to thwart our hustling brethren, the more competitive games were played *out of the bag*. That is the dominoes were placed in a bag and then shaken up. The players then picked their seven out of the bag, supposedly unable to see or feel the difference. However, Pop was a magic man as well as con man and he could mark and feel at the same time!

Ken carried on: 'We were ower the moon and with fifty quid a piece in our pockets, we were gonna party like kings. We stopped to drink a few more beers and not look like we'd skinned them and left. A few looked as if they fancied a go but I mentioned a few of the handy lads from the West End I knew and they shut up. But Pop couldn't be happy could he, the daft bugger. He always has to show off his magic show. So after another two pints he starts playing card tricks with them and pulling cards out of their pockets, showing them the card they chose in another gadgy's pocket and then the daft twat pulls a table tennis ball from behind one big ugly twat's ear. ****'s sake, it all kicked off. I hit the ugly one, Pop hit one ower the head with the domino board and we legged it outta the bar, chased down Gateshead high street and we jumped on a bus heading into Newcastle. The bastard used to do that to me every time we went out.'

Indeed, Pop couldn't stop. I played him for ten pence one day in the Club. I shuffled the board rigorously and violently so he couldn't see the tiles. We both picked up and played. He won...he'd picked up 7 blancs!

Roker Pier and the Blast Beach

I was not too interested in Greyhound racing, whippets or dominoes but what I loved was to spend time fishing with my father. The fondest memories I have of Dad are fishing, either in or around London on holiday at my aunty's in the lovely summer heat or fishing off Roker pier in the freezing autumn and winter days and nights.

We fished off Roker, Hendon, South Shields and Seaham piers and also under Alexandra Bridge in Sunderland for sea fish. Under the bridge there were then many flat fish - *flatties*. We caught Dabs, Plaice, Lemon Sole and Flounder all of which were delicious to eat. If I fished with the lads from school, Eeyore Alan, Natty and Jammy mainly, and we had no money to buy lug or rag worms from Tennick's tackle shop in Roker Avenue we'd buy the cheaper bait, kippers, herring or mussel and use that. Such sea food was cheap then. Digging for lugworm and ragworm with a long bladed spit was backbreakingly hard work particularly in the beds in Shields on the Tyne at the Black Middens. Massive rag worms were to be had there as well as on the beaches of Whitburn and Roker. All this bait was no use without fish and those days there seemed to be plenty.

Climbing onto Roker pier those days was a peril as the whole fence was covered with barbed wire with huge metal spikes. It wasn't open to the public like now and we were trespassing but the lighthouse keeper who cycled up every day didn't bother with us. Nor did the local police. It was only when storms hit and someone was washed off you were given any hassle. The lighthouse keeper had an underground tunnel to walk through in storms from his house on the beach to *the roundhead* and up into the lighthouse. Sometimes he would evacuate us through this if the storms got too bad.

Fishing through the night was the real adventure and the best time. But even in summer it was cold and we had no car, so Dad and I had to get off the last bus and wait through the night even if it was

259

desperately cold until the first bus to get home. The whisky in his tea didn't do much good some freezing nights for sure.

I fished with a tortured Eeyore Alan during the coldest night of 1973. We left school in Washington and went to Sunderland with our fishing gear. We sat in *The Park Inn* until about the last bus and with five or six Newcastle Exhibition beers in us took the bus to Dawdon, down the east coast past Seaham. Dawdon, like Easington Village (set of *Billy Elliott*), and Horden, had a pit that went out under the sea and the coal waste and slag was dumped directly into the sea off huge chair lift hoppers. If you have seen the iconic film *Get Carter,* this is where Michael Caine dumps the baddy before he is shot (oops sorry if I spoiled it). Never mind the continuity error only us locals sussed that he must have chased on foot the baddy from the Jarrow slacks on the Tyne across South Tyneside, Sunderland and the River Wear for approximately fifteen miles in only five minutes to end up at the blast beach. However, despite the lack of geographical accuracy I'd recommend it; it's a great movie of its seventies genre and I believe our Ken was in one gangster scene as an extra.

The beach at Dawdon was called the blast beach as all of the coal polluted beaches were on that part of coast. It was like the planet scene from *Alien 2* or what was left of Iwo Jima after John Wayne had nuked it. Nothing grew there - there was no life. It was just coal slag and driftwood but for some unknown biological or piscatorial reason the cod fish loved it, especially at night and in the freezing cold of winter, so Alan and I were off to catch them – or so we thought.

As we got off the double-decker bus with our beach caster rods, duffel coats and haversacks the driver turned and said: 'Are yeah two young buggers daft or summit. Can youse not hear the waves man?'

Now, as the sea was way off through the actual pit and pit yard at the bottom of a huge cliff that we had to descend in the dark, we hadn't even thought to listen. So, fearing he might be correct we put our heads out of the door and heard a distant roar. The bus driver laughed at our shocked faces and said: 'Best of luck lads: this is the last bus yaem though. I pity you daft buggers. I'll be tucked up in beed at the back of our lass's arse soon; warm as toast. So long suckers.'

And he drove off. We walked through the pit buildings and down towards the cliffs. With the beer still affecting our judgement we were confident that even if the sea was well-up we'd catch fish. We didn't even worry about the plank that spanned a gap in the cliff from which it was certain death if you fell. During the miner's strikes of the previous year we'd hauled bags of sea coal wrapped across bike frames up those cliffs. Sea coal and the odd Post Office telegraph pole being the only fuel most of us had. It burnt slowly and gave little heat but at least warmed the ovens to cook from and helped us survive. It was also the only form of heating for many of us during the later year long final strike of 84/85.

The coal has gone now and with the coal went the slag and the waste so now the beach has been reclaimed by nature and is beautiful and sandy. It is a nominated heritage site and haven for sea and marram grasses and bird life. Now they won't film *Alien 2* or *Get Carter* on the beaches I fished but carry out environmental conservation programs. Post-industrial development has improved the environment and health of people in ways we could never have contemplated all those years ago when we saw the desolate and coal waste strewn beaches as a natural part of work and play.

Now budding young lovers should visit these beautiful beaches as part of true love bonding. I took my darling wife there in our first throes of courtship in the seventies when it was still the *Blast Beach* – a real man's beach with pure coal slag and no form of biological life, or indeed any sentience. She sat frozen on coal slag in the barren featureless desert huddled around a sea coal fire and knitting me a woolly jumper. It was a grey, freezing cold winter's day with the wind howling in from the East. I caught two codling all day and was chuffed. She caught double pneumonia but agreed to marry me. She got a good un when she got me, don't you agree? I always was a romantic chap.

Even now forty-four years later she sits knitting while I fish for carp in the rain. How life changes though. Now she has a comfy chair, and umbrella and a lovely lady brings her a hot bacon sandwich and a steaming hot cappuccino. There are even clean, nice toilets she will actually use; a momentous event because she has been traumatised by outside toilets ever since in the throes of first love I took her to watch Sunderland at Roker Park, not long before going fishing on *The Blast*. It seems the ghastly state of only one ladies' loo in a stand for 10,000 people and the lads' peeing onto terraces with their by-product flowing copiously down the steps into her nice open-toed sandals put her into some form of post traumatic shock concerning outside toilets and football. She never went back to watch the lads (a crafty plan by her loving partner you may say). As you will know by now, I spoil her rotten now but I miss those good old football days you can read about in *Relentless Misery* when you could get bubonic plague from the meat pies and cholera from the toilets.

Back to the coldest night of 1973. Alan and I descended the cliff realising that indeed the mocking bus driver was correct - the sea was massive. It had not calmed as we thought it must over the last two days after the North Easterly November gale that had blown all week had abated. We attempted to fish but the waves were too large and constant. So we made the decision to walk to Seaham harbour and fish the pier and if the waves were coming over the pier we would try the *green wall* in the harbour. The zone between Dawdon blast beach and Seaham was called colloquially *the chemical beach*; we had no idea why, except it was like the blast beach - horrible. But in the pitch dark, ten degrees below freezing and half pissed we stumbled into pits and crevices carrying our rods and bags. Then, above the roaring huge sea crashing on the coal strewn beach I heard a cry, 'Help David!'

I looked around and couldn't see Alan but heard another pitiful lonely sob in the dark freezing night: 'Help! I'm bloody sinking.'

I looked to the right and could make out his dark shape but only half his size. I switched on my torch and there he was up to his waste in some form of what must have been chemical waste, slowly sinking. I couldn't help but laugh. This was turning out to be some night. But Alan kept pleading pitifully for me to help as he sank so overcoming my mirth I began to pull him out of the deadly ooze. Finally, he lay on the black coal beach covered in some form of green luminescent nuclear waste which glowed in the torchlight. I howled with laughter again. Funny enough Alan, who remains the most laconic man I know, didn't laugh but went into his Eeyore mantra that I love even to this day. 'Ah just kna'd that would happen to me. Ah just kna we'll get nee fishing noo.'

And indeed he was correct. I caught one codling off the green wall and we froze to death. Hence a ghost writer is writing this. Sorry, but we only nearly froze to death. We were so cold that we packed up and curled up in a woodpile on Seaham docks. We were yards away from Timmy's coble and lay frozen, Alan soaking and his teeth chattering all night with only the radioactive green glow of his body to give us light and we waited for the first bus. The coldest night in 1973 was also the longest for us; but they were happy days for sure. These were days when no one cared if beaches, chemical waste, piers or cliffs were death traps for us all. Luckily, we have moved on.

Ken, Cecil, Pop and the club lads were all ageing gunfighters by the time I was in my late teens and we were growing more into following football, pubs and rock music and hopefully girls. Whippets, greyhounds and dominoes and even freezing to death fishing on nuclear waste covered beaches were becoming passé to us. Slowly, the new Generation X of the seventies and eighties were becoming enlightened, moving towards new Woke and BAME-friendly environments that normal human beings saw as, well, normal. However, for history's sake and for posterity and to show how far we have moved on with gender equality and diversity I will tell of the time that the village broke the chains of unintentional racism and moved down the long road to tolerance.

CHAPTER EIGHTEEN
IGNORANCE AND DIVERSITY

London and Lambton Lion Park

There is no doubt that we had childhoods sheltered from multicultural life. I can't remember ever seeing anyone from a different country, religion, creed or indeed of any colour but pale white or burnt red from too much sun on Roker beach. The first foreigners to go to Shiney Row were my dad in the 40's, Mr Osman, the local Methodist preacher who was Lebanese and his son Thomas who was a year older than us but relentlessly tortured for his olive colour and ethnicity by some at Shiney School. Then the Chinese takeaway arrived in '71 followed a few years after by the Bangladeshis but they did not integrate into this weird community. I was the only youth from my part of the village who could claim to have met anyone different because I holidayed in multicultural London when Dad could afford the overnight bus from Sunderland Park Lane bus station for his annual two weeks holiday.

We stayed at Aunty Win's in Kilburn or Aunty Rene's in Paddington. That was until Aunty Winn moved out to the posh house in Pinner, when we had luxury and I had my own bedroom for once. When we stayed in London I played with my cousin Raymond and his mates in the park play areas between the houses or in Regents Park. A lot of the young kids were black lads of West Indian parents and I played football with them every summer holiday. As I was quite good I got on well with them and they accepted me into the teams and other games. I was of course a total curiosity to the Cockneys as I guess they were to me. My accent caused some communication problems but on the whole we all had similar poor upbringings, life-styles and a love of football. We became good friends, even pen pals and I looked forward to meeting them when we could come again each summer.

When I got home I was always asked: 'What are the darkies like Davey? Are they the same as us then?' I am not trying to be controversial with my choice of phrases but it was the case then that folk were ignorant and many actually were just curious. They weren't trying to be offensive – well, some were simply thick, but a lot of us didn't have any knowledge of the real world or whether a word which our own mothers and fathers would say could be seriously insulting in the wider world. One of these simple folk was *Empty Heed*.

In the early seventies Safari Parks became the trend and our esteemed aristocrat Lord Lambton decided to copy his fellow privileged peer the Marquis of Bath and Jimmy Chipperfield who opened the first safari park in the belted Earl's Longleat Estate. Lambton opened up Lambton Lion Park on his land right next to Shiney Row. Madness we all thought - the lions haven't a chance with the lunatics who prowled and poached the Lord's jungle gills and hamlets.

And they didn't, because not long after he opened up, the lads threw ladders and branches over the fences and cut the chain link to let out the animals both for fun and to have a pop at them. Gussy loved it and wanted to catch a couple of monkeys to add to his growing menagerie in his camp around the Front. A zebra was found in my sister Margaret's house in Burnmoor, right opposite the Park. Lucky for the lions they didn't escape - like the Mother Goose and Widow Twanky, they'd not not lasted long once the club turned out at closing time.

TINKER
Watered Beer and 'Tinkers'

There were few Nobel Prize winners in Tinker's bar the day when *Empty Heed* and his like became emancipated and broke the chains of ignorance and it remains etched in village folk lore.

That day as usual *Tinker*, the landlord of *The Wheatsheaf*, was sitting in the bar playing dominoes with some of his regulars. *Tinker* was a character. He was once a pitman, now a raconteur, voyeur of village life and massive piss taker. We were related to him through our Mark's side. Even though his name was Jack, the bar was always called *Tinker's* by locals and still is even so many years after this wonderful man died. It was once a *Nimmo's* house and then a *Cameron's* from Hartlepool brewery house, famous for *Strong Arm* beer. It remains still the pub of choice for the maniacs of the area. It always was.

In Ken's and Snack's hay day the windows went out most nights I was told. In my day it was similar, Snack was still active then, as were Digger and his lads. Then as the years rolled by, we had Billy Wilson and all his crew with scorpions and tarantulas in a fish bowl on the bar and a savage Rottweiler guarding the outside toilets and back door. In this era we witnessed the pièce de résistance when the local gangster, Buck, bought a round of drinks, took out a handgun and blew his brains out in front of us all. These days the cage fighters who train in the ring up the road built by my nephew maintain the tradition of extreme violence and mayhem built up over fifty years. You can't beat quaint British pubs for tradition and hospitality.

Look up *Tinkers* on YouTube. It's there. My nephew a very young, under age Hedgie is there: an aged, but still large Snack; *Willy the Mag*, Tucker, Starkie, young Nebs and many more characters. It's a throwback to a world when such behaviour was classed as normal – I guess normal as in a Jack Nicholson movie.

Now back to finish our story of early 70's understanding of racial tolerance and diversity. *Tinker*, was playing dominoes, smoking his famous pipe and *Empty Heed* was sat in the corner. *Empty Heed* was, pretty well defined by his nick named. People were talking about the new Lambton Lion Park and *Tinker* was winding them up as was his wont. He mentioned that the park employed white hunters who were thought to be allowed to catch and eat the animals as part of their salary package. Everyone nodded at this sagacity from the elder raconteur. *Empty Heed* looked even more puzzled and anxious and *Tinker* sensing a chance to rip the piss shouted over: '*Empty Heed*, has thoo ever seen a darkie?'

He knew the answer of course but was fishing to amuse the more intelligent and worldly customers who were playing dominoes with him.

Empty Heed responded looking even more tortured. 'Nah, Tinker. I've hord aboot them from the lads down the pit. Live in Africa divn't they.'

Tinker smiled and winked at his customers and took a puff of his pipe. 'Nah Empty Heed not noo. They are all ower the place. Even some born here man.'

Empty Heed responded. 'What! Here? In Shiney? What they deeing here man? What they look like Tinker ?'

Tinker answered taking a long puff at his pipe and winking again at a young Digger sitting opposite him before playing his double six domino and winning the game as usual: 'They're black and wear white hunter hats and khaki shorts.'

'Black! What, like we are after a shift?' Empty Heed asked, referring to the coal dust that habitually covered them all after work.

Tinker winked and shuffled the dominoes again. 'Nah Empty Heed, their skin is actually black man. Black arl ower. Even their dick.'

'Bloody hell man! Ah'd love to meet one. Bet they've got some canny tales to tell Tinker. Ah've nivva been tee Africa. Nivva been past Howton (Houghton-le-Spring)'

'You'll meet one, if they let them out of the Lion Park on their day off.'

Tinker took another puff of his pipe and Empty Heed went into his trance, not really of this world.

Sometime later the door opened and into the bar came a large, very well dressed gentleman in a grey suit, white shirt, red tie and black brogues carrying a briefcase. It was unusual in the village to see anyone in a suit except the older men like my dad who always wore suits on Sunday lunchtime to go to the Club. He must have been a travelling salesman who stupidly thought he'd pop into a quaint pub for a libation on a hot day and chose *Tinkers* – the poor deluded man. However, the most usual feature of this unfortunate traveller was that he was black!

The co-incidence was unbelievable really, Tinker winding Empty Heed up about the origin and behaviours of our friendly people of colour and then someone of colour actually walked in. To my knowledge this had never happened before in the village and never in the pub. The gentleman looked around and asked in a perfect cockney accent where the landlord was; by the way anyone non-local was viewed as and therefore Southern and Cockney, even if they came from Hartlepool.

Tinker got up and told him that he was the landlord and walked behind the bar to serve the man. It was like the Clantons had walked into the bar in Tombstone before *the Gunfight at the Ok Corral*. Life stopped. The dominoes stopped chattering, people stopped taking drags on their cigarettes and absolute silence reigned as they all looked towards *Empty Heed* who was staring at the man as if he had seen a ghost. His face was a picture of awe and his eyes usually half shut and bleary were bright and shining as if he'd seen the Angel Gabriel in Bethlehem.

The man asked for a pint of Cameron's Best Bitter. Tinker gave him Ordinary of course, always suitably watered down in the underground cellar casks for the underage lads like me that he allowed to drink in the back room. He also gave his weak beer to strangers and charged them a penny more. The man paid and started to drink his well-earned pint. He had obviously had a long drive that morning and looked in need of refreshment. Tinker looked mischievously over at Empty Heed and winked and nodded his head towards the visitor, as if to say: *Look here's one, just like I told you.*

Empty Heed in a burst of enlightenment and curiosity that belied his normal wit and intelligence got up out of his seat in the corner window - the window where people were thrown through most nights - and approached the thirsty salesman.

Everyone waited in anticipation, silence cracking the air. He tapped the man on the shoulder and as the man turned to look down on him, Empty Heed asked his never forgotten question: 'How man, is thoo a darkie?'

People in the pit villages of East Durham always spoke Bible English my old Geordie colleague from Newcastle, Big Don, used to tell me when he came to drink over in Shiney in *The Oddfellows*. He thought it amusing to listen to Geordie Williamson (*Willie*), one the village's best preachers, talk his *Thous* and *Thees* and *Thoos*. Now, whether our friend from the South in *Tinkers* bar that afternoon understood Bible language and the pitmatic *Thoo* or not is important but he seemed to understand that his ethnicity was in question. Everyone sat and watched for what seemed an eternity. Tinker took another puff of his pipe, glancing at his customers in quiet satisfaction that his wind up had worked. Our visitor looked at Empty Heed who was staring at the man in astonishment still and the visitor looked up and down his own body and took his hand off his beer and replied: 'Well, mate, I guess I must be.'

Empty Heed stared, gob-smacked and then as if he had discovered Archimedes' law of displacement, he nodded his amazingly thick head at the man and gave his own *Eureka*: 'Champion! Ah thowt see. Ah always wanted to meet one. Thanks marra,' And he shook the bewildered man's hand, turned around and sat down again.

The stranger shook his head as his new found *marra* (friend/workmate) sat down and drank up his pint. Tinker put down his pipe and asked if wanted another drink.

'No thanks. I think I'll head off back to civilisation if that's all right.'

He picked up his briefcase, took a look at Empty Heed who was staring at the wall in his corner looking puzzled at the mysteries of the metaphysical universe, his life's ambition fulfilled. The stranger shook his noble dark head in pained disbelief at the asylum he'd unfortunately entered and left. I doubt he ever went to Shiney again.

Yes. It was a mad house, *Tinkers*, and as I admitted before all of us then, not just Empty Heed, were to different extents ignorant of other people, cultures, languages and behaviours.

GEORDIE
Mackems and Geordies

The story of Empty Heed's first encounter with his *White Hunter* reminds me of the xenophobia in a racial incident some years after we all became much more correct in our language and behaviour. It happened when I entered purgatory and actually had to work. Workers on Tyneside in England, like a lot of areas, were pretty militant and also could be extremely parochial and xenophobic. Tyneside wouldn't let workers from Sunderland (less than nine miles away) work in their shipyards and they'd strike at the blink of Jimmy Hoffa's concrete eye. Parochially, this is put down to the hatred between *Mackems* (Sunderland people) and *Geordies* (from Newcastle) referencing their two football teams, but basically most was pure job protection arising from a territorial hierarchy bordering on tribal. A classic example was what happened to a lovely man and scaffold manager who worked for me.

George was a *Barnardos Boy* (an orphan who was taken into the care of Doctor Barnardo's organisation) and along with his sons, grew up in one of the hardest areas of Sunderland, Hendon Docks. Marvellous man, husband and father but hard as nails. He had to be, he was black and there weren't many black lads in Sunderland, even in post-Empty Heed days.

When I first met him he told me that he'd found prejudice was rife in this corner of England. I sympathised with him but wasn't surprised as to me as few locals had been educated in multicultural alignment. For most of those I grew up with the only black person they had seen was their father when he came back from the pit covered in coal dust.

George carried on. 'Dave, when I first worked on the Tyne I faced so much prejudice. They used to drop welding rods on me heed. They would spit at me, me car was trashed and I was attacked by a couple with a baseball bat after work in the car park. Mind you, I kicked **** out of them.'

As you do, I thought. Oh the wonders of a Hendon dockland and a Banardo's upbringing - not unlike Flashman in *Tom Brown's School Days* and his upbringing in that other bastion of English society, Rugby school.

'Aye, Geordie, I'm sorry to hear that son. It must have been hard being black, mate?'

'Davey man, you daft bugger! It wasn't coz I was black, they had nee bother aboot that man. It was coz I was a *Mackem*.'

To explain, in football, *Mackem* was a term for people who came from Sunderland and supported Sunderland AFC. In the heartlands of the Tyne shipyards, our Geordie faced a tribal prejudice of a different kind to that of his colour, something he was used to.

Very soon after Empty Heed became enlightened I too sought my own road to Damascus and left the very sheltered and bizarre environment I had surrounded myself in for eighteen years and headed off to a very multicultural and gender diverse life as a student at Manchester University.

CHAPTER NINETEEN
MANCHESTER UNIVERSITY AND LOVE

MRS ASHMAN
Shiney Library and Dr Doolittle

I finished secondary school in 1974 and gained the A level grades I needed for University. I had spent many hours studying in the library at the end of my street and as I write this now I can still remember the joy and the excitement of the library being built all those years ago in the sixties. I already loved books and read them at home in bed borrowing them mainly from the small school collection and the thought of at last having our own village library was amazingly exciting to some of us street kids. We used to play football each one of us as a different character from either *Mr Twink* or the *Dr Doolittle* books. Harmless, and I know before you say it, not what you'd expect from *real schoolboys*. But we were young then and we made sure none of the big boys, or heaven forbid, the girls, saw us being soft! This reminds me, some behaviours you never forget because I still look around 360 degrees when my wife tries to make me hold her hand in public. 'Who knows,' I say. 'Someone I know might see us.'

I used the new library to read every book series I enjoyed. Sometimes the library or school didn't stock them all so I used to save up pocket money and go the *Hill's* book shop in Sunderland to buy them. I moved on from saving bird's eggs, cigarette brand packets, and chewing gum cards to collecting books. As a co-incidence my wife was doing exactly the same thing many miles away in the foreign and barren world of Yorkshire (well not exactly the same collections obviously). She saved her pocket money and part-time work money to buy books but her mother wouldn't let her read anything until she had done her chores and only in bed with a torch as her mother, a real Yorkshire woman, had a simple principle - you should sleep in bed and be too tired to waste time reading after hard graft.

I bought books on many things and I read further volumes in Shiney library. I studied in there throughout my O levels and A levels, mainly because it was warm in winter, especially during the mining strikes and the power strikes of the early seventies when we had no heat or light. Later, as it was quiet, I also spent time during my University breaks in there.

A couple of years ago, I met Fay - Mrs Ashman then, a lady not a great lot older than me who had worked there from leaving school - now made redundant. She had been there since I was a young man. I met her in *The Oddfellows Arms*. Anyway we talked about how the library had helped and guided many to a better life in many ways. She remembered me fondly as the young teenager and then man who frequented and studied there throughout his academic life, days without Google, the Internet or multiple choice questions.

Recently, I also met Fay's partner, Ray Larsen, a very funny crazy human being in *Tinkers* along with Hedgie my loving nephew, *Geordie the Mag*, Snack's daughter and many of the other last old gunfighters of Shiney who still refuse to go quietly into the night. I had my youngest son with me taking him for the first time to Tinkers. Sadly for him, the people in there, both men and women, have very few teeth left for him to practice his budding Dentistry on and definitely not the money for expensive orthodontic tooth replacements. They'd only be kicked out again anyway.

We drank to the old days and to those who have faded away, tragically many not as peacefully as they and their loved ones would have wished, but I raised my glass higher to Fay and her colleagues and for that library because it moulded me and many like me. It was pulled down to make way for another cheap shop and those who shut it and all the others are no better in my mind than those politicians that burned books or closed the pits and shipyards.

University and Strange People

In autumn 1974, the library was still there, I'd won my place at University and now I was ready to take a life changing step. My dad walked me to the Number 39 bus stop to get the bus to Newcastle and take a train to Manchester and start college. We shook hands and said goodbye - no hugs, kisses or emotion those days, but I saw a fierce pride and happiness in his face. He was so proud that I was going. Few people did from the village then. Students from low income backgrounds could only attend by the grace of a full educational Government grant for fees and living.

My father and mother that warm autumn morning in late September had no idea what I was doing or what it entailed or where I was going. Everything about school, exams, UCCA, university was beyond them; all they ever wanted was me to be happy. Unconditional love;

something I was too young and also too thoughtless to understand then.

My father's only desire and that of the fathers and mothers of many of my pit village friends was that he would do anything so that I did not have to go down the pit. I was lucky, and to this day I thank him for his encouragement, patience and rehabilitating financial support for my education because not only did it mean I did not have to go down the pit, it meant I had a range of choices. So many people do not. And that is a stain on all of us. We should strive to give our children a choice. Too many times in my lifetime we have failed collectively as a government of the people, by the people and for the people to do this. I can only pray that one day a government will see the sense and a way forward.

Back in 1974 there weren't many choices for working class kids. I was one of the lucky ones; I never realised then how fortunate I was but very soon I did as strikes and unemployment hit hard and changed the lives of so many people I knew. Not much choice when uneducated, broken and on the dole. Thank you Dad, those nights reading books to me and long walks talking about life before you went off for your Sunday pint; they gave me a choice – all the money in the world couldn't take that from me.

I knew nothing about choice as I climbed onto the Number 39 bus and waved goodbye to that sad, loving, man. I would not be back until Christmas and contact would only be by letter as we had no phone. All through that lonely first term I waited to get my letter from my dad. It made me so happy, a great pleasure that has long gone. I met Gary and Eeyore Alan at Newcastle Central Station. Gary was off to Salford University and Alan to UMIST. We were all heading off to the unknown having hardly ever left the pit villages we grew up in. When we arrived in Manchester it was pissing down. When we left three years later it was pissing down. In the meantime, it pissed down. Something I gather that hasn't changed since the Seventies.

We soon split up and Gary went off to find his bus and Alan and I got on ours to head to our halls of residence. He got off at Oxford road and I headed on down past the University, through Rusholme and onto Fallowfield. I walked for ages in the rain, lugging my huge suitcase around the halls of residence trying to identify my flat. Eventually I knocked on the door and a lovely big brown eyed girl opened the door to find a bedraggled and soaked, long-haired, bearded tramp standing there. As I looked into the flat I could see girls things drying on the radiator. I was both puzzled and mildly excited. I was supposed to be sharing the flat with seven other boys. Four upstairs and four downstairs in individual bedrooms with a common bathroom and lounge and kitchen…there shouldn't be girls in here surely?

And sure enough there weren't - wrong flat. But she introduced herself with a lovely Yorkshire lilt and with an amazing co-incidence we found out that we both were on the same course. There you are Gill…I told you I'd make you famous.

I went next door to my own flat and pushed the bell. A very dark lad opened the door and spoke to me in halting, African English. I have to say I was a bit like Empty Heed; it was a bit of shock to me. You didn't meet many Kenyans in Shiney. He invited me in. My bedroom was next to the door so I entered and put my suitcase down. The walls were white-washed, breeze block concrete, one small bed and a desk and window. But it was a room I thought and I needed to dry off. So I went to the shared bathroom and dried myself off and changed. I then went into the communal kitchen cum lounge and sat at the table was the African lad and another foreign lad who introduced himself in broken English as Pablo from Venezuela. For an hour we stared at each other trying to make conversation but unable to communicate. My Geordie pitmatic was unintelligible those days and I couldn't make out a word of what they said. I looked at my watch and it was 5 pm and thought *This is going to be a long, long term and when does the bar open?*

I heard the front door open and a loud couple of voices, banging and shouting and then the bedroom door next to the lounge opening. A few minutes of noises and English voices and the door opened up and in came a tall, long, strawberry blond-haired lad and a bubbly, curly blonde-haired girl. The boy looked at the three lonely and probably frightened souls sat around the table. 'Hi I'm Paul and this is Jude my girlfriend. Is the bar open yet?' he said putting his hand out.

I took his hand and replied: 'Davey: I'm not sure when it opens but was told maybe 7 pm. But there's one I saw in Fallowfield down the road, *The Friendship*, I think that's five thirty. Let's gan now if you want?'

'Do you want to come?' Paul asked our fellow flat mates.

'We don't drink.' Was their astonishing reply – well it was astonishing to my new found drinking mate Paul and certainly to me.

'For ****'s sake man why did you come to England then?' Paul asked, plainly shocked.

'To study,' said Pablo.

Paul shook his long hair in despair and amazement and Jude came over to the two foreign students and patted them gently as if they were sick or suffering puppies. I turned, uninterested in foreign teetotallers and as I left the room said: 'Come on then we're missing opening time.'

So it began, three years of booze, sex and music, with a little study in between for some of us.

Paul never did a lot of studying to my knowledge. He did Sociology or some namby-pamby non-science course where studying was irrelevant. If they ever went to lectures it would in the University Student Union bar where the social science lecturers were permanently ensconced anyway discussing the causes of rampant poverty and alcoholism and drug abuse in Moss Side whilst getting stoned and pissed themselves.

Indeed, Paul quickly sussed that the route to happiness and a successful career in music, which was his goal, was not through a first-class honours degree but by joining the social events committee and getting himself elected Social Secretary. Then the following year the hope was to be selected for the job of all jobs, Events Officer, a salaried sabbatical position. This was the Holy Grail of all social science students; no study, no work, just free concert tickets, booze, drugs and a ticket to the music business.

Over the three years I was there I saw that some of the past Events Officers and Social Secretaries had been there at University for decades. Some I think were made Emeritus professors of dodging real work. Paul, in awe of these people, longed to become a Professor of events management and prolong his time in student paradise.

Student Unions and Punk

Paul had thousands of LPs and a music system that was state of the art. I had a transistor radio as that was all I could fit in my suitcase. He also knew John Peel and had met Eric Clapton, his hero, a few times. Music was his way to happiness and as social secretary for the Students' Union he met many bands and had the power with the Events Officer, which he eventually became, to make or break emerging bands. Punk was just emerging in the mid-seventies. Personally I was still very much into progressive rock and electric folk but Paul persuaded me to come and watch this new band he had booked called *The Stranglers*, who were playing what we now know was a more sedate forerunner to the wild punk of *The Sex Pistols* and *The Clash*. We duly turned up on a Saturday night at the Union and listened to about two songs from this wonder band when Paul and his committee (not unlike the Club and Snack) paid off the band by unplugging the sound system. I often wonder if *The Stranglers* ever did another gig and became famous!

I met the *Lindisfarne* lads at the Saturday night show, very drunk on brown ale, all of us and a bit late playing due to the consumption but still I can see us all swaying and singing: *We Can Swing Together* as we did back home in the North East at house parties when at school. And then my favourite meet of all time - I talked to Melanie Safka – loved her and her music since early school: *Candles in the Rain, Peace Will Come,* and *Leftover Wine* - listen to them and weep. Music that united not divided...yes, the music hadn't died that first year in 1975.

Anoraks and Physics

Over the next few days the whole flat filled up. John was next to my bedroom. A quiet older lad from Southport who ran a care home with his mother and we were to become good friends. Above us a dental student arrived - like the two foreign students he never drank, so obviously I can't remember him.

Then Michael arrived.

Michael was a tall, gangly curly-haired youth in a huge red quilted anorak, which was in some way still in fashion then. He was what these days you would call *an anorak* or *geek.*' He was studying Physics and was not unlike *Sheldon* off *Big Bang Theory;* highly intelligent with dysfunctional social interpersonal skills, as my Asperger's expert wife informs me now, but to us simple folks he was simply crackers. Drink was not a friend to Michael - he went over the top if he had any, which was anytime we took him out or he decided to bring a few bottles of Woodpecker cider back to his room. It was a perpetual battle to stop him getting beaten up as, wearing his brown Marks and Spencer slacks, a long-sleeved shirt buttoned up to the neck and his huge red anorak, he practised his courtship technique of fixing on a girl, any girl even if with a lad, dancing extremely close, throwing his arms and huge long legs in the air. I saved his arse many a night from irate boyfriends and I loved him purely because he was different and a bit crazy - especially, when he built us a telly out of spare parts.

He told us he had built many electronic gadgets back home - he even built a spy camera, long before surveillance cameras and CCTV was invented, which he hid in his parents ceiling light. We did begin to wonder about Michael when he told us this. Most of us had no desire to even think about our parents at grips never mind watch it!

Sadly, despite having a brain the size of a planet, Michael failed his first year exams and we never saw him again; a casualty who failed to adapt to college life and learn how to study on his own for choosing a terribly hard and unfair science subject course with professors who expected you have the brain of Richard Feynman to pass. This is a lesson to anyone thinking of borrowing fifty grand to get a degree and then a postgraduate life of huge student debt, unemployment and misery - never choose Physics.

Maine Road and Rastafarians

I struggled on weekends if I wasn't playing football because most students didn't drink during the day or they went out late at about 8 or 9 pm and drank one pint.

I was becoming very homesick so I started going over to watch Manchester City play on Saturday afternoons to kill time. Maine Road was across Platt Park and through Moss Side. Those days Moss Side was known as the roughest, most dangerous place in Manchester. To me it was just another great place to drink. I used to have a few in different bars before the match and after the match I went to a pub which, like a lot of Moss Side then was full of Rastafarian types. I could play very good darts and I started to take money off them. For some obscure reason, they seemed to like me and I went there most Saturdays as I went to matches over a year or so. Maybe it was the accent and the long hair and beard. The Jamaican accent was very similar to mine for sure! But I made some canny friends in there. Everyone normal I met back in Halls of Residence used to think that I had lost the plot to go there as the reputation was one of extreme violence, extortion, drugs and gang warfare. I naively told them they should come up at Christmas with me to visit Shiney Row.

When The Boat Comes In and Bobby Thompson

Those days my accent was strong, Durham, *pitmatic* bible speak, I guess. To me and to everyone I knew it was a Geordie accent and I was a Geordie to anyone I met. I loved the North East culture and still do.

Bobby Thompson, the *Little Waster*, had pit village and shipyard life down to a fine art, hilariously funny with a lot of pathos, mixed with self-depreciation of the poverty and struggle to provide a living. He was a friend of our Ken. He came from Fatfield, the same place as the goalkeeper *Jordan Pickford*, and *Alan Price* of *The Animals* rock band fame. Ken and Bobby had worked together down the pit before Ken took to crime and fleecing posh women and Bobby took to the stage and fleecing agents and punters by not turning up. He became famous on TV, lost it all, became a liability for agents trying to book him and then resurrected his career in the seventies. He is sadly a bit unintelligible to most of the rest of the world and the life he describes has mostly gone. But please look up his videos on YouTube. It says a lot about the times this book is about.

In Manchester, Gary, Alan and others I met from the North East were Geordies, no matter what team you supported. And the girls loved it. Mainly because the two hit TV programmes at the time were *When the Boat Comes In* and *The Stars Look Down,* both depicting life in the North East pits after the first war which frankly wasn't much different to what I'm describing in this epic of the fifties and sixties. The girls loved to hear the accent. They'd ask to hear us say, *Toast and butter* - which came out as *Toe-est and boetta* – or to sing the *When the Boat Comes In* theme song.

> *Dance ti' thy Daddy, sing ti' thy Mammy,*
> *Dance ti' thy Daddy, ti' thy Mammy sing;*
> *Thou shall hev a fishy on a little dishy,*
> *Thou shall hev a fishy when the boat comes in.'*

This was a better *knicker dropper* than Cherry B and Cider! The rest of the song is about drink and the hope of more cheap fish, particularly haddock, bloaters and salmon; you'd need a big wallet to buy them these days for tea.

Drink was then and still is a big part of North East culture and I tell a tale of those days to prove it. The end of term I brought John and his mate from Sandbach, Phil, back home for a weekend. They couldn't believe the sight in *The Manor's Club*, Newcastle, after I'd picked them up from the 2.00 pm train at Central Station on a Friday. We got in about 2.20 pm and it was packed, hundreds of men in a smoke-filled room. The tables were full of *Newcastle Brown Ale* drinkers and they had never seen so much *Broon'* and so many men in a bar on a supposed working weekday. You see, it was the height of decadence in

Manchester to drink *Brown Ale*. The posh students thought they were on crack cocaine or LSD if they had one bottle. It was the Absinthe of beer to the University intelligentsia. Here in Newcastle it was just normal daily food in vast quantities and a sure route to Ward 17 in the Royal Infirmary. My publisher Andrew is certain he came with me and another friend Colin Megson one weekend and was similarly amazed at the place, but the drink has numbed my memory of that.

I was shocked that evening when we got to our house because on the TV was an advert for the merits of moderate drinking. I couldn't believe what I was seeing. After all I'd told the lads and lasses in Manchester about our famous drinking culture. The ad showed a few lads getting on a double decker bus in Newcastle and spotting a mate at the back sitting with his girlfriend.

'How man its half pint Harry!' one lad shouts and points at the mate who obviously didn't believe in drinking himself senseless.

'Harry man thoo should have been with us last neet,' another shouts as they walk up to him.

'Bet thoo wishes thoo could drink like us man. Last neet we wez comatose on the lash, mortal man. It wez mint. We canna remember a thing.'

Harry's girlfriend grabs and holds his hand and smiles lustfully looking into his eyes. Then she turns to the lads and says: 'We can. Can't we pet?'

Thankfully it made little impact on beer sales – or romance, North East style.

EDDY
Edgehill College and Soccer Hooligans

I became homesick in Manchester so I headed over the East Lancs Road to Edgehill College, Ormskirk where Eddy was studying Physical Education to be a teacher. *Chuckle, chuckle.* Studying for God's sake? The place was a heaven for young men. Seven girls to every boy, sport every day, a bar that sold cheap beer and discos most nights. I never left for weeks. I played semi pro-football in Liverpool and earned a bob or two for my beer. I also played college football and some basketball and then one day I was volunteered by Eddy to play *that girls' game*, hockey. Well, I thought it was for girls until I realised how fit the male players were, and skilfull and hard. Sadly, I wasn't up for people smashing me with balls and sticks, which should only happen outside

Shiney Row Club or the Chinese, so I reverted to Friday night type and was sent off for chasing an Indian lad around the pitch trying to brain his turban covered head with my hockey stick. I stuck to football and fair fights without sticks after that.

Eddy's tutor was a man called Wally Edge, a very interesting man as he'd taught Paul McCartney and George Harrison at The Liverpool Institute High School. They'd had a real soft spot for the man and nicknamed him Cliffy, a name he'd keep forever; it would be wouldn't it, Mr Edge! He is also pictured on the cover of George's album Dark Horse. Less interestingly than his Beatles connection, one day he saw me sat in the bar one afternoon after five weeks of knowing me and said: 'Davey what are you doing here? Shouldn't you be in the Educational Psychology lecture with Eddy?'

'Why?' I replied, taking a drink from my pint.

He looked puzzled and said that this was a teacher training college.

I said, 'I know, I'm at Manchester University Medical School'.

He sadly shook his head, walked away saying: 'I should have known if you were a mate of Eddy's...'

The bank in Ormskirk also asked me why I didn't move my account from my home in Manchester if I was studying in Edgehill and I told them the same as I'd told Wally Edge. Like him, they just shook their heads.

When I returned to my Oak House flat in Fallowfield, Paul and John had packed up my stuff to send back. They thought I'd gone home. They thought I couldn't wait until Christmas in a few weeks to get back home and be with fellow football fans. Actually they were right.

Eddy and me went to many Sunderland away matches from college over those years and still do. The terraces were as hard as the managers and crackerjack players then too. In the seventies going to a game was dodgy and some places dodgier then others. My book Relentless Misery is all about supporting football teams over sixty years and the crazies we met and crazy things we all did. Needless to say, the games at Manchester were where I had most fun, or terrors - both were inextricably linked. Eeyore Alan who came to Uni with me was a strong Magpie fan, along with Davey Rutter and a lot of other North East football team lads I played with, as was my oldest friend Paul from Shiney. I had gone to Sunday school with Paul - his father was a Methodist minister at the chapel and Sundays for Paul were difficult as he had to follow a strict day of worship and abstinence from TV, play or fun. It was hard for Paul as he lived in the posh houses, and had the stigma of wearing glasses and being a church lad. Therefore, with the usual stereotyping by the lads, he was classed as soft. He was my best friend and I used to look after him when he was little. He failed his eleven plus so he didn't go to the grammar school but had to endure the torments of Shiney Row Secondary Modern School. But as he grew older he became a fit strong young man, joined the army cadets, then the Marine cadets and eventually the Paras and could well look after himself. He used to visit me in Manchester and I would be obliged to go to the match with him and Eeyore Alan if the team were playing Manchester United.

Paul was staying with me when Newcastle played United on a Wednesday night. Alan and Paul persuaded me to go along with a lad we lived with called *the Gargoyle*, so named because that was what he was. He was short, hump-backed and with a long, twisted face on a massive head covered with coarse wirey hair which he never washed in all the time we knew him.

'Urgh...I don't need to wash - it has natural oils,' was his charming excuse. Also he never ever slept. If you came in anytime during the night, he was awake and sat on the bed in a Buddha like position. He said he didn't need sleep. His eyes bulged like *Marty Feldman* and I suspected he had an overactive thyroid but he would dismiss this notion with his usual guttural, primeval, 'Urgh'. He only had a couple of pairs of white (well, grey-stained) baggy underpants and the dirty pair he used to store at the base of his bed. And always, every minute of the day, he was listening to the seventies hit song, *Where Do You Go to My Lovely* by Peter Sarstedt. It was on his record player constantly, day or night. The guy whose bedroom was next door to him hated him with a passion and he had taken to recording him at the toilet. He told Alan and me that the sounds emanating from in there were inhuman and not of this world and went on for hours. So he taped the sounds and played them back to us. Dear God, the memory haunts me still. Joyfully, the tragic end of Peter Sarstedt and that song was a moment of great joy to us all.

It began when Stan came to visit. Stan came down for a party. He was by then the alter ego of *Sid Vicious* of *The Sex Pistols*. In the middle of the night about 3 am we were in my bedroom where all of us were kipping and all you could hear were the constant strains of *Where Do You Go to My Lovely*. Alan told Stan that this had tormented everyone for months. Stan said no more but walked out the room and down the stairs. All we heard was the teeth-clenching screech of a needle being scratched across the record and then perfect silence. Stan came back upstairs and explained. He had walked in on the horrible sight of the Gargoyle sitting on the bed in his Buddha position, naked except for grey baggy underpants, his red bulging eyes and staring intensely at him. Stan had walked over to the record player, crashed the needle arm across the record, taken the disc off the turntable and thrown it out of the third floor window into the street below. He did all this in silence and turned around and came back upstairs leaving *the Gargoyle* mortified and gargling, 'Urgh'. So ended the nightly Sarsted torture.

But *the Gargoyle* was of some use – he had a handgun, a Beretta with a magazine and real bullets but the firing pin had been filed down and for some insane reason decided to take it to the match. Pulling it out saved them all from a good kicking when confronted by several violent United hooligans on an Oxford Road bus. One more bizarre incident in that fine football-supporting city.

Coffins and Tommy Ducks

We often drank in a famous bar called *Tommy Ducks*. It was in town and opposite the Midland Hotel in East Street. It was good for a couple of reasons. The first and main one is that you could get a lock in there after the Student Union bar shut at 3 pm. This was long before the pubs were allowed to open all day. The second reason for its fame was that it had girls' underwear stapled on the ceilings supposedly by grateful female customers. Mind you it also had a glass-topped coffin in the bar.

We were welcomed in there and came to realise that the police drank there too as well as more than a few villains. Also the cast of *'Coronation Street'* imbibed there too and members of the cast had added their knickers to the collection on the ceiling. I couldn't get too excited by *Ena Sharple's* drawers mind!

I enjoyed *Tommy Ducks* right up until the weekend of a Newcastle match when the landlord took the side of the lunatics who had just been released from Strangeways Prison against poor old me and Eeyore Alan. And I lost all respect I may have had left for Greater Manchester police the next day when, like the landlord, they made it clear that they hated Paul and me as Geordies and allowed a mob of their team's *firm* to hunt us down on the street in plain sight without lifting a finger to save us.

I've never been a fan of Manchester polis since and certainly not after they let a mob of National Front skinheads batter some of my less street-wise fellow students senseless when we were peacefully demonstrating outside Barclays Bank on Oxford Road against the bank's support of Apartheid in South Africa – a hard lesson learnt, and one for today's revolutionary youth - simply, if you are going to risk the wrath of a mob of right wing fascist thugs who may contain many trained by the British army or police or Milwall football club then at least take a few along who can fight.

DOCTOR FOZZARD
Schizophrenia and Tomatoes

Outside of football matches, I did do some studying but really not until the final two terms of the final year. You could to do this then. Now people seem to have to work continuously to get their degrees. This indolence and aversion to work was unfairly rewarded as I gained an upper second which pissed off my peers on the course. First class science degrees were not given out those days unless you actually were Einstein.

We had some really good tutors at the Stopford Building Medical School and some strange ones. Our Professor specialised in neuropharmacology and diseases of the mind. It was alleged he may well have personal experience of such disorders and he certainly went missing for periods, whether to medical conferences or the nut house, I can't possibly say. Certainly he loved to tell us how to trick the criminal justice system.

His favourite tale was how to persuade the police that you were crackers when you had maimed or chopped your partner up. He had discovered, whether from personal study or not who knows, that if you stuff your face with hundreds of tomatoes there is a chemical marker in them that mimics the one seen when they test for Schizophrenia; a sure fire way to *avoid the chair* through diminished responsibility. You dear reader may have use of this pharmacological gem one day and thank me for it.

His other classic was how to cure the reactive depression caused by having to eventually face the music of final examinations after three years of drunken and drug crazed idleness, sex and sloth. His cure? Eat several tons of bananas. Bananas are loaded with a precursor to 5-hydroxytryptamine (5HT) and in the mid 70's a lack of 5HT in the brain was thought to be the cause of reactive depression so by adding vast quantities of it to one's brain it might well cure you. It would not actually do the study you should have completed over the previous three years but you would feel very, very happy when you failed, or got a third class ordinary degree.

Prozac and Rabbit Stew

Doctor Barry Cox was a great tutor, full of comedy and he made lectures and practical lessons fun. He specialised in real 5HT research. He was not as bananas as the Prof and he moved off some time later to join a big Pharma company. I believe he made several steps towards the discovery of a 5HT agonist, now the solution to hundreds of millions of people's anxieties and woes across the world. It is called Prozac. I still prefer bananas.

A lot of the time we researched on animals. Sad I know but necessary. Students themselves were paid to take Stage 1 Clinical Trials of new drugs. We got decent beer tokens by putting ourselves in the forefront of research. The beer I think killed any side effects of the test drugs. The animals were humanely killed before dissection and I saw no reason to waste the rabbits as they could make a good stew and normally we couldn't afford meat. Well, we did eat meat pudding and chips from the chippy after a gallon of beer so maybe that's an exaggeration.

Meat puddings are a Lancashire thing and I miss them a lot. *Gobblin* or *Frey Bentos* tinned meat puddings are not the same. As an aside, I could open a *Fray Bentos Pudding* or steak and kidney pie tin using a mechanical tin opener. My older son when a student a couple of years ago, despite having a brain the size of a planet, had no idea how to open the *Fray Bentos Steak and Kidney Pie* tin I had donated to him and his starving flat mates. Why? Because as he told me afterwards, 'They don't have a ring pull on them Dad.' It appears he tried knives and forks, screwdrivers and finally did what all the young uns these days do, he YouTubed it. Sure enough there is a video on that cyber wonder world of another student whose parents had to post him a video of how to use a mechanical tin opener. The mind boggles at what they teach our kids these days, don't it!

Ring pull tins had not been invented when we were Cubs or Scouts or just camping out and trying to open tins with one of the devices in our Swiss Army knives. Normally you'd slice the end of your thumb off. And this now makes me think my son had a point. *Why do Fray Bentos not use ring pull tins?* For sure, their corned beef needs an easier way to open it for God's sake. That pre-Enlightenment Iron Age opening device is lethal. How many people have bled to death on badly opened corned beef tins? When you pick up the tin and there is no metal key thing attached or when the thing snaps off half way around and you try to dig the meat out with your Swiss Army knife and slip and lose your last opposable thumb. This leaves you unable to hold your mobile phone which is useless anyway because you yet again fail to remember is it 999 or 111 or what the **** is the mobile phone number to press for emergency? And you finally fall to floor frothing at the mouth. As you bleed into unconsciousness you remember the famous *Sun* headline in the Falkland War when we sank the Belgrano - *Gottcha.* Then you realise that all along the Argies have been planning this. Only the British are daft enough to eat corned beef or steak and kidney puddings out of tins anyway so let's make them lethal to open and *kill 'em all.* As you slowly bleed to death on your kitchen floor and approach eternity you realise the clever Argies have finally got their revenge for the Belgrano...*Gotcha, you English bastard.*

Those days at Manchester there were no ring pulls, and we had lost our Swiss Army knives, so sick of eating pudding and chips from the chippie, I also tried to make guinea pig stew. However, there's not really much meat on rodents. My flat mates at the time were not impressed with my stews as they worried about the drugs which might have been within the poor creature. Have to say it never affected us, except maybe *the Gargoyle* - it may well have been the source of his horrible screaming and panting during his hour long bowel movements. Sorry mate, I was only trying to cure the world's sick.

Like my son, other young people may not understand terms which to us were commonplace. In *The Brass*, a new pub here ran by two gay young men, Jamie and Byron, who are trying hard to introduce my fellow wrinklies to the brave new world of *Woke* understanding, the young barperson, Harvey, made me think again about terms that are being thrown into the dustbin of history. A few tourists came in and one asked this young man if there was a fruit machine in the pub. He finally raised his head from his Smartphone (a most unusual occurrence because even Steve the boxer with his gentle prompting - 'Matey, get your arse off that phone and pour us a round before I thump you,' - struggles to break his undoubted concentration) and said the immortal words, 'This is a pub. We don't sell fruit. Mrs Tibbs around the corner will sell you a banana or anything you want.'

You may laugh, but really, like the ring pull can, if the only gaming machine you know is one that looks like a Boeing 737 cockpit and you need a degree in Advanced Mathematics to use it, why would you say anything else – indeed. We chuckled at what the lad would have said if they'd asked for a one-armed bandit. Would he have directed them to the police station?

I mentioned the episode of the Argentinean corned beef tin cyber plot to my fellow ancients. Charlie agreed vehemently with my conspiracy theory. Furthermore, he was adamant that the Government was in a plot with tin makers to make ring pull tins impossible for us old folks to open.

'The bastards are trying to starve us to death buoy. They hope to save billions on the pensions. Those pensioners who bloody Covid don't kill off they'll get anyway, because they will starve them to death. I spent three days with no food last week because with my arthritis I couldn't pull the ring open on my tin of beans or the tins of tuna. Finally, I had to get my old tools out and hacksaw the tops off!' Indeed, it is not easy when your bones get old, which was confirmed that same morning before the pub (which was my 66th birthday by the way). I had been typing my next mega book, a timeless classic for children, *Tommy's Last Wish* and listening to worship music on YouTube, as is my wont. Before each song the advertisements were for coffin dodgers in this order: first *A cure for Arthritis*, next *A cure for Prostate Cancer* and then, the crème de la crème and the ignominy of it all - they use some bloke with the most irritating fake Geordie posh voice to tell me *how to plan a cheap funeral*. How do they know that! How do they know it's the day I finally get my bus pass! And this, after years of being the only one on the bus everyday heading into the town to drink ale and the only one who pays real money – why didn't Google send me a message saying, 'Happy Birthday young man, here's to many, many healthy years of using your bus pass to travel the UK and drink even more good ale'? Instead, they know full well I'm starving to death because I can't open ring pull tins of beans, I piss three times a night because my prostrate can't cope with the *Jail Ale* and my *Co-Op* funeral plan won't even pay for a gallower and cart to ferry me to the river Styx while my triple lock pension increase which has just been stopped won't even pay for the pennies for the Ferryman. The bastards - how DO they know these things?

Oh dear, my head has gone again; best move on to happy days in Manchester.

Doctor John Fozzard was my first tutor and he was like a mentor to me as he understood that I was, well, different, and had problems with life down there. He was an expert in his field and also liked a beer. His father won the black pudding championship every year from his butcher's shop in Bingley so he was a real *bait* man. He insisted I see him after I returned from my first Easter break. I turned up and he steamed into me. It seems one of my fellow students had had a difficult time and particularly over the Easter holidays she had become extremely depressed. He remonstrated with me as he said I should have helped her though the year as everyone seemed to look up to me as mentor or leader. I struggled with that notion. I'd hardly been there to mentor or lead anyone as I lived perpetually in debauchery at Edge Hill teacher training college! Anyway I committed to try to help her and I found out where she lived and called on her that night.

KATHRYN
Death and Redemption

When she opened the door she was visibly shocked as if Charles Manson had come knocking. You see every time she had seen me I was pissed or causing some violent altercation. I had actually fancied her since the first day I saw her at our matriculation six months previously but every time I saw her at parties or dances I did something mad - mainly vomiting or fighting. Curiously, she never seemed interested in such behaviour from such a Greek God - she was a Southerner I guess and posh and that was never a good sign. But this evening she finally invited me in and we talked through the long evening and as a result we became friends and then partners. This changed my whole attitude to living away and I saw a reason to stay in Manchester and I finally started working for the first year exams.

Before meeting Kathy I had decided to leave Manchester and had told my father so when he took me to the bus stop to come back after Easter. I wanted to get a job and earn money and be like Davey, Stan and my other working mates. I was sick of having no money and wanted to earn my way and to help him and mam with my board and keep. He nodded at me and lovingly shook my hand. He held on tightly and looked sadly at me. He had tears in his eyes. 'Son, whatever you make your mind up to do, we will always be here for you. Think about it son, if you are not happy then come home. I will always be proud of you whatever you do.'

The bus turned up and I got on. I watched him walk away and saw his shoulders droop and move up and down. I had never seen him cry before and I was fated never to see him do it again. Then on my return to what I thought would be my last term, through Dr. Fozzard's bollockings and mentoring direction and the meeting with Kathy, I changed my mind and got stuck into the Prozac bananas to cheer me up and get me through the exams.

I came home after exams and took a job working at the gas mask brickworks hell again. Kathy was coming up in a few weeks to see me. Poor lass had never been North of Manchester. Her Sister was a doctor, her brother-in-law a lawyer and her father seemed to own half of a City listed plc. God knows what she would think of us.

Sadly she never came when planned as my world ended, never to be the same again. Dad died suddenly.

FLORENCE TAN

'The trails of the world be countless, and most of the trails be tried; You tread on the heels of the many, till you come where the ways divide; And one lies safe in the sunlight, and the other is dreary and wan, But you look aslant at the Lone Trail, and the Lone Trail lures you on'.

Robert Service

I was passing over the death of my father because I was going to add that in an epilogue along with a path I took to redemption much later on in my life, a large part of which was a long lasting psychological consequence of that death. However, death is part of life for each and every one of us, young and old, and is particularly difficult to understand when we are in the throes of the joy of our youth. So I must tell of the unhappy events after that day in 1975 which unknowingly changed my life and say a bit about how it affected me later.

In 1969 that great band Family sang, *The Weaver's Answer*, about an old man looking back on the tapestry of his life that the Weaver had

288

woven; threads of gold and black on his loom. Many of the golden ones of mine and I hope yours I have shared already in this masterpiece. However, my father's death was the black thread in my tapestry which followed me through my life and was first woven the day the music really died which was not when Buddy Holly died in Don McLean's 1970's classic *American Pie'* but when my father passed away.

It was Timmy who told me he was dead with a simple sentence: 'Ya fatha's deed Davey.' That was it; no sorry, no tears, no comforting words. He had put his head through Davey Rutter's old Ford Cortina's window and he told me the tragic news.

Four days earlier I had ran the quarter mile to the phone box to call the ambulance and helped carry my father into it and then into hospital after he had collapsed into my bedroom on getting up for work at 5.00 am. He'd had a stroke. I visited him that Sunday night and believed he was getting better. I had told him two days previously that I had finally passed my first year exams, was happy at last and had found a friend in Kathy which had changed my mind about leaving University so I'd be returning to Manchester. I am certain to this day that he smiled through his pain and inability to speak.

But two days later on that Sunday, Timmy's Dad had been with us in hospital early evening and as we looked at Dad in bed comatose and breathing heavily he told me to go and get a couple of pints with Davey and Stan and go home. He'd look after my dad for a while longer. I now know that he had seen men die and knew what was coming but then, in my youth and ignorance, I didn't know these things and thought he was sleeping.

That week was terrible and I went missing in bars in Newcastle and Sunderland with my wayward cousin David from London. Then Friday came when they brought Dad back to the house. I didn't want to see him cold and lifeless but my family made me come back. It was what men do I was told. The next morning was the funeral and I still refused to see him in his coffin. But in the end my grieving mother said I should be the last to see him before the men came to screw the lid down. All the family and the women from the two streets were sat there gossiping and chatting as if nothing was wrong. They had seen it all. Most had laying out sheets in their bedroom drawers to lay out the dead; even my own mother laid out dead neighbours. Death was real and normal to them.

It was unreal and a nightmare to me. I just couldn't think that way but I took a huge breath and entered the back room where he was lying. I walked over and looked at the open coffin. He looked blue and cold but I leant down and kissed his forehead, the first time in my life I can remember kissing my dad. It was a cold, unforgiving, and life-changing kiss for me. I lifted the veil over his face and looked at him one last time and said: 'Sorry Dad, I should have told you before this.' And as I was about to say the words I'd never said before, *I love you,* a hand came past me and lifted the veil. 'Aye pet, he looks lovely disn't he.'

I turned around at this unwanted and unexpected intrusion. My Auntie Edna had come in and decided she fancied a last look, totally oblivious to my wish be the last to see him.

'The lads have come to screw him doon now David. Best you gan and look after yeah mam.' And she dropped the veil over his face.

And that was it; my last moment on this earth with my beloved father. The lads' came in and started the eternal screwing. I stared at the closed coffin for a few seconds and whispered: 'Goodbye Dad.' And I went back to face the chattering hoards in the other room.

The funeral passed with me holding my mother up most of the time. She broke down when the coffin wouldn't fit and struggled to be lowered into the small hole in Burnmoor graveyard. I wiped her tears and stood erect and proud.

The church service was awful for me, *The Lord's My Shepherd* and *Abide with Me*, a eulogy from a vicar who didn't even know him and loads of people who I really didn't want to talk to or see. I saw it all through, looking after my mother without a tear as I had to be strong. I was now the man of the family and it's what you did. Only in the quiet of my bedroom after Mam had settled down and the old wives were saying how great the funeral had been and how well he looked in his coffin and telling my mam she was looking good in her new black frock and how nice the ham and pease pudding sandwiches were and the men were getting blooted in the Club, did I break down. My wonderful cousin John came and put his arm around me and said nothing, a simple arm of comfort - *it's what men do.* And we all ended up in Shiney Club that night, listening to *the turn*, the odd tear from sisters and friends, and the usual potential fight, and that was that.

But it wasn't was it.

The loss of Dad, that funeral day and the cold, lifeless body in the coffin never left me. I had never grieved; it wasn't what men did. I didn't do much to help my mother afterwards. I went back to the norm, got on with things and thought about my problems. I never did much when I heard her crying in her bedroom at night. *She was tough enough* I thought. We all were in our family surely? No hugs, kisses or expressions of love to my mother to help her through. It took years to understand how we both should have reached out and touched each other. The broken can be healed but I never believed that then.

One year later my twenty year old cousin Raymond was killed in a bicycle accident in Paddington; tragic for parents who adored him as an only child and for all of us who knew how much he meant to them. They grieved terribly, turned his room into a mausoleum, something dead in their hearts from then on until they passed away much too early, two broken people.

The same year my Uncle Joe died and then Uncle Jim and Uncle Tom blew their brains out rather than suffer a long, breathless end with their black, coal-dust shattered lungs. And we trooped of to a cold, soulless church yet again.

The next year Paul, my best friend was killed in the Paras at twenty-one years old. I had been born the same time and we had laid next to each other in the maternity ward. We were like brothers. Now in the late seventies his Nana, Mrs Littlefair, knocked on my door, I opened it, she looked at me and said quietly, without emotion: 'Tell ya Mam our Paul's deed. Killed yistada.'

And she walked away.

Like Timmy, Auntie Edna and all of the folks those days, death was a fact, people showed little emotion - you just got on with it.

At Paul's funeral, Marcus who worked and studied with me cried and cried; he had never had tragedy in his life and had grown to love the North East and my great friends. Paul's Methodist preacher father took his grieving wife's hand and placed hers and his onto the coffin upon which was a single item, Paul's crimson Parachute Regiment beret. He turned and looked pointedly at us all and without emotion, he called out: *The Lord giveth. The Lord taketh. Blessed be the name of the Lord.'*

I stood head bowed amazed anyone could bless anyone when in such pain. I felt anger and shame that he had made his grieving wife endure such a show of what I considered personal self-gratification and clearly delusion. At the crematorium the soldiers of his regiment played the

Last Post as the coffin and Paul disappeared into the closing curtains and the black hole of eternity.

Back home at our house we all got pissed. Paul's brother who had joined the Navy and was only seventeen years old broke down and I had to phone his father to come and console and take him home, drunk as he was. Derek arrived, sober and serious, but surprisingly he was very calm and not angry at his now only son being led into the debauched ways of his brother's best friend.

However, I was angry by now and challenged him on his faith and how he could believe such nonsense given how great a Christian he was and how he'd put Paul through all that nonsense in his early years. Surely his God would look after him of all people, a preacher, yet he had lost his son. How could his God justify that? The reality was that I was also selfishly angry that my own father had been taken so early, Raymond, my uncles and now Paul all in three years. In my own selfish, self-centred grief I had to take out my pain on someone, and why not Derek and his mythical God?

Derek was calm and assuring, despite my anger and insensitivity, and looked me straight in the eyes with a look of absolute certainty and peace that I still see now. He held my hand and quietly said: 'Jesus' love has taken our Paul to where he is now. He is happy finally at peace. Paul was meant for better things than the pain he experienced in this world. One day I hope you will see that.'

Bullshit I thought and told him so. 'It's nothing but a comfort thing to you, no one else. Look at your son over there, wrecked and in tears, he's not in any peace. He's in real pain, like all of us. I just can't get how you can believe that.'

'David, all I can do is keep praying for you and that one day you will understand His love.' He stood up and he put his arm around his young son and very respectfully said thank you to my mam and walked him away. I last saw him at his son's wedding a couple of years after and have never seen him since and now as I write this I regret that sincerely. He was a golden hidden thread that the weaver had woven throughout my tapestry of life. I see it now, the golden thread, clearly, even as my own eyes grow dim; a way, a truth, a life and a light that never fades. Sorry Derek I never saw it until late but I am certain you will know that.

After the tomes related in this book, I followed the sunlight trail that Robert Service's poem at the beginning of the section described and was blessed with a wonderful family, friends, workcolleagues and an amazing wife by my side. But I often strayed from the sunlight path and took the Lone Trail which inevitably for me was to lead to the dark path of anger, lust, greed, violence and self destruction. I guess too many sins to mention here. At fifty, I was an angry frustrated man, still searching for healing over my father's death and an answer to questions that increasingly tore my head and senses apart; why had I thrown my talents away, the meaning to my life and my worth on this earth. Questions that I already had the answer to but I never knew that until guided there years ago by one person's small gift of great love. That person was a complete stranger, a wonderful Singaporean Chinese lady who asked one day when I was in a real mess with my life, at the end of my tether and couldn't see a way out: 'Can I pray for you?'

For me - a foreigner, a stranger, a broken man; Why bother with me? But she did. And I owe that lady, Florence Tan, more than I can say. Because like Mother Theresa said, she showed me that: *Not everyone can do great things but everyone can do small things with great love.*

And that random act of kindness from a caring person, holding my hands and praying for me while I cried and healed sat at the back of a Church I had never attended in forty years, changed my life. But I think now that I will leave the build up to that story for another time, another platform and another audience. You'll think I'm getting soft! I'll be holding our lass's hand in public next.

To conclude this later life redemption, it was Florence Tan's gift of kindness that revealed the knowledge of what Paul's dad, Derek, had prayed for all those years ago for me; simply, that we can all be redeemed because of an unconditional Amazing Love. And the night before my precious meeting with Florence it was my loving wife who forgave me my failures through one long night of confession and counselling in the humidity and heat of Singapore. Many failures in the main I finally understood caused by my longing for something I could never have - sharing with my father the material wealth and wonderful experiences my success, career and marriage had brought me - sharing things that both my father and I could only have dreamed of in the years of my youth through his struggles with poverty and life. I came to understand through that long night that all those material things or my career achievements had never much mattered to me if I couldn't repay him for his sacrifices or share with him my beautiful family which he would never see. I saw now that all my weakness and failure to come to terms with his passing manifested itself too many times as angry self destruction and in my selfishness I often just gave up everything I'd achieved, lost the will to continue and hurt myself and others. I shouldn't deserve this luck and love. I followed that Lone Road to dependency and selfishness. Losing my job too many times through unacceptable behaviour, hurting people who cared for me, always seeking that elusive answer to what worth my life had been to anyone. It was my wife's forgiveness and love and Florence's small act of great kindness that I finally came to understand the wonder of Christ's perfect sacrifice for me – for me, a sinner. And I saw The Weaver's answer on the great tapestry of life for the first time.

I haven't earned it, nor do I deserve it, but through His sacrifice I have been blessed with a wonderful life and precious family
An Amazing Love indeed

An amazing love that showed me the way, the truth and the life and a debt I try to repay in my own small way. I continue to fail too many times for comfort. The pain and troubles of life do not go away because I found faith, nor do the doubts or questions about it. As an extended Shiney Row family we have since suffered more terrible pain with my nephew's tragic suicide and with past hurt to my own family that I still find hard to explain or endure. I often become deeply sad on my far too often dark days when all I hear is silence when I ask the question, *Why them and why wasn't I able to help?* However, what carries me through these black days is the faith that even in the silence, if like me you are a lost sheep, He listens, and will come for you and reunite those you have loved.

'He is the One who never leaves the one behind.'

Yes, a wonderful life, blessed by my own guardian angel, my beautiful wife. Count your blessings Davey. And these days I do. But in the summer of '75 after Dad's death I didn't.

It was long difficult summer for me and then Kathy wrote to say that she would not return to Manchester and was taking up a place in London to study Medicine. This was almost a bonus for me because even though I was becoming very attached to her, I was struggling with going back for my second year as I really wanted to stay and earn money and help my widowed mother.

My mother had seven pounds fifty pence a month pension from Dad's work and that's all. She had worked as a cleaner for a very rich and posh woman but had dropped a heavy silver salver tray on her foot which has caused major and continual blood circulation problems and after a bilateral sympathectomy couldn't walk or stand for long periods anymore. So, in the end I told my mother I'd stay. She had never ever in her life lost her temper or shouted at me but she did then. She told me that my dad had worked seven days a week for my opportunity, he was so proud and how could I even think about not completing it for him. I agreed to think about it and went to the Club, as you do. Next thing I know our Timmy and Mark came in, asked me outside and threatened to give me a hiding if I gave up. Both said they would look after Mam and I'd go back and make the family, friends and the village proud.

I guess the thought of broken legs finally did it and I returned in the autumn.

Once back in Manchester, Kathy came up every weekend as she had promised and we enjoyed the time so much. But sadly my mind was shot. Dad's death was still painful and it really hit me on my own living in a Clyde Road, West Didsbury shit-hole that my new flat mates Pete and Clive had found. I was supposed to share a room with Paul too but he bunked in with his new girlfriend in her flat. I ended up selfishly finishing with Kathy but then staying with an even posher lass from the top girl's school, Roedean – she and her brother from Eton are both famous now but I gave her up too, much to her distress. I was in a bit of a mess.

And the new digs didn't help.

These were the days when landlords could do what they liked. The Landlord and Tenant Act of 1985 was ten years away and even I say, one of the better pieces of legislation from Lady T and her government. The place was rancid: one small *pay as you go* gas wall fire which I couldn't afford and no other heating. The bath was brown stained and the taps emitted rusty, stained freezing cold water. The whole place stank of must and damp. There were mice and vermin in it. I grew to like a certain friendly brown mouse and took to feeding it and having late night conversations with it. And as I moved on from my broken relationships, it did me a great favour one freezing night.

I had brought a lovely lady back from college and after a few beers with the local criminals in *The Midland Hotel* bar we retired to my hovel.

She was not impressed by the place. Also being of sound mind and strangely chaste for those post-swinging sixties, liberated pre-AID's days, despite my valiant attempt at persuasion, did not want to climb into my bed and chose Paul's empty one. With a deep frustrated sigh, I accepted the inevitable. disappointment. Then I noticed my mouse run across the room to the open sewer which was large hole where my hand basin waste pipe entered the wall. Thinking quickly, I turned out the light and started to scratch the floor.

My lovely friend whispered through the darkness, 'David, what's that noise?'

'What noise? I can't hear anything,' I said.

She went silent. A few minutes later I scratched the floor again, but a bit louder.

'There it is again. What is it David?'

'Oh that might be the mouse. He comes out at night. If you're frightened, why don't you climb in with me?' I whispered, deviously and hopefully.

'No. I'll be alright here. It's only a mouse.'

Frustrated yet again, I thought about just sleeping but well men are men and young hormones are, well, hormones. Two minutes later I scratched again much louder and threw a beer mat over at the bed.

'Oh! David what was that. It jumped up on the bed I think,' she shouted.

Through the gloom as my eyes were adjusting I saw she'd sat bolt upright.

'No can't have pet. The mouse can't jump that high. Mind you the rat that lives under the bed might. Let me come and see.'

'Bugger that, I'm coming over there.' Cue one semi-naked, very posh attractive girl running on tiptoes in the darkness straight into the arms of a caring, compassionate Greek god. Sadly, her fear of rodents didn't change her sound mind and chaste decision to abstain from the pleasures of the flesh. Another frustrating night despite the cunning scratching rodent ploy – however, you may like to try it one night. It will work for any gender or sexual orientation, as boys these days are soft of course and might well be scared of mice. However, I'm not sure if in this Hashtag MeToo world you might get banged up in the slammer for it. But it's worth a bash. Prince Andrew has a good lawyer if you need one.

The landlord came up every month in his Jag from London to collect the five pound a week rent from this horrible house and all the others he owned. I hated the place and became depressed with it all. I had Rastafarians above me, who, very like *the Gargoyle*, played one song over and over. All day and night, the bloody thing boomed through the ceiling - *No Woman No Cry* by Bob Marley and the Wailers. The rise of Reggae in the seventies was lost on me because of that one song; for like *Where Do You Go To My Lovely'* it haunted my every waking moment. Sadly, it was to lead to the inevitable violence as one night I had a meltdown at 4 pm in the morning, ran up the stairs, smashed on their door and firmly nutted the first one of them to open the door. Surprisingly, my action paid dividends because when I returned from medical school the next night my Jamaican neighbours had gone. I guess I was very lucky as those days that I knew nothing of *Yardies* or gang warfare, rampant knife crime or Frenchtown. I only knew of a *Redemption Song*, Shiney Row-style. Two days later a horde of Chinese moved in and *No Woman No Cry* was exchanged for a constant thumping on the ceiling as they practiced Kung Fu and the remorseless sounds as they chopped endless vegetables for their Oriental bait . Sometimes you are better off with the music and neighbours you know.

Derek and Clive Live and Head, Hands and Feet

Clyde Road was purgatory. Even the police wouldn't go there. When we lost a stereo stolen from the apartment, Clive went to the police station in West Didsbury where they told him kindly to go to *The Midland Hotel* and buy it back. Indeed we drank there even though we knew the place was jam-packed with the criminals of Manchester. We decided not to annoy them and ask for our music player back.

Clive introduced me to Bruce Springsteen and the first album I heard was *Born to Run*. I followed up with both his earlier ones and *The Boss* became a regular player in the stable we lived in along with *Jackson Browne, Bad Company, Roxy Music, Hatfield and the North, Supertramp, Wishbone Ash, Fleetwood Mac, Head Hands and Feet* and many, many more brilliant bands that flowed constantly throughout that time and space. Punk took over in a massive way and we were blessed with great music which helped get you through the squalor, cold and rodents.

Cult art for us was the LP and acts from Peter Cook and Dudley Moore. *Derek and Clyde Live* was brilliant satire - lines forever etched in the memory. The student union regularly showed the movies of Barry

Mackenzie - *The Adventures of Barry Mackenzie* and *Barry Mackenzie Holds His Own*. These were our milestones of movie art, culture and literature. You can stick your Ingmar Bergman and Swedish misery and your Barrie Norman film reviews up the Great Divide. As Sir Les Patterson, Minster of Australian Culture, said, spilling his Foster's can down his vomit and beer stained white suit, 'We Australians have a special culture.' Indeed, they do, Skippy.

It was like moving to Palm Beach when I finally left the hell of Clyde Road in my third and final year and reunited with Eeyore Alan in a house in Withington. I shared a bedroom with him. Even in my early morning misery I chuckled most days when I woke up at the tens of *Time Form* horse racing statistic books that covered his bed like a paperwork duvet. He spent every waking hour trying to mathematically calculate a system that would beat the bookies and win him that early retirement even before he started work. 'Ah just knaar it'll nivva work before those bloody exams,' he'd cry out, throwing a Time Form across the bed then realise he was two hours late for his tutorial on Complex Numbers.

And indeed, even now after a lifetime of work he is hoping to develop it...but like the man at St James Park whose only bucket list wish is *To see Newcastle United win a trophy,* Alan just knaars: 'Nee body lives that long.'

I suddenly woke up to the fact that Alan's mythical system wouldn't stop me having to get a job. More importantly, Mr *Van Morrison*, I had met my own beautiful *brown eyed girl* who would change my life and with many *soft words on a Sunday morning* she brought me out of my academic self-destruction. It was time to try to regain the lost years of study and focus on getting that degree of which he would have been so proud.

To my surprise and eternal thanks to all who encouraged and taught me I managed to achieve that highest goal. I was offered PhD research positions in leading Universities but I chose to go back home to the North East as my mother was lonely and had little money and a position at Sunderland Polytechnic School of Pharmacy offered a real salary as a Research Assistant and Lecturer and at last I could support my mother.

MARCUS
Terry Wogan and J.R. Ewing

I began lecturing at the Sunderland School of Pharmacy and studying in the dungeon of the ancient Galen Building for a PhD on the effects of chemical entities to cure asthma, derivatives of which were eventually to become the infamous blue pill, Viagra. I wish I'd known then that my ICI 63,197 compound could change the sex lives of millions as I'd have made millions and would not be sat here typing this at 5 30 am in the vain and desperate hope that when the vaccine kills off that Chinese bug I can pay for a flight out of this geriatric purgatory and away from crazy Gus and...the endless rain and smiling weather forecasters all winter and every hour on telly. Tell me why do they smile when they show storm after bloody storm, flood after flood hurling across the Atlantic? I'd wipe that smile off their smug faces.

And the endless antique, home buying, quiz and bloody reality shows and now as soon as I come to the end of writing this epic, I'm locked up in my own home yet again and probably banged up by the local Old Bill if I break lockdown and walk down to the empty prom and buy mesel a Mr Whippy with monkey's blood...well..there you go my *heed* has gone again.

So, as I didn't make the Viagra millions, and the quartile royalty check for the other books has arrived today and will buy me about three pints, when Boris opens up the boozers up again I will spend it. I will head down to the pub and see if Yorkie's plan to grow geese for Christmas on my dearest's lawn is financially viable, without divorce or the Old Bill banging me up again when they find out where the goslings came from.

Where was I? Yes...stuck in the Pharmacy School dungeon.

The only thing I remember nice about being stuck in the Tower of Sunderland cells during this three year period of the good times I'm writing about is listening to Terry Wogan. I loved him. His Irish craic was the only reason I switched on BBC Radio 2. A generation brought up on Radio Caroline, Radio One, John Peel, Whispering Bob Harris, didn't listen to Radio Two did they? Well some of us did, but only for Wogan and only for the piss-take. His chatter about some records made me chuckle every dark, bleak winter morning, especially his love of Jormans (Germans). He took the piss relentlessly about their lack of humour, their waging war record and their inability to produce any meaningful song (apart from *The Scorpions*, who are excellent I must admit). I loved his early morning banter with his producer about the German song, *The Lighthouse Across the Bay*. Listen to it. It is German angst and romance at its best. It's Teutonic melody makes the *Horst Wessel* SA marching song seem like Julie Andrew's *spoonful of sugar*. It was the inspiration for *The Iron Chancellor* character in my *Turkey and Easter Egg*...well, some of it was!

Another great song of his was *Me and the Elephant* by Gene Cotton. It used to bring Wogan to tears...and me.

Another 70's and 80's classic, 'Dallas' of course made him famous. His character assassination, nick-names and general humour about a supposedly serious portrayal of the Oil Industry, big business greed, corruption and sexual infidelity were masterful in many eyes. *Swellen* (Sue Ellen, the pouting, angst ridden wife of JR, the wife – cheating, scheming, evil tycoon) was a particular favourite of his. As was *the poison dwarf*, (small in height, if disproportionate of bosom, as were the bosoms of all the girls in Dallas) J.R.'s diminuitive niece. Then there was *Miss Ellie, Jock*, the lovely *Pam Ewing, Cliff Barnes* and of course the tortured *Bobby*, who died, was resurrected and I think died and rose again. This resurrection was all for the sake of the script and viewing figures and not the redemption of the world. *Bobby* was dead for a whole series but one day he walked out of the shower, resurrected and into the healing bosom of the gorgeously, full figured *Pam*. Who the hell wouldn't? Maybe Mary Magdalene possessed similar healing assets because as *Mott The Hoople* sang in 1973 I would have *rolled away the stone* with broken arms to be resurrected by Pam.

Wogan managed to make *Dallas* the most watched programme on telly and his *Who shot JR?* early morning cameos were priceless. Ten years later I met my own version of JR, not unlike the screen one in lots of ways, and I also was nearly shot in Texas myself - happy days indeed.

However, back in the dungeon of Sunderland Jail I was not so happy. Work was not really what I was made for; I was beginning to realise that. Fellow prisoners, Marcus and Peter also didn't seem to like work much more I did, but Peter is now I gather a millionaire in the City. And Marcus ended up smuggling bibles into China, a spiritual leader and healer.

And me? Well you know what happened by now - a life of purgatory working with insane crazy people and now it's come to living on book royalties of three pints a month and drinking them with even more crazy people...so stick in there folks with the task ahead, *Eat that Frog* every day and look what you can achieve.

Savoury Dips and Pumphrey's Wine Bar

I did introduce Marcus to *slavery dips*. These were pure cholesterol fat dipped in pure cholesterol gravy soaked baps, buns, rolls or stotties or whatever you wish to call them. Ibbotson's the butcher in Vine Street made them and every day we both left the dungeon pit to buy two each for lunch, dressed in our white coats; me with my surgical instruments in my top pocket. Some days when the test tubes and guinea pigs and our respective Professors got too much we would take the slavery dips to the local boozers, *The Borough, Ivy House, Museum Vaults, Beehive* and drink beer with the cholesterol saturated delicacy.

Marcus drove a Triumph Bonneville bike those days, most of the time pissed. How the hell we survived, I'll never know. He was a good looking and wild young man; girls were attracted to him and him to them. A cracking man and friend then and lost to me for thirty years until we connected through the cyber world and I was amazed he'd found the way and was a Pastor. But those days in the dungeon he was wild and he introduced me to *Pumphrey's* the first wine bar in Newcastle. He had secured a job there at nights after working chopping up his white mice liver in the dungeon during the long day. He told me that it was heaving every night with men and girls. It was unknown those days for real men to drink wine so I had to see why sensible males would even think about a place like this. Surely not in Newcastle!

We took his bike over after a few beers in the Felling where he lived and I was amazed that the wine place was heaving - men who were mainly in suits and girls who were not like the normal Friday night Toon lasses, these were slim, had clothes on and didn't have tattoos, or purple and blue legs (the effect of extreme winter cold on the naked flesh of under-dressed lasses).

Here I was introduced by Marcus to a large Cockney guy in a snappy suit. After a drink or two he invited me to come and see him the next day once I'd admitted I was looking to get out of the purgatory of research and lecturing to disinterested students who really only wanted to be back in *The Museum Vaults* drinking their grant money away. I wanted to start earning real money, so academia was not for me. He told me he was head of sales for a company called Xerox and they were about to launch something that would revolutionise the world; a device

301

which would send pictures and words over a telephone line. I had to get in on this.

Next day I visited him in his huge office. I had never been in an office; labs; dungeons, the odd police cell and bars were my comfort zone. And I had never seen so many graphs on walls showing sales figures, units sold, pounds earned and people hunched on phones and desks looking at green sheets of computer paper. These were days before personal computers or mobile phones folks: can you believe it, no Wi-Fi, Microsoft Windows or Google.

My drinking mate sat me down and his lovely secretary gave me a cup of coffee. He opened up with in his strong cockney accent without any small talk or introduction. 'Now then my son, why do you want to sell tin boxes?'

This knocked me back. I didn't want to sell tin boxes. I wanted to do something that was exciting, technologically advanced, world breaking, make a huge impact on society and give me such a great boost in life and job satisfaction. And I told him this.

'Well son. I guess you better just **** off back and find another aspirin or something to cure the clap or some shit like that. See all those people out there?' and he pointed beyond his glass office walls to the suited men and women beavering away on phones. 'They don't give a monkey's about saving the world. They only want to be rich. And if they don't get rich, I don't get rich and that means I fire them.' He looked deep into my astonished and disappointed eyes. 'Son, my advice is to go back to that lab and finish what you started. When you realise what this life is about then give me a call again and we'll have a glass of fizzy in Pumphrey's. Thanks for coming.'

And so ended my first interview trying to get into real business...and *Fax machines?* What hell were they? I consoled myself that they would never sell anyway.

OUR LASS
'Rocky' and Cosa Nostra Flats'
I eventually did finish the doctorate just like the cockney sales manager advised. I did it for my father's memory with no intention of carrying on in research. I never did sell fax machines nor did I get extremely rich, and nor did I save the world's sick. Mrs Thatcher came and went, the milk went forever, so did the pits, the shipyards and the steel works. The pit villages and ship building towns lost their heart and

soul. The Working Men's and Miner's Welfare clubs gradually closed, the football never got any better, and I made and lost great friends and family. And the real disaster and hell of all hells was that I had to do real work.

I joined an American Pharmaceutical giant a couple of weeks after the month both my dearest and I and Prince Charles and Lady Diana got married. I was on the dole and I guess Charlie wasn't. My first real employer was bigger than Pfizer those days; long before they stole the multibillion dollar sales of my dungeon discovered Viagra! And long before the multibillion Covid vaccines which will save the world and make them even more than the male penis erector pill has. The Paradise of Youth was lost forever and the times were changing, work took over and, unlike Kitty and Jack in *Contracting for the Devil,* I never escaped it. But all was not lost; I had met my love, my life, and she gave me three wonderful children and a love and life I really do not deserve. My angel on earth, - the only place *where peaceful waters flow.*

I met her for the first time as I have already mentioned with my first girlfriend in *The Red Lion* pub in Withington, Manchester. Those days the pub was owned by Noel Burrows, who was the UK crown green bowling champion. The pub had its own crown green and we tried to play many times when pissed. I was much better at darts which I played every early evening in the small bar with the suited guys who came in from work, with the tradesmen in their work clothes and with the doctors and nurses from the Christie cancer hospital up the road. Most nights I earned my beer money from them playing *501* or *Killer.* I spent these winnings there and in the chip shop over the road where meat pudding and chips was the diet of choice.

We lived five minutes from the pub. The house was owned by a Manchester landlord, *Cosa Nostra Flats.* One night we watched *World in Action,* an ITV investigatory journal/criminal exposure programme, which was bent on exposing our esteemed landlords as Don Corleone clones - secret TV footage showed them setting dogs on starving widows and evicting destitute refugees. It showed huge guys with baseball bats and German shepherds battering long-haired students like us to death. We all looked shocked - surely not our landlord? Then one day not long after the TV exposure we got a letter through the post from them. Our neighbours, poor souls (I apologise abjectly for our behaviour if you are still alive my poor dears) had complained too many times about our antics. The letter from the Consigliore went something along these lines:

It has come to our attention that you have been disturbing the kind and true residents in your vicinity. Particularly, we are referred to the fact the noise starts around the closing time on afternoons and nights of the Red Lion public house. Incidents of urinating from the third floor window, our garden gate being used as a weapon in an altercation last Saturday night, repetitive Peter Sarstedt music emanating from the second floor all night and day and records being thrown out into the street. Also reports of horrible screaming coming through the bathroom window each night. We have a list of many more incidents of anti- social behaviour. Unless you desist in this behaviour and restore the house to its original state we shall be forced to take action. We are certain that you will understand what the action may be and we are also certain that you would not want us to take those steps. We are proud of our record of resolving disputes amicably and without resort to extreme measures.

You will understand that we strive to help in any way. We shall however be calling around to interview your neighbours and visit you all in the near future.

We have no doubt that you will oblige with our request and look forward to your co-operation.

Yours sincerely,
Luca Brasi
Head of Customer Compliance

It was time to leave. And we did, but not until final exams were over. This was our last term at University and my new love and I had developed a strong relationship after I had raised the courage to ask her to come and see the movie *Rocky* with me at the Odeon picture house on Deansgate. I still remember leaving the pictures with all the other guys, everyone bouncing on our toes, shadow-boxing, mimicking Sly Stallone as we jogged along the road with our girlfriends. I tried to impress her when we were back in the house with my Stallone inspired one-handed press-ups; my back has been knackered ever since!

As the exams ended and the results rolled out I realised that I had fallen in love with her but really didn't know how to cope as she was staying and I was leaving. I feared for the uncertain future I had in front of me and didn't want to burden myself or her with that uncertainty so we agreed on Victoria Station as I left for home that we should end the relationship. Romantic writers would have a field day with the emotions of both of us displayed and the pathos of the fume-filled station. *Farewell My Lovely* and *Brief Encounter* was nothing compared to our goodbye.

As I sat on the train I thought of the first time I had come down to Manchester three years ago. Life had changed and was changing. Dad had passed away - no more fishing, long walks and talks in Lord Lambton's estates, bus stop meetings or farewells. I couldn't meet him in the Club on a Sunday like all my other friends did with their fathers. Mam was on her own, very miserable and skint all of the time, rapidly becoming a recluse and dependent on *Valium* sleeping pills. Friends were scattering over the country and some overseas in the Army and in real danger. I really didn't want to go home but I knew I needed to be with my mother in her loneliness and poverty to support her. And now my only real love had come and gone. It wasn't a great trip.

When I arrived back I gratefully ate another of my mother's massive dinners for tea. I told her I was off to the Club to think about things - as you did. Several Fed Best pints later and a word of advice from the wonderful friend of my father, and now I, Ted Kelly, I put my coins into the Club phone, pressed button A...

...And I called my future wife, the mother-to-be of my beautiful children.

GRATEFUL THANKS

To Skippy, my pedantic Aussie mate and Dave the original mad professor who both tried valiantly to keep me politically and grammatically correct

To Terry Greenwell, RIBA, Shiney Row and Washington Grammar School's Frank Gehry, for his cracking cover artwork

To Lord Ned Lambton, 7th Earl of Durham, for his kind foreword

Printed in Great Britain
by Amazon